THE LETTERS OF

Claudio Monteverdi

Portrait of Monteverdi by Bernardo Strozzi (1581–1644), painted *c.*1635
on panel 98×75 cm. Vienna, Musikverein, from Oscar Strakosch
collection

THE LETTERS OF
Claudio Monteverdi

Translated and Introduced by
DENIS STEVENS

Revised Edition

CLARENDON PRESS · OXFORD
1995

Oxford University Press, Walton Street, Oxford OX2 6DP
Oxford New York
Athens Auckland Bangkok Bombay
Calcutta Cape Town Dar es Salaam Delhi
Florence Hong Kong Istanbul Karachi
Kuala Lumpur Madras Madrid Melbourne
Mexico City Nairobi Paris Singapore
Taipei Tokyo Toronto
and associated companies in
Berlin Ibadan

Oxford is a trade mark of Oxford University Press

Published in the United States
by Oxford University Press Inc., New York

British Library Cataloguing in Publication Data
Data available

Library of Congress Cataloging-in-Publication Data
Monteverdi, Claudio, 1567–1643.
[Correspondence. English]
The letters of Claudio Monteverdi / translated and introduced by
Denis Stevens. — Rev. ed.
Includes bibliographical references (p.   ) and index.
1. Monteverdi, Claudio, 1567–1643. 2. Composers—Italy—
Correspondence. I. Stevens, Denis, 1922–   . II. Title.
ML 410.M77A4 1995 782'.0092—dc20   [B]   94-40349
ISBN 0-19-816414-9

1 3 5 7 9 10 8 6 4 2

Typeset by Best-set Typesetter Ltd., Hong Kong

Printed in Great Britain
on acid-free paper by
Biddles Ltd.
Guildford and King's Lynn

. . . for Anthony, Daphne, Michael
and in memory of W.J.S. and E.R.S

Preface (1980)

THROUGHOUT the many years during which I worked on the source-materials of Monteverdi's music with a view to publishing, performing, or recording it in a way that might more clearly mirror his true intent, it never occurred to me that the editorial problems I had to face and resolve might also be found (though in greater number) in his literary legacy, especially his correspondence, in so far as it had survived. I referred to a few letters from time to time in order to understand certain questions posed by the music, but it was not until the early autumn of 1964 that I began to feel the need for a complete and fully annotated English version of all the letters thus far discovered, whether in Mantua or elsewhere.

I find, in the voluminous file of correspondence concerning this project, two communications from friends whose constant encouragement over the years ranks as one of the prime reasons why I have been able to complete the work. One is a typically courteous and helpful reply (3 November 1964) to a question I asked of Federico Ghisi in Florence; the other, a letter (11 January 1965) from Albi Rosenthal—musician, linguist, and bibliophile extraordinary—mentions my 'only too justified suggestion that [Monteverdi's] whole correspondence should be translated into English (obscure as some passages may be here and there!)'.

And there, I suppose, it all began. The foolhardiness of superannuated youth persuaded me that the task could be finished in fifteen months, but a life divided between teaching, research, performing, travelling, and a zestful family decreed that the term would be fifteen years. They proved to be eventful and difficult years, but I was gradually able to collect and work on the materials wherever and whenever leisure permitted me to do so. I constantly reminded myself that, generally speaking, things take longer and cost more than they should, and this being so, my first duty here is to thank those organizations and foundations whose generosity sustained my labours: the Accademia Monteverdiana, the American Philosophical Society, the Charlotte Brechemin Foundation, the Chapelbrook Foundation, La Fondazione G. Cini, and the Rockefeller Foundation. It was during a residency at the Rockefeller Foundation's Study and Conference Center in Bellagio, Italy, that the basic work of translation was completed. I gratefully acknowledge assistance far beyond

[vii]

the call of duty not only from the genial Director of the Center, Dr William C. Olson, but also from one of its first advisers, Sir Herbert Butterfield. Finally, I wish to express my sincere thanks to the staff of all the libraries in which I worked, and to all colleagues and friends who in any way assisted me.

D.S.

Santa Barbara, 1979

Preface (1994)

IN this new edition, certain changes and revisions affecting letters and commentaries have been made in the light of newly published information in books, articles, and reviews, and through private communications from colleagues who read the 1980 edition with constructively critical eyes. I am especially grateful to Dr Tim Carter.

One further letter (no. 122), discovered by Carlo Vitali, was first published by him in *Nuova rivista musicale italiana*, 14 (1980), 410–12. The newest and most extensive biographical information appears in Paolo Fabbri's *Monteverdi* (Edizioni di Torino, 1985) and in its English translation by Dr Carter (Cambridge University Press, 1994).

My own contribution to the ever-widening view of Monteverdi's life now covers in some detail the events of his early years in Cremona and Mantua, especially in so far as they were influenced by his family, his studies, travels, friends, and patrons. It was indeed fortunate that he was born in the city of luthiers, and gained his first impressions of musical life in two lively, vibrant, but essentially different areas of Lombardy.

Various attempts have been made since 1885 to provide readers with an Italian text of the letters, and this has finally been achieved by Dr Éva Lax of Budapest. Her *Claudio Monteverdi: Lettere* (Olschki, 1994) is an accurate and complete edition of immense value. My special thanks go to her for many years of generous advice in the matter of textual interpretation and philological background.

In 1962 Oxford University Press published my edition of *Il Combattimento di Tancredi e Clorinda*, and now, nearly a third of a century later, they have agreed to publish the present volume. My appreciation extends also to Bonnie J. Blackburn, Leofranc Holford-Strevens, Helen Foster and Bruce Phillips who in many and various ways have helped to see this revision through the press.

D.S.

London, 1994

Contents

[xi]

Synoptic Table of Letters

Mantua

Cremona

Mantua

Venice

Venice

Parma

Venice

Parma

Venice

Illustrations

Plates

Figures

Introduction

. . . poichè gli errori quasi annelli di catena l'uno con l'altro s'abbracciono

WHEN Ferdinando Gonzaga, sixth Duke of Mantua, wrote those words to
Monsignor Soardi at the papal Curia in the early autumn of 1616, he was
thinking not as the poet he so ardently wished to be, but as the politician
and potentate that chance had forced him to become. The errors to which
he referred, interlinked and inseparable like cause and effect, were no
errors of scansion or syntax, but of judgement or administration; and he
already sensed, perhaps, that the end of the chain would mean the end of
his House, as indeed came to pass not long after his death.

He could never have guessed, nor would he have wished to consider,
that in years to come the political errors might be outstripped at least in
number by the unbelievable mistranscriptions of certain documents then
being filed away in his own archives, yet such was the case when, in
1929, the first reasonably complete collection of Monteverdi's letters
was published in Italy under the aegis of G. F. Malipiero, to whom all
admirers of Monteverdi owe so much. And though Malipiero, like
Rawdon Brown who edited the voluminous *Calendars of State Papers—
Venice* for the Rolls Series, found it expedient to hire assistants, in neither
case was their work in the demanding field of palaeography properly and
carefully checked.

Some of the more misleading of the mistakes in the *Calendars* were
pointed out by Alessandro Luzio in his catalogue of the Archivio Gonzaga
(ii. 118), but those in Malipiero's edition of Monteverdi's letters went
unnoticed and uncorrected for many years, with the result that translations into other languages compounded the confusion in the Italian text.
Ironically, the earlier though less complete collections of letters transcribed and published by Davari in 1885 and Prunières in 1926 frequently
offer more reliable readings than some by subsequent editors. The diplomatic transcription by Dr Éva Lax (Olschki, 1994) now places our understanding on a reliable foundation. The lack of this in earlier years made life
difficult, as I discovered in 1966 when I began to assemble photographic
copies of every known letter or document written by (or dictated by)
Monteverdi.

[1]

Handwriting and Literary Style

Monteverdi's handwriting is a common form of chancery cursive used widely as a book hand or an epistolary hand. Its lively character, elegance, and speed of movement admirably reflect the spontaneity of a creative or a communicative mind, and in the particular variety cultivated by Monteverdi—an offshoot of *cancellaresca testeggiata*—the effect is heightened by the long-looped ascenders and other decorative features, especially noticeable in capitals. As is customary in this hand, the vowel *e* is open, like *c* with a detached top, and it is often confused with *c* or *i*. When Monteverdi began to go to school about the year 1573, he may have had access to some such book as the *Essemplare* published at Rome in 1560 by Gianfranco Cresco da Milano, but naturally over the course of years his handwriting underwent changes and modifications brought about by the need for haste, or by the onset of arthritis.

With regard to literary style, there is much to interest the connoisseur of humanistic prose, for Monteverdi's flow of words not infrequently bears comparison with the best of his music. One senses in many of the longer letters that same white heat whose fusion of improvisation and formal discipline brought into being a taut masterpiece such as the *Combattimento* or the chaconne *Zefiro torna*. The subject is heard, then soon enmeshed in the inexorable counterpoint of subsidiary themes, developed and extended by means of parenthetical allusions, followed by a return to the subject and the drive towards the final cadence. His letters in many ways mirror his music.

The firm foundations of Monteverdi's construction and syntax lie deep in the soil of classical Latin, with its balanced elegance and clear sentence-structure. The overall structure, however, is humanistic in its passionate flux and its dependence not so much on ablative absolutes as on participial clauses that push the main verb far into the body of the letter. Sentences are lengthy and convoluted, relying much on shorter segments and sub-junctive verbs for contrast, as well as on most of the popular figures of speech and not a few grammatical tricks, which sometimes give the impression of having been put there to test the translator.

In the introduction to Letter 18, which consists of one extremely long sentence, beautifully balanced and punctuated, an attempt has been made to analyse the internal structure in such a way as to show its clarity and logic, its movement and meaning. The same technique could be applied to most of the other letters, apart from those belonging more to the category of brief memoranda or covering notes.

If there is one master-key to the locked-in design of Monteverdi's prose, it must be sought in his punctuation—either as actually written or as implied by context and syntax. Those of his glossators who never tire of complaining about his lack of punctuation demonstrate at the same time their total unfamiliarity with the autographs, where punctuation marks abound even though they are faint to the point of being barely discernible in a photocopy. In making my translations I have come to the conclusion, after many years of experiment and at least four major revisions, that it is better to resist the temptations of the short cut whereby long sentences are cut into short ones, and retain at all costs the far-reaching thrust of the original sentences. This has been achieved by using not only commas and semicolons as points of division for subordinate clauses, but also parentheses and dashes, all these being deployed within or without one another as the particular sentence demands. I trust that readers will not be deterred by this method, which—if it occasionally places a strain on the span of comprehension—at least has the virtue of preserving unchecked Monteverdi's flow of arched symmetry.

Letter 6 offers a splendid example of powerfully moving paragraphs set forth in a climactic sequence, all of which could easily be missed (and has been missed by most translators) through breaking up the flow of thought and failing to establish the key-word 'fortune' which leads in each new point of the writer's argument. It would have been possible to translate this, or any other letter, in such a way as to project an image of a suave, urbane, businesslike man pleading his case before a magistrate: nevertheless it seemed more in keeping with Monteverdi's character (as revealed by his style) to preserve all those locutions and circumlocutions, all the hyperbole and meiosis, indeed everything that contributes towards the rounding out of a true portrait.

Range of Topics

Apart from giving us a clear picture of the composer's personality, as it developed over the last forty-two years of his life, the letters reveal sharply focused details of his professional career, in addition to colourful vignettes of some of the musicians and courtiers he knew and with whom he collaborated. What results is a fascinating panorama of social conditions, especially in so far as they affected a busy musical director and composer working in Mantua, Venice, and Parma at a crucial time in the history of music. The span of the letters (1601–43) coincides with the burgeoning years of Italian opera, together with its cognates the ballet, *torneo*, and intermezzo. One finds here discussions of operatic aesthetics and problems of staging, matters pertaining to casting and orchestration, the day-to-day relationship with patrons and librettists, not to mention the troubles and trials of duplicating full scores long before the days of photocopy.

Other letters, which frequently occur in groups, deal with topics such as the hiring of wind-players; the vocal ranges of singers (also their timbre and skill in ornamentation); actors of the *commedia dell'arte* and their petty jealousies; alchemy as a kind of innocent hobby rather than a serious or full-time activity; the numerous worries attendant upon the education of sons in a city known for its libertine way of life; health and sickness as it affects creative work and travel; finance seen from many aspects—from that of the struggling composer, trying to make ends meet and anxious for his just reward (part of which he never received), from the point of view of the ever-bargaining musician, whether singer or instrumentalist or instrument-maker, and from the later and loftier vantage of a successful man who can command considerable sums of money in special fees and commissions.

As for musical politics, Monteverdi is never hesitant to draw aside the curtains and show us what really went on in the courts and churches where, to the outsider, life must often have seemed to be suspiciously rosy. Rival factions, corrupt officials, backbiting and slander, all can be seen with a clarity that is totally unflattering and sometimes frightening. Monteverdi is tricked by his employers, insulted by one of his musicians, forced to work at a pace that he does not relish; yet at other times he is happy with small successes—a helping hand for his sons, a concert that went well, a prestigious invitation to compose occasional music for a noble wedding.

Over and above the daily round, which might include a robbery at gunpoint or threats from the Inquisitor, there are generous portions of the letters that help us to understand what Monteverdi was doing as a musician. He mentions works that have survived—*L'Orfeo*, *Arianna*, *Il Combattimento*, *Tirsi e Clori*—and makes our ears tingle with accounts of scores that were never completed or never begun, like *La finta pazza Licori*, which might have been the first comic opera; or works that were lost, such as the Mass and Vespers for Christmas in St Mark's; *Armida*, the parergon to *Il Combattimento*; stage works and ballets, madrigals and motets, canzoni and intermezzi; and fortunately there are some that can be identified with a reasonable degree of certainty even though their names do not appear—the two Petrarch madrigals from Book VI, the motet for the feast of Our Lady of Mount Carmel, the intermezzi for *Le tre costanti* (whose existence has hitherto never been noticed apart from an isolated footnote), the eight-part *Dixit Dominus* considered as a five-part composition by previous investigators, and some of the motets for special feasts and occasions.

Problems of Identification

Monteverdi often mentions his friends, relatives, and colleagues in an offhandedly cryptic manner—here a surname, there a Christian name, now a title or rank, and sometimes a completely oblique reference which at first defies every attempt to identify the person concerned. Over a period of ten years I built up a card-index of these names, compiling biographies and tracking down identities to the best of my ability, and ending up with well over a hundred characters who ran the gamut from fame to obscurity. I owe much to the lists and references compiled for the Archivio Gonzaga in Mantua by Stefano Davari, a source that was also used by Domenico de' Paoli in his partial list of persons cited, this latter being the first published attempt at a *personalia* for the letters as a whole. But there always remained some two dozen personages whose identity continued to elude me until I was finally able to visit Cremona, Mantua, and Venice with sufficient time to complete the necessary research.

It was only then that I found it possible to track down the Mantuan medical doctors Bertoletti and Bruschi; the singers Amigoni, Bisucci (the 'young man from Bologna'), Lazerini, Tarroni, and others; the composers Bianchi (lurking under the name 'Giulio Cesare Cremonese') and Ignazio Donati; the organist Grillo—not mentioned by name, though Monteverdi tells us on the last day of 1622 that one of the organists of St Mark's had passed to a better life a month and a half ago, a casual remark that helps us to suggest an approximate date of 15 November for Grillo's death, so far undocumented in the standard works of reference. Other characters in the drama, many of them obscure but important, come from all walks of life and numerous professions: among the musically inclined patricians we have Bembo, Giustiniani, and Mocenigo; the imperial resident Rossi whose penchant for the archicembalo type of harpsichord is documented elsewhere; Giovanni Spiga, jeweller to the Gonzaga court; and the mysterious 'Signor Bergamaschino' whose real name was Antonio Callegari. Add to these the real men hiding behind civic and ecclesiastical titles—doges, abbots, deans, bishops, and cardinals—and the stage suddenly becomes peopled with an almost unbelievable variety of rich and poor, weak and powerful, famous and infamous. The circle of Monteverdi's friends and acquaintances was nothing if not wide.

A related but independent problem of identity arises when we try to ascertain the recipients of certain letters. It was Monteverdi's custom (though not an invariable one) to take a single-sheet letter, fold it, seal it, and write the name of the addressee on the back: in such instances the name can easily be found even though the ink may have faded. Other letters were tucked into packages of music, while others still, several pages long, were originally enclosed in some form of envelope or folder, which (with the name of the recipient) has long since been discarded.

When there is no name or ancillary clue, it seems to be a matter of guesswork whether the letter was intended for Chieppio, Iberti, Striggio, or Marigliani; or whether the true recipient was a cardinal, a duke, or a prince. Certainly there is substantial divergence of opinion between Davari, Prunières, Malipiero, and Paoli in the matter of identifying each *destinatario*, yet evidence in most cases can be found in the wording of the salutations beginning and ending each letter, as well as in the honorifics used in the body of the letter. Generally speaking, each person is addressed in a manner consistent with the demands of court etiquette, retaining that form of address until his rank or office changes—prince to duke, or cardinal to duke, or count to marquis. Monteverdi errs only two or three times in the extant batch of 127 letters, and then only because he was forgetful of a recent change in rank or situation. His guidelines are therefore highly reliable, and the translations attempt to mirror the hierarchy of titles in such a way as to clarify at all times the issue of identity.

Table of Salutations

DUKE or PRINCE

Serenissimo [mio Singolar] Signore et Padron Collendissimo
[My] Most Serene [and Particular] Lord and Most Respected Master

DUCHESS

Serenissima Signora et Padrona Collendissima
Most Serene Lady and Most Respected Patroness

CARDINAL

Illustrissimo et Reverendissimo Signore mio et Padron Collendissimo
My Most Illustrious and Most Reverend Lord
and Most Respected Master

FOREIGN DUKE, PROCURATOR, MARQUIS, YOUNGER SON OF DUKE

Illustrissimo et Eccellentissimo mio Signore et Padron Collendissimo
My Most Illustrious and Most Excellent Lord
and Most Respected Master

COUNCILLOR, FIRST RANK

Illustrissimo mio Signore et Padron Collendissimo
My Most Illustrious Lord and Most Respected Master

COUNCILLOR, SECOND RANK

Illustrissimo mio Signore et Padron Osservandissimo
My Most Illustrious Lord and Most Esteemed Master

COUNCILLOR, THIRD RANK

Molto Illustre mio Signore et Padron Osservandissimo
My Very Illustrious Lord and Most Esteemed Master

The unusual form of address, 'Molto Illustre et Reverendissimo mio Signore et Padron Collendissimo' (appearing at the head of Letters 124 and 125), corresponds almost exactly with that used by Count Bardi when writing to G. B. Doni in 1634, and it is therefore certain that Monteverdi's two letters about aesthetics and theory were directed to Doni's attention when he was Secretary to the College of Cardinals, even though his name does not appear.

Various honorifics employed in the course of a letter can also help to resolve a question of identity. Their function and significance are dealt with in the appropriate introductions, especially in those cases where attributions may be dubious. In translating these medial references, abbreviated by Monteverdi as 'V.E.Ill.ᵐᵃ', 'A.V.S.', 'V.S.', and so on, I have followed his own example and abbreviated the English equivalent, so that instead of using—perhaps twenty times in any one letter— the cumbersome expression 'Your Most Illustrious Lordship', I have simply used 'Your Lordship'. In Letter 5, addressed to Cardinal Ferdinando Gonzaga, 'V.S.Ill.ᵐᵃ et Rev.ᵐᵃ' is short-circuited to 'Your Eminence'.

Location and State of the Letters

Widely scattered though the letters may be, the vast majority—111 out of 127—are precisely where one would expect to find them: in the Archivio di Stato at Mantua. The Gonzaga, whatever their faults, employed conscientious archivists, thanks to whose efforts it is now possible to reconstruct, from day to day, the throbbing life of a city-state through its greatest era. Even more material would have been at our disposal if other Mantuan recipients of the composer's letters had kept them safe and sound in a strong-box. He certainly wrote to his relatives there: father-in-law, brother-in-law, and his son Massimiliano after he had set up a medical practice. He must have had frequent communication with his lawyer Bagozzi and other officials of court, city, and chapel. The musicians Campagnolo, Dognazzi, Rubini; the entire Basile family—Adriana, her husband, and sisters—could have received dozens of letters from Monteverdi in Venice. Yet nothing survives of all this, nor do we have copies of letters sent to him, apart from a handful of brief memoranda in the Venetian archives.

The four letters to the Duke of Bracciano are also where one would expect them to be: in the Orsini archives, whence they were transferred to the safe keeping of the Archivio Capitolino, Rome. In the Archivio di Stato, Venice, are four more letters addressed by Monteverdi to the Procurators of St Mark's, and to the Doge Francesco Erizzo. In Florence, the city where G. B. Doni was born and died, are two letters undoubtedly addressed to him, which passed from his family to the collector Basevi, who in turn gave them to the Conservatorio.

Logic leaves the scene, however, when we come to explain the present location of five letters addressed to the Marquis Bentivoglio, who lived at

Ferrara when Monteverdi was working on the music for the Farnese wedding in Parma. These five travelled by various means to Forlì, Naples, Bologna, Paris, and Oxford; a sixth letter (no. 121), formerly in the Heyer collection at Cologne, may now be in New York City, but is still untraced at the present time.

Another untraced letter is listed by Carlo Valbianchi in *Raccolte e raccoglitori di autografi in Italia* (Milan, 1901), 186. No date or description is offered, but the name of the owner is given as Cavaliere Dottore Luigi Azzolini, of Via Principe Amadeo 56, Rome. Inquiries directed to this address revealed nothing of the present whereabouts of this letter, though it may possibly have been one of the three at Naples, Bologna, or Paris, since the recent provenance of these remains unknown. It is reasonably clear that certain letters were taken from the archives in Ferrara and subsequently sold privately as soon as it was realized that a Monteverdi autograph could fetch an attractive price, yet the happy outcome is that they are still in safe hands. And that, in the long run, is what really matters.

The letters are written on paper of various sizes, ranging from 18 × 26 cm to 20 × 28 cm, and they consist either of a single folded sheet (resulting in the sizes given above), or in a page torn from the bifolium. Sometimes Monteverdi tore the written page away from the blank one in such a way as to obscure words at line-endings. In the longer letters, he added single or folded pages as required. Those at Mantua are kept in a special Monteverdi file, established by Davari, and with the main batch are two written in 1608 by Baldassare Monteverdi, the composer's father. On each wrapper and letter, a number has been printed in order to preserve the correct sequence of pages. The idea of the special file (*cassetta*) apparently arose because of numerous requests made by visiting scholars who wished to study letters written by artists, architects, and musicians attached to the court.

The uneven distribution of letters over the last forty-two years of the composer's life offers sufficient proof of the fact that vast numbers of them have been lost, perhaps irretrievably. It works out that, on average, we have only three letters from each of the years in the period spanned by the first and the last extant letter; plainly the total of 127 is but a fraction of those that he must actually have written.

[9]

Table of letters in each year

(no letters are extant for years omitted from this list)

1601	1	1617	7	1627	26
1604	2	1618	2	1628	5
1607	1	1619	6	1630	2
1608	2	1620	27	1632	1
1609	2	1621	6	1633	1
1610	2	1622	7	1634	1
1611	2	1623	4	1637	1
1613	1	1624	1	1643	1
1615	4	1625	4		
1616	4	1626	4		

Assuming that many readers will begin by dipping into the letters rather than reading them through from first to last, I have placed each commentary before the letter concerned in order to set the scene, explain the characters briefly, and discuss any particularly difficult problems of interpretation. The commentaries will, I trust, help the reader to appreciate more readily the subtle overtones of each letter in addition to its overall significance in relation to Monteverdi's life.

Finally, a word in defence of Monteverdi, who has not only been accused of omitting punctuation, but also of misquoting titles and misspelling names. In fact he did nothing of the sort. All the so-called 'Monteverdi errors' derive from scholars who transcribed his handwriting incorrectly. In the following translations, however, his idiosyncratic way of spelling personal and place-names has been standardized, since a too rigid adherence to old spellings and dialect forms would have erred on the side of pedantry.

Bibliographical Information

At the beginning of the preface to each letter, there will be found: place and date of writing; addressee (enclosed in square brackets if deduced from internal evidence); library or archive, location, and pressmark; number of folios preserved; number of pages on which letter is written; enclosure (if any); references only to published versions of *Italian* text. (For details of authors and books, see Bibliography.)

NB. Identification of persons mentioned in letters (footnotes with al-phabetical references) are repeated throughout the book as an aid to those readers who may wish to study individual letters. Some duplication with the commentaries was deliberate in order to allow them to be read as a running narrative.

Monteverdi's Life to 1601

Cremona

THE city of Cremona, set amidst fertile plains on the banks of the River Po, may have been dominated politically by Spanish rule in Milan, but it constantly fostered and displayed noteworthy artistic independence, one small facet of which was destined to change the musical world at large. By 1545 the Amati family living in the neighbourhood of San Faustino was already concentrating its skills on shaping and perfecting the new violin, although older stringed instruments such as the viols were still in demand among the more conservative type of musician.

It was a son of Cremona, Agostino Licino, who composed two books of canonic duets (1545 and 1546) for 'viole, violoni & altri stromenti simili', as he says in the dedication of his second book, laid humbly (as was the custom) at the feet of his protector Benedetto Guarna. String music was already international. A composer from Cremona publishes books in Venice, dedicates them to a *molto magnifico patron* from Salerno, and the only surviving copies are in Munich! Writing in unusually discursive fashion, Licino mentions several members of the Guarna family by name and suggests that his 'musical alphabet', despite its simplicity, might prove useful as a change from *primera*, the popular card-game depicted so vividly in music some years later by the elder Alessandro Striggio of Mantua, a virtuoso string-player himself.

Why did the Cremonese succeed in the gradual improvement of their stringed instruments and their music, while others lagged behind? Because they worked extremely hard, through long hours and lean times. They worked to live, and loved to work, and their children, who were many, grew up to the sweet sounds of instruments and voices. Vocal music was also widely cultivated, at first in an ecclesiastical cadre; and many of its proponents sought the protection of a church or an order, as did Lucrezio

This account of Monteverdi's life prior to 1601 is derived from many of the sources drawn upon for the later Mantuan and Venetian years: Ademollo, Bertolotti, Canal, Coniglio, Davari, Vincenzo Errante, Fabbri, Fenlon, Litta, Monterosso, Pontiroli, Santoro, Sartori, Giorgio Sommi-Picenardi, Guido Sommi-Picenardi, Tagmann, and Vogel.

Quinzano, who was born about 1556 in Cremona and later became a Cistercian monk. His frenzied dedication to work of many kinds was of such intensity that he became ill and died when comparatively young, although an eight-part setting of *Duo seraphim* in Vienna's National Library proves him a minor master even so. That same liturgical text was known to another son of Cremona, yet to be born— Claudio Monteverdi.

A sure sign of Cremona's growing artistic tendencies appeared in the several meetings, at first informal, that took place in the late 1550s between three learned men, Pietro Martire Ponzio, Giovanni Battista Mainoldo, and Sigismondo Picenardi, with a view to establishing an *accademia* where discussions could be held and concerts given. These plans finally bore fruit in 1560 when the Accademia degli Animosi came into being and took for itself the motto *In casus omnes*.

Poets and literary men made frequent contributions to this new platform for the city's intellectuals, and as time went on they were joined by musicians, notably Giovanni Sinibaldi and his daughter Anna, both renowned string instrumentalists, Giovanni Francesco Mainero, the organist and organ-builder, and the young Marc'Antonio Ingegneri. By 1565 Ingegneri, a composer and teacher from Verona, was also well known as a virtuoso string-player. Residing in the district of San Pantaleone, he enjoyed the protection of nearby Carmelite fathers in San Bartolomeo, who were known to take especially good care of violinists and violin-makers. Later he was to pass on his mastery of musical arts and his skill in violin-playing to Claudio Giovanni Antonio, first-born son of Baldassare Monteverdi (a barber-surgeon) and his wife Maddalena Zignani, who came from a family of goldsmiths. They were married during the early months of 1566 in the same parish that sheltered the Amatis.

Claudio Monteverdi, baptized at the church of SS. Nazaro e Celso on 15 May 1567, was destined to make original and lasting contributions to the art of string-playing. He sought out and perfected such emotional underscorings as percussive pizzicato and its complete opposite, the long slow bow-strokes of melting beauty. Musically aroused, he could produce shattering martellato strokes, and he probably encouraged a discreet use of vibrato, which in one of his letters he described as a very pleasing effect. Like his teacher Ingegneri he accepted the fact that his string-writing would take second place to his vocal endeavours, the simple reason being that whereas vocal music had been cultivated far and wide for many centuries, the playing of stringed instruments was not yet a settled feature of the musical landscape.

In his mature years he would go to St Mark's, Venice as director of music, and the year of his birth saw the publication of a book of ricercari by Claudio Merulo, who then held the position of the basilica's first organist. In Mantua, where Monteverdi would make an indelible impression, his future mentor Giaches de Wert brought out the first secular publication of his Mantuan career.

By 1568 Camillo Mainero (brother of the organ-builder Giovanni) was organist of Cremona Cathedral, while Germano Pallavicino, organist of San Francesco, was shortly to leave for Mantua. If Cremona could nourish a young artist, he would have to export himself should he wish to make progress in the musical world.

An active and upwardly mobile Cremonese group came from the Morsolino family—Giovanni Battista, Antonio, and Omobono—and all three played minor roles in Monteverdi's unfolding and growing career. But despite Mantua's proximity and its many opportunities for musical practitioners, it was also known to be a hard centre of scandal and libertinism. De Wert, the very man whose passionate madrigals and noble church music were to inspire many musicians, became involved with the Ferrarese singer and poetess Tarquinia Molza, from whom he was eventually separated by order of the duke.

On 16 May 1571 a daughter, Maria, was born to Baldassare and Maddalena Monteverdi, and on 31 January 1573 a son, Giulio Cesare. He followed his elder brother in a musical career, first at Mantua, then as organist in Castelleone and in Salò, where he was struck down by the plague in 1630. Their mother died in 1576, leaving the father responsible for three children below the age of nine, and not surprisingly he remarried in the following year. His second wife, Giovanna Gadio, bore him three more children but survived only for a few years. The burden on the family as a whole was not diminishing, but the elder son already showed remarkable signs of musical aptitude.

By cutting through side streets and hurrying down what is now the Corso Matteotti, Claudio could be at the cathedral in a little over five minutes, and there he learnt not only to sing and take part in the choral services but also to develop his ability as a player of the viols and—more important—the violins that were being perfected only a short distance away by the Amati family. His teacher in this absorbing and challenging world of music was the newly appointed *maestro di cappella*, Marc'Antonio Ingegneri, a native of Verona, where the young student found one of his first patrons.

Ingegneri, a versatile and inspired individual, played both the old and newer type of stringed instruments with amazing skill. In addition he ranked as a fine choral conductor and an above-average composer. Little wonder that the Monteverdi boys worked so hard and achieved such early distinction—especially Claudio, whose progress was so rapid and brilliant that he unwittingly drew upon himself the envy of other local musicians, young and old. He hints at this in his dedication of the *Sacrae cantiunculae* (1582) to Don Stefano Canini Valcarenghi, whom he calls upon for protection against the slanderous tongues of his jealous detractors. Such is ever the experience of youthful genius.

A general census took place in 1576, and from it we can see that Cremona was a growing city of nearly fifty parishes and a total population approaching 36,000. Among them could be found a vast variety of trades and professions—just over three hundred, including about forty teachers, some of them specialists in music and singing. Although only one instrument-maker is named, Andrea Amati, there were five players in five different parishes: Giovanni Carubello, B. Albricho, Faro Tinto (a lutenist), Camillo di Barozi, and one who is an unnamed *sonador*—the Spanish term indicating the instigators of the census.

The fashion for ensemble music in four parts, distantly anticipating the string quartet, began to make itself increasingly apparent in the years when Ingegneri was developing his orchestra at Cremona cathedral. Cristofano Malvezzi, director of music to the Grand Duke of Tuscany, launched a set of ricercari (one by the singer and composer Jacopo Peri) in 1577, and Giorgio Mainerio of Parma followed in 1578 with a light-hearted collection of dances in Hungarian, Venetian, French, English, German, and Flemish styles. Not to be outdone or outshone, Ingegneri then produced his second book of madrigals, ending with two *arie di canzon francese per sonar*. Three anthologies, all containing four-part instrumental music.

What he wrote for Cremona, however, was Christmas music, and the prefects were so pleased with what they heard that they granted him a special payment of 62 imperial lire for the magnificent concertos and sonatas performed in the cathedral in 1578. That year, the Duchess of Milan and her courtiers, returning from a visit to Loreto, spent an entire week in Cremona, staying with friends in the Santa Agata district, and she may well have heard some of the rehearsals. The chamber orchestra and its repertoire had at last found favour in the ears of the clergy, nobility, and laity.

By 1579, when Chiara Maximilia was born to the Monteverdis, concerts were on a regular footing. In 1580 Ottaviano Cantù, an eminent councillor, gave a speech referring to the old practice of employing a cornettist, pointing out that this had fallen into disuse because the proper fees were not paid. A better player being thereupon hired, he at once agreed to a new annual contract obliging him to take part in all the cathedral concerts.

Ingegneri, his fame and fortune growing, married Margherita Soresini on 22 January 1581, the witnesses being three of his musical colleagues. On 7 February Luca Monteverdi was born, and if this were not enough to enliven the family, there was the state visit, late in February, of Prince Vincenzo Gonzaga, whose ill-fated marriage to Margherita Farnese would take place on 2 March. If his stay in the city was brief, he let it be widely known that his prevailing passion, apart from women, was for music. Every connoisseur of the art knew of his renowned groups of singers and instrumentalists in Mantua, and it is not impossible that he listened intently, as was his wont, to the virtuosi of Cremona, among whose younger members was Claudio Monteverdi, about to send to Angelo Gardano (Ingegneri's Venetian publisher) his very first collection of church music: the three-voice *Sacrae cantiunculae*. This work and his next four bore the legend 'pupil of Ingegneri'.

While Prince Vincenzo dallied in Cremona, another of his later collaborators, Giovan Battista Guarini, in Ferrara had begun to sketch *Il pastor fido*, and that too would affect Monteverdi. In the mean time purely local events faintly threatened the peace of the cathedral organ loft, for the frequent concerts calling for the union of stringed instruments and organ (a point of authenticity too often forgotten today) meant that either the strings had to tune up or the organ to be tuned down. Ingegneri, as a string-player, was first to suggest the latter solution, and the prefects discussed the issue at their meeting on 19 January 1582.

The proposed 'abbassamento' of the organ soon brought up other problems, for it was found that some pipes did not sound as they should, that the bellows could not always be relied upon, and that other pipes were markedly defective. Ingegneri, together with the organist Camillo Mainero, sent a memorandum to the prefects requesting prompt action in view of concert commitments. One idea led to another, and in stating the need for new pipes there was also an appeal for a tremolo, either to supply the vibrato that was lacking in the string tone or to agree with it if in fact it already existed.

By the time Monteverdi's little books appeared, the organ question had been submitted to Giovanni Battista Morsolino, a Cremonese serving as organist in Bergamo. Finally none other than Graziadio Antegnati, one of the most famous organ-builders of the age, became involved, and the documents began to pile up in the cathedral archives. Despite the prevailing problem of reconciling string and organ pitch, the Christmas concerts continued and Ingegneri's vital role in them was once again praised by the cathedral authorities.

On 29 January 1583 Filippo Monteverdi was born, the last child of Baldassare: he eventually played a more important family role than some of his immediate predecessors. Claudio, with such an auspicious beginning to his career as a composer, could hardly fail to continue in the same vein, and 1583 saw the publication of his four-part *Madrigali spirituali*, dedicated to Antonio Fraganesco, one of the leading figures in Cremona's council, in which he fulfilled the role of 'decurione'—an official in charge of ten men. A quarter of a century later, Monteverdi would see many of his secular madrigals reissued with sacred texts supplied by his friend Aquilino Coppini, and later on still the *Selva morale e spirituale* would feature sacred and secular works with Italian texts.

But there was as yet no instrumental music from his pen. Composers of vocal anthologies occasionally slipped in one or two pieces suitable for ensembles, as did the Apostolic Protonotary Lodovico Agostini in *Il nuovo echo* of 1583, with its 'Intramezzo' and 'Fantasia ad imitatione del Signor Alessandro Striggio', both for five parts. As for the organ discussions, they finally wound down in the summer months, with Ingegneri and his colleague Fadosio Malnepote beating a discreet retreat but maintaining that the idea of lowering the organ pitch was due not so much to pressure from the string-players as to please the citizens who came to the cathedral to listen. A face-saving document was duly drafted, and the entire excursion gently vanished into obscurity. Its message to posterity is, however, very clear: that those involved in concert-giving were prepared to go to considerable lengths to ensure the collaboration of strings and organ.

From Milan came an order forbidding barber-surgeons to poach on the preserves of medical doctors. If this pronouncement initially caused some resentment, it appears to have been circumvented by allowing the lesser ranks to qualify in some measure and add to their names the prefix 'dottore'. Baldassare must have been duly relieved, as doubtless were many of his colleagues in Cremona.

By April of 1584 Guarini was devising a fetchingly erotic scene about blind man's buff for the third act of *Il pastor fido*, but admitted to Vincenzo Gonzaga that it was but an idea for a dance, so far without words or music. The Striggio family, at this time resident in Mantua, were invited by Alfonso d'Este to stay at Ferrara for three weeks to listen to the ladies' concerts, and off they went, Alessandro, his wife, and their 11-year-old son Alessandrino, who would later write the libretto for Monteverdi's *Orfeo*. But stage music was as yet far from Monteverdi's mind.

In October he was overjoyed to see his third work, the *Canzonette*, published in Venice with a dedication to Pietro Ambrosini, a member of a Bolognese family by that time solidly established in Cremona. Ambrosini may have been an art-lover, for Monteverdi states that just as a painting by a little-known artist can gain prestige from the place where it is displayed, so too can a musical composition be enhanced by its association with a famous man. Nor was the analogy with art fortuitous. Cremona could hardly fail to be proud of the Campi family—Giulio, Bernardino, Antonio, and Vincenzo—for all were gifted and versatile artists whose mature classicism placed them on a high level of excellence, while the long-lived Sofonisba Anguissola (1527–1625) ranged widely in her search for pictorial ideas and subjects, which included her own self-portrait.

The art of dancing was widely cultivated in Italy, and Monteverdi would write at least four ballets during the course of his early life. Vincenzo's sister, Anna Caterina Gonzaga, witnessed a ballet at Ferrara in February 1585, with words by Guarini and music by Ippolito Fiorino, scored for violins, harpsichords, and organs, which struggled to make themselves heard above the sound of the dancing. In the following year, 1586, Monteverdi (by then 19) spent a great deal of time perfecting his first essay in five-part harmony, the *Libro primo de madregali*, to be published in 1587, with a dedication to Count Marco Verità dated 27 January.

Marco Verità and his brother Gasparo lived at Verona, where they were influential in the Accademia Filarmonica. Remembering that Ingegneri was Veronese, it is highly likely that this introduction came through him, and possible also that Monteverdi had contacted the city where as a young and promising practitioner he might become eligible for employment. Marco Verità appears as one of the interlocutors in Pietro Ponzio's *Dialogo della musica* (1595), and he was also the dedicatee (together with his brother) of a book of *Capricci e madrigali* by Paolo Fonghetti in 1598, and of the *Giardinetto de madrigale e canzonette* by various authors published in 1588.

Almost contemporary with Monteverdi's *Primo libro* was the formation of a ladies' ensemble by Vincenzo, who became fourth Duke of Mantua and Monferrato on 22 September 1587, and the publication of Tasso's *La cavaletta*, a work begun two years previously, and which exhorts Striggio, Wert, and Luzzaschi to bring back true *gravitas* to the madrigal, avoiding the flighty and the frivolous. His message was not always heeded, for Vincenzo enjoyed the lighter secular music of Gastoldi, Wert, Pallavicino, Rossi, and Baccusi. From 1588 until 1591 all those composers brought out secular collections, and all enjoyed an ever-increasing reputation. The state of the Mantuan treasury, which under the new duke authorized such expenditure on the arts, was succinctly conveyed in a report to Venice by her ambassador to Mantua, Francesco Contarini, in 1588.

Mantua

At 22 Monteverdi was ready to leave home. He had four publications to his credit, ten or a dozen years of experience as a violinist and singer, a growing acquaintance with the harmonic possibilities of the *viola bastarda* or lyra viol, and a fair comprehension of the tough nature of the musical profession. His old teacher Ingegneri was ailing. Florence, with its plans to outshine the smaller courts in the intermezzi for Bargagli's play 'La Pellegrina', reached as far north as Mantua for its hired instrumentalists (the two Striggios) and as far south as Rome for its singers. Monteverdi may have travelled there. He definitely travelled to Milan, where in 1589 he met Jacomo Ricardi, a native of Lodi who had served as the Milanese Resident in Rome. A lawyer by profession and music-lover by inclination, he accepted the dedication of Monteverdi's *Secondo libro de madrigali* in the early days of 1590. Monteverdi clearly played for Ricardi, for he refers in his writing to 'the feeble motion of my hand on the viola', which was probably the understatement of the year.

This time the support of an important statesman outside the orbit of Cremona paid off, although not in the form of an invitation to Milan. Instead there were inviting sounds from Mantua, perhaps an echo of Duke Vincenzo's visit to Cremona eight years previously. If the actual date of Monteverdi's departure is unknown, his letters make it clear that his service at Mantua must have begun in 1589. In the new book of madrigals, he describes himself for the last time as a pupil of Ingegneri, and the style of the compositions has already moved to another level.

Music in Mantua was also at a higher level than at Cremona. The duke employed a large number of musicians on a regular basis, and invited eminent guests from time to time—usually female singers in whom he professed an amiable if not amatory interest. Indeed his favourite lady, Agnese del Carretto, Marchioness of Grana, was a singer and poet of no mean accomplishments, and held court at the Palazzo del Tè where she surrounded herself with poets and musicians. One of the former, Muzio Manfredi, was so moved by a performance that he wept openly, and was rewarded by the loan of Agnese's handkerchief. The emotional content of the madrigals must have been potent and persuasive.

Ippolito Baccusi came to the cathedral as organist in 1590, while the duke ordered a harpsichord from Venice, and a salary roll prepared about the same time named Monteverdi as a member of the court ensemble along with half a dozen violinists and ten singers.

Among the violinists was Salomone Rossi, and the singers included the two sisters from Vicenza Lucia and Isabetta Pellizari, Francesco Rasi (who was later to sing the title role in *Orfeo*), Pandolfo Grandi, Bassano Casola from Lodi, and Giovanni Battista Marinone. Duke Vincenzo provided them not only with a salary, but with food, unusually scarce in that year in many parts of Italy due to the famine, which Mantuan plans had managed to ward off. Towards the end of the year Agnese del Carretto was busy organizing and rehearsing *Il pastor fido*, casting Francesco Campagnolo, a future virtuoso tenor, as Silvio. It was not by chance that the child she had by Vincenzo bore the same name, yet the production did not thrive, and Guarini had to be called in to attend to some of the crises.

Cardinal Bellarmine later insisted that the play had corrupted more sons of the church than either Luther or Calvin, and little wonder, for the poet's own scenario for the intermezzi still preserved in Ferrara mentions not only naked nymphs but naked old men, all of whom might perhaps be allowed to cover their parts with a thin veil. Instruments they had in abundance: bagpipes, strings, flutes, cornetti, reed pipes, and recorders. Guarini was still writing letters to the duke about it as late as May.

Monteverdi, by June, had more important things on hand, for it was then that he saw the publication of his *Terzo libro de madregali*, with a dedication to Vincenzo Gonzaga stressing the fortunate introduction to his service through 'the noble exercise of the viola'. The madrigals already show a turn towards the virtuosic element resulting from the magnificent singers at court. The composer, who would have kept in touch with Cremona, heard that Ingegneri had died on 1 July and his position taken over by Rodiano Barera.

The year 1593 was darkened by the continuing feud between Mantua and Parma, for Ranuccio Farnese had never forgiven the slight to his sister when Vincenzo abandoned her and married Eleonora de' Medici. But the quarrelsome noblemen were reconciled, in so far as they could be, late in July 1594, and Monteverdi, who always tried to stay well away from trouble, further explored his vein of secular vocal music. He contributed four canzonette to a collection of works by other Cremonese composers, notably Antonio and Omobono Morsolino, published by Amadino in Venice. Copies were sent by Valeriano Cattaneo in late December to Vincenzo's sister, who had become the wife of Duke Alfonso II d'Este.

Duke Vincenzo, called upon to join an alliance against the marauding Turks who were already on the way to Buda and Pest with a fair-sized army, summoned his Mantuan troops and set out for the plains of Hungary, doubtless attracted by visions of military glory. He and his army left Mantua in June 1595, with a small *cappella* directed by Monteverdi. Francesco Gonzaga, Bishop of Mantua, blessed the troops and all who travelled with them, and the journey took them first across Austria and then by fleets of barges down the Inn and the Danube.

While the army proceeded directly to join the imperial troops, Vincenzo left by a slightly divergent route that took him and his large retinue of personal servants, bodyguards, and chapel to Linz and Vienna. He took part in festivities involving noble relatives and princes, and also found time to put down an insurrection over arrears of pay by distributing largesse on a generous scale. He met Archduke Matthias on 16 Spetember, and shortly afterwards announced himself ready to do battle, aided by Aldobrandini and the papal troops who had come to join them.

Fortunato Cardi, a Mantuan court secretary who accompanied the expedition, wrote of an impressive ceremony on the eve of battle when Vincenzo, wishing to transport the cultural cast of his dukedom to the neighbourhood of riverside Visegrád (Plintenburg), attended a vespers service at which Monteverdi provided the music. His colleagues included Padre Teodoro Bacchino (a castrato despite his cloth), Padre Serafino Terzi (bass), Giovanni Marinone (another bass, not identical with the later Marinoni 'detto Giove', who compiled a memorial volume, *Fiori poetici*, after the composer's death), Padre Valerio—a chaplain from Ferrara, who probably sang alto—and possibly one other.

This ensemble could certainly have done justice to some of the five-voice settings published much later in Monteverdi's anthologies of 1641 and 1650, where the more backward-looking examples could well be survivors of this very expedition. Fortunato Cardi's account claims that Monteverdi was considered separately as a director and had in his charge five musicians; in this case the ensemble could even have performed six-part compositions. Conjecture, however, is of less importance than the firm knowledge that music resounded meaningfully in those distant parts, and may have redounded more to the credit of the duke than did his military exploits, the inconvenience and embarrassment of which drove the Italians back to Mantua by November.

The death of Giaches de Wert on 23 May 1596 created a musico-political shift that was eventually to move the courtly scene away from chamber music and towards drama. Benedetto Pallavicino followed him in office, forming a strong team with Gastoldi, who was already at Santa Barbara. More violinists joined the orchestra, notably the Rubini brothers, Giovanni Battista and Ottavio, whose arrival in 1597 provided two more composers as well as two more string-players.

Mantuan composers began to gain fame abroad. Five of them—Wert, Baccusi, Pallavicino, Rovigo, and Gastoldi—were represented along with five of Monteverdi's madrigals from books two and three in Kaufmann's anthology, *Fiori del giardino di diversi eccellentissimi autori*, issued in Nuremberg in 1597. Still only 30 years old, Monteverdi had stepped beyond his country's bounds as regards publication, and his knowledge of the likelihood of this useful export may have helped him decide on marriage, which followed two years later. Before then, however, he had to contend with a major ceremonial event at court, the baptism of Leonora Anna Maria in 1598, the last daughter of Vincenzo and Leonora and the future empress of Austria. Music there must have been, but no signs of it have come down to us in the published works of Monteverdi. Not all occasional music survived, and very little of it formed part of the regular repertoire.

The great artistic event of the year was the definitive production of *Il pastor fido*, which this time benefited considerably from techniques employed in Ferrara and—at least in Gastoldi's music for the *Gioco della cieca*—in Florence. The ballet sections had been worked out and developed with skill and persistence without obliging performers to sing and dance at the same time. Hidden choruses provided the necessary music, supported by audible instrumental groups and their continuo departments. A topic of courtly conversation for many years, the persistent pastoral had at last become a reality, and within a decade the brightest light in Mantuan musical drama would be invited, or rather commanded, to supply a new and epoch-making entertainment on a libretto by Alessandrino, no longer diminutive but a respected official in the Gonzaga administration. *Orfeo* would not be a spoken drama with musical interludes, but an opera, a 'work' in its own right. In that same year Ferrara was annexed by Pope Clement VIII, and the way was now clear for Mantua to triumph over Florence, if such a deed were possible.

Mantua's actors, on a level of importance with her musicians in far-off days, have tended to fall into oblivion, whereas composers are still remembered through those of their works that are still performed today. Yet an occasional quirk of confusion such as mistaken identity can sometimes prolong an actor's image, and this happened to Tristano Martinelli, the greatest Arlecchino of his day. On 29 April 1599 Duke Vincenzo appointed him chief actor at court, and he later enjoyed a career that took him to France, where he was widely admired and appreciated. Although somewhat older than Monteverdi, his physiognomy was sufficiently similar to the composer's to cause Domenico Feti's portrait of Martinelli to be mistaken for Monteverdi even in fairly recent years.

The violinist Giacomo Cattaneo, along with the Rubinis, Barberoli, Barbimoli, Farina, and Frolandi, was a colleague of Monteverdi's from the 1590s onwards. The irrepressibly gregarious nature of practising musicians is such that one usually expects a few stray strands of social intercourse by way of relaxation after rehearsals and concerts. It was doubtless in this manner that Monteverdi became aware of Cattaneo's daughter Claudia, and they were obviously attracted to each other besides being bound by shared musical interests.

When they were married in 1599, by permission of the duke, their small stage was set and lit within the vastly larger one that was Mantua, and the forty-two years of correspondence which we have from Monteverdi's pen was about to flow forth soon after the opening of the new century.

LETTERS
and
Commentaries

THE FAMILY OF VINCENZO I GONZAGA

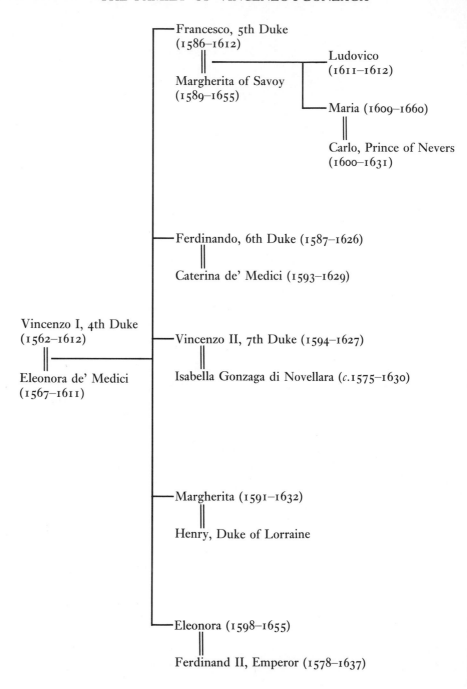

Francesco, 5th Duke
(1586–1612)
‖
Margherita of Savoy
(1589–1655)

Ludovico
(1611–1612)

Maria (1609–1660)
‖
Carlo, Prince of Nevers
(1600–1631)

Ferdinando, 6th Duke (1587–1626)
‖
Caterina de' Medici (1593–1629)

Vincenzo I, 4th Duke
(1562–1612)
‖
Eleonora de' Medici
(1567–1611)

Vincenzo II, 7th Duke (1594–1627)
‖
Isabella Gonzaga di Novellara (c.1575–1630)

Margherita (1591–1632)
‖
Henry, Duke of Lorraine

Eleonora (1598–1655)
‖
Ferdinand II, Emperor (1578–1637)

I

Mantua, 28 November 1601
to Duke Vincenzo Gonzaga, at Kanizsa

Mantua, Archivio Gonzaga, Cassetta 6, fos. 77–8. Bifolio: 3 pp. and address

Davari, 82; Malipiero, 127; Paoli, 17; Fabbri 1985, 66; Lax, 13

Two perversely fascinating features in this letter—which is not an autograph, but a fair copy by a scribe—tower above all the rest. One is that the letter could never have reached the besieged town of Kanizsa,[1] a few miles east of the present border between Croatia and Hungary, where Monteverdi believed Duke Vincenzo and his army to be stationed; the other is that because the date of Pallavicino's death has been placed twenty-nine weeks too soon in every musical dictionary prior to the *New Grove*, certain matters have been totally misunderstood, and the motives of the writer questioned.

Opinions as to the style and content of the letter vary from Paoli's 'a minor masterpiece of tact'[2] to Redlich's epithets—'typical . . . expressive', 'malicious'.[3] Truth to tell, Monteverdi was neither tactful nor malicious: he was absolutely honest and outspoken, and he can usually be relied upon when his latter-day commentators cannot. Shortly after his marriage to Claudia Cattaneo on 20 May 1599,[4] the composer had been sent on a journey to northern Europe as a member of the Duke's musical retinue. He managed to avoid the slightly later and definitely less pleasant trip to the marshes of southern Hungary when Vincenzo, convinced of a personal need for military glory, set out from Mantua on 18 July 1601, at the head of troops that were destined to join papal forces, Florentine mercenaries, and German *Landsknechte* in a frontal attack on the Turkish army under Hannam Pasha.

Monteverdi had a valid excuse for staying in Mantua, for his wife was expecting her first child, and on 27 August at the church of SS. Simone e Giuda the infant was baptized and given the names Francesco Baldassare, out of deference to Prince Francesco (represented at the church by another Francesco, 'Illustrissimus D.

---

[1] Now Nagykanizsa; it was known in Italy at that time as Canisa or Canissa.

[2] Paoil, *Monteverdi*, 77.   [3] Redlich, 13, 170.

[4] Gallico, 'Documents', 71. Eugenius Cagnatius, one of the witnesses, is the Eugenio Cagnani who wrote the *Lettera cronologica* addressed to Duke Francesco on 19 Feb. 1612. This letter praises Monteverdi and Striggio for their *Orfeo*, in which Francesco Rasi, the virtuoso tenor, appeared. Although there is no specific mention of the role he took, his voice and his artistic stature make it clear that he must have sung the part of Orpheus. For the complete text of the letter, see *Mantova: Le lettere*, ii. 621.

Franciscus de Odinis', as the records have it), and to the composer's father Baldassare Monteverdi. In the mean time, the two gentlemen quietly blocking Monteverdi's path to promotion were very much alive: Gian Giacomo Gastoldi,[5] who was in charge of the music at the ducal chapel of S. Barbara, and Benedetto Pallavicino, responsible for Vincenzo's private chapel and chamber music.

Vincenzo discovered something of the nature of his campaign problems long before he reached the field, for his sojourn in Graz soon revealed the existence of jealousies, both petty and tremendous, over the matter of who was going to give orders to whom. It was in fact an ill-disciplined and disparate army with too few cannon and too many commanders, and by the time it had reached Kanizsa the Turks knew that they had little to fear. After further bickering over matters of rank and authority, Vincenzo managed to make a sortie, but without gaining any significant tactical advantage over the enemy. Then he began to be troubled with an old ailment—a sore knee which confined him to his tent and gave him time to think of other methods of attack. Hopelessly addicted to the lures and promises of alchemists, whom he maintained at court in considerable numbers, he wrote to Mantua urging them to invent a new kind of cannon-ball that would dispense soporific or poisonous gases within the Turkish stronghold.

Nothing resulted apart from additional expense, but as time went on the weather at Kanizsa deteriorated and even Vincenzo (who should have been well looked after) took to complaining about conditions of total discomfort. His young secretary, Alessandro Striggio, the future author of the libretto for Monteverdi's *Orfeo*, found the hot days and freezing nights extremely hard on such as were used to a more temperate climate, while his superior, Annibale Chieppio, wrote to Eleonora Gonzaga that torrential rains had soaked his mattress.[6] Nor was morale improved by increasingly deadly Turkish fire and the arrival of German reinforcements whose commander, Colonel Roswurm, made it quite clear that Vincenzo's army and command were alike unsatisfactory.

The once proud but now humble Duke had only just written to his master of revels, Federico Follino, outlining a splendid series of tableaux depicting the siege and capture of Kanizsa, for performance at the following carnival (1602). Yet nothing could be done but give the order to strike camp, and by sheer irony the Mantuans were already leaving the scene of muddy misfortune when, on 28 November, Follino sent his letter about the superb scenario he had devised,[7] and Monteverdi sent his request to be appointed Director of Music. Neither letter reached Vincenzo at Kanizsa, because he was already on his way westward, but they may have come into his hands at Graz, or at some point nearer home territory. The bedraggled army arrived in Mantua on 18 December after a tiresome winter crossing of the Brenner Pass, and jubilation yielded place to feelings of relief. Everybody concerned wanted to

---

[5] For Gastoldi's position, see Jeppesen, 317–19, where the correct dates of birth and death are given: 1554–1609 (4 Jan.). Note that the reference 4/1 1609 is written in the European style—day, month, year.
[6] Errante, 'Forse che sì', 56.   [7] Ibid. 106–9.

save face, and to this end considerable trouble was taken to convince other principalities of Vincenzo's good intentions if not of his bravery.[8]

The central part of the letter lists four names—Striggio, de Wert, Rovigo, and Pallavicino—in a context that suggests some kind of succession in which Monteverdi had hoped to have some part or interest. The elder Alessandro Striggio, who died on 29 February 1592 in the district of Cervo,[9] enjoyed the status of a greatly admired but unpaid musical servant of the Gonzaga court. Giaches de Wert was titular Director of Music at S. Barbara from about 1582 until his death on 6 May 1596, the bulk of his later work being madrigalian or dramatic.[10] Francesco Rovigo, who had returned to Mantua in 1591 after a lucrative spell at Graz, excelled as an organist but was also adept in the composition of sacred and secular vocal music.

Although Monteverdi, as singer, violinist, and composer, struck a somewhat different figure from his predecessors, and perhaps for that very reason was considered unsuitable to succeed them, he had evidently made some previous efforts to secure an appointment because he uses the word 'persevere', and later the expression 'to seek once more'. It must be emphasized that he was not applying for the Directorship of Music at S. Barbara, for this was held by Gastoldi. His request to the Duke was for control over the music in the Duke's private chapel, which travelled with him at all times, and in the wide and loosely defined area of chamber music. That request was granted, and on 10 April 1602 the Duke also conferred Mantuan citizenship upon Monteverdi and his family.[11]

[Address:] To the Most Serene Lord, my Most Respected Lord, the Lord Duke of Mantua, Canisa

Most Serene Lord, my Most Respected Master,

If I did not hasten to ask personally of Your Highness's good grace, on this occasion of Pallavicino's[a] death, for the musical appointment which Signor Giaches[b] formerly had, perhaps envy in the designs of others might, to my detriment, use such obvious ploys[c]—more akin to rhetoric than music—that tainting Your Highness's good will towards me they could give you to believe that this arose from some fear of my incapacity, or from

---

[8] Coniglio, 376.

[9] Documentary information kindly communicated by Professor Pierre Tagmann.

[10] For a complete account of his life and works see MacClintock, *Wert*.

[11] Although the original decree was lost, a new authorization was issued by Duke Carlo in June 1628. See Davari, 84.

[a] Benedetto Pallavicino.   [b] Giaches de Wert.

[c] *sifatti modi* has a pejorative meaning in this context.

some excessive self-assurance; and therefore I was waiting ambitiously for what (unworthy servant that I am) I should have affectionately requested and sought out with special humility.

Furthermore, if I did not also try to seize the chance of serving Your Highness as often as an occasion presents itself, you would have particular reason to complain justly of my negligent service; and similarly my poor knowledge not seeking (to good ends) greater opportunity for showing itself to your most refined musical taste as of some worth in motets and masses too, you would have just cause to complain of me.

And finally, the world—having seen me persevere in Your Highness's service with much eagerness on my part and with good grace on yours, after the death of the famous Signor Striggio,^d and after that of the excellent Signor Giaches, and again a third time after that of the excellent Signor Franceschino,^e and again (lastly) after this of the competent Messer^f Benedetto Pallavicino—could with reason murmur of my negligence if, not because of my skill but because of the loyal and singular devotion I have always maintained in regard to Your Highness's service, I did not once more seek the position now vacant in this quarter of the church, and did not in all respects ask most eagerly and humbly for the aforementioned title.

For all the above reasons, then, and perhaps for those which—to my good fortune—your kindness could add (since you have never disdained to hear my humble compositions), I ask beseechingly to be Director^g of Music both of the chamber and of the church; which post, if your kindness and grace will so honour me, I shall receive with the humility that befits a feeble servant when he is encouraged and favoured by a great prince as is Your Highness, to whom I bow and make a most humble reverence, daily praying God for the greatest contentment that a devoted and loyal servant can most affectionately wish his lord.

from Mantua, 28 November 1601

Your Most Serene Highness's

most humble and most grateful servant

Claudio Monteverdi

---

^d Alessandro Striggio, the elder.   ^e Francesco Rovigo.

^f Following a threefold repetition of *Signor*, the word 'Messer' slightly downgrades Pallavicino (along with the word 'competent').

^g The old form *mastro* is used.

2

Mantua, 27 October 1604
to Duke Vincenzo Gonzaga, at Casale Monferrato[1]

Mantua, Archivio Gonzaga, Cassetta 6, fos. 81–2. Bifolio: 3 pp. and address

Prunières, 231; Malipiero, 129; Paoli, 21; Lax, 14

The three years that separate Letters 1 and 2 were eventful for the entire Monteverdi family. Confirmation of his court appointment and Mantuan citizenship in 1602 must have sounded to the composer like an overture to a new era, and his personal feelings were to some extent mirrored in the art of music itself. On 2 April 1602 Lodovico Grossi da Viadana dedicated to the Marquis Alfonso d'Este a work that was destined to change the future course of church music—the *Cento concerti ecclesiastici*, whose *falsobordone* figurations were later to appear in Monteverdi's *Dixit Dominus* of 1610.[2] The general growth of interest in basso continuo possibilities led Duke Vincenzo (see Pl. 1) to add an organ and a lute to his collection of instruments.[3] Monteverdi's improved social position and salary encouraged him to leave his father-in-law's house in the parish of SS. Simone e Giuda, and take up residence nearer to the ducal palace. If the location of this house cannot now be accurately ascertained, it is nevertheless clear that it must have been in the parish of S. Pietro, whose baptismal records show the names of the composer's daughter, Leonora Camilla (who did not long survive), and of his second son Massimiliano.[4]

Presumably this move took place late in 1602, for by 20 February 1603—when the infant daughter was baptized—Monteverdi's family had already taken up residence in their new parish. Leonora, named after the Duchess, had as godparents Count Giulio Caffino (who was represented by his son) and Countess Polissena Gonzaga, daughter of Prince Francesco Gonzaga of Castiglione delle Stiviere.[5] Although composers were considered of less importance than singers, Monteverdi's name was linked with that

---

[1] Casale Monferrato was the governmental seat of large territories assigned to the Gonzagas of Mantua by the Emperor Charles V in 1536. These territories, although providing a massive buttress between Savoyard Turin and Spanish Milan, brought endless trouble to the Mantuan administration, yet it was during Vincenzo's reign that conditions were at their best. He fortified Casale at vast expense, and either he or his ministers paid frequent visits to the city, whose cathedral has in recent years disclosed unsuspected musical treasures.

[2] Viadana: *Cento concerti ecclesiastici*, ed. C. Gallico (Kassel, 1964).

[3] Bertolotti, 80 (letters of Girolamo Stauber and G. M. Lugharo, 1602).

[4] Gallico, 'Documents', 68.   [5] Coniglio, 482 (and Tavola 3).

1. Vincenzo I Gonzaga, fourth Duke of Mantua. Anonymous oil painting.
Soprintendenza alle Gallerie di Mantova. Photo: G. Giovetti, Mantua

of the virtuoso tenor Rasi in a letter from Arcangiolo Manara of Verona to the Duke of Mantua, both musicians being praised for their excellence, especially as theorbo-players.[6] Above all, Monteverdi was surrounded by friends, among whom the cornetto-player Giulio Cesare Bianchi, also a native of Cremona, was later to occupy the 'casa Monteverdi' in that city and publish Claudio's Litany of the Rosary and several of his motets.[7]

On 1 March 1603 Monteverdi dedicated his Fourth Book of Madrigals to 'the most illustrious lords and most respected masters of the Accademici Intrepidi of Ferrara', assuring them of his perpetual esteem and obligation for the many favours granted to him and to his musical colleagues.[8] That sense of indebtedness is also reflected in his choice of poetry by Arlotti, Moro, Rinuccini, Tasso, and above all Guarini, a sure indication of his awareness of much extra-Mantuan literary culture, as well as a reliable guide to the extent of his participation in the Ferrarese production of *Il pastor fido* in 1595.

Duke Vincenzo, constantly on the lookout for further additions to what has been referred to—not without some justification—as his musical harem, began a negotiation in June 1603 with the papal singer Paolo Faconi from Mantua[9] who promised to supply (ostensibly for musical ends) a talented soprano aged 13, by name Caterina Martinelli. Her father, suspecting that Vincenzo's interest extended to matters other than musical, did not wish to run the risk of having Caterina sent back from Mantua on some trumped-up charge of insufficiency, so he wrote to the duke's ambassador in Rome and requested that at a time appropriate to all concerned a doctor and a midwife should provide verification of the girl's virginity.[10] Vincenzo, put on his guard, suggested that in order to allay suspicion Caterina should stay at the house of Monteverdi, 'our Director of Music, who has a wife and other relatives'. And so, towards the end of the summer, the composer's already large household acquired yet another member: a charming guest, pupil, and perhaps babysitter. Claudia, then beginning her third pregnancy, would have been glad of a little help.

A son, Massimiliano Giacomo, was born to the Monteverdis in May 1604, and at his baptism on 10 May Count Ottavio Massimiliano di Collalto represented the Archduke Maximilian as godfather, the godmother being the 13-year-old Princess Margherita, whose proxy was Vittoria Nuvolona. The house was becoming a little more crowded, a little less peaceful. Chapel and chamber music kept the composer fully occupied, yet somehow he had to find the time for thinking and writing about his reply to Artusi's nagging pedantry.[11] In the preface to his Fifth Book of Madrigals, Monteverdi promised to publish his theory of the *seconda prattica*, but when the time came in 1607 it was a polemical rather than musical document, and in his brother's hand rather than his own.

---

[6] Bertolotti, 81. Monteverdi's instruments were the violin, viola, and viola bastarda, but his favourite was the theorbo.

[7] Pontiroli, *Monteverdi*, 52.   [8] Paoli, 387–9.   [9] Frey, 445.

[10] Ademollo, 37 (letter of 28 June 1603).   [11] Palisca, 'Artusi', 133–66.

[33]

By the end of October, when Monteverdi wrote his letter to the Duke, the situation was considerably less bright than it had been six months earlier. He could deal with critics, manage his family, work at his music, and watch anxiously over his already ailing wife; but living without money was no easy matter. His own wages, along with those of Claudia and her father Giacomo Cattaneo, had not been paid for five months. The villain was Ottavio Benintendi (or, as Monteverdi spells his name, Belintento)[12] the court treasurer, whose irresponsibly dishonest behaviour caused a lawsuit to be brought against him in 1609.[13]

The composer's anxiety, frustration, and righteous indignation burn through almost every line of the letter. He knows that the blame lies neither with the Duke nor with his President of the Magistracy,[14] and he is not afraid to name the culprit and describe his uncooperative and unpleasant attitude. He even goes so far as to suggest a way in which the nefarious practices of treasury officials might be successfully circumvented—by paying the wages directly from taxes and tolls levied in the district of Viadana, at that time an important Gonzaga dependency.[15] It is not only the blocking of funds that upsets him. Bad as that may be, the waste of time and the inroads made on a busy working day are worse. Monteverdi makes it plain that an artist cannot be expected to function efficiently unless he is guaranteed a reasonably peaceful life.

[Address:] To the Most Serene Lord Duke of Mantua and Monferrato, my Lord and Master, Casale Monferrato

Most Serene Lord, my Most Respected Master,

As a last resource[a] it is indeed proper that I appeal to Your Highness's infinite virtue, since it is that which in the end directs your will concerning the salary granted to me by your kindness. I therefore kneel before you with the greatest possible humility, and beg you to be so good as to cast your gaze not upon my boldness (perhaps) in writing this letter, but rather[b] upon my great distress, which is the reason for my writing; not upon the Lord President,[c] who on numerous occasions has given an affirmative order so very kindly and politely, but rather[b] upon Belintento,[d] who never wanted to carry it out except when it pleased him, and now that

---

[12] An ironic pun that Monteverdi did not dare to make in his letter to the Duke.   [13] Davari, 98.

[14] Possibly this was Alessandro Striggio, who held the post in 1613 according to the third edition (Mantua, 1613) of G. B. Basile's maritime fable *Le avventurose disavventure*.

[15] Gallico, 'Dazi', 242.

[a] Salary, as opposed to ordinary allowance (*provigione ordinaria*—see Letter 6) such as bread, meat, fish, oils, and candles.

[b] *si bene* for *bensì*.   [c] Alessandro Striggio.   [d] Ottavio Benintendi.

it has come down to this, I have almost had to accustom myself[e] to being beholden to him—and not to the infinite virtue of Your Highness, who through his boundless good will grants favours even to servants of little merit such as I am compared with the widespread regard for Your Highness's great merit—even though (what is more) he behaved badly to me when he did not want to give me such payments.

This humble petition of mine comes to you with no other aim but to beg Your Highness to kindly direct that I receive wages amounting to a total of five months, in which situation my wife Claudia and my father-in-law[f] also find themselves, and this sum grows even larger since we do not see any hope of being able to get hold of future payments[g] save by the express command of Your Highness, without which support all that I have been building up will be ruined and undone, since misfortunes continue to overwhelm me day in and day out, and I have not the means to remedy them.

Nevertheless, to obtain these payments (at least of one month only, if not all) I have used nothing if not prayers, humility, and politeness morning and night, by virtue of which exertion I have lost and am still losing practically all the time for study that I ought to devote to the taste and requirements of Your Highness, finding myself as I do in a responsible position and favoured by you, and yet I can obtain nothing.

If I am worthy to receive it of Your Highness's infinite virtue, I beg you from the bottom of my heart to grant me this particular favour which is not only[h] that I be paid, but—this I shall feel each time as an even greater favour—that I not be paid by the hand of this Belintento, for I am sure that Your Highness could find someone other than him who would give me some satisfaction,[i] at least in words if not in deeds, at least in honour if not in results, at least once if not every time. Nor do I know why this man goes on behaving thus towards me.

If this favour of yours were to extend over the customs duties of Viadana,[j] we should be entirely satisfied; and I being thus assured by Your Highness's infinite virtue and by the many other outstanding graces and kindnesses granted to me, hope also to be favoured (by virtue of such graces and kindnesses) with that which I have requested of Your High-

---

[e] *usar termine*, lit. to get used to the condition (or state).   [f] Giacomo Cattaneo.
[g] *future [paghe]*.   [h] *non solo [questa volta ma] . . . ogni volta.*
[i] *che non doperasse* (the *non* being pleonastic).   [j] The place, not the composer.

ness. Being capable of no more, I shall pray that Our Lord grant a long life to Your Highness, to whom I bow and make a most humble reverence.

from Mantua, 27 October 1604

Your Most Serene Highness's

most humble and most grateful servant

Claudio Monteverdi

3

Cremona, December 1604
[to Duke Vincenzo Gonzaga, at Mantua]

Mantua, Archivio Gonzaga, Cassetta 6, fo. 84. Folio: 2 pp. Enclosure: ballet music

Prunières, 232; Malipiero, 131; Paoli, 24; Fabbri 1985, 68; Lax, 16

Although this is one of the very few letters bearing no indication of the day on which it was written, we may safely assume that the composer was at his father's house in Cremona for the Christmas season. The lack of any special greeting for Christmas or the New Year indicates that the letter probably belongs to the early part of December, in which case it might be dated five or six weeks later than Letter 2. Monteverdi's periodic absences from Mantua did not relieve him of his duties as a composer, even though he may have enjoyed some respite from rehearsals and performances.[1] On this occasion the Duke asked him to write a ballet score on the subject of the moonstruck shepherd Endymion, celebrated under various guises in ancient Greek legend and revived in Monteverdi's lifetime by such poets as John Lyly[2] and Ascanio Pio di Savoia, whose intermezzi for the festivities at Parma in December 1628 contained a scene about the love of Diana and Endymion.[3]

Monteverdi's music has not apparently survived, but it was presumably intended for performance during the carnival season of 1605, some aspects of which were

[1] The next five letters, all from Cremona, contain references to work (mainly composition) expected of Monteverdi by his employers. Letter 4 (1607) to Iberti is about madrigals; no. 5 (1608) to Cardinal Ferdinando Gonzaga about an unnamed piece of music, probably secular; no. 6 (1608) to Chieppio mentions a return to toil in Mantua; no. 7 (1609) to Striggio discusses a monody which can be rearranged as a madrigal; no. 8 (1609) to Striggio assesses the personality and music of Galeazzo Sirena.

[2] *Endimion, the Man in the Moone* (1585). There are several varying versions of the story, but the combination of love, eternal sleep, and the goddess of the moon is discoverable in most of them.

[3] See Letter 105. Notwithstanding Monteverdi's reference to Endymion, the name does not appear in the printed libretto, which simply uses the word *pastore*. The date of this letter, given as 1617 (though Monteverdi must have intended to write 1627), misled many into thinking that an intermezzo entitled *Gli amori di Diana e di Endimione* was written for Parma in 1617 (Paoli, *Monteverdi*, 219, 220, 236). Order was brought out of this confusion by Frank Walker in a communication to *Music and Letters*, 29 (1948), 433–4. But by a strange coincidence an *Endimione* was under discussion at Mantua late in 1615 (Ademollo, 232; Davari, 114), apparently the work of Duke Ferdinando. There is no way of telling whether this was a *favola* or a ballet, but Striggio refers to it as if it were already in existence, and in consequence, the possibility of its being identical with the *Endimione* of 1604 should not be ruled out. Ferdinando, 17 at the time and a precocious poet, often collaborated with Monteverdi.

described by the mannerist painter and designer Federico Zuccharo (c.1539–1609) in *Il passagio per Italia*.[4] He singles out for special comment the music he heard at the Palazzo del Tè, where the acoustics of the Sala dei Giganti produced sweetly reverberant harmonies.[5] Although he may well have met Monteverdi, he neither mentions him by name nor describes anything resembling the ballet *Endimione*, which, if it consisted only of two *entrate* and two *balletti*, must indeed have been a short work; but in all likelihood the sections discussed by Monteverdi were parts of a larger plan, whose musical portions might even have been divided between several composers, as was sometimes the custom in Mantua.

Monteverdi mentions four sub-sections in this ballet: an *entrata* and a dance for the stars, an *entrata* for the shepherds, and a dance for the stars and shepherds together. He has begun work on the dance for the stars, and his plan for alternating the orchestral colours and the dancers seems to be as follows:

A	tutti	all the stars
B	strings *a 5*	first pair of stars
A	tutti	all the stars
C	strings *a 5*	second pair of stars
A	tutti	all the stars

The brief cheerful tune (A) is to return like a refrain when the string quintet has finished its contrasting air, or airs, for these may have varied in the manner suggested (B, C) even though the bass remained identical.[6] Something very similar to this plan can be seen in his ballet *De la bellezza le dovute lodi*,[7] which definitely dates from the late Mantuan period since it appeared in the *Scherzi musicali* of 1607. In spite of its being a sung ballet (which *Endimione* could also have been) it relies to a considerable extent on the alternation of keys, moods, and tempi, a feature which is obscured in the modern printed edition.[8]

Another important matter mentioned by Monteverdi is the orchestration he intends to use. In this respect he shows us a mind that is orderly as well as artistic: when all the stars dance all the instruments play, and when only two stars dance the strings are heard alone. He never specifies the make-up of the tutti, but it was obviously composed of strings, woodwind, and possibly brass. In a letter dated some seven years later and addressed to Prince Francesco (no. 12, 26 March 1611), Monteverdi talks about a newly recommended wind instrumentalist whose alleged abilities are remarkably varied: recorder, flute, cornetto, bassoon, and trombone. In addition he can even play violins and viols. Undoubtedly therefore the tutti consisted of instruments such

---

[4] Bologna, Bartolomeo Cocchi, 1608.

[5] Ademollo, 52. He also mentions that a whisper in one corner of the room could be clearly heard in the opposite one, though inaudible at the centre. Doni (ii. 171) discusses a comparable acoustic phenomenon in the ducal palace.

[6] As in the *entrate* for *Il ballo delle Ingrate* (1608).

[7] Malipiero edn., x. 62.

[8] After the final cadences at 'fior d'amore' and 'contra beltade' there should be a repeat of the first *balletto*. Failure to observe this results in a string of unrelieved tripla sections. See Stevens, 'Ballet', 359–60.

as these, and true to the manner of French ballet music, the texture was five-part with a correspondingly rich middle register, like that of the slightly later *Ballo delle Ingrate*.[9]

Of the people mentioned in the letter, the composer's younger brother Giulio Cesare had by 1604 left the cathedral of Mantua for a place at court, and Giovanni Battista the dancer (no further name is given) was in all probability in charge of the choreography as well as a star in both senses of the word. De' Paoli suggests that the 'Jseppe Ballarino' mentioned in connection with the projected performance of *Il pastor fido* in 1592 might be the same man in spite of the slightly different name, but there is no proof of this and no reason to believe that the same choreographer remained in charge over a long period of years.[10] The end of the letter, with its strongly worded plea for consideration in regard to the amount of work expected of him in a short space of time, shows that serious problems over salary payments were not the only troubles that beset Monteverdi in the autumn and winter of 1604. His health and strength, impaired by overwork and by the insalubrious emanations from Mantua's marshes, had fallen to a low point and could only be restored by proper rest. This the Gonzaga had no intention of granting him.

My Most Serene Lord and Most Respected Master,

Ten days ago I received from the courier a letter from Your Highness commanding me to compose two *entrate*, one for the stars that have to follow on the moon, the other for the shepherds who come on after[a] Endymion; and likewise two dances, one for the aforementioned stars alone, and the other for the stars and shepherds together.

And so, with a most eager desire to obey and carry out Your Highness's commands as promptly as possible (which I have always possessed and done, and will possess until I die and ever shall do), I set to work first on the music for the stars. But not finding among the instructions how many there must be to dance it, and wishing to compose it on an alternating plan, as it would in my opinion have been novel, delightful, and pleasing—that is, having first of all a short and cheerful air played by all the instruments and likewise danced by all the stars; then immediately the five viole da braccio taking up a different air from the first one (the other instruments stopping) and only two stars dancing to it (the others resting); and at the end of this duo section, having the first air repeated with all the instru-

---

[9] Not published until 1638, in the Eighth Book of Madrigals.   [10] Paoli, 348.

[a] Follow on; come on after: the use of the frequentative *seguitare* suggests that there is a continuation of action rather than a following in somebody's footsteps.

ments and stars, continuing this pattern until all the said stars have danced two by two—but not having had the actual number, and this information being essential (if indeed Your Highness takes pleasure in this type of interspersed arrangement as I mentioned), I have in consequence put off doing it until I know; and in order to find out, I have written to Signor Giovanni Battista[b] the dancer, so that he can give me the exact number through my brother.

Meanwhile I have composed this piece, which I am now sending off to Your Highness, for the shepherds and the stars. Indeed, my Most Serene Lord, I have composed it with that habitual devotion and ready willingness to serve you[c] which I always have had and always shall have, yet certainly not with the consent of those physical powers (ready and accustomed to doing my will) that I have enjoyed in the past. For they are still weakened from past exertions, and so feeble that neither through medicine, nor dieting, nor giving up studies have they been restored to their initial strength, even though partly so.

I hope nevertheless to recover them with the Lord's help, and when this comes about (if it please His Divine Majesty) I shall then beseech Your Highness for the love of God never to burden me again either with so much to do at once or in so short a time, for it is certain that my great desire to serve you[d] and the great exertion involved would inadvertently draw me to my life's abridgement; but this life being prolonged will serve Your Highness and benefit my poor children. Therefore Most Serene Lord, if Your Highness were now to find that I have served you neither in finesse nor in speed as perhaps you expected and as it was my wish to do (as indeed I have always wished), do not blame my goodwill or my inclination, for both the one and the other will always count as the highest grace and highest favour whatever Your Highness may be so kind as to command them, to whom bowing down I make a most humble reverence and pray Our Lord for your every perfect happiness.

from Cremona, December 1604

Your Most Serene Highness's

most humble and grateful servant,

Claudio Monteverdi

---

[b] Giovanni Battista Ballarino.   [c] *servirlo*, referring to *Signore*.
[d] *servirla*, referring to *Altezza*.

4

Cremona, 28 July 1607
to Annibale Iberti,[1] at Genoa [Sampierdarena]

Mantua, Archivio Gonzaga, Cassetta 6, fos. 87–8. Bifolio: 2 pp. and address. Enclosure: madrigal

Davari, 87; Malipiero, 133; Paoli, 27; Fabbri 1985, 122; Lax, 18

A period of slightly more than two and a half years separates this letter from the previous one, and during that interval Monteverdi cast and recast the twin dies of opera and madrigal in such a way that their imprint would change irrevocably the future course of musical history. Several of his settings of passages from Guarini's *Il pastor fido*, written in all likelihood for a performance of that bothersome but epoch-making pastoral at Mantua in 1598, were surreptitiously copied and given into the hands of the enemy at Ferrara later in the same year. The fulminations of Canon Artusi[2] unleashed a bitter controversy that was to be subdued neither quickly nor easily; and if Monteverdi was slow to anger, he also took his time before publishing those pastoral excerpts—disguised now as madrigals—in his Fifth Book, whose dedication to Vincenzo Gonzaga bore the date 30 July 1605.

This musical vessel of fortune, bold in its harmonies and daring in its use of continuo instruments for the last six items, was buoyed up and sent on its way by two poems, both apparently innocuous, the one referring to Claudio and the other to Monteverdi.[3] They were the work of a Carmelite father, Cherubino Ferrari, theologian to the court of Mantua and a close friend as well as an ardent champion of the composer. Ferrari was not, perhaps, a great poet; but he took cheerful advantage of his cloth to prod the Duke into recognizing Monteverdi's plight, asking for 'love, grace, and favour' in return for a heartfelt gift. In the light of Letter 3, this plea from a third party takes on a special meaning. So too does the reference to Cerberus and Hades in the second poem, which none of the cognoscenti would read without thinking at once of Artusi barking away in Bologna.

In any event, the Duke seems not to have overburdened his director of music on receiving a presentation copy, handsomely bound, of Book Five. He engaged himself

---

[1] This is the first of many letters to Iberti.

[2] A pertinent extract is given in Strunk, 393–404. See also Palisca, 'Artusi', 133–6.

[3] These poems are so obviously conceived as a pair that it is difficult to understand why Barblan, in his excellent biography, deals with them separately and considers the first to date from a much earlier period. See Barblan, 'La vita', 20, 26 n. 28, 43.

[41]

for several months in a rather unusual piece of musical diplomacy, attempting to bring back to Mantua a Portuguese organist, Juan Leite Pereira, who had been ordered to return to his native country and to the silence of the cloister. Vincenzo, by distantly manipulating agents, friends, and cardinals, persuaded the man to leave Rome without papal permission, but he was still not back in Mantua by February of 1606.[4] In that same month, from Pisa, Prince Ferdinando Gonzaga sent details of a battle and a ballet to his brother Francesco in Mantua.[5] It was already carnival time, and the brothers vied with each other in producing various kinds of courtly entertainment. Of the two, Ferdinando was the poet and musician, Francesco the schemer and organizer.

Mantua had not seen a really grandiose theatrical venture since *Il pastor fido*, and it was therefore with a feeling of excitement and expectancy that Francesco conferred with one of the younger court secretaries, Alessandro Striggio, whose father had been a famous musician in former times. Striggio offered to write a new version of the Orpheus legend, and the idea was accepted with alacrity. But he would need a composer with considerable experience of the stage, and the Florentines (especially Marco da Gagliano) were not always available. Sigismondo d'India had wandered in and out of Mantua without making a profound impression, for his best work was yet to come. Salomone Rossi, relieved in August 1606 of the obligation to wear a yellow sign on his hat, thus became one of the most privileged members of Mantua's Jewish community; but he was at his best in chamber music. For a stage piece, there was only one possible choice—Monteverdi.

The composition of *L'Orfeo, favola in musica* must have taken almost an entire year. Letter 4 shows that even a five-part madrigal demanded a full week of Monteverdi's time, especially since he liked to work only in the morning and the evening.[6] The opera may have been completed by mid-November, when his wife Claudia wrote a pathetic letter to Annibale Chieppio begging for financial help from the supposedly wealthy tax area of Viadana.[7] Then began the copying of parts, engagement of singers, and planning of rehearsals. With Francesco Rasi in the title role, success was virtually assured, but there was a tremendous amount of work to be done. Monteverdi was once more totally involved in a production that broke new ground and taxed his physical resources to the uttermost.[8] It was first performed on 24 February 1607, but by early summer he and his ailing wife and children were back in Baldassare's house in Cremona.

In gallant contrast to this sad and impoverished family, Vincenzo and his courtiers set out for a summer spree at Sampierdarena, at that time an unspoilt beach in the

---

[4] Bertolotti, 85.   [5] Ibid. 86.

[6] See the letter of Antonio Goretti to the Marchese Bentivoglio, 27 Nov. 1627, cited in the commentary to Letter 115.

[7] Cf. Letter 2. Claudia begs that the Duke 'may grant that our salary be paid from the taxes of the town of Viadana, which favour being received will be the most significant of all' (Mantua, Archivio di Stato, Busta 2705. Letter dated 14 Nov. 1606).

[8] For the most complete and detailed account of *L'Orfeo* see Iain Fenlon's 'The Mantuan "Orfeo"', in Whenham, 1–19 (and the Appendix of letters, 167–72), and Carter.

vicinity of Genoa. In a short space of time they spent 100,000 scudi, according to a Venetian official named Benedetto Moro, who told the Senate in no uncertain terms of the displeasure registered by Vincenzo's impoverished subjects.[9] An infinitesimal portion of that largess was presumably allocated to Don Bassano Casola and a group of singers under his direction, who had accompanied the court to the seaside in order to give concerts from time to time. It was a male voice group, to judge by Monteverdi's description, with—in all probability—castrati, a male alto, and the usual tenor and bass.[10] No instrumentalists are mentioned, and it is therefore likely that the music enclosed with the letter called only for a group of unaccompanied voices.

Of special interest is the deep concern shown by Monteverdi for the proper rehearsal of a new and unfamiliar work. He does not hesitate to ask a senior court official to be sure to hand over the music well in advance, so that Bassano Casola can teach the singers their parts.

Since he promises to send 'the other sonnet' as soon as possible, the two compositions—both settings of sonnets and for unaccompanied voices—might be considered as a pair, based on poetry by a single author. But no name is hinted at, and no incipits are given. The manuscript *partitura* that accompanied the letter has been lost. Yet Monteverdi was not in the habit of sending away his new compositions without first making a copy for himself, and undoubtedly this copy would be kept in readiness for the next madrigalian publication.

This was Book VI (1614), which contains settings of various types of poetry, seven of which are sonnets. The ones written for Sampierdarena must be among this group; and it so happens that five of them are scored for voices and clavicembalo obbligato, while the other two are a cappella—the glorious settings of *Zefiro torna* and *Ohimè, il bel viso*, both by Petrarch.[11] While this identification cannot be proved absolutely, it is reasonably certain that these are the links between the sad summer of 1607 and the book that followed seven years later—the only one of the nine books of madrigals that lacks a dedication. None was needed, for the dominant note of Book VI is lamentation and reverent homage, and the Petrarch sonnets are from that part of his canzoniere 'in morte di madonna Laura'.[12]

On 10 September 1607, the composer's wife Claudia died. She was buried in Cremona cathedral, but since she was not a native of the city her remains were later transported to San Nazaro.

[Address:] To my Most Illustrious Lord and Most Respected Master, Signor Annibale Iberti, Councillor of His Most Serene Highness, Genoa

[9] Errante, 'Forse che sì', 25–6.   [10] Ibid., 31.

[11] See Pirrotta, 42; Stevens, 'Necklace', 371–2.

[12] Anthony Pryer brings persuasive musical evidence in favour of a composition date c.1607 in his forthcoming study, 'Monteverdi's Madrigals'.

My Most Illustrious Lord and Most Respected Master,

As soon as His Highness[a] left Mantua, I too went away—to see my father in Cremona, where I still am—which is why I did not receive Your Lordship's letter earlier than the 20th of this month, and so on seeing His Highness's commission, I straightway began setting the sonnet to music, and was engaged in doing this for six days, then two more what with trying it out and rewriting it. I worked at it with the same devotion of mind[b] that I have always had in regard to every other composition written by me in order the more to serve His Highness's most delicate taste.

But I did not work with comparable physical strength, because I was a little indisposed. Nevertheless I hope that this madrigal is not going to displease His Highness, but if by chance (to my misfortune) it were to obtain an unfavourable[c] result, I beg Your Lordship to tender my apology based on the abovementioned reason.

Here then is the music I have composed; but you will be doing me a kindness by handing it over, before His Highness hears it, to Signor Don Bassano[d] so that he can rehearse it and get a firm grasp of the melody together with the other gentlemen singers, because it is very difficult for a singer to perform a part that he has not first practised, and greatly damaging to the composition itself, as it is not completely understood on being sung for the first time.

I shall send Your Lordship the other sonnet, set to music, as soon as possible—since it is already clearly shaped in my mind[e]—but if I should spin out the time even a little, in His Highness's opinion, please be good enough to let me know and I shall send it at once. And with this conclusion, making a humble reverence to Your Lordship and praying that you may count me among your servants, I pray Our Lord for your every happiness.

from Cremona, 28 July 1607
Your Most Illustrious Lordship's
devoted servant
Claudio Monteverdi

---

[a] Vincenzo, fourth Duke of Mantua.
[b] *affetto d'animo*, in contradistinction to physical strength: *forze di corpo* (next paragraph).
[c] *contrario*.   [d] Bassano Casola, *vice-maestro di cappella*.   [e] *nella mente mia nella sua orditura*.

5

Cremona, 26 November 1608
to [Cardinal Ferdinando Gonzaga, at Mantua]

Mantua, Archivio Gonzaga, Cassetta 6, fos. 92–3. Folio: 1 p. Enclosure: music

Prunières, 233; Malipiero, 134; Paoli, 31; Lax, 20

According to Prunières, this short covering letter was intended for Chieppio: Santoro, however, opts for the Duke.[1] But the form of address suits neither, for it contains the word 'Reverendissimo', which Malipiero associates with some unidentified ecclesiastic. De' Paoli was the first to guess correctly that the recipient was Cardinal Ferdinando Gonzaga, and although no proof is offered, it may be found in Letters 10 and 11, both of which share the same form of address as this one, as well as mentioning musical compositions.

At this point in his career, Monteverdi knew only one cardinal who was also a composer, and that was Ferdinando, eldest son of the Duke. Beginning in January 1608, a rich repertoire of letters from Cini, Gagliano, Peri, Rinuccini, and G. B. Strozzi—all Florentines—bears an identical salutation,[2] for on 24 December of the previous year Ferdinando had been created a cardinal.[3] 'Eccellentissimo' gave way to 'Reverendissimo'; yet this was the same young man who wrote page after page of poetry and music, and who appeared with his two brothers on the stage with all the aplomb of a professional actor.[4]

If Ferdinando generally favoured the Florentines, his brother Francesco came forward as a champion of Monteverdi by encouraging the production of *Orfeo*. The composer must have remained in Cremona at least until 10 August 1607, when he was elected a member of the Accademia degli Animosi.[5] He then went to Milan so that his friend Cherubino Ferrari could hear parts of the opera, which prompted an enthusiastic letter from the music-loving theologian to Duke Vincenzo.[6] But the return to his father's house, and to the illness and death of his wife, drove from his memory the triumphs of the past and cast a deep shadow over the future.

---

[1] Santoro, *Monteverdi*, pl. xxiii, facsimile.
[2] See especially Davari, App. II, 173–83; Ademollo, 53–71, 82–6.   [3] Ademollo, 58.
[4] These words of Beltrame are cited by Ademollo, 60.   [5] Sommi, *Monteverdi*, 22.
[6] Davari, 86. On 8 Mar. 1608 Ferrari wrote about his experiences in theatrical entertainments of various kinds in a letter to the Duke of Modena, mentioning also that Monteverdi used to confer with him about his compositions (Prunières, 210 n. 59).

Among the many friends who sent messages of sympathy and condolence was Federico Follino, a talented deviser and chronicler of court entertainments. In his letter of 24 September he begged Monteverdi to return to Mantua and compose music for the forthcoming wedding festivities of Francesco Gonzaga and Margherita of Savoy, thus earning for himself the greatest fame on earth.[7] If this high-pitched promise played some part in persuading the sorrowing composer to collaborate in the festivities, it is also possible that he agreed knowing that only a total involvement in work would ease his pain.

Discussing plans with Francesco on 9 October, he realized how much there was to accomplish in a relatively short time, and therefore implored his princely patron to write to the Duke with a view to obtaining at least some of the poetry within a week.[8] Although Monteverdi and Rinuccini were close friends, court procedure had to be strictly followed: composer to prince, prince to duke, duke to secretary, secretary to poet, and then the same in reverse. The libretto did not arrive in a week; but in less than a fortnight Rinuccini himself arrived, and both composer and poet were able to talk over their problems at first hand.

At this time Monteverdi was giving music lessons to the young singer Caterina Martinelli, who at first lodged with him and his family, later moving to another house on 7 November 1606. While learning the role of Ariadne, she fell a victim to smallpox and died on 8/9 March 1608.[9]

Francesco remained at the very centre of attention for the first six months of 1608. The formal wedding in Turin on 19 February was followed by festive music and theatrical entertainments, but these were almost completely overshadowed by the Mantuan productions of May and June—*Arianna, Il ballo delle Ingrate*, and the intermezzi for Guarini's play *L'Idropica*. Ferdinando, however, was by no means neglected or forgotten: several of his contributions to a much-revised *Dafne* performed during carnival time brought him much artistic credit as well as duly honouring his ecclesiastical rank. He was constantly in touch with poets and composers in Florence, leaving the Mantuan contingent largely in the hands of his brother.

This may help to explain why, towards the end of the year, Ferdinando suddenly turned to Monteverdi for assistance. The idea had been put into his mind just over a year before, when Francesco Cini—hoping that his *Tetide* would be included in the festivities of 1608—wrote to Ferdinando suggesting that Peri might compose the main recitative and arioso sections, and Monteverdi the choral parts of the intermezzi and the solo and choral passages for the gods.[10] While nothing ever came of the project, Cini's idea about saving money by utilizing the services of Mantuan musicians may well have prompted Ferdinando to think of Monteverdi, especially since a highly respected young singer, Francesco Campagnolo, had

[7] Davari, 88.

[8] Davari, 88 n. 2, from which it is clear that Francesco wrote the letter on the day following his interview with Monteverdi.

[9] Ademollo, 44–5.   [10] Davari, 177.

just reported to the Cardinal that Florentine music was ugly and their musicians vicious.[11]

The exact nature of Ferdinando's commission is not known, but Monteverdi's unusually prompt delivery of the music suggests that the text was not a long one. In an eloquently persuasive letter of 27 November, the composer's father had begged the Duchess Eleonora to intercede with the Duke and grant an honourable release for a servant in such a low state of health, and in due course Chieppio sent a suitably worded reply.[12] It is therefore unlikely that Ferdinando would have expected Monteverdi to set the libretti being prepared for Mantua by Gabriello Chiabrera, who described them as 'two little stories to be sung and acted'.[13] Perhaps it was a commission to set one of Ferdinando's own poems, of which there was no dearth.

My Most Illustrious and Most Reverend Lord, and Most Respected Master,

No less ready than desirous to serve Your Eminence,[a] I began—as soon as the footman arrived—to carry out your commission for the piece of music I am sending you. And although I can truthfully say that because of my indisposition (from which I have not yet recovered) due to the heavy tasks undertaken yonder[b] in recent days, Your Eminence will not be served in precisely the way I would wish, may my goodwill be accepted all the same through your clemency. Assuring you that I could receive no greater favour than ever to serve Your Eminence (to whom in conclusion I bow most humbly), I pray Our Lord grant you that happiness which is appropriate for so great a prince.

from Cremona, 26 November 1608
Your Eminence's
most humble and most devoted servant
Claudio Monteverdi

[11] Ibid. 93 n. 2 (31 Oct. 1608, on returning from the wedding festivities of the son of the Grand Duke and Maria of Austria).

[12] Santoro, *Monteverdi*, 75. A previous letter to the Duke (9 Nov.) elicited neither acknowledgement nor reply.

[13] Ademollo, 84.

[a] The normal address for a cardinal is used here although Monteverdi repeats the longer form of address used for the salutation.

[b] *costì*, meaning 'over there in Mantua'.

6

Cremona, 2 December 1608
to Annibale Chieppio, at Mantua

Mantua, Archivio Gonzaga, Cassetta 6, fos. 95–6. Bifolio: 3 pp. and address. Enclosure: a letter from Federico Follino

Davari, 94; Vogel, 429; Prunières, 233; Malipiero, 135; Paoli, 33; Fabbri 1985, 150; Lax, 20

Certain aspects of this letter (exceeded in length only by no. 49) have posed a series of strange problems for earlier biographers of Monteverdi. The usually reliable Prunières assumed that the addressee was Striggio,[1] although his discussion of the content more correctly stresses the role of Chieppio, whose name appears on fo. 96ᵛ. But the letter could hardly have been written 'straight off at a sitting',[2] for it begins with a clear statement that the day on which the missive was started was 30 November, and it closes with the date of 2 December. Obviously written over a period of nearly three days, it undoubtedly cost its author a great deal of worry and anxiety, for Chieppio, although a self-made man of considerable wealth and influence, was of comparatively humble origin and had always entertained feelings of warm regard for the composer.

Prunières also mentions a letter from Monteverdi to Chieppio, written on 26 November, 'which has not been discovered'.[3] This brief remark, however, indicates that the source of the confusion goes back to Letter 5, said to have been addressed to Chieppio on that date,[4] although in fact the recipient was Cardinal Francesco Gonzaga.

What actually happened was as follows. Monteverdi's illness and retirement to Cremona in the summer of 1608 virtually cut him off from service at court, although he did send a piece of music and a reply to the Cardinal's request, as is now clear. But by that time Baldassare's letter had already reached the Duke (9 November)[5] and discussion was in progress as to the advisability of allowing Monteverdi to succeed to the Directorship of Music at S. Barbara, since Gastoldi was seriously ill and had only a few months to live. Such an appointment would have meant a higher salary and less work; and at this stage of his career Monteverdi ardently desired a change from the exorbitant demands of theatrical composition. But in the end the post was given to Antonio Tarroni.[6]

---

[1] Prunières, 233; Letter IV. [2] Ibid. 90. [3] Ibid. 211 n. 77.
[4] Ibid. 233, Letter III. [5] Facsimile in Santoro, *Monteverdi*, pls. xxiv–xxv.
[6] Jeppesen, 319; Tagmann, 381–2.

The day after Monteverdi had sent the Cardinal his music, Baldassare wrote another letter to Mantua, this time to the Duchess Eleonora (27 November)[7] begging her to intervene with her husband and secure an honourable dismissal for the ailing Claudio. Unfortunately, Eleonora and the Duke were not on the best of terms, and she probably used the letter as an excuse to upbraid him for the unceasingly licentious extravagance shown towards his lady singers, and the relative neglect of his composers. Thus taunted, and driven to anger, the Duke must have asked Chieppio (possibly on 29 November) to send off a letter at once to Monteverdi, ordering him to return to court. The letter certainly arrived on the last day of the month, and both father and son, on reading it, must have realized that their perfectly reasonable requests had been turned into explosive material because of the tense situation at Mantua, for which of course neither of them was responsible.

The appeals from Baldassare to the Duke and Duchess having failed, the direct approach was the only remaining possibility, and this explains the length and the tone of Monteverdi's letter to Chieppio. It is a last-ditch type of letter, in which the composer makes excellent use of his knowledge of rhetoric to build up a colossal case against the Gonzaga and against those responsible for court administration. After all, he was then 41 years old, with numerous publications and several spectacular performances to his (and his employer's) credit; yet his salary and perquisites were not much better than those of the fifty archers who formed part of the Duke's bodyguard.[8] Their salary in 1608 was 180 scudi per annum, plus free accommodation. Monteverdi earned 200 scudi and had to pay for his own lodgings.[9]

In addition to providing for his family, he had had to look after Caterina Martinelli as a guest and pupil. His letter makes it plain that somebody put it into the Duke's head to save money by awarding an increase of salary (to 300 scudi) and immediately planting upon him another pupil and lodger, the young tenor Francesco Campagnolo. When he objected, they sent Campagnolo to someone else's house and reduced Monteverdi's salary by 60 scudi, so that he was left with only 240. At about this time the poet Chiabrera[10] was granted an income of 300 a year, though he (like Monteverdi) practically had to sue to obtain it. Three years later Adriana Basile—admittedly a great artiste—was to enjoy an annual income of 2,000 scudi, in addition to a palatial residence, jewellery, furniture, and countless additional rewards.[11]

If the Gonzaga and their treasury officials could possibly swindle the artists on whose remarkable talents they so liberally feasted, they would do so on the slightest excuse. Even as late as 1628, when the city and dukedom alike were well on the way to perdition, the brothers Giovanni Battista and Orazio Rubini were sent as musical emissaries to the imperial court, at that time in Prague, for the wedding of the King of Hungary. But on arrival there, the musicians found that instead of being paid in thalers (as they had been promised by order of Carlo of Nevers) they were given florins, which they did not want.[12]

---

[7] Facsimile in Santoro, *Monteverdi*, pls. XXVI–XXVII.   [8] Errante, 'Forse che sì', 25.

[9] 1,197 lire (Davari, 98) = 200 scudi, since the Mantuan scudo was then worth 6 lire.

[10] Ademollo, 182.   [11] Ibid. 175.   [12] Quazza, *La guerra*, i. 95.

In the first part of his letter to Chieppio, Monteverdi describes his ailments, which seem to have ranged from a serious type of migraine headache to a case of shingles. He was almost certainly not exaggerating, for Benvenuto Cellini is known to have fallen ill from the fetid air of the marshes, and lost no time in cursing the city and leaving it.[13] There follows a splendid display of rhetoric, in which the word 'fortune' governs a whole series of 'if' clauses, and places before Chieppio a pent-up list of genuine grievances involving interference with salary and perquisites, loss of commissions and a pension, livery of poor quality, and much hard work with little reward.[14]

Monteverdi shows a remarkable familiarity with the salaries and savings of other famous musicians, probably because the putative worth of others in any given field of human activity has never ceased to interest those who may feel, perhaps with some justification, that they are less well off. In the case of Palestrina and de Monte, it was probably based on hearsay; but he may have known fairly reliable sources of information for Marenzio and for the two Ferrarese composers, Luzzaschi and Fiorino. Rovigo, who served at Mantua for a time, presented no problem.

But the outlook for Monteverdi in Mantua appeared as gloomy and forbidding as did the Styx to Orpheus in his own music-drama, then barely two years old. Marco da Gagliano, who visited Mantua to provide one short intermezzo for Guarini's L'Idropica, had drawn the equivalent of Monteverdi's annual salary for a mere two months' work. No wonder there is a note of indignation in a letter whose necessarily courtly language scarcely bothers to conceal the true reason for his wanting to be dismissed.

All that can be said is that the letter made its point and the outcome was successful, and in all of this Chieppio's kindly interest may perhaps be perceived. On 19 January 1609, Vincenzo Gonzaga, fourth Duke of Mantua and Monferrato, decreed that his most famous musician should receive an annual pension of 100 scudi,[15] and a week later his pay was increased to 300 scudi per annum.[16] But the paymaster was still Benintendi; and the struggle for the pension continued until the year of the composer's death.

[Address:] To my Most Illustrious Lord and Most Esteemed Master, Signor Annibale Chieppio, Councillor of His Most Serene Highness, Mantua

[13] Barblan, 'La vita', 83 n. 78. The fact, cited from Bertolotti, that many Mantuans lived to a ripe old age merely demonstrates that the natives (among whom Cellini and Monteverdi should not be numbered) had become to a large extent immune.

[14] Paoli, 37 interprets the reference to Vincenzo's request for music as a commission for *Orfeo*. But this opera was written for Prince Francesco and the Accademia, not for a wedding. What Monteverdi is referring to is surely the Duke's demand for theatrical works to be performed at the wedding festivities of 1608.

[15] Tiepolo, 136, after Monteverdi's own copy submitted to the Venetian Signoria in 1643.

[16] Davari, 98.

My most Illustrious Lord and Most Esteemed Master,

Today, which is the last day of November, I received from Your Lordship a letter from which I learned of His Highness's[a] command: that I come as soon as possible to Mantua. Most Illustrious Signor Chieppio, if he orders me to come and wear myself out again, I assure you that unless I take a rest from toiling away at music for the theatre, my life will indeed be a short one, for as a result of my labours (so recent and of such magnitude) I have had a frightful pain in my head and so terrible and violent an itching around my waist, that neither by cauteries which I have had applied to myself, nor by purges taken orally, nor by blood-letting and other potent remedies has it thus far been possible to get better—only partly so. My father[b] attributes the cause of the headache to mental strain, and the itching to Mantua's air (which does not agree with me), and he fears that the air alone could be the death of me before long. Just think then, Your Lordship, what the addition of brainwork would do. If His Highness orders me to come and receive graces and favours from his kindness and clemency, I tell Your Lordship that the fortune I have known in Mantua for nineteen consecutive years has given me occasion to call it inimical to me, and not friendly; because if it has done me the favour of receiving from His Highness the Duke the honour of being able to serve him in Hungary, it has also done me the disfavour of saddling me with an extra burden of expense from that journey, which our poor household feels almost to this very day.

If fortune called me[c] to His Highness's service in Flanders, it also crossed me on that occasion by making my wife Claudia, living at Cremona, bring expense to our household with her maid and servant, she having at that time still only 47 lire a month from His Highness, beyond the money my father gave me.

If fortune did me a good turn in that His Highness the Duke then increased my allowance from $12\frac{1}{2}$ scudi in Mantuan currency to 25 a month, it also went against me by making the aforementioned Lord Duke decide subsequently to send me word, by Don Federico Follino, that out of this increase he intended that I should pay the expenses of Signor Campagnolo, then a boy, and because I did not want this trouble it was necessary for me to give up 5 scudi a month for those expenses, so I was left with the 20 scudi which I now have.

[a] Vincenzo Gonzaga.   [b] Baldassare Monteverdi.
[c] *se m'ha fatto chiamare*. The subject of this and the next five paragraphs is *fortuna*.

If fortune favoured me last year by making the Lord Duke invite me to assist with the musical events for the marriage, it also did me a bad turn on that occasion by making me perform an almost impossible task, and futhermore it caused me to suffer from cold, lack of clothing, servitude, and very nearly lack of food (through the stopping of my wife Claudia's allowance and the onset of a serious illness), without my being in the slightest degree favoured by His Highness with any public mark of esteem, though Your Lordship knows very well that the favours of great princes help servants both in regard to honour and what is useful to them, particularly on an occasion when there are visitors.

If fortune granted me a livery from His Highness, to wear at the time of the marriage, it also let me down badly by making me have it of cloth which was woven from silk and floss-silk, with no overcoat, no stockings and garters, and no silk lining*d* for the cloak, wherefore I spent out of my own pocket 20 scudi in Mantuan currency.

If fortune has done me a favour by letting me have so very many opportunities of being commissioned by His Highness, it has also caused me this loss, that the Lord Duke has always spoken to me about hard work, and never about bringing me the pleasure of something useful.

If lastly (to go on no longer) fortune has looked kindly upon me by making me think I had a pension from His Highness of 100 scudi in Mantuan currency from the captaincy of the piazza,*e* it showed its black side even then because when the marriage ceremonies were over there were not 100 scudi but only 70 (along with the loss of my extra fee and loss of money from the previous months), as if perhaps it were amazed by the 100 scudi being too much; and those added to the 20 I am getting made about 22 ducatoni*f* a month. If I had received them what should I then have set aside for the use of my poor sons?

Orazio della Viola would have had to work very hard to get an income of 500 scudi a year, without the usual perquisites,*g* if he had nothing but the aforementioned every month. Similarly Luca Marenzio would have had to work quite hard to become as rich, and likewise Philippe de Monte

---

d *fodra di cendado.* Sometimes spelt *zendado*, and known as sendal (a silken material).

e *capitaniato della piazza.* The office giving control over the main square and the merchants who profited from it.

f Venetian gold ducats, worth approximately 12.5 per cent more than the corresponding Mantuan coins.

g *provigione ordinaria*, referring to allowances of goods as opposed to salary (*ultima provigione*). Cf. opening sentence of Letter 2.

and Palestrina, who left his sons an income worth more than 1,000 scudi. Luzzaschi and Fiorino[h] would have had to work quite hard to get an income of 300 scudi each, which was then left to their sons; and lastly (to say no more) Franceschino Rovigo would have had to toil away to save 7,000 scudi, as he did, if he had nothing but the aforementioned wages, which hardly suffice to pay the expenses of a master and servant and clothe him; for I don't know about his having two sons as well, which is the case with me. So, Your Lordship, if I have to draw the conclusion from the premisses I shall say that I am never going to receive graces and favours at Mantua, but rather expect (if I had come) to receive the final blow from ill fortune.

I know full well that His Highness the Duke has the very best of intentions towards me, and I know that he is a very generous prince; but I am extremely unlucky at Mantua, and this Your Lordship will discover from the following account, for I do know that His Highness—after the death of my wife Claudia—made a resolution to leave me her allowance. However, on my arrival in Mantua he suddenly changed his mind and thus gave no such order (unluckily for me), wherefore up till now I happen to have lost more than 200 scudi, and every day I go on losing. He also decided—as I said before—to give me 25 scudi a month, but lo and behold he suddenly changed his mind, and unluckily for me five of them fell by the wayside; so that my ill fortune, Your Lordship, is openly acknowledged to be at Mantua.

What clearer proof do you want, Your Lordship? To give 200 scudi to Messer[i] Marco da Gagliano who can hardly be said to have done anything, and to give me nothing, who did what I did. Therefore I beg you for the love of God, Most Illustrious Signor Chieppio, knowing that I am unwell and unfortunate in Mantua, please let me have an honourable dismissal from His Highness, for I know that from this I shall derive true happiness. Don Federico Follino promised in one of his letters, inviting me from Cremona last year to Mantua for the wedding preparations—I tell you he promiscd me what Your Lordship can see in this letter of his that I am sending you; and then at the end of it all nothing happened, or if indeed I had something, it was 1,500 lines to set to music.

[h] Luzzasco Luzzaschi; Ippolito Fiorino.
[i] Messer: used in the pejorative sense, as with Pallavicino (Letter 1).

Dear Sir, help me to obtain an honourable dismissal, for it seems to me that this is the best possible thing, because I shall have a change of air, work, and fortune; and who knows, if the worst comes to the worst, what else can I do but remain poor as I am? As regards my coming to Mantua to secure my dismissal with His Highness's kind approval, unless he wish it otherwise this much will I do, assuring Your Lordship that I shall always proclaim His Highness as my lord and master, wherever I am, and I shall always acknowledge him with my humble prayers to Almighty God; more than this I cannot do. Then when it comes to considering the graces and favours received time and time again from the Most Illustrious Signor Chieppio, you may be sure that I never think about this matter without blushing, remembering how troublesome I have been to you; but where my feeble powers cannot reach, at least my heart and voice will succeed in proclaiming your infinite kindnesses and my everlasting indebtedness to Your Lordship, to whom (as I close) I bow and kiss your hands.

from Cremona, 2 December 1608

Your Most Illustrious Lordship's
ever most obligated servant
Claudio Monteverdi

7

Cremona, 24 August 1609
to Alessandro Striggio, at Mantua

Mantua, Archivio Gonzaga, Cassetta 6, fos. 99–100, Bifolio: 3 pp. and address

Prunières, 236; Malipiero, 139; Paoli, 40; Fabbri 1985, 154; Lax, 25

This is Monteverdi's first extant letter to Alessandro Striggio, then a court secretary and councillor of the same rank as Chieppio, whom he had accompanied on the expedition to Hungary in 1601. Both were addressed as 'osservandissimo', whereas their senior Iberti was 'collendissimo'. As a musician (and therefore a mere servant in the court hierarchy) Monteverdi was extremely careful to observe the correct forms of address and salutation, and the niceties of this procedure frequently assist in determining the identity of the recipient.[1]

After two weeks Striggio sent a reply, which the composer received on 9 September, dating his answer 10 September. Letters 7 and 8 should thus be considered as a pair, and an isolated pair at that, for they are the only two letters of Monteverdi that seem to have survived from the year 1609. Both letters discuss wind-players among other topics, for Prince Francesco wanted to take with him, to Casale Monferrato, an ensemble of cornetts and trombones that could be used for outdoor events as well as for music at mealtimes.[2] But the letters have suffered serious misinterpretation in English and French, as well as Italian, because Monteverdi's carefully drawn distinction between Vincenzo and Francesco—'il Serenissimo Signor Ducca' and 'l'Altezza Sua del Signor Principe'—has been overlooked or ignored.[3] The prince was still in pursuit of wind-players eighteen months later, as is clear from Letter 12.

Monteverdi acknowledges receipt of words to be set to music, but in no way indicates that Striggio is the author. Although composer and poet had already collaborated on *Orfeo*, and were to join forces in 1620 for the production of *Apollo*,[4] the verses referred to here are almost certainly by someone else. Marc'Antonio Ferretti had sent a pastoral play to the duke in the early autumn of 1609, adding a prologue

---

[1] See also introduction to Letter 5.

[2] Monteverdi's familiarity with wind instruments and their players may to some extent have been due to his friend and pupil Giulio Bianchi, a virtuoso cornettist on the Mantuan musical staff.

[3] Prunières, 212 n. 79; Paoli, 40 where it is suggested that the Duke, rather than his son, is troubling Monteverdi over the matter of the wind band.

[4] But not *Tirsi e Clori*, whose text is 'marinistic' (Pirrotta, 49). Marini was at the court of Carlo Emanuele I, Duke of Savoy, from 1608 until 1615, and his poetry was especially admired there and in Mantua.

which he enclosed in a letter of 23 September, but there is no mention of music.[5] Monteverdi's earlier experiences with Guarini's pastoral had taught him that it was perfectly feasible to set poetry in the form of an aria and later arrange it for vocal quintet,[6] and he was later to do the same kind of transformation trick with the 'Lament of Arianna', which delighted the Venetians but earned the disapproval of Giovanni Battista Doni.[7]

Nevertheless there is a strong possibility that the verses chosen by the Duke were by one of the poets favoured by him at that time, such as Gabriello Chiabrera or Giambattista Marini. In this case one would expect to find a suitable candidate for the composition in question among the arias or madrigals subsequently published among Monteverdi's various collections. But no monodic setting by Chiabrera is to be found there; and the only solo piece based on Marini is *Tempro la cetra* (Book VII), which does not lend itself to an arrangement for ensemble. It is possible that Monteverdi, after sending a copy of the aria to Striggio, reworked it for five voices and published it in 1614—the next convenient occasion—when Book VI appeared. This contains several five-voice settings of Marini's poetry, and the music is known to date from the composer's last five years in Mantua.[8]

In the second paragraph, Monteverdi makes it clear that he is now referring to Prince Francesco, for he has asked his brother Giulio Cesare to present to 'L'Altezza Sua *del Signor Principe*' a specially bound score of *Orfeo*, because a parcel of advance copies was already on its way from Amadino's press in Venice. The composer, being in Cremona, left the binding and presentation arrangements to his brother, but thought it advisable to have Striggio, as librettist and court secretary, say a few words at the appropriate time. The 23-year-old dedicatee, presumably impressed and justifiably proud, must have realized that the sponsorship of a major work seldom falls to the lot of so young a patron.

Still referring to the prince,[9] Monteverdi goes into the complicated business of engaging a wind band. Fees, conditions, and repertoire occupy his mind at first, for he is anxious to ensure that they are not overpaid (the family trio asks for as much money

---

[5] Ademollo, 85.   [6] See the *Pastor fido* madrigals (*sic*) in Books IV and V.

[7] Doni, ii. 98 (new pagination after Index). '. . . composto a più voci dal medesimo Monteverdi, a richiesta di un nobile Veneziano'. The names of three Venetian noblemen occur in Monteverdi's correspondence: G. M. Bembo (Letter 41, 1620), who is said to have held regular musical evenings; Lorenzo Giustiniani (Letters 72–6, 1622) for whose wedding in 1630 Monteverdi wrote *Proserpina rapita*; and Girolamo Mocenigo (Letter 96, 1622; Letter 118, 1628), his special patron, for whom he wrote the *Combattimento*. Although Giustiniani was too young to have commissioned this by 1611, Bembo was active in 1613, but the most likely candidate is Mocenigo, who was just 27 at the time of the première of *Arianna*. Another reference of Doni generously exonerates Monteverdi: '. . . non ha colpa il Signor Baudio [*sic*] . . . in haver ridotto in Madrigali il lamento della sua Ariadna, più per compiacere ad altri, che a se stesso, come egli medesimo in una sua lettera confessa'. Doni may be referring to a letter in his own possession, for although the Lament is mentioned in Letters 19 and 124, Monteverdi discusses neither the polyphonic version nor his reasons for making it.

[8] Pirrotta, 43.

[9] 'al detto Serenissimo Signor principe'. Francesco, the first-born son of the Duke, was also addressed as 'Serenissimo', as may be seen from the dedication and preface to *Orfeo*.

as the composer himself was earning only five years previously), and he shows concern about their technical standards in both light and serious music.[10] Monteverdi was nothing if not a conscientious agent, as this and subsequent letters clearly demonstrate, nor was he unaware of the sensitive political problems attendant upon the enticing of musicians from the employ of Don Pedro Enrique de Acevedo, Count of Fuentes and Governor of Milan.[11]

[Address:] To my Most Illustrious Lord and Most Esteemed Master, Signor Alessandro Striggio, Most Worthy Councillor of His Most Serene Highness, Mantua

My Most Illustrious Lord and Most Esteemed Master,

I received a letter from Your Lordship together with certain words to be set to music, as a commission from His Highness,[a] and they arrived yesterday which was the 23rd of this month. I shall start to work on them as soon as possible, and when they are all done I shall inform Your Lordship or bring them myself to Mantua, because I want to be back in service shortly. I thought first of setting these words for a solo voice, but if later on His Highness orders me to rearrange the air for five voices, this I shall do.

I have nothing else to tell Your Lordship except about *Orfeo*: I hope that tomorrow, which is the 25th, my brother[b] will receive the finished publication from the printer,[c] who will send it to him by the courier from Venice which arrives tomorrow, as it happens. And as soon as he receives it he will have one copy bound and will give it to His Highness the Prince,[d] and when he does so I beg Your Lordship to put in a few words with the Prince, conveying to him the great desire I have in my heart to prove what a very devoted and very humble servant I am, and explaining that I give little to His Highness (who deserves much) really because of lack of opportunity rather than through any defect of spirit.

[10] For further information on wind-players in Mantua, see Cavalcabò, *passim*.

[11] b. Zamora 1525, d. Milan 1610. After distinguished military service in Italy, Portugal, and France, he moved on to administrative duties, serving as Governor-General of the Low Countries (1595), Captain-General of the Spanish Army (1596), and Governor and Captain-General of the State of Milan (1600). He was a close friend of Cardinal Borromeo.

[a] Vincenzo, fourth Duke of Mantua.   [b] Giulio Cesare Monteverdi.
[c] Ricciardo Amadino.   [d] *L'Altezza Sua del Signor Principe* (Francesco Gonzaga).

On this same occasion you will also be doing me a kindness by letting the said Prince know that I have spoken to those cornett- and trombone-players, as he commissioned me to do, and that they told me they will come and serve His Highness, but on these two conditions: one, that they would like to be helped by His Highness with letters of request to the Count of Fuentes[e] (or to whom it may concern) so that they can draw[f] some wages which fall due after the Count of Fuentes leaves for the state of Milan; and so that Your Lordship may understand, these wages are due because they play in the castle[g] at Cremona. And the other point is that the father and two sons who play all the wind instruments would each like 12 scudi a month. I objected to this at once, and told them that His Highness would go up to 8, with which (it seems to me) they should be contented. They have not said either yes or no about it.

The two others, because they are not as competent as these three, could I believe be had for less salary. They play together well and readily both dance and chamber music,[h] since they practise every day. I shall be waiting for a reply about this, and whatever His Highness commands, that will I do, but I shall not go beyond his instructions. So with this I close, making a reverence to Your Lordship, and I beseech you to maintain me in your good graces.

from Cremona, 24 August 1609
Your Most Illustrious Lordship's
devoted servant
Claudio Monteverdi

---

[e] Don Pedro Enrique Acevedo, Conde di Fuentes.   [f] *scodere* (*riscuotere*).
[g] Castello di S. Croce.   [h] *et da ballo et di musica*.

8

Cremona, 10 September 1609
to [Alessandro Striggio, at Mantua]

Mantua, Archivio Gonzaga, Cassetta 6, fos. 102–3. Bifolio: 4 pp.

Prunières, 237; Malipiero, 140; Paoli, 43; Lax, 26

There existed, in the Cremona of Monteverdi's day, two kinds of wind band: the *pifferarii* (city waits) who played in the streets and for special ceremonies, and the quintet of cornetts and trombones whose task it was to provide music at the castle. The latter group did not hesitate to confide in the composer when he asked them how they would break their contract, should the need arise. But before Striggio could ascertain Prince Francesco's wishes regarding the players, His Highness wrote directly from the Gonzaga summer palace at Maderno,[1] inviting Monteverdi's comments on the organist and composer Galeazzo Sirena, a fellow citizen of his at Cremona. This letter, delivered on 4 September, gave him less than a week to sound out Sirena, whom he had known for many years; but when Striggio's letter about the wind band arrived on 9 September Monteverdi replied at once, for he had already interviewed the self-opinionated young organist of S. Agostino and had begun to ask himself what, if anything, lay behind Francesco's urgent request for information.

Francesco and Margherita, resting at Maderno after the birth of their daughter Maria on 19 July, were looking forward from a temporal if not an emotional point of view to their return in the autumn to Casale Monferrato. The problems of governing this small yet highly fortified outpost of the Gonzaga empire demanded—at any rate for the greater part of the year—the presence of a capable prince, and since Francesco was the first-born he was the obvious choice. His younger brother Ferdinando, doting upon his musicians and poets, was at that time persuading Sante Orlandi to collect singers for him,[2] or reading a new play *Amaranta pescatrice* sent to him from Giovanni Villifranchi in Florence.[3] The carnival of 1610 demanded attention.

Although principally concerned, as a patron of musicians, with his wind quintet (which rears its corporate mouthpiece once again in Letter 12), Francesco also worried about his chapel and in particular about its organist. Rumour had reached him that Sirena might be suitable for the vacant position, so he wrote to Monteverdi requesting an opinion as unbiased as might be hoped for in the circumstances. It is

---

[1] The palace, of which nothing now remains, was built by A. M. Viani at an estimated cost of 100,000 gold scudi. It was accessible from Mantua by road or by boat, via the Mincio and Peschiera.

[2] Bertolotti, 91.   [3] Ademollo, 85.

generally assumed that Monteverdi read into this request more than was really intended, it being 'typical of . . . his suspicious character that he should have feared that Sirena's appointment might endanger his own position as Director of *all* the music at Mantua'.[4]

But he shows less suspicion than anxiety—a well-founded anxiety when one considers the unreliable state of the Gonzaga exchequer combined with the volatile characteristics of their mentality. They were a strange and fickle dynasty, liberal at one moment and parsimonious the next; and the sands of their time were fast running out. A widower with two young sons to care for, Monteverdi feared that a new organist for Francesco's chapel might eventually qualify for the title of Director of Music, and when the prince succeeded to the dukedom, then what would happen? Francesco would have to decide whether to take over his father's appointee, or replace him by somebody else—possibly younger and more adaptable—from his own entourage.

Yet Monteverdi knew perfectly well that Sirena was no match for him. He had heard the man play during the ceremonies of the Accademia degli Animosi on 27 September 1609[5] and had listened attentively to some of the music at S. Agostino. As opposed to Monteverdi, whose numerous published works included five books of madrigals and an opera score, Sirena had nothing in print. Monteverdi's first large-scale collection of church music was already at the printer's, but Sirena's masses would not appear until 1626.[6]

And so, assuming the unusual role of music critic, Monteverdi writes of the works he has heard, telling Striggio that although the music sounds well it is difficult to perform. He adds that Sirena is clever but conceited, and barely conceals his sarcasm when he refers to the man's being well endowed both in the poverty and conviction of his ideas—a sharp-pointed zeugma that surely stemmed from his early training in rhetoric. But Monteverdi is nothing if not fair, for he praises Sirena's instrument-making, his wind music, and some aspects of his musicianship. He has even asked him to come and live in Mantua for a trial period so that the prince, on one of his frequent return visits to the city, might judge for himself.

But Sirena would hear nothing of it, and by the beginning of the new year Francesco had gone on to Turin while Striggio had taken his place temporarily at

---

[4] *Monteverdi Companion*, 31. It should be noted that Monteverdi never controlled all the music at Mantua, for there were sizeable musical establishments at S. Barbara and S. Pietro with which he had nothing to do.

[5] Sommi, *Monteverdi*, 34–5.

[6] In Ercole Porta's *Vaga ghirlanda* (Bologna, 1613) the motet *Salvum me fac* is said to be based on a 'tenore di Galeazo Cremonese', who may be identical with Galeazzo Sirena. See Sartori, *Bibliografia*, i. 190–1. Other than this, his first publication appears to be the motet *O amantissime et dulcissime Jesu Christe* in Bonometti's *Parnassus musicus Ferdinandaeus* of 1616. A book of masses appeared in Venice (Gardano) ten years later, and by this time he had been appointed organist of Cremona Cathedral, where his music for ceremonial occasions seems to have elicited great admiration. Two such events are described in the Bresciani MSS (Pontiroli, 'Musicisti', 170) with specific mention of works for five and six choirs singing in angelic harmony. According to Bresciani, Sirena died in 1636 (ibid. 157).

Casale. Yet they continued to correspond about *Orfeo*, which indicates that Monteverdi was still very much in their minds.[7]

My Most Illustrious Lord and Most Esteemed Master,

On the 9th of this month I had a letter from Your Lordship enjoining me not to engage those wind-players without further advice, but rather to keep them buoyed up with a little hope. This much I did, and this much I would have done without being advised; in any event I shall so continue with greater confidence now that I have it as an order. I said to these people three days ago: 'If the commander or governor of the castle knew that you wanted to leave, would he give you permission?' They replied that not only would he not give permission, but he would hinder them in every way so that they could not leave. 'And if the need should arise, how would you leave?' They answered: 'We would go without saying anything.' I did not discuss the matter futher; but Your Lordship has now heard about the difficulties of their departure.

On the 4th of this month I also had a letter from His Highness the Prince,[a] written to me from Maderno.[b] This mentions that I am to enquire whether a certain Galeazzo Sirena, composer and organist, would come and serve His Highness, and what salary he would like; and that I am to let the said prince know about his capability and intelligence. And because I am very well acquainted with the said Galeazzo—indeed he comes daily to see me at home, so that through this I know him intimately—I performed this task as soon as the commission was received.

The man at once replied that he had no mind to go and serve princes, but was keen to go and live in Milan as Director of Music at the church of La Scala[c] (especially since certain Milanese singers promised to make that post available to him), because with a chance like that he says he could earn his living by teaching, making music for the city, composing for the nuns, and having guitars and harpsichords made for sale; and so by this means he would hope to become rich in a short time.

To this I replied that I wanted him to think a little about what I had said to him, and then if he did not wish to enter the service of that prince, he

---

[7] Bertolotti, 92.

[a] Prince Francesco.   [b] Now known as Toscolano-Maderno, on the western shore of Lake Garda.
[c] Santa Maria della Scala.

[61]

might at least tell me what excuse I should offer. So, after seeing him several times and nothing having come of it, I thought it proper to write to Your Lordship as to who this man is, so that you may inform His Highness; for if I insist on waiting until Galeazzo answers me and then write to His Highness, I am afraid he may think that by being tardy I am negligent in doing what he commands.

I therefore tell Your Lordship that this Galeazzo is a man 37 years old, poor, with a wife and children, a father who works as a labourer in the carriage and sedan-chair*d* trade at Poggio, and a mother very much poorer who has to spin at the mill all day. This man has an all-round talent, and when he concentrates he does not do badly. He set himself to make a psaltery and made it very well; he set himself to make a theorbo and again he made it very well, and likewise a harpsichord and many other hand-made things. In music he is certainly intelligent, but self-opinionated; and he insists that whatever comes out of his head is the most beautiful of its kind, and if others are not quick to say so, he himself is the first.

Of his work I have only heard—from two eight-part masses—the Kyrie and Gloria of one, and all of the other except the Sanctus and Agnus (for more than this he has not composed), and a Credo from another four-part mass, a twelve-part *Dixit*, and some four-part canzonas to be played on stringed or wind instruments, these being very practical, technically well worked out, and of a certain novel invention. As for the masses and *Dixit*, however, they are written in a style that is certainly opulent but difficult to sing, because certain voice-parts and rests are hunted down,*e* which greatly tires and worries the singers.

I genuinely believe that he would still accommodate himself to what His Highness is looking for, but since I have not heard any of it—any of his work in this vein—I prefer not to give my opinion, because I rather think that before he could gain familiarity with the theatre it would cost him no little effort, having spent his time on music of the ecclesiastical type; and even in this he still finds it hard to be successful with his own works, since he tends to be stubborn.

So, knowing him to be very well endowed both as regards the poverty and the conviction of his thought, and not being sure that he would give complete satisfaction to His Highness, I said to him: 'Since I know that

---

d scranne da poggio   *e* va cazzando (= cacciando)

you would want to be well paid, and so that His Highness may know upon whom he has to lay out such moneys, it will give you little trouble to do what His Highness commands. Consequently, if you would like to go and live in Mantua on a trial basis for three months and there display your worth, I will see to it that you are given a room, service, food, and something of a gratuity as well; and in this way you can arrange the contract yourself.' But to this he replied that he did not want to, so I added: 'You do not have anything in print about which an opinion can be given concerning your worth, nor do you even want to come on trial, nor have you ever composed theatrical music; so how can one possibly form any idea of this without first-hand knowledge?'

As Your Lordship has realized, he is of this nature: he has ample conviction but no idea of making himself liked by the singers, for those in Cremona are not happy singing under him, although they respect him; and he readily speaks ill of a third party. Next, about his organ-playing: he performs in accordance with his knowledge of counterpoint, but certainly not with elegance of hand, since he has not the touch to bring off runs, trills, appoggiaturas, or other ornaments, and he himself admits to not making a profession of it, although he plays the organ in S. Agostino here in Cremona; but he does this because he is poor.

After two or three days he asked me to tell him (if he were to go and serve His Highness) whether the prince wanted him as his Director of Music, or for some other post, to which I replied that I did not know his intention. So, Signor Striggio, I thought I would write to Your Lordship a few words about the things that make me uneasy, because I mean the prince is entitled to do just what seems right and pleasing to His Highness, but by taking either him or others as Director of Music (if indeed he wants to give him such a title, and that I don't know), on the death of the Duke, and should Almighty God allow me to survive—the prince having a Director of Music—what would you wish me to do: go away from Mantua then?

I want to find out, if you please, Your Lordship (in that discreet manner which I know will be better seen to by you than explained by me), whether His Highness has this intention, so that I may know what to do. Forgive me if I have been too long, but blame my ignorance which has prevented me from learning to speak concisely. And so with this I remain your devoted servant, and I kiss your hands, praying that you may keep

[63]

me in your good graces, and letting you know that I shall soon be in Mantua.

from Cremona, 10 September 1609
Your Most Illustrious Lordship's
devoted servant
Claudio Monteverdi

9

Mantua, 9 June 1610
to [Duke Vincenzo Gonzaga, at Maderno]

Mantua, Archivio Gonzaga, Cassetta 6, fo. 106. Folio: 2 pp.

Prunières, 239; Malipiero, 144; Paoli, 48; Lax, 30

The year 1610, like its predecessor, yields only two letters from Monteverdi's pen, but this time they are both directed to members of the Gonzaga family. In January, Prince Francesco was temporarily absent from Casale on a visit to Turin, leaving Striggio to look after certain of his official and personal interests. Among the latter, music and theatre continued to occupy pride of place, as may be seen from correspondence in late January and early February. Francesco sent the words of a ballet, to be set to music, and asked about the arrival of certain court musicians. A postscript exhorts the busy secretary to send off a copy of the score of *Orfeo*, although it is not clear whether a performance of the opera was being considered at that time. On 4 February Francesco adds that he is still awaiting the costumes and the musicians, as well as Ercole Marigliani, then a junior secretary who shared Striggio's interest in the composition of libretti.[1]

Since by 1610 Striggio had been assigned to Casale Monferrato, and was later to become much involved with political affairs in Milan, the letters usually assumed to have been addressed to him from 1610 until 1615 must be reallocated. Continuing troubles with Savoy and Spain forced the Gonzaga to deploy their diplomatic forces with increasing care and cunning, and when Striggio left Mantua his place was taken by Iberti, whose career abroad had come to an end in 1612, leaving him free to supervise the correspondence with Venice and Germany.[2] Monteverdi, who was based in Venice from 1613 onwards, would therefore keep in touch with Iberti.

Duke Vincenzo, after a series of arduous and protracted negotiations with the singer Adriana Basile of Naples, could finally look forward in the spring of 1610 to the arrival of this highly talented artiste and members of her immediate family. Ottavio Gentile, a diplomatic agent in Rome, sent word to the Duke of her passage through that city,[3] where Cardinal Ferdinando also heard her and reported on her excellence both as singer and instrumentalist. By the time she and her retinue had departed for Bracciano, Florence, and Mantua, the Cardinal had become ecstatic.[4]

---

[1] Bertolotti, 92.   [2] Quazza, *Diplomazia*, 43; Coniglio, 426.
[3] Ademollo, 122.   [4] Ibid. 127.

It is difficult to understand how the Duke, as recipient of letters couched in a steady crescendo of enthusiasm, could bear to think of any other singer when 'la prima donna del mondo' was already on her way northwards; but he may have been planning the formation of a very special and highly virtuosic madrigal group—a vocal coronet whose most resplendent gem should be none other than Adriana. A messenger had therefore been sent from Maderno (where Vincenzo and a handful of his courtiers were enjoying the cool breezes of the Lago di Garda) with a letter for Pandolfo Grandi,[5] one of the best tenors among the court musicians, informing him that in addition to reserving his own services he should find the best possible contralto even if it meant engaging a newcomer.

Grandi, born in Modena and still in touch with musicians there, naturally contacted one of them when the letter arrived, but was bound to ask Monteverdi's opinion regarding the man (for a contralto part could then, as now, be sung by a male alto) since the Director of Music was ultimately responsible for the quality of the ensemble. This explains Monteverdi's concern not only for the vocal ability and agility of the candidate—whose name is not given—but also for his effectiveness in a madrigal group. A broad hint of the haste in which the audition was arranged emerges from the remark that the man was obliged to leave for Maderno before an *ad hoc* group could be formed.

This letter is in some ways a pendant to the previous one, for both reveal Monteverdi's critical aptitude: one deals frankly with a composer and organist, the other with a singer, whose good and bad points are expertly analysed and assessed. Within a fortnight of receiving this audition report, the Duke heard of the safe arrival in Mantua of Adriana, and hurried to Porto where she had already been welcomed by the Duchess. Antonio Pavese, writing to Cardinal Gonzaga on 25 June, exulted in the beauty of the diva's voice and mentioned that of all who listened admiringly none was more moved than Monteverdi.[6] Before the end of the year he was to travel to Florence and Rome, but even their finest singers failed to impress him as did Adriana Basile.

My Most Serene Lord and Most Respected Master,

I was entrusted by Messer Pandolfo[a] (on behalf of Your Highness) with hearing a certain contralto, come from Modena, desirous of serving Your Highness, so I took him straightway into S. Pietro[b] and had him sing a motet in the organ-loft. I heard a fine voice, powerful and sustained, and

---

[5] He served from 1591 until at least 1621 (Jeppesen, 318) and his name appears in later salary lists (MacClintock, *Wert*, 48; Bertolotti, 97). In 1618 he contributed two works to Malgarini's *Motetti* dedicated to Scipione Gonzaga of Bozzolo.

[6] Ademollo, 155.

[a] Pandolfo Grandi of Modena.   [b] The cathedral in Mantua.

when he sings on the stage^c he will make himself heard in every corner very well and without strain, a thing that Brandino^d could not do as well.

He has a very good *trillo* and decent ornamentation,^{e} and he sings his part very surely in motets, so I hope he will not displease Your Highness. He has a few small defects, that is to say, he sometimes swallows his vowel a little, almost in the manner of Messer Pandolfo, and sometimes sends it through his nose, and then again he lets it slip through^f his teeth, which makes the word in question unintelligible; and he does not really strike the ornamentation as would be needful, nor does he soften it at certain other places.

But I am of the sure opinion that he could rid himself of all these things as soon as they are pointed out. I have not been able to hear him in madrigals, because he was all ready to set out and place himself at Your Highness's disposal, so that I am reporting to Your Highness what I have heard him in, and since you have ordered me to do nothing else, I end my letter here, making a most humble reverence to Your Highness, and praying Our Lord that he may long keep Your Highness in good health and in His good grace.

from Mantua, 9 June 1610

Your Most Serene Highness's

most humble and most grateful servant

Claudio Monteverdi

---

^{c} *sena* (= *scena*). ^{d} Antonio Brandi, a male alto.
^{e} *gorgia*. ^{f} *sdrussilare* (= *sdrucciolare*).

IO

Mantua, 28 December 1610
to [Cardinal Ferdinando Gonzaga, at Rome]

Mantua, Archivio Gonzaga, Cassetta 6, fos. 108–9. Bifolio: 3 pp.

Prunières, 239; Malipiero, 145; Paoli, 51; Fabbri 1985, 155; Lax, 31

The lack of an address on this letter has inspired various guesses concerning the identity of the recipient. Davari, the first to discuss its contents, suggested that Monteverdi was writing to the Mantuan ambassador in Rome, Aurelio Recordati,[1] but although the opening salutation would indeed be adequate for an ambassador, the content of the letter stresses the fact that the composer's son Francesco is a vassal of the Gonzaga family, and under the special protection of the recipient. This points clearly to a member of the family; and since the second part of the letter dwells on musical topics, in particular the artistic liaison between the singer Adriana Basile (see Pl. 2) and Cardinal Ferdinando Gonzaga, the most likely candidate would appear to be Ferdinando.

If Monteverdi could, with perfect propriety, ask for one of the Cardinal's songs, he would hardly hope for such a gift from an ambassador who was neither poet nor composer, or from Striggio (as Malipiero would have it), for at that time the Duke's councillor was assisting Prince Francesco at Casale Monferrato. What is more, Monteverdi's request for urgent help in persuading Pope Paul V—or the Cardinal in charge of the datary—to award a bursary to his son can only have been aimed at someone with powerful connections in Rome, preferably a Gonzaga and a musician.

In addressing the Cardinal, Monteverdi made one of his very rare errors, for the opening salutation lacks the essential word 'Reverendissimo'. Nevertheless the honorific used in the body of the letter—'V.S.Illma'—agrees with that in his other letters to the Cardinal.[2]

In order to place the letter in its proper context, some understanding of the Cardinal's interests and movements is desirable. Overshadowed to some extent by his elder brother, Ferdinando nevertheless led an active life in Rome, writing poetry and music (including verses in praise of Adriana Basile and songs for members of his own musical establishment), as well as keeping in touch with musicians in Venice, Mantua, and Florence. Ottavio Rinuccini, writing to him from Florence on 24 June 1610, bestows the highest praise on a duet and some arias of Monteverdi, admired by

---

[1] Davari, 100.   [2] Letters 5 and 11.

2. Adriana Basile. Engraving by Niccola Peretty. Florence, Biblioteca Nazionale Centrale

everybody but particularly by Jacopo Peri.[3] At about this time Adriana, having arrived safely in Mantua, informs the Cardinal of the satisfactory completion of her journey and requests some of his compositions, to which he replies on 3 July promising to enclose a copy of *Vita della mia vita* and another new song that might not displease her.[4]

Acknowledging the letter and music on 15 July, Adriana points out that instead of two songs she received only one, whose title is *Care pupille amate*. Thus cheated of a cardinal composition, she asks for a special favour that will surely make up for it—a piece of wood from the True Cross, which he can surely obtain from Cardinal Borghese.[5] Alas, the Cardinal is ill and the relic unobtainable, so Ferdinando sends her some trinkets, for which she is extremely grateful. But still she asks for songs,

---

[3] Davari, 99.   [4] Ademollo, 156.   [5] Ibid. 158.

preferably light-hearted ones like a frottola (a rather late appearance of this term), or a canzonetta.[6]

While this amiable banter continued its leisurely progress, Monteverdi was preparing for his journey to Rome, where he planned to take a copy of the newly published Mass, Vespers and Motets (dedicated to the Pope), and sound out the datary regarding financial aid for his son's education.[7] By the middle of September, Prince Francesco had written to his brother about the composer's visit, requesting hospitality and help. Duke Vincenzo added his support, sending commendatory letters to the cardinals Montalto and Borghese, both of whom were not only musical but liberal in their patronage of musicians. They replied in due course, promising to assist Monteverdi in so far as they were able.[8]

On 25 September Adriana sends a very strange letter to Cardinal Ferdinando: he must have forgotten her, surrounded as he is by those ravishing Roman sirens. Of course, she sings poorly compared with them, but she can never forget his kindness to her, she cherishes *Care pupille amate*, she asks for more songs of the same kind, and looks forward to seeing him at Mantua.[9] Her remark about the sirens is, of course, a thinly veiled reference to her great rival, Hippolita Marotta,[10] whose talents and graces were indeed admired by the Cardinal, among countless others. Lively comparisons of the two singers were to continue at least until 1620, when the Este princess Giulia Felice wrote that although La Marotta had a better voice she was not so attractive, whereas La Basile possessed charm of countenance and of voice.[11]

Cardinal Ferdinando, anxious perhaps to allay the fears and calm the ruffled pride of his father's favourite singer, travelled to Mantua and spent the latter part of October renewing acquaintances at court and singing duets with Adriana, possibly to Monteverdi's accompaniment. But early in November the Cardinal left his ancestral home, pausing at Ponte di Lagoscuro to write her a personal letter of thanks and good wishes.[12] Continuing to Rome, he arrived shortly before Monteverdi and was able to effect all the introductions the composer and his patrons had hoped for. On his return, however, Monteverdi realized that he had accomplished much less than he set out to do, and as soon as the Christmas festivities were over he put pen to paper and wrote to the Cardinal about the matter of the bursary.

He ends Letter 10 with a comparison of Hippolita Marotta, Francesca Caccini (who sang for him in Florence), and Adriana Basile, to whom without any hesitation he awards the palm. She delights the audience's ears and eyes when she is tuning up,

---

[6] Ademollo, 160. The author believes that 'Signor Giuseppe' refers to Monteverdi, and this could possibly have resulted from a slip of Adriana's pen. At that time the composer was indeed concentrating on secular music of a predominantly serious nature, to be published later in Book VI (1614), as we know from Bassano Casola's letter (Davari, 99).

[7] See Bassano Casola's letter of July 16 (Vogel, 430) and Fenlon, 'Vespers', 381.

[8] Vogel, 356, gives brief extracts from Cardinal Montalto's letter of 23 Nov. and Cardinal Borghese's letter of 4 Dec.

[9] Ademollo, 161.　　　[10] Cametti, 111–23.　　　[11] Ademollo, 264.　　　[12] Ibid. 161.

even before she has opened her mouth. But there is a discordant note: Monteverdi tells how Adriana, on hearing him reiterate the praises bestowed *in absentia* by the cardinals Montalto, Borghese, and Gonzaga, suddenly became very jealous and accused Cardinal Ferdinando of holding La Marotta in higher esteem, this being the reason why he still withholds his songs in spite of ceaseless entreaties. At this point Monteverdi takes matters in hand, and (possibly because he suspects strained relations between the prelate and the artiste) implores the Cardinal to send him a song, if he will not send one to her. This request was granted by the middle of the following year, as Letter 11 will show.

My Most Illustrious [and Most Reverend] Lord and Most Respected Master,[a]

With this letter of mine I am beseeching God with every heartfelt emotion that He grant Your Eminence a good beginning for the New Year, with very good means[b] and the best possible outcome for every one of your most splendid thoughts; and that He grant me always an opportunity for merit in Your Eminence's favour, with the aid of which I am most certain to enjoy, before I die, the happiness that I hope for, by seeing my son in the Roman seminary with a benefice from the church to pay his board and lodging,[c] I being a poor man. But without this favour I could not hope for anything from Rome to help Franceschino,[d] who has already become a seminarian in order to live and die in this calling under the protection of, and as the most humble servant of Your Eminence; being (as he is) a vassal of the Most Serene House of Gonzaga, born of a father and mother who served Their Highnesses for a long time, and of a marriage solemnized with the special consent of His Highness Duke Vincenzo. For if Rome, even with Your Eminence's favour, were not to help him, he and another brother of his would remain poor, so that they would hardly be able to get to the New Year with bread and wine, if I were to die.

I shall look out for some simple benefice or other that can bring in a stipend sufficient to obtain the satisfaction of this need from His Holiness,[e] if Your Eminence will be so kind as to try and assist both him and me at

---

[a] Monteverdi, usually most punctilious and consistent in his mode of address, omits the customary *Reverendissimo*.

[b] *mezzo*, in this context an almost untranslatable pun, since the word forms part of the 'beginning . . . middle . . . end' phrase which grows naturally out of the New Year's greeting.

[c] *donzena* (= *dozzina*).   [d] Francesco Monteverdi, then 9 years old.   [e] Pope Paul V.

the same time (as I hope from your infinite virtue), either with His Holiness or with Monsignor the Datary;*f* otherwise, fearing that I troubled you too much when I was in Rome, I would not dare to ask him again for any favour.

Before I left Rome I heard Signora Hippolita*g* sing quite well; at Florence I heard the daughter of Signor Giulio Romano*h* sing quite well and play on the theorbo-lute and harpsichord, but at Mantua I heard Signora Adriana*i* sing, play, and speak extremely well. Even when she is silent and tunes up, she has qualities to be admired and worthily praised. I was compelled to assure her how much the Most Illustrious Lords, cardinals Montalto and Borghese*j* honoured and esteemed her, and even more so how much Your Eminence did. In reply to this praise from Your Eminence she said: 'Signora Hippolita has qualities more estimable than I have in the sight of that gentleman, for indeed I have heard about the infinite praises he gives her.'

Concerning this I went to great trouble to make her believe the opposite, but apparently I did not obtain the desired result, for she added: 'If Cardinal Gonzaga held me in his esteem as you think he does, he would have made me worthy of one of his beautiful songs, so that I could sing it.' Dear Sir, make me worthy of one of them so that I may undeceive her with this proof, at which point I pray you also to give Signor Sante*k* the task of sending me the cantata with accompaniment for two arch-lutes, promised me by Your Eminence, so that I can let His Highness hear it one Friday evening in the Hall of Mirrors. For all of this I shall remain a most grateful servant to you, and here by way of conclusion I make you a most humble reverence and kiss your hands.

from Mantua, 28 December 1610

Your Eminence's

most humble and most grateful servant

Claudio Monteverdi

f *Dattario*, the cardinal supervising the office charged especially with examining the fitness of applicants for papal benefices.

g Hippolita Marotta, whose patron was Cardinal Montalto.

h Francesca Caccini; Vogel, 357 n. 2, wonders whether this particular reference might also include Settimia, but she had married Ghivizzani in 1609 and they lived in Lucca. Monteverdi had already heard her sing, for she undertook the role of Venere in the *Arianna* première of 1608.

i Adriana Basile.   *j* Monteverdi writes 'Perretti' instead of 'Borghese'.

k Sante Orlandi, at that time Director of Music to Cardinal Ferdinando Gonzaga.

II

Mantua, 22 January 1611
to [Cardinal Ferdinando Gonzaga, at Rome]

Mantua, Archivio Gonzaga, Cassetta 6, fos. 118–21. Bifolio: 3 pp.

Davari, 133; Prunières, 240; Malipiero, 149; Paoli, 57; Lax, 33

In Letter 10 Monteverdi had begged Cardinal Ferdinando for one of his compositions in order to heal what seemed to be a breach, or put right what threatened to be a misunderstanding, between two musicians who really admired each other. Touched perhaps by Monteverdi's message of good will for the new year, the Cardinal decided to think about it; but he had written to Adriana already and had received no reply. He wrote again and again, with the same result. Was the diva sulking because he had praised her rival? Eventually she replied on 11 January 1611, explaining that his earlier letters must have gone astray,[1] but her excuse seems to have fallen on deaf ears.

Monteverdi, however, was far more fortunate, for he received from Rome not just one song but two, along with a covering letter whose appreciative comments gladdened his heart and raised his spirits.

Five months later, from Florence, Ferdinando assured Adriana in a dignified and courtly manner that he was still anxious to see her in order to enjoy once more her delightful conversation.[2] But he still did not offer the hoped-for song. His journey to Florence seems to have been undertaken principally for musical reasons, for he had been in touch with Peri about an unfinished opera based on Francesco Cini's *Tetide*,[3] and probably hoped to renew his contacts there among poets and musicians. The letter to Mantua, with the two madrigals, must have been sent about five days after his note to Adriana; and just as she was disappointed, so was Monteverdi overjoyed at what he read.

Writing of events in Mantua, Monteverdi describes for him the weekly concerts in which Adriana took part, praising her to the skies and stressing the number and the quality of the guests. They included the Duchess Eleonora, who then had barely four months to live, and her husband Duke Vincenzo, who would survive her only for a brief span.[4] The Lady Isabella of San Martino, widow of Don Ferrante Gonzaga by whom she had several children, and sister of Alfonso Count of Novellara and Archbishop of Rodi, was destined to play a major role in the convulsive events leading up to the War of the Mantuan Succession. In five years' time she would still be attractive

---

[1] Ademollo, 162 (letter of 11 Jan. 1611).   [2] Ibid. (letter of 16 June 1611).
[3] Davari, 183.   [4] She died on 8 Nov. 1611, Vincenzo on 11 Feb. 1612.

enough to charm the Duke's youngest son (also named Vincenzo) into a matrimonial adventure that shook the House of Gonzaga, rattled the Roman Curia, and provided gossip and scandal for all the courts of Europe for the best part of eight years.[5]

Monteverdi, after paying lip-service to high society, then moves into the infinitely more fascinating field of music, revealing to the Cardinal one of his favourite methods for the realization of a continuo madrigal. The musicians from Casale Monferrato (probably the Rubini brothers)[6] are to play the theorbos, whose independently rippling chords will be borne up by the gentle tone of a small organ with wooden pipes, and above this lush harmonic foundation the voices of Adriana and Giovanni Battista will express the text and melodies of the Cardinal's madrigal *Ahi, che morire mi sento*.[7] But the name of the composer is to be withheld until after the performance.

It has sometimes been suggested that the mysterious 'Don Giovanni Battista' could be Adriana's brother G. B. Basile.[8] He was a thoroughly respectable poet, but there is no evidence of his ability to sing; and even if he could, the mildly honorific 'Don' would be hard to explain. In 1633, for instance, when he was raised to the status of court gentleman, the documents nowhere refer to him as 'Don'.[9] But those in minor orders, such as Monteverdi's colleagues Bassano Casola and Antonio Tarroni, were often called 'Don', and since G. B. Sacchi was in Mantua at this time and later applied to Striggio for a chaplaincy at the cathedral, he may be the singer in question.[10]

Once again Monteverdi's insistent pleas for a benefice that would support his son clearly demonstrate the kind of knowledge with which a petitioner would be well acquainted. In April a Mantuan musician at Novara applied to Duke Vincenzo for a vacant canonry,[11] and it might well have happened that the news reached Monteverdi. He asks the Cardinal for help, presumably in Rome, but if his figures regarding the Novara income are correct (or nearly so),[12] it seems from the available records that the bishopric was not, in fact, vacant at that time.

During the summer, Margherita gave birth to a son, Lodovico, who would assure (as everyone thought) a male line of descent for the Gonzaga. The Cardinal, however, being somewhat in the shadow of his elder brother, decided to go to Naples, where he received a letter from Adriana begging him to wait there until she herself journeyed

---

[5] Errante, 'Il processo', recounts the affair in considerable detail, based on the evidence of documents in the Archivio Gonzaga and elsewhere.

[6] The term *casaleschi* often appears in Mantuan documents as a kind of description or nickname for the brothers Rubini (Giovanni Battista and Orazio), who served as violinists at the Gonzaga court as early as 1597, and were also known as composers (Bertolotti, 73). One of the motets in Malgarini's anthology of 1618 is by 'G. B. Rubino Casalasco del Violino', and their competence in composition may account for their prowess on the theorbo. For other references to them as violinists, see Paoli, 59; Quazza, *La guerra*, ii. 95; Bertolotti, 103.

[7] Among later settings of this poem are those by G. Stefani (1623), and Francesco Monteverdi (1624).

[8] Paoli, 59.   [9] Ademollo, 199.   [10] Bertolotti, 92, 97.   [11] Ibid. 93.

[12] Eubel, iv. 262: Carolus a Basilica Petri was succeeded in 1593 by Ferdinandus Taberna, who died in 1615. There is nothing to suggest that the episcopal succession was interrupted in 1611. The cathedral of Novara had three dignitaries and thirty-two prebends, the annual income being 8,500 scudi romani.

south in October.[13] She then left for Casale, G. B. Sacchi left for Rome,[14] and Ferdinando went to Paris to attend the obsequies for Henri IV. While staying there, he received letters from her and from Jacopo Peri, who wanted to see Maria de' Medici once again,[15] and he listened to some of the latest court airs by Guédron, which made their way back to Mantua towards the end of November.[16] In some ways the year had ended better than he hoped it would, for Adriana was sweet-tempered once again and the cares of state seemed to remain at a comfortable distance.

My Most Illustrious and Most Reverend Lord and Most Respected Master,

I have just now received Your Eminence's very kind letter together with the two most beautiful madrigals set to music; and I read and reread the letter, I at once sang the music to myself over and over, and kissed the one and the other again and again with extreme rejoicing, seeing in that letter how great Your Eminence's affection is towards one of his lowliest servants, as I am, who deserve nothing.

Every Friday evening music is performed in the Hall of Mirrors. Signora Adriana[a] comes to sing in concert, and lends the music such power and so special a grace, bringing such delight to the senses, that the place becomes almost like a new theatre. And I think that the carnival of concerts will not end without His Highness the Duke[b] having to post guards at the entrance, for I swear to Your Eminence that in the audience this last Friday there were not only Their Highnesses the Duke and Duchess,[c] the Lady Isabella of San Martino,[d] the Marquis and Marchioness of Solferino,[e] ladies and knights from the entire court, but also more than a hundred other gentlemen from the city too.

On a similar splendid occasion I shall have the theorbos played by the musicians from Casale,[f] to the accompaniment of the wooden organ (which is extremely suave), and in this way Signora Adriana and Don Giovanni Battista[g] will sing the extremely beautiful madrigal *Ahi, che morire mi sento*, and the other madrigal to the organ alone. Tomorrow I

---

[13] Ademollo, 164.   [14] Bertolotti, 93.   [15] Ademollo, 189.   [16] Bertolotti, 93.

[a] Adriana Basile.   [b] Duke Vincenzo.   [c] Vincenzo and Eleonora.

[d] Isabella di Novellara, sister of Count Alfonso and widow of Don Ferrante Gonzaga di Bozzolo.

[e] Cristierno Gonzaga di Solferino and his wife Marcella, née Malaspina.

[f] *casaleschi*, a word used by Mantuans to denote the inhabitants of Casale Monferrato in general; and here referring probably to the Rubini brothers (Orazio and Giovanni Battista).

[g] Giovanni Battista Sacchi.

shall take the aforesaid compositions and present them to Signora Adriana, and I know how precious they will be to her, yet I do not want to tell her the composer's name until she has sung them. I shall then send a report to Your Eminence of the entire outcome.

I shall not fail to see to it that Franceschino my son,[h] and Your Eminence's most humble servant, may learn three virtues: first, to serve God with all diligence and fear; second, the art of letters; and third, a little music, for until now it seems to me that he manages both *trillo* and ornaments quite well, so that by means of Your Eminence's support he may obtain from God and His Holiness[i] the favour which I beg for him every day in my feeble prayers.

I do not know, Most Illustrious Lord, whether it would be too bold of me to ask you—the bishopric of Novara[j] being vacant, which has an income of 8,000 scudi—whether you would be kind enough to put in a word here about the allowance for this son of mine, since it would pay for his board and lodging, amounting to at least 100 gold scudi. If in fact I have been too forward in troubling you, forgive me for the love of God, but if I could indeed receive the favour, what content I would feel in my heart! It would seem as if I had acquired all the gold in the world.

Dear Sir, if it is possible through your boundless grace, help me; and it depends more upon your infinite kindness in doing me a favour, than upon my merits—for I know very well that I have within me nothing but what is born of your infinite goodness. And so I bow to Your Eminence and make a most humble reverence, and I pray Our Lord for your every perfect happiness.

from Mantua, 22 January 1611
Your Eminence's
most humble and most grateful servant
Claudio Monteverdi

[h] Francesco Monteverdi.   [i] Pope Paul V.
[j] Novara, a cathedral town twenty-nine miles west of Milan.

12

Mantua, 26 March 1611
to [Prince Francesco Gonzaga, at Casale Monferrato]

Mantua, Archivio Gonzaga, Cassetta 6, fos. 115–16. Bifolio: 3 pp. Enclosure: music

Davari, 134; Malipiero, 147; Paoli, 54; Fabbri 1985, 67, 173; Lax, 35

The addressee of this letter is usually assumed to be Duke Vincenzo Gonzaga, for the salutation 'Serenissimo' and the plentiful references to 'L'Altezza Vostra Serenissima'[1] normally refer to the Duke, as in the first three letters. But there was one other member of the family who had the right to this form of address, as is proved by Monteverdi's preface to *Orfeo*, whose opening and closing salutations agree exactly with those of the present letter. It was in fact sent to Prince Francesco (see Pl. 3) at Casale Monferrato, where Giulio Cesare (the composer's younger brother) was rehearsing the music he had written for Ercole Marigliani's *Il Rapimento di Proserpina*, for performance on 29 April 1611.[2]

Since it is clear from Letter 7 that the engagement of wind instrumentalists was of special concern to Prince Francesco, whose normal place of residence at this time was Casale, Monteverdi's new report on a candidate for the band confirms the identity of the recipient. Additional proof lies in the composer's reference to the prince in quoted speech (which he often uses in his letters for greater effect),[3] and to his own brother.

The intermediary between the prince and the composer was Giulio Cesare Bianchi, a native of Cremona, a well-known cornetto-player, a composer of modest attainments, and a former pupil of Monteverdi who was his senior by about ten years.[4] Although their careers diverged, the men remained on friendly terms, and in 1620

---

[1] The final one, just below the date, is given as 'V.S. Illma' by Malipiero and De' Paoli. Davari transcribed it correctly.

[2] Solerti, *Albori*, i. 157.   [3] As in Letter 10, to Cardinal Ferdinando.

[4] Sommi, *Monteverdi*, 35 n. 38, citing the Bresciani MSS in the Libreria Civica of Cremona, vol. xxviii (*Uomini insigni di Cremona*), mentions that Bianchi served the court of Mantua for many years, played the cornetto in his native city, and dedicated his two publications to Pope Paul V and Cardinal Montalto. He also spent some time in Piacenza. This material is also reproduced in Pontiroli, 'Musicisti', 167. The same article (169) enlarges on the duties of wind-players at Cremona, in an undated entry probably not much later than 1616: 'in the Piazza Maggiore two choirs of trumpets began to play, then four drummers and a pair of pipers went back and forth in turn, now one playing, now the other, for the entertainment of the people'.

3. Francesco IV Gonzaga, fifth Duke of Mantua. Anonymous engraving. Soprintendenza alle Gallerie di Mantova. Photo: G. Giovetti, Mantua

Bianchi published two books of church music containing forty-two of his own compositions and seven by his teacher.[5] In a census of 1637 he is named as the lessee of Monteverdi's house in Cremona,[6] so they must still have been in touch during the last years of their lives.

It is not known who the young musician was, or whether he was eventually appointed, but perhaps he was pressed into service for the *Rapimento*, whose purpose was to celebrate the prince's birthday and possibly the birth of a second child to Margherita. That child, christened Lodovico, might have saved the House of Gonzaga from extinction, but an attack of smallpox brought his life to an end at the tender age of eighteen months.

[5] RISM 1620[3], *Libro primo* (Paris, Uppsala); 1620[4], *Libro secondo* (Frankfurt, Warsaw).
[6] Pontiroli, *Monteverdi*, 52.

The life of Duke Vincenzo was not in every respect a shining example for his three sons to follow. Each of them inherited, to a greater or lesser degree, his love of extravagance and his lack of concern for the future, yet they also displayed a laudable enthusiasm for the arts and an almost naïve belief that the kind of existence led by their actors and musicians was entirely satisfactory. The Gonzaga tended to pay the lowest possible fees (except to famous lady singers), at the same time demanding the highest possible standards. Although Monteverdi's young candidate claimed to play several instruments, he was reminded that the prince would wish to hear—both indoors and outdoors—a wide range of music drawn mainly from vocal sources.[7]

Of the three sacred works sent by Monteverdi to the prince, the first has been erroneously cited in all but one of the available versions of the letters. Davari correctly gave its title as *Dixit a 8* in 1885, but ever since then it has reappeared as *Dixit a 5*, raising the problem that no such psalm, scored for this number of voices, can be discovered anywhere among the composer's surviving works. There is no doubt whatever about the accuracy of the figure '8'; and in any event no self-respecting composer of Monteverdi's day would set the first of the Vesper psalms for less than eight voices divided into two choirs. His first essay of this kind, in the 1610 anthology, presupposes three distinct groups—a six-part choir, six soloists, and a consort of as many instruments with organ continuo. It may well date from 1595.

The *Dixit* sent to Francesco was probably one of those published later in the *Selva morale* of 1641, or in the posthumously edited collection of 1650.[8] As for the two-voice motet for the Elevation, perhaps the most likely works are *O bone Jesu* (Donfrid, 1622) and *Venite sitientes* (Calvi, 1624), for none of the other duets refers to Our Lord or to the Blessed Sacrament. The choice is even more limited with regard to a five-part motet in honour of the Virgin, for one work only corresponds to this designation: *Exultent caeli et gaudent angeli*, in Calvi's anthology of 1629. As in Letter 4, Monteverdi urges that the music be properly rehearsed before it is performed— a warning which would be unnecessary except in a society accustomed to hurried decisions, inevitable confusion, and the constant risk of under-rehearsed interpretations.

My Most Serene Lord and Most Respected Master,

Your Highness left instruction with Messer Giulio Cesare[a] the Cremonese (who plays the cornetto) that if someone could be found who would play the recorder, cornetto, trombone, flute, and bassoon—for want of a fifth part in Your Highness's wind band—you would be pleased to take him on.

---

[7] The term 'canzoni francese' could of course refer to the instrumental canzoni available in numerous publications of the time.

[8] Note that the first *Dixit* of each collection contains some of the same material, although they begin differently. The earlier version is without doubt the better of the two.

[a] Giulio Cesare Bianchi.

I therefore approach with this letter of mine to let Your Highness know that there is a young man here of about 26 or 28 (I do not know whether he is passing through or has come on purpose) who can play on the aforementioned instruments very readily at least, and with assurance, because I have heard him play both recorder and cornetto; moreover, he says that he can also play the gamba and the viola.

At first glance I find him full of great probity and good manners. On my own initiative I sounded him out concerning his requirements in case it should happen that Their Highnesses[b] might be pleased to engage him. Never, as far as I have been able to ascertain, has he wanted to come down to any other particular than this: that if he were worthy of such a favour, he would consider all that might be given to him as great good fortune, since he has no other or greater desire than to learn, and to serve, and to become fit to be allowed to serve.

As is my custom, I sounded him out and told him: 'If His Highness the Prince were pleased to take you on, this gentleman very much likes not only to hear a variety of wind instruments, he also likes to have the said musicians play in private, in church, through the streets,[c] and atop city walls; now madrigals, now French songs, now airs, and now dance-songs.' And he told me in reply that he would do everything, as he will always consider it great good fortune, this becoming fit to be allowed to serve the likes of Their Highnesses in some way. He says that he will stay in Mantua for Easter; consequently, Your Highness can give such instruction as may please you in this matter.

At this point in my letter I am also praying that Our Lord grant you a happy Easter, and I beseech you to be so kind as to accept the *Dixit* for eight voices which Your Highness ordered me to send, together with which I am also sending you a little motet for two voices to be sung at the Elevation,[d] and another for five voices for the Blessed Virgin. Once Holy Week is over I shall send a couple of madrigals, and anything else that I understand may be to Your Highness's taste.

You will do me a special kindness by letting my brother[e] see these compositions a little before Your Highness may condescend to hear them, so that my brother, the singers, and the players can—as a group—get acquainted with the melody of the said songs, for Your Highness will then

---

[b] Francesco and Margherita.   [c] *dietro alle vie.*
[d] *levazione di N.S.*   [e] Giulio Cesare Monteverdi.

be less offended by this feeble music of mine. And so with this I make a most humble reverence and pray Our Lord, with the greatest and most fervent feeling of which I am capable, for the consummation of your every most generous thought, and the maintenance of your perfect health.

from Mantua, 26 March 1611

Your Most Illustrious Lordship's

most humble and most grateful servant

Claudio Monteverdi

13

Venice, 12 October 1613
to [Annibale Iberti, at Mantua]

Mantua, Archivio Gonzaga, Cassetta 6, fos. 122–3. Bifolio: 4 pp.

Prunières, 241; Malipiero, 151; Paoli, 62; Fabbri 1985, 178; Lax, 37

An unusually long interval separates Letters 12 and 13. Those two years and seven months, full of terror and chaos for the Gonzaga, were difficult and decisive for Monteverdi and his younger brother. They must often have wondered what would become of them when the Duke died,[1] and when he did fall ill quite suddenly, and die (quite unreasonably) almost in mid-carnival of 1612, their fraternal concern for the future undoubtedly increased. But Claudio was ready to exercise his practical turn of mind, and less than a month after Vincenzo's solemn and splendid funeral, a memorandum was despatched to Francesco, fifth Duke of Mantua, asking for assistance in the same old matter of a benefice for the 12-year-old child who had been named in honour of the new ruler.

Monteverdi deserves to be admired for his sheer persistence. He had pleaded with the Pope, pursued the Datary, cajoled at least three cardinals, enlisted the support of Duke Vincenzo, and now he was applying to Francesco, who obligingly wrote a letter of recommendation to Aurelio Recordati in Rome. The request was passed on to the Cardinal of Santa Cecilia, but the benefice, alas, had already been disposed of.[2] When the news arrived towards the end of March, disappointment dominated the Monteverdi household, but there was no time for regret because the Duke and Duchess had already planned their birthday celebrations, and a ballet had to be prepared for performance at their villa in Porto on 7 and 8 May.[3] The following month was largely taken up by the coronation ceremonies.

In the mean time, Enzo Bentivoglio of Ferrara, well known to Monteverdi as one of the leaders of the Accademia degli Intrepidi (and his future collaborator in Parma), had devised a tourney for the insatiable Gonzaga.[4] This was almost certainly postponed because of Vincenzo's death, and later reworked with assistance from Francesco in order to celebrate the election of the Emperor Matthias in July.[5] Although the documents reveal little, Monteverdi would surely have been involved as

---

[1] See the penultimate paragraph of Letter 8.   [2] Davari, 100.   [3] Ademollo, 197.

[4] Guido Bentivoglio to his brother Enzo: 'del torneo che V.S. prepara di fare ad instanza del duca di Mantova, io non so che dirmi'. Letter dated 11 Feb. 1612 (Panigada, 430).

[5] Arnold, 25.

director if not as composer, and he may have been helped by Giulio Cesare, who had already provided music for Francesco at Casale.[6]

Something, however, was amiss. On the very day (20 July) when Antonio Pavese reported on the brilliant concourse of personages, the most famous soprano in the whole of Italy complained to Cardinal Ferdinando that she hardly ever saw her new patrons and was tired of being cooped up indoors.[7] To the modern observer, the situation seems devoid of rhyme or reason. But there is a constantly recurring syndrome in the pathology of power politics, whereby the death or deposition of a ruler very often results in the displacement of those known to have been his favourites. Perhaps this happened in Mantua in the summer of 1612, for Adriana had been brought to the city by Vincenzo, just as Monteverdi had many years before. Francesco appears to have had very little to do with Adriana, possibly because he knew of her musico-literary liaison with his brother Ferdinando, but on one occasion he sent her fish that he had caught in Modena, and some fresh fruit; his wife, languishing at Goito, begged Adriana to come and sing to her and help while away the time.[8]

Francesco's indifference with regard to Adriana's personality and musicianship can to some extent be understood. But it is difficult to fathom his reason for terminating the employment of Claudio and Giulio Cesare Monteverdi on 30 July.[9] Since their musical competence can hardly have been in doubt, one wonders whether the indus- trious brothers had somehow become involved with the Farnese, upon whom Francesco declared war in that same month of July in order to avenge an insult to his late father. Although Monteverdi's relationship with the court of Parma was not to begin in earnest for another fifteen years,[10] the slightest hint of artistic commerce would have been enough to arouse Francesco's wrath.

One of the first tasks given to Sante Orlandi, temporarily placed in charge of the Duke's private music, was to write to Ferdinando in the hope that he could find a successor to Monteverdi among the musicians he knew so well in Rome. The Cardinal promptly suggested Giovanni Francesco Anerio, but news of the vacancy had already reached Ferrara, where Pietro Maria Marsolo, Director of Music at the cathedral, at once applied for the post by sending letters and compositions.[11]

Monteverdi, after returning to his father's home in Cremona for the month of August, went in September to Milan, where in all likelihood he called on his friends Cherubino Ferrari and Aquilino Coppini.[12] He was also in touch there with Alessandro Striggio, at that time on a diplomatic mission involving negotiations with the new Governor, the Marquis of Ynojosa.[13] But the tongues of envy, engorged by scandalous rumours attendant upon Monteverdi's departure from Mantua, began to

[6] Solerti, *Albori*, i. 157.   [7] Ademollo, 194.

[8] Ibid. 195. A letter unknown to Ademollo, and referring to Adriana, was recently discovered in Ferrara. See Reiner, 'Angioletta', 32–3.

[9] Santoro, *Monteverdi*, 83. See also Soardi's letter of 31 July, and Orlandi's of 3 Aug. (Davari, 104).

[10] See Lavin, Reiner, Nagler, *passim*.   [11] Davari, 105–7.

[12] Sartori, 'Monteverdiana', 401.   [13] Quazza, *Diplomazia*, 43.

spread further falsehood by accusing him of a desire to usurp the post held by Vincenzo Pellegrini at Milan Cathedral.

To make matters worse, Duke Francesco was informed that Monteverdi had brought disgrace upon himself by bungling a performance of liturgical music in the Duomo. The Duke thereupon ordered Campagnolo, the well-known tenor, to contact Striggio and find out the truth,[14] and when the reply came back it was clear not only that Monteverdi had never interfered with the cathedral music, but that his many concerts given in private homes had met with the utmost success and approval.[15] This correspondence proves that his friends and former patron in Mantua were still very much concerned to vindicate the glory of his reputation.

In late November an epidemic of smallpox broke out in Mantua. One of the first victims was Lodovico, the infant son of Francesco and Margherita, and the only legitimate heir to the house of Gonzaga. Lodovico died on 3 December, and less than three weeks later his father followed him to the grave. Mantua and its rulers were at the threshold of disaster. Ferdinando, accompanied by his Director of Music Sante Orlandi, hurried back from Rome and assumed control. Before the end of January he was deeply embroiled in politics, Carlo Emanuele of Savoy being determined to undo Striggio's good work by persuading Milan to join him in an attack on Casale Monferrato. In addition, although the marriage that should have united Mantua and Savoy had been dissolved by the death of Francesco, his widow whimsically maintained that she was pregnant, and if she brought forth a son it would be he who should succeed to the dukedom, and not Ferdinando.

Amid such widespread tension, music at Mantua began to suffer. Paolo Faconi, however, continued to procure singers for the Cardinal-Duke, casting around Rome for sopranos, altos, tenors, and basses as if nothing at all had happened. On 9 February 1613 he wrote to Ferdinando about a talented young choirboy who greatly desired to be castrated.[16] And on 16 March, the ever-musing brother of Adriana published the third edition of his maritime fable, *Le avventurose disavventure*, dedicating it to 'Alessandro Striggio, Conte di Corticelli, et presidente dignissimo del ducale magistrato di Mantova'.[17] The new and interesting emergency, heightened by Margherita's departure from Mantua and by her father's attack on Casale, compelled Striggio to leave for Milan once more, his place being taken by the aging Iberti, whose diplomatic career abroad had come to an end.[18]

If the late Duke had taken little interest in Adriana, his youngest brother Vincenzo soon began to show that he wished to make amends by writing to her from Casale and Nice in a pleasantly bombastic way about his military exploits.[19] There is no mention of music and no reference to his former teacher Monteverdi, whose whereabouts at this time are a matter for conjecture. He was probably at Cremona with his father and his two sons, while his brother lodged and worked in nearby Castelleone.

In distant Venice, on 10 July, the death occurred of Giulio Cesare Martinengo, Director of Music at St Mark's. Long ailing and impoverished, he left a sorry legacy of an inefficient, depleted choir and a somewhat soiled reputation in the eyes of the

---

[14] Vogel, 430 (doc. 9); 26 Sept. 1612.   [15] Davari, 104; 10 Oct. 1612.   [16] Bertolotti, 90.
[17] Ademollo, 201.   [18] Quazza, *Diplomazia*, 43.   [19] Ademollo, 202.

procurators, who lost no time in requesting of the ambassadors and residents at Rome, Padua, Vicenza, Brescia, Bergamo, Milan, and Mantua information about possible candidates for the vacant position.[20] Even at this stage they mentioned that Monteverdi's name had already been put forward, so that their request was largely concerned with obtaining assessments of his musical ability. These comments presumably took precedence over all the other material submitted, for the procurators did not even bother to make a short list: they simply invited Monteverdi, who gave public proof of his competence on 19 August. The work he chose was the six-part mass *In illo tempore*, published in Venice three years previously. It was rehearsed at S. Giorgio in the morning, with instrumentalists doubling the choral parts, and performed at St Mark's in the afternoon, to the accompaniment of two organs.

Monteverdi, appointed without delay and reimbursed in the amount of 50 ducats by way of expenses,[21] returned to Cremona in triumph and spent part of the sum on a new serge coat whose warmth, alas, he was destined not to enjoy, for he was robbed near Sanguinetto, on the road from Mantua to Este, when travelling back to Venice with his sons and maidservant. Even now, the flat and lonely countryside takes on a somewhat sinister aspect in the twilight. The attack by three ruffians may have been carefully planned, for the courier (whose behaviour Monteverdi found highly suspicious) certainly knew of Monteverdi's appointment at St Mark's, and of his intention to remove himself, his family, and all his goods from Mantua to Venice. Since there were no other passengers, and nobody carried weapons for protection, it was an easy robbery; and the courier probably collected his cut on the return journey. But Monteverdi lost almost everything he possessed, and wrote at once to Iberti for financial aid.[22]

Although the letter contains nothing of musical importance, it throws considerable light on travelling conditions in Lombardy at that time, focusing sharply on the methods of attack adopted by teams of robbers. It even tells us something about their out-of-date firearms,[23] whose main purpose apparently was to intimidate and not (fortunately for the history of music) to kill.

My Most Illustrious Lord and Most Respected Master,

I am writing to let Your Lordship know how, being in the company of the Mantuan courier and leaving with him*ᵃ* for Venice, we were robbed at Sanguinetto*ᵇ* (not in the actual place, but rather two miles away from it) by three ruffians—bandits—in this manner. Suddenly from a field adjoining the main road there came two men of a brownish complexion,*ᶜ* not much

---

[20] Arnold, 'Succession', 208; see also Arnold, 202 (Doc. 3).   [21] Arnold, 202 (Doc. 1).

[22] The use of 'Collendissimo', the absence of Striggio in Milan, and the assignment of Venetian affairs to Iberti point to him as recipient. There is also the fact that Monteverdi admits to having written already to the Lord President of the Magistracy, an office then held by Striggio.

[23] For further details see Stevens, Communication, and Gallico, 'Assalito'.

ᵃ *partendomi con esso lui* (pleonastic).

ᵇ Sanguinetto: four miles east of Nogara, between Legnago and Nogara.   ᶜ *chiera* (= *cera*).

beard, and of medium height, with a long musket apiece (the flint-wheel type) and its firing-pin down. Then, one of these approaching on my side to frighten me with the musket, and the other holding on to the bridle of the horses—which went along quietly[d]—they drew us aside into that field without saying a word.

And making me kneel down as soon as I had alighted, one of the two who had the muskets demanded my purse, and the other demanded the cases from the courier. They were pulled down from the carriage by the courier, who opened them for him one by one, that assassin taking what he liked, and having everything given to him promptly by the courier. I was still on my knees all the while, guarded by the other one who had a gun, and in this manner they took whatever they wanted, as the third of the three assassins, who had a spike in his hand and had acted as look-out, was continuing to do this, making sure that nobody should enter from the road.

When they had well and truly turned over all the goods, the one who was looking into the things obtained from the courier came up to me and told me to undress myself because he wanted to see whether I had any other money. On being assured that I did not, he went over to my maid-servant for the same purpose, but she—helping her cause with all manner of prayers, entreaties, and lamentations—made him leave her alone. Then, turning to the things and the cases, he made a bundle of the best and finest, and while looking for something to cover himself with he found my cloak—a long one of serge,[e] brand new—which I had just had made for me in Cremona.

He said to the courier, 'Put this cloak on me'; but when the assassin saw that it was too long for him, he said: 'Give me another one'. So he took my son's, but finding it too short, the courier then said, 'Look, master, it belongs to that poor seminarian—give it to him'; and he complied. The courier also found the said boy's suit and did the same, and then when he asked with many entreaties for the maidservant's things as a gift, the ruffian handed them over to him. They made a huge bundle of the remainder, took it on their shoulders,[f] and carried it away. Then we picked up the things that were left and went off to the inn.

---

[d] *andasevano* (= *se andavano*) by metathesis.   [e] *rassa* (= *rascia*, from Rashka, in Yugoslavia).
[f] *a bazzolo* (from Cremonese *bazzol* = yoke).

On the following morning we filed a charge at Sanguinetto, then we left (I being much upset) and reached Este.[g] We took a boat for Padua, which held us up all Thursday[h] night and nearly the whole of Friday in silt, nobody worrying about the fact that we finally got away at two in the afternoon,[i] in heavy wind and rain, on an uncovered barge, and with none other rowing in the stern but our courier, who made a really hard job[j] of it. We arrived at Padua, but it was as much as we could do to get in by seven in the evening.

After rising early on Saturday morning to leave for Venice, we waited more than two hours after sunrise to get under way, and during the time we were in Padua, the courier put his arm in a sling saying that this happened because of that business about the cloaks, when he was robbed. I, knowing that nothing of the coachman's was touched or even looked at, was beside myself, to say the least. This act of the courier aroused suspicion among all who were with us, because they had previously seen him without any injury at all.

And there was someone in the Padua boat who said to the courier, 'What kind of tale is this, brother?', and being about to add further words (I would say, perhaps, as a jest) the courier dropped out of the conversation. So we reached Venice at six on Saturday evening while he was joking and laughing; then he stayed for barely two hours and left again for Mantua. This was the affair in detail; and because the other Mantuan courier was here at my house reproaching me by saying that he understood I suspected the last courier, I told him in reply that I suspected nothing and that I take him to be a good man. But it is true that he did do that act you know about—putting his arm in a sling on Saturday morning because of the incident that happened on the previous Wednesday evening, and yet nobody touched him and he was rowing all day Friday.

I am writing to let Your Lordship know that I suspected nothing about this man, because if such a thought were to have entered my mind I would at once have given notice of it to Your Lordship. I am really saying that in regard to this act of the courier's—putting his arm in a sling—he gave us something to think about, and if there is something to be thought about, I

---

[g] Este: the point at which travellers left the road to embark for Padua via the Canale di Battaglia, and then on to Venice via the Brenta, in the *burchiello* that was celebrated in music by Banchieri's *La barca di Venezia per Padova* (1605).

[h] *giobia* (= *giovedi*).   [i] For *ore italiane* see Talbot, 60.   [j] *bona fatica* (ironic).

leave it to the very prudent opinion of Your Lordship, for as for myself I think of nothing and look for nothing unless from the hand of God. I assure you, Most Illustrious Lord, that they robbed me of more than a hundred Venetian ducats in goods and money.

When I was in Mantua, I enjoyed the favour from the Lord President[k] of having six months' salary, and I am also due for another, due three months ago. I told him of my great misfortune. If you were to try and put in a good word for me with the Lord President (although I know that the Lord President's kindness is great), I would regard it as the greatest favour because, Sir, I have infinite need of it. And here making a most humble reverence to Your Lordship I pray God for your every true happiness.

from Venice, 12 October 1613

Your Most Illustrious Lordship's

most humble and most grateful servant

Claudio Monteverdi

[k] Lord President [of the Magistracy], at that time Alessandro Striggio.

14

Venice, 22 August 1615
to [Duke Ferdinando Gonzaga, at Mantua]

Mantua, Archivio Gonzaga, Cassetta 6, fo. 131. Folio: 2 pp.

Malipiero, 156; Paoli, 74; Lax, 40

The Gonzaga could not forget Monteverdi, and even if they tried to do so they were constantly reminded by the musically inclined members of other houses of the rare artist they had lost. In December 1613 Francesco de' Medici wrote to the Cardinal-Duke (see Pl. 4) asking for a copy of *Arianna*, which was duly sent and acknowledged before the year was out.[1] But Monteverdi had been obliged to turn his back on music-drama, at least for a few years, being fully committed to the re-establishment of order and discipline in the choir of St Mark's. One troublesome character named Domenico Aldegati tilted at a fellow singer in 1613 and many years later insulted the maestro himself.[2]

The lack of time and inclination for festivities at Mantua in 1614 was largely due to the pressing problems at Casale, which drained both the energies and the financial resources of Ferdinando and his government.[3] With Striggio away and Iberti in his place, less growth occurred in the field of artistic endeavour and the Mantuan virtuosi went off to other cities and countries. Francesco Rasi, the tenor who had sung the title-role in *Orfeo*, spent some time in Austria and may even have repeated his Mantuan success when the opera was given at Salzburg in 1614.[4] Adriana was still unhappy, having been prevented by the Duke from visiting Verona whither she had been invited by a marquis.[5]

A sympathetic and concise description of Ferdinando's character at this stage in his career comes from the pen of Giovanni da Mulla, the Venetian ambassador in Mantua.[6] 'He is of medium height, abstemious in his habits (unlike some of his close relatives), delicate of complexion, handsome, with a kind face full of dignity. He seems healthy and would be even better if he kept away from his favourite court doctor. Often he is heard to say that he has no other refreshment or solace than music, and that without this he would die. His natural inclination is towards poetry and music: he sleeps little, and it is thought that ideas come to him in the night, since every morning he wakes up with some new artistic project.'

---

[1] Davari, 123.   [2] Prunières, 213. See also Letter 126.   [3] Coniglio, 413.
[4] Antonicek, 267; Einstein, 'Emissär', 31.   [5] Ademollo, 204–7.
[6] Errante, 'Il processo', 648.

4. Ferdinando I Gonzaga, sixth Duke of Mantua. Anonymous engraving. Soprintendenza alle Gallerie di Mantova. Photo: G. Giovetti, Mantua

One morning he dwelt upon something of greater import than mere music or poetry. Having recently met Camilla, the beautiful young daughter of one of his statesmen, Ardizzino Fàa, he allowed himself to fall in love with her and—purple or no purple—to speak of matrimony, although she was far below his rank in rulership and well beyond the pale as far as Rome was concerned. But he proceeded at first with caution, letting it be known that he intended to renounce the cardinalate in order to be properly crowned as Duke. Since a wedding called for music, the secretaries began to busy themselves and finally succeeded in persuading Girolamo Frescobaldi to leave Rome and come to Mantua for an annual salary of 600 scudi, just twice the sum earned by Monteverdi in his final years at court.[7]

[7] Bertolotti, 91.

Monteverdi, not yet under consideration as a contributor, was in any event beginning to enjoy the first-fruits of success in Venice. He was even noticed by the minor lutenist, Pietro Paolo Melii, who dedicated to the new Director of Music a galliard entitled 'La Claudiana' in his *Intavolatura di liuto attiorbato*, published in Venice in 1614. The choir at St Mark's was settling down, and it may have been in June or July of 1614 that Monteverdi's Sixth Book of Madrigals appeared, unique in its lack of a dedication yet enshrining works that commemorated the passing of his wife Claudia, and of the singer Caterina Martinelli. Angelo Grillo, abbot, then regent of the monastery of S. Nicolò del Lido, wrote in August 1614 to thank the composer for sending a complimentary copy,[8] and later continued to proclaim the beauties of this new publication in a letter to Fr. G. B. Magnavacca.[9]

Most of the madrigals date back to Monteverdi's last six years in Mantua and are emotionally and artistically inseparable from his experiences there. The part-books, devoid of the usual subservient genuflection to a princely patron, must have made a doubly deep impression on the Mantuans, and especially upon Ferdinando, who turned a deaf ear to the Florentine blandishments of Giovanni del Turco,[10] looking southwards to Naples for Margherita Basile, sister of Adriana, and eastwards to Venice for the composer whom his late brother had stupidly let go. He was determined to marry Camilla Fàa, and with Monteverdi, Frescobaldi, and Margherita Basile on hand the wedding could be celebrated with the finest music in Italy.

Plans for the wedding were, if not well advanced, at least taking shape;[11] and to this end the Duke had written a libretto which he hoped Monteverdi would set to music. But since the manuscript seems not to have survived, and further discussion is lacking, the entire matter may be relegated to the limbo of Mantuan projects that were mooted but never brought to fruition.

On 6 February 1615 Ferdinando wrote to Adriana Basile's mother asking for the assistance of Margherita, a younger sister of Adriana and a singer of considerable promise. Again there is a certain urgency in his insistence that the wedding must take place soon, but the Neapolitan family, either resisting or failing to understand pressure of this kind, did not send Margherita on her way until April.[12]

During the latter part of February, and after protracted negotiations, Girolamo Frescobaldi arrived in Mantua.[13] A native of nearby Ferrara, he was no stranger to Lombardy, yet what he saw and heard in Mantua was enough to send him scurrying back to Rome after a stay of barely three months. No wonder Monteverdi was not anxious to return. By staying on in Venice he was able to contribute special music for Holy Week at St Mark's, where his son Francesco sang solos. Although the composer earned an extra 50 gold ducats (and his son earned ten),[14] he had no immediate plans to publish a large-scale anthology of church music. But the occasional publications of

---

[8] Letters of Angelo Grillo (edn. of 1616), iii. 127, quoted in Einstein, 'Grillo', 177; Grillo, 461.

[9] Einstein, 'Grillo', 177–8; Grillo, 461–2.   [10] Davari, 108.   [11] Ademollo, 209, 212.

[12] She arrived in Mantua at the end of April, and Ferdinando announced this in his letter of 1 May to Cornelia Basile (ibid. 209).

[13] Bertolotti, 91.   [14] Arnold, 36.

others sought to include one or two of Monteverdi's motets, an auspicious beginning being made by the duet *Cantate Domino* in Bonometti's *Parnassus Musicus Ferdinandaeus*.[15] Dedicated to the archduke Ferdinand, later to become the emperor Ferdinand II and the husband of Eleonora Gonzaga, this anthology shows that other composers besides those in the Graz court circle were anxious to maintain their connections with the Habsburgs.

If Monteverdi sought to honour the Archduke, others were intent upon honouring the composer. Tarquinio Merula's preface to his *Canzoni a quattro*, dated 1 June, does not mention a specific dedicatee, but the ninth of the canzoni is inscribed to his fellow Cremonese, Claudio Monteverdi. A much later work of Merula, the *Quarto Libro delle Canzoni da Suonare* (Venice, 1651), would contain a further tribute in the form of composition for two violins and continuo entitled 'La Monteverda'.[16]

In Mantua, Ferdinando was still toying with musical projects but grew rapidly tired of Margherita Basile, whom he gave in marriage to Ettore Cattaneo Dadi on 27 June.[17] The Duke's generous mood even extended to Margherita's brother Lelio, granting him part of the pension funds of Eugenio Cagnani, an eminent Mantuan citizen who had been a witness at Monteverdi's marriage.[18] But by the beginning of August, Margherita had fallen from ducal grace,[19] the treaty signed between Mantua and Savoy on 20/21 July had become somewhat confused, and Ferdinando was still determined to marry Camilla Fàa in spite of all opposition. Monteverdi undoubtedly knew of this, and while writing about his arrears of payment thought it not inopportune to enquire about possible commissions.

My Most Serene and Particular Lord and Most Respected Master,

As Your Highness knows very well that Duke Vincenzo of blessed memory was kind enough to do me the favour of giving me 100 scudi a year, or rather a fund from which I might conveniently draw the aforementioned annual income, I therefore—never having received the said fund from the ducal exchequer, whose duty it is to give it to me—have always resorted to having notes made for me every six months in arrears, and these being promptly handed over, I have even received the money, except for two.

I have applied several times, with the help of my father-in-law,[a] to the Most Illustrious Lord President of the Magistracy,[b] that he might authorize reimbursement for these two also, in view of the fact that in the decree

---

[15] See *Collected Works*, ed. Malipiero, xvi. 409; also Federhofer, 167.

[16] Sartori, *Bibliografia*, i. 212, 412.   [17] Ademollo, 211.

[18] Ibid. 213; Gallico, 'Documents', 71.   [19] Ibid. 214.

[a] Giacomo Cattaneo.

[b] Perhaps no longer Striggio, who would have been more helpful had he not been absent in Milan.

the exact words appear as follows: 'meanwhile commanding the President of our Magistracy that he carry out this our donation and obligation without any other mandate or commission, this being our well-considered wish'.*c*

But my father-in-law having reported back to me that giving the order is the prerogative of Your Highness (according to a new general rule imposed by you), and I being forced by dire need—as it is now time to lay up provisions for the entire year—as well as being assured of the infinite kindness and humanity of Your Highness, have plucked up courage to come and beg you (as is my wont) and implore you from the bottom of my heart, that you may please be so kind as to order that the said sums due to me be handed over, so that I may support the two sons*d* I have with me at no little expense, desiring as I do that they learn the virtues in a more than mediocre fashion (these sons having been born and bred in Mantua), and that you may make me worthily able to enjoy the outstanding favour that Duke Vincenzo, my particular lord—who is in heaven—granted me.

And likewise I beseech you with the same heartfelt emotion to be so kind as to make me worthy from time to time of a few commissions, so that I can make it clear to the world and to my own self that, although a very lowly and feeble servant, I am not utterly unworthy of Your Most Serene favour. May God long maintain Your Highness both in health and in His grace, and may He grant me merits worthy of Your Highness's commands, to whom I make a most humble reverence.

from Venice, 22 August 1615

Your Most Serene Highness's

most humble and most grateful servant

Claudio Monteverdi

c Monteverdi quotes this from his own copy of the document, which he kept until the year of his death (see Letter 127).

d Francesco, aged 14; and Massimiliano, aged 11.

15

Venice, 6 November 1615
to [Annibale Iberti, at Mantua]

Mantua, Archivio Gonzaga, Cassetta 6, fos. 133–4. Bifolio: 3 pp.

Prunières, 244; Malipiero, 158; Paoli, 76; Fabbri 1985, 214; Lax, 42

It is hardly to be wondered at that the composer's entreaty of 22 August fell on deaf ears, for the plans concerning Ferdinando's marriage to Camilla Fàa—not to mention his renunciation of the cardinalate—occupied the entire court throughout the summer months. Although it was to be a secret marriage, almost everyone in Mantua, as well as a considerable number of outsiders, received daily intelligence of the proceedings. The Franciscan composer Lodovico Viadana sent music from Ferrara,[1] and numerous local musicians were doubtless involved in the entertainments mentioned by Lelio Arrivabene in his letter dated 4 November to the Duke of Urbino.[2] A previous letter from Arrivabene had already informed him that the wedding was imminent,[3] although there were few signs of approval because of the social gulf between the Duke and the beautiful commoner.

Amidst all the rumours and court gossip, one that seemed to concern Monteverdi was relayed to him by the Capuchin friar, Cesare Cattaneo, brother of the composer's late wife. Little is known about Fra Cesare, except that he went to Egypt in 1621 and brought back a monkey, but he was almost certainly a member of the Capuchin Convent in Mantua.[4] Since it was comparatively easy for preaching friars to gain access to the lower court echelons, it may have been there that Fra Cesare heard (or thought he heard) about an authorization from the Duke granting Monteverdi his *fondo*. This fund was probably swallowed up by the wedding disbursements, but Monteverdi applied for it once again to the Duke in Letter 18, sent in July of the following year.

Although the pseudo *fondo* was constantly and flagrantly used by the Gonzaga as a carrot before the donkey's mouth, it is quite clear from the anxiously cooperative tone of Letter 16 that the composer really thought that a bank draft was on its way. Whenever they wanted something from Monteverdi, they would allow a rumour to circulate concerning the capital fund, knowing full well that one of his relatives would report the information to Venice. By raising his hopes, the Gonzaga would be sure of a speedy and affirmative reply when they sent their commission.

[1] Bertolotti, 95.　　[2] Ademollo, 216.　　[3] Ibid. 214.　　[4] Bellonci, 221.

My Most Illustrious Lord and Most Respected Master,

Impelled by the heavy expenses that I am obliged to meet in bringing up my sons[a]—desiring that they learn to read, write, grow up in the fear of God, and become a credit to society, on account of which most necessary considerations I have always had to maintain them and their tutor in my own lodgings, so that they and he have been costing me more than two hundred ducats a year—and finding myself with three hundred ducats from St Mark's and one hundred thanks to the donation granted me by Duke Vincenzo[b] of happy memory, but not being able to have that hundred (which I sorely need), I had recourse in one of my letters to the infinite kindness of His Highness Duke Ferdinando,[c] a month ago or more.

And I had a reply from my brother-in-law the Capuchin[d] to the effect that Your Lordship has in hand not only my letter but also an authorization due to His Highness's clemency, enabling me to enjoy at last not only the hundred scudi I am owed by the ducal exchequer for past instalments, but also possession of the fund from which I may conveniently draw that annual income. You may rest assured that when I heard from my brother-in-law that Your Lordship had obtained this order, I at once hastened to thank God for such a remarkable boon, and I was overjoyed, knowing to what an extent Your Lordship has always been my protector and patron.

I am not going to tell you about my past ailments, which I still feel in my head and body because of the great suffering I underwent with *Arianna*, nor am I going to tell you about the two sons born and bred in Mantua (for indeed Duke Vincenzo was responsible for my marriage), nor that I left that Most Serene Court in so sorry a plight—by God!—as to take away no more than 25 scudi after being there for twenty-one years; nor in conclusion am I going to recount anything else to Your Lordship because I know that you are very well and completely informed.

I shall only ask, with unceasing prayer, that you may please be kind enough to arrange for me so to be comforted by this blessed fund from which I could draw these blessed hundred scudi, as to enjoy a token of my labours, and of the grace of Duke Vincenzo's glorious memory, and of the

---

[a] Francesco, aged 14; and Massimiliano, aged 11.   [b] Vincenzo Gonzaga, fourth Duke of Mantua.
[c] Ferdinando Gonzaga, sixth Duke of Mantua. The letter referred to is no. 14, sent two and a half months previously.
[d] Fra Cesare Cattaneo (see also Letters 18 and 71).

assistance to support my poor sons; and also to show these musicians who serve the present Duke that just as they are both favoured and honoured (as I well know), so too were those who served Duke Vincenzo.

Dear Sir, I beg you for the love of God to try and assist me in this matter, which will maintain at one and the same time my sons, my honour, and the spirit and splendour of Duke Vincenzo; for indeed God ordains that wages may not be withheld from a poor servant from night until morning, and the city of Venice and others too will indeed see that I am well thought of in a place where at present people are surprised because they see nothing.

I do not know what else to say, other than to turn once more to Your Lordship's goodness, on which I rely for my every comfort. Wherefore I do not and shall not fail—neither I nor my poor sons—to pray God for your every most lofty exaltation, and for the fulfilment of your every honourable desire. And here making a humble reverence to you I kiss your hand.

from Venice, 6 November 1615
Your Most Illustrious Lordship's
most grateful servant
Claudio Monteverdi

16

Venice, 21 November 1615
to [Annibale Iberti, at Mantua]

Mantua, Archivio Gonzaga, Cassetta 6, fos. 136–7. Bifolio: 3 pp.
Enclosure: four scenes from *Tirsi e Clori*

Davari, 109; Malipiero, 159; Paoli, 79; Fabbri 1985, 204; Lax, 44

Although the manuscript of the ballet *Tirsi e Clori* has not survived, the Archivio
Gonzaga preserves not only the present letter but also a covering letter, written on the
same date, from the Mantuan Resident in Venice, Camillo Sordi.[1] In it, he tells
Cavaliere Annibale Iberti (whose name and title are given in full): 'today Monteverdi
has promised to let me have a copy of a ballet so that you may give it to His Highness.
If he does send it, as I hope he will, it will be attached to the envelope; and he offers
to add to it and write in whatever will be to His Highness's taste. He will also send a
description of the way in which it ought to be sung and played.'

This covering note therefore ranks as a rare example of an account of a letter about
to be written by Monteverdi; and when the letter and the music arrived at the
Resident's office, they were almost exactly as promised. The letter having been
written in a hurry, some of the words are difficult to decipher, especially between lines
37 and 40. Their correct interpretation is however a matter of unusual importance
since we are dealing with a precious piece of evidence as regards performance practice,
both general, as it affects the Baroque continuo, and particular, as it concerns *Tirsi e
Clori*.

Since Monteverdi sent the musical draft fitted to a text already given to him (or
found by him), his willingness to change it is proof of the continuing practice whereby
verses could be removed from a composition and new ones substituted.[2] Unfortunately we do not know whether Ferdinando retained the original text or added
another; and if another, who wrote it.[3] The verses published with the music in Book
VII are unlikely to be Striggio's, for the letter from Sordi makes it clear that the
recipient and co-ordinator was Iberti.

Five days before the letter was written, Ferdinando had ceased to be a cardinal. As
if to compensate the family honour, his brother Vincenzo was nominated, but he
never went to Rome, nor did he wear the biretta. He had other irons in the fire, in

[1] Busta 1547, E xlv, no. 3 (kindly communicated by Professor Pierre Tagmann).
[2] Another example of this, involving Giambattista Guarini, is given in Kirkendale, 46.
[3] See Pirrotta, 49.

particular an attractive widow, Isabella di Novellara, who lived at San Martino dall'Argine, not far from Mantua. Monteverdi, who had been presented to her at concerts in the ducal palace, mentioned her name to Ferdinando in his letter of 22 January 1611, but nobody in Mantua at that time had the slightest idea of the scandalous decade ahead of them.[4]

My Most Illustrious Lord and Most Respected Master,

His Highness[a] of Mantua's Most Illustrious Resident[b] dwelling in Venice, very much my master, commissioned me recently through Your Lordship's letter (at the command of His Highness of Mantua, my particular Lord) to set a ballet to music; but the commission did not go into any other detail, unlike those of the Most Serene Lord Duke Vincenzo—may he be in glory!—who used to demand of me such productions either in six, eight, or nine movements, besides which he used to give me some account of the plot, and I used to try to fit to it the most apt and suitable music and the metrical schemes that I knew.

However, believing that a ballet of six movements[c] should turn out to be to His Highness's liking, I straightway tried to finish the enclosed, of which two movements were lacking; and this in fact I began in recent months in order to present it to His Highness, thinking that I would be in Mantua this past summer for certain business affairs of mine.

While I am sending it off by the hand of the Resident to Your Lordship, to present to His Highness, I also thought it a good idea to accompany it with a letter of mine addressed to Your Lordship, to tell you at the same time that if His Highness should want either a change of tune in this ballet, or additions to the enclosed movements of a slow or grave nature, or fuller and without imitative passages (His Highness taking no notice of the present words, which can easily be changed, though at least these words help by the nature of their metre and by the imitation of the melody), or if he should want everything altered I beg you to act on my behalf so that His Highness may be so kind as to reword the commission, since, as a most devoted servant, and most desirous of acquiring His Highness's favour, I shall not fail to carry it out in such a way that His Highness will be satisfied with me.

---

[4] Errante, 'Il processo', *passim*.

[a] Ferdinando, sixth Duke of Mantua.   [b] Camillo Sordi.   [c] *Tirsi e Clori* (Book VII).

But if by good fortune the enclosed should be to his liking, I would think it proper to perform it in a half-moon, at whose corners should be placed a theorbo and a harpsichord, one each side, one playing the bass for Chloris and the other for Thyrsis, each of them holding a theorbo, and playing and singing themselves to their own instruments and to the afore-mentioned. If there could be a harp instead of a theorbo for Chloris that would be even better.

Then having reached the ballet movement after they have sung a dialogue, there could be added to the ballet six more voices in order to make eight voices in all, eight viole da braccio, a contrabass, a spineta arpata, and if there were also two small lutes, that would be fine. And directed with a beat suitable to the character of the melodies, avoiding over-excitement among the singers and players, and with the understanding of the ballet-master, I hope that—sung in this way—it will not displease His Highness.

Also, if you could let the singers and players see it for an hour before His Highness hears it, it would be a very good thing indeed. It has been unusually precious to me, this present opportunity, not so much for showing myself very prompt in obeying His Highness's commands, which I so much desire and long for, as to commend myself to Your Lordship as a loyal servant, praying that you may wish to maintain me, and condescend to command me. Here I make a humble reverence to you and pray Our Lord for your every true pleasure and happiness.

from Venice, 21 November 1615

Your Most Illustrious Lordship's

most affectionate servant

Claudio Monteverdi

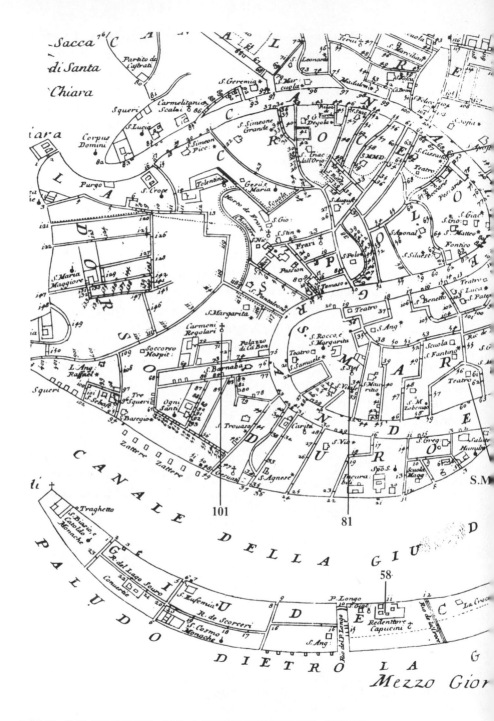

MAP OF VENICE AT MONTEVERDI'S TIME

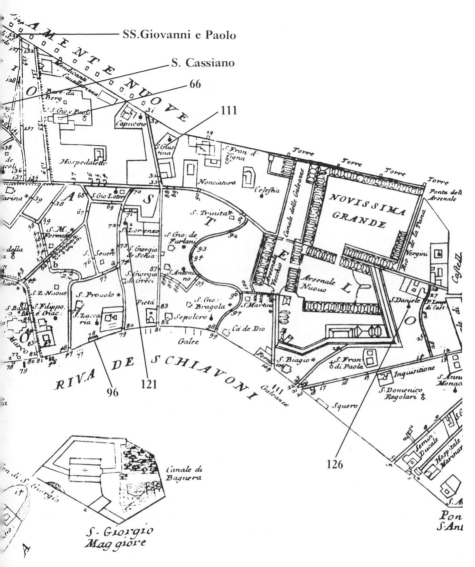

SS.Giovanni e Paolo

S. Cassiano

66

111

96   121

126

Opera-houses in which Monteverdi's operas were produced:
SS. Giovanni e Paolo — *Le nozze d'Enea con Lavinia*, 1641;
L'incoronazione di Poppea, 1642). S. Moisè — (*L'Arianna*,
1639, 1640). S. Cassiano — (*Il ritorno d'Ulisse*, 1640).

Numbers are those of letters indicating places mentioned in them:
Letter no. 58. Redentore; 66. SS. Giovanni e Paolo; 81. S. Stefano;
96. Palazzo Mocenigo; 101. Carmine; 111. S.Giustina; 121. S. Lorenzo;
126. S. Daniele; *passim*: S.Marco.

17

Venice, 28 November 1615
to [Annibale Iberti, at Mantua]

Mantua, Archivio Gonzaga, Cassetta 6, fo. 139. Folio: 1 p.

Malipiero, 163; Paoli, 82; Lax, 46

Ferdinando did not neglect to look elsewhere for talent, since it was common knowledge that although Monteverdi was a genius, he could behave in a somewhat erratic manner, working at his own pace and sending in material late. His Highness accordingly sounded out the Neapolitan composer, Muzio Effrem, and on hearing that he would be willing to come and work in Mantua, sent him 300 scudi for travelling expenses.[1]

My Most Illustrious Lord and Most Respected Master,

I have at hand Your Lordship's advice as to how you not only received the ballet,[a] but also presented it to His Highness; and as it is reported that what little His Highness[b] has deigned to hear gave him pleasure, I am greatly comforted by this news, since with all my heart I desire not only to serve His Highness with all promptness, but also that my service may turn out to be to His Highness's liking.

I am now looking forward to hearing how the remainder has pleased him, or whatever His Highness commands, because if I am to be made worthy of new commissions I shall not fail to accomplish once more, with all my spirit and powers, whatsoever shall be commanded of me. In the meantime, I beg Your Lordship to maintain me as your servant, praying that you make me worthy of serving you; and here I make a humble reverence to you and pray Our Lord for the utmost of your every true contentment.

from Venice, 28 November 1615
Your Most Illustrious Lordship's
loyal servant
Claudio Monteverdi

[1] Bertolotti, 96.

[a] *Tirsi e Clori.*
[b] Ferdinando, sixth Duke of Mantua.

18

Venice, 27 July 1616
to [Duke Ferdinando Gonzaga, at Mantua]

Mantua, Archivio Gonzaga, Cassetta 6, fo. 142. Folio: 1 p.

Prunières, 245; Malipiero, 164; Paoli, 83; Lax, 47

Unusual in its appearance, this letter, in the hand of a professional scribe, tells a story that is only too familar. Monteverdi, wishing to make an impression upon the reluctant Ferdinando, spent money that he could ill afford on a piece of carefully prepared calligraphy, the main reasons being that the cost of living in Venice was on the rise, and his growing sons needed a full-time tutor. That was the best and safest way to have them educated. At the same time he had probably begun to petition the procurators for an increase of salary in view of his success in reorganizing and improving the music at St Mark's, and this increase—from 300 to 400 ducats—was granted on 24 August.[1]

Meanwhile he complained about his lack of basic sustenance in the hope of wringing a contribution from Ferdinando, now crowned sixth Duke of Mantua and fourth Duke of Monferrato in lavish ceremonies which took place in San Pietro as well as in the ducal palace on 5 and 6 January. This coronation being but the formal recognition of an accepted fact, it is doubtful whether it improved Ferdinando's temper or increased his liberality. His secret marriage to Camilla Fàa continued to cause hostile reactions both within and without the court and city of Mantua, while his younger brother's election to the cardinalate unfortunately coincided with an infatuation for Isabella di Novellara, widow of Ferrante Gonzaga di Bozzolo,[2] a member of one of the many smaller rival branches of the main tree. It was a tense beginning to a chain of events leading to a distant but unavoidable disaster.

Life was certainly more peaceful in Venice, whose musical presses paid occasional tribute to Monteverdi's growing reputation. On 1 May 1616 the Cremonese composer Pietro Lappi dedicated a collection of canzoni to Giovanni Pietro Ghirardello, the number of parts ranging from four to thirteen. The last piece, a canzona *a 13*, bears the title *La Monteverde*;[3] but whether it was composed as a present for Monteverdi or a birthday greeting to his son (who had his thirteenth birthday in 1614) is a matter for

---

[1] Sommi-Picenardi, 156.

[2] Also known as Isabella di San Martino dall'Argine, the name of her residence. See Letter 11.

[3] Lappi's publication (in a complete set of part-books) is preserved in Verona, Biblioteca Capitolare.

conjecture. It might even have commemorated the year in which Monteverdi arrived in Venice.[4]

It is often stated that Monteverdi's prose is breathless, that it lacks punctuation and phrasing; but in fact he takes unusual care to balance his cadences, carrying over into epistolary prose some of the props and designs he uses so effectively in his music. This letter consists of but one long sentence, its various parts set off one against another according to the rules of rhetoric; yet in spite of its length there is a sense of purposeful flow, of gathering momentum, which carries the reader through a maze of propositions and statements to a climax of fervent intensity. Although it probably had no effect whatever upon Ferdinando, it remains a masterpiece of literary composition in this particular vein, and could be analysed as follows:

1.0 financial crisis
1.1 very great need of
    1.1.1 bread
    1.1.2 wine
    1.1.3 other things
1.2 impoverishment
    1.2.1 mainly because of educating sons
        1.2.1.1 born there (*costì*) in Mantua
        1.2.1.2 living here (*costà*) in Venice
    1.2.2 also because of high cost of living
2.0 plea to Duke
2.1 Monteverdi begs with the greatest
    2.1.1 sincerity of which he is capable
    2.1.2 humility that he owes
3.0 desired result of plea
3.1 that the Duke may order payment to be made
    3.1.1 at least for three semesters
    3.1.2 later of the capital sum
4.0 the Duke's reply to the Capuchin
4.1 this man, Monteverdi's brother-in-law
    4.1.1 knows the composer's dire needs
    4.1.2 offers his own fervent prayers
5.0 Monteverdi's own prayers
5.1 he asks the Lord to grant
    5.1.1 happiness for the Duke
    5.1.2 grace for himself, to remain a servant
6.0 closing reverence.

In short: 'my financial position impels me to beg you that you order payment of interest and capital. God bless you.'

---

[4] The fact that numerology played an important part in such tributes may be verified in many of the contributions to the *Fiori poetici* collected and published after Monteverdi's death by his friend Marinoni.

Most Serene Lord and Most Respected Master,

The very great need in which I find myself, Most Serene Lord, having necessarily to provide my poor house with bread, wine, and many other things; and being impoverished mainly by having to educate my sons[a] (born and bred over in Mantua) for whom, on account of the dangerous liberty here in Venice, I have been bound to maintain a tutor, and in addition by the high cost of living which prevails in the city—all this impels me to beg you, with the greatest sincerity of which I am capable, and the greatest humility that I owe you, that you do me the favour of ordering that at least the money from the past three semesters (which I am owed by the Treasury) be handed over to my father-in-law;[b] hoping later through your innate goodness to be favoured at the first opportunity (in recompense for the long service devoted to this Most Serene House) by the capital of these moneys, since—with Your Highness's singular clemency—you were so kind as to reply in this sense to my brother-in-law the Capuchin,[c] who knowing my dire needs was urged by compassion to offer Your Highness the most fervent prayers; and in the meantime I shall always pray Our Lord that He grant Your Highness a most happy state, and that He may lend me grace to be ever and always recognized by you as a lowly servant; and with this ending I make a most humble reverence to Your Highness.

from Venice, 27 July 1616
Your Most Serene Highness's
most humble and most devoted servant
Claudio Monteverdi

[a] Francesco (nearly 15 years old), and Massimiliano (12).
[b] Giacomo Cattaneo.   [c] Fr. Cesare Cattaneo.

19

Venice, 9 December 1616
to [Alessandro Striggio, at Mantua]

Mantua, Archivio Gonzaga, Cassetta 6, fos. 144–5. Bifolio: 4 pp.

Davari, 112; Vogel, 432; Prunières, 246; Malipiero, 165; Paoli, 86; Fabbri 1985, 206; Lax, 48

Two days before Monteverdi received his increase of salary from the grateful procurators of St Mark's, his erstwhile pupil Prince Vincenzo applied for a marriage licence from the Bishop of Cremona. Vincenzo, possessing more braggadocio than brains, appears to have been banished from court because of some minor scandal, possibly concerning his behaviour after he reluctantly became a cardinal; and by a singularly unfortunate choice he was sent off to Gazzuolo, where the Gonzaga had an elegant villa. Less than four miles away, in the village of San Martino dall'Argine, there lived an attractive widow named Isabella with whom the much younger Vincenzo proceeded to fall in love. Had she been an ordinary widow, nobody would have raised an eyebrow, since affairs of this kind were as common in the history of the Gonzaga as were good deeds in the lives of the saints.

Isabella's husband had been a vociferous member of a rival clan of the Gonzaga, and by Don Ferrante she had borne eight children, one of whom—Scipione—was at that time Prince of Bozzolo, though only in his early twenties.[1] There may have been political as well as amorous reasons for the new liaison, for as Ferdinando's power weakened so did his enemies (especially his own family) seek to strengthen their own hands. Although Ferdinando and his younger brother were often at loggerheads, both were yet capable of behaving with disastrous stupidity and to some extent they shared each other's foibles. If Ferdinando could contract a secret marriage, so would Vincenzo.

His first move was unsuccessful, because the Bishop of Cremona (in whose province Gazzuolo lay) refused the licence for the very good reason that the names of those desiring to be united in holy matrimony were for some strange purpose not divulged. Vincenzo, determined not to be outwitted, went straight to the Bishop of Mantua, who by great good fortune was a Gonzaga,[2] and very soon the coveted licence and

---

[1] Coniglio, 476. Scipione enjoyed an annual income of 30,000 scudi (Ademollo, 231).

[2] Monsignor Francesco Gonzaga, who was baptized Annibale, but changed his name in 1563 on completing his novitiate as a Franciscan (of whose order he later became head), lived from 1546 until 1620, by which time he had 'passed to a better life' (Letter 49). His arrival in Mantua in 1593 saw the beginning of a one-

widow were in his grasp. The ceremony took place in Isabella's house before a few friends, the officiant being the parish priest and the most prominent guest the Archbishop of Rodi, who also happened to be Count of Novellara and Isabella's brother.[3] When the news reached Ferdinando in his country place at Porto, he is rumoured to have said: 'Povera mia casa!'

He then accused the Bishop of Mantua, a stern Franciscan, of deliberately helping Vincenzo to marry Isabella, thereby bringing disgrace upon the family by encouraging a 'dama ordinaria' to consort with a prince. But the bishop was none other than Isabella's brother-in-law, for he had been born at Gazzuolo and continued throughout his life to take a friendly interest in all that went on there.[4] Gaining no satisfaction, Ferdinando dashed off a letter of complaint to Monsignor Soardi, Mantuan Resident at the Papal Curia. But it was too late: the Vatican recognized the legality of the marriage, while at the same time censuring Vincenzo for his cavalier treatment of the purple.[5]

While Ferdinando was trying to challenge the situation with one hand and put down recurring troubles at Casale with the other, Vincenzo led an almost captive existence at Goito and the court became daily more and more agitated. Striggio was recalled from Milan not only to exercise his considerable powers of diplomacy, but also to inject an element of reassuringly splendid entertainment into a time of tension and anxiety. The excuse for this new involvement with music and theatre was the coming marriage of Ferdinando and Caterina de' Medici, the unfortunate Camilla Fàa having been conveniently banished to a convent.

It was difficult, however, to bring into being entertainment fit for a ducal wedding when Mantua lacked a major composer, and its only lady singer of international renown was about to sell her house and leave. When Ercole Marigliani, then a court secretary at Casale, wrote to Adriana Basile on 5 November concerning the sale of her property at Piancerreto, she replied on 23 November apologizing for the delay and thanking him for his advice.[6] At about the same time Ferdinando, also at Casale, received a letter from Striggio outlining the various possibilities, which included a fable by Scipione Agnelli (*Le Nozze di Tetide*), another by Francesco Rasi (*Ati e Cibele*), and a third by Ferdinando (*Endimione*).[7]

At the end of the letter, Striggio says that he has not so far given any other instructions to Monteverdi, who went off to Venice to await the Duke's commands. This seems to indicate that the composer was in Mantua in the early autumn, and he may indeed have used part of his salary increase to subsidize a journey to Cremona, where his aged father still resided, after which he returned to Venice via Mantua. There he would have met Striggio for the first time in many years, and they would

man campaign against lascivious and corrupt behaviour, in which unfortunately music and other forms of entertainment were included. See C. Sacco, *Vita e sante attioni dell'Illmo et Rev^mo Monsignor F. Gonzaga* (Mantua, 1624).

[3] Errante, 'Il processo', 647.   [4] Coniglio, 360.
[5] 17 Sept. 1616 (Errante, 'Il processo', 651–2).   [6] Ademollo, 221.
[7] Ibid. 232. For Rasi's unusually dramatic career, see Kirkendale, 'Rasi', *passim*.

undoubtedly have discussed the possibility of further collaboration along the lines of *Orfeo*. The change in salutation from 'osservandissimo' in the two letters of 1609 to 'collendissimo' in the present letter shows that Monteverdi was aware of the fact that Striggio had been made Count of Corticelli in 1612.[8]

Apparently Monteverdi was not yet aware of the disillusionment of Adriana Basile and her sisters. He cheerfully looks forward to their singing, even composing, the music for the three Sirens; and he probably could not have dreamed of more suitable artists. The letter reveals his highly critical attitude regarding the libretto, in contrast to his friendliness towards the Basile sisters, and to Francesco Rasi and Francesco Dognazzi. These he could trust: but he was not so sure of the poet Agnelli, although he had set his verses before in the *Lagrime d'amante al sepolcro dell'amata*, written in 1610 and published in Book VI (1614).

It has not so far been noticed that Striggio reached similar conclusions to those of Monteverdi on a preliminary reading of the fable, which seems to have been written in a hurry. That same letter of Striggio (22 November) mentions 'Agnelli's agile muse', unable even to wait for the Duke's commands; and it goes on to criticize the sheer length of some of the soliloquies, which could prove tedious if every word were set to music. The practical man in him also drew attention to the difficulties of staging a maritime fable, with its attendant need for water and ships.

In a comparably practical frame of mind, Monteverdi criticized the fact that many of those soliloquies would have to take place in parts of the stage where lutes and harps would not sound well, even if there were three of each.[9] For the composer of Monteverdi's time, each stage had its heaven, air, and earth,[10] and instrumentalists as well as singers had to be ready to perform at whatever point the play might dictate. The 'air' of the stage mentioned here corresponds with the terminology of Letter 22, where Monteverdi uses the phrase 'in cielo et in terra della sena'.

He is rightly critical of the issue regarding the west and north winds, for since they do not speak, they can hardly be made to sing. Yet he points out, in a prophetic sentence, the ease with which instrumental music can imitate winds, sheep, and horses, and even though examples of such musical onomatopoiea were rare in his own time, they came into their vivid own with Tchaikovsky's *Francesca da Rimini*, Strauss's *Don Quixote*, and Wagner's *Ring*.

My Most Illustrious Lord and Most Respected Master,

I received Your Lordship's letter from Signor Carlo de' Torri[a] with most hearty rejoicing, also the little book containing the maritime fable *Le*

---

[8] For a dedication to him as Count of Corticelli, dated Mar. 1613, see Ademollo, 201.

[9] When Monteverdi repeats the word 'armonie' he seems to mean continuo instruments.

[10] MacClintock, *Wert*, 185; Guarini, 263 ff.

[a] Probably a Mantuan gentleman visiting Venice, bringing with him Striggio's letter and a copy of the libretto.

Nozze di Tetide. Your Lordship writes that you are sending it to me so that I may look at it carefully and then give you my opinion, as it has to be set to music for use at the forthcoming wedding of His Highness.[b] I, who long for nothing so much as to be of some worth in His Highness's service, shall say no more in my initial reply than this, Your Lordship—that I offer myself readily for whatever His Highness may at any time deign to command me, and always without question honour and revere all that His Highness commands.

So, if His Highness approves of this fable it ought therefore to be very beautiful and much to my taste. But if you add that I may speak my mind, I am bound to obey Your Lordship's instructions with all respect and promptness, realizing that whatever I may say is a mere trifle, being a person worth little in all things, and a person who always honours every virtuoso, in particular the present Signor Poet[c] (whose name I know not), and so much the more because this profession of poetry is not mine.

I shall say, then, with all due respect—and in order to obey you since you so command—I shall say first of all in general that music wishes to be mistress of the air,[d] not only of the water; I mean (in my terminology) that the ensembles described in that fable are all low-pitched and near to the earth, an enormous drawback to beautiful harmony[e] since the continuo instruments[f] will be placed among the bigger creatures[g] at the back of the set[h]—difficult for everyone to hear, and difficult to perform within the set.

And so I leave the decision about this matter to your most refined and most intelligent taste, for because of that defect you will need three theorbos instead of one, and you would want three harps instead of one, and so on and so forth: and instead of a delicate singing voice you would have a forced one. Besides this, in my opinion, the proper imitation of the words should be dependent upon wind instruments rather than upon

---

[b] Ferdinando, sixth Duke of Mantua.

[c] Scipione Agnelli, who later became a solid historian and Bishop of Casale Monferrato.

[d] *padrona del aria*. Almost certainly a pun.   [e] *armonie*, in the general sense of music.

[f] *armonie*, in the specific sense, meaning those instruments whose task it is to fill in the harmonies. Note the reference to the actual instruments a little later.

[g] *fiati*. Although *fiati grossi* can mean heavy breathing, this does not fit the context; and Monteverdi can hardly be referring to wind instruments since he discusses them a few lines later and gives them a rounded description—*istrumenti da fiato*—about which there can be no doubt. The creatures are, of course, the Tritons and sea-gods.

[h] *aria della sena*. The stage of Monteverdi's time had its heaven and earth; and a third region consisting of space at the back, in which the softer instruments did not sound well.

strings and delicate instruments, for I think that the music of the Tritons and the other sea-gods should be assigned to trombones and cornetti, not to citterns or harpsichords and harps, since the action (being maritime) properly takes place outside the city; and Plato teaches us that 'the cithara should be in the city, and the tibia in the country'[i]—so either the delicate will be unsuitable, or the suitable not delicate.

In addition, I have noticed that the interlocutors are winds, Cupids, little Zephyrs, and Sirens: consequently many sopranos will be needed, and it can also be stated that the winds have to sing—that is, the Zephyrs and the Boreals. How, dear Sir, can I imitate the speech of the winds, if they do not speak? And how can I, by such means, move the passions? Ariadne[j] moved us because she was a woman, and similarly Orpheus[k] because he was a man, not a wind. Music can suggest, without any words, the noise of winds and the bleating of sheep, the neighing of horses, and so on and so forth; but it cannot imitate the speech of winds because no such thing exists.

Next, the dances which are scattered throughout the fable do not have dance measures. And as to the story as a whole—as far as my no little ignorance is concerned—I do not feel that it moves me at all (moreover I find it hard to understand), nor do I feel that it carries me in a natural manner to an end that moves me. *Arianna* led me to a just lament, and *Orfeo* to a righteous prayer, but this fable leads me I don't know to what end. So what does Your Lordship want the music to be able to do? Nevertheless I shall always accept everything with due reverence and honour if by chance His Highness should so command and desire it, since he is my master without question.

And so, if His Highness should order it to be set to music, I would say that—since deities have more dialogue than anyone else in this fable, and I like to hear these deities singing gracefully—as regards the Sirens, the three sisters (that is, Signora Adriana and the others)[l] would be able to sing them and also compose the music, and similarly Signor Rasi[m] with his part, and Signor Don Francesco[n] as well, and so on with the other gentle-

---

[i] *cithara debet esse in civitate, et thibia in agris* (*Republic*, 3. 399 D 7–9).

[j] The principal character in *Arianna* (Monteverdi–Rinuccini), first performed in 1608 at Mantua.

[k] The principal character in *Orfeo* (Monteverdi–Striggio), first performed in 1607 at Mantua.

[l] Adriana Basile and her sisters Margherita and Tolla.

[m] The tenor, Francesco Rasi.

[n] Don Francesco: Don Francesco Dognazzi, who became Director of Music at Mantua in 1619.

men; in this way copying Cardinal Montalto,[o] who put on a play in which every character who appeared made up his own part. Because if this were something that led to a single climax, like *Arianna* and *Orfeo*, you would certainly require a single hand—that is, if it led to singing speech, and not (as this does) to spoken song.

I also consider it, in this respect, much too long as regards each of the speaking parts, from the Sirens onwards (and some other little discourse).[p] Forgive me, dear Sir, if I have said too much; it was not to disparage anything, but through a desire to obey your orders, because if it has to be set to music (and were I so commanded), Your Lordship might take my thoughts into consideration. I beg you in all affection to regard me as a most devoted and most humble servant to His Highness, to whom I make a most humble reverence, and I kiss Your Lordship's hands with all affection and pray God for the fulfilment of your every happiness.

from Venice, 9 December 1616

> Your Lordship's (to whom, most affectionately, I wish a
> happy holiday) most humble and most grateful servant
> Claudio Monteverdi

[o] Alessandro Peretti Damascene, grand-nephew of Pope Sixtus V, and a musician of some note who helped Monteverdi on several occasions. The play referred to is Giacomo Cicognini's *Amor pudico*.
[p] *ragionatella*.

20

Venice, 29 December 1616
to [Alessandro Striggio, at Mantua]

Mantua, Archivio Gonzaga, Cassetta 6, fo. 147. Folio: 2 pp. Enclosure: List of scenes in *Le Nozze di Tetide*

Prunières, 247; Malipiero, 168; Paoli, 90; Fabbri 1985, 209; Lax, 51

The delightful confusion of the opening paragraph suggests either that Monteverdi had genuinely tried to find out what was happening at Mantua (and failed because of postal losses), or that he was slightly worried over Striggio's failure to reply and was beginning to put it down to the somewhat outspoken nature of his comments in Letter 19. As it turned out, both Striggio and the Duke agreed with the composer about the intractable poetry of Agnelli's libretto; but (unknown to Monteverdi) their usual rapidity of communication was hindered by the absence of the Duke in Casale, where he was attempting to deal with a resurgence of political problems engineered by the House of Savoy.

A tentative scheme for this exchange is as follows. Monteverdi's letter of 9 December probably reached Mantua on the 12th, whereupon Striggio—after thinking the matter over for a day or so, and looking again at the libretto—wrote to Ferdinando at Casale. This letter, which may no longer be extant, carried an endorsement of Monteverdi's strictures, and the Duke could have been considering what plan to adopt from about 18 to 20 December. We know that he wrote to Striggio on 21 December, agreeing that Agnelli's poetry was too hard to go with a musical setting, and asking for something more mellifluous to be chosen.[1]

This letter would have arrived about 24 December, and Striggio may have been unable to convey its message to Monteverdi until just after Christmas. One thing is certain—his letter arrived in Venice on 30 December, crossing with Monteverdi's dated the 29th.[2] Striggio also wrote to the Duke, pointing out that Agnelli—already sensitive to the situation—had rapidly produced a sketch for another fable, *La congiunta d'Alceste e di Ameto*.[3] If Ferdinando likes it, Striggio will send a copy at once to Monteverdi, who would apply himself to it more readily than to *Tetide*. Rasi's *Ati e Cibele* will be ready in a week, and Ferdinando's *Endimione* is anxiously awaited.

---

[1] Davari, 114.   [2] See Letter 21, first paragraph.

[3] Davari, 114. In footnote 2, perhaps the date should be 29 Dec. rather than 19, since Striggio's letter seems to be a reply to the Duke's.

Monteverdi's account of the time spent on the Mass for Christmas Eve (which was expected of the Director of Music annually) makes one wonder what happened to the manuscripts of twenty-nine masses written during his Venetian period, if indeed he really composed a new one every year. Presumably cast in the form of large-scale *concertato* masses intended for a major feast, they cannot possibly coincide with the a cappella work in the *Selva morale*, which otherwise preserves only the Gloria of the Thanksgiving Mass of 1631 and part of its Credo as examples of the more elaborate type of Venetian church music then in fashion. One would hardly think it possible to 'lose' twenty-nine Christmas masses by the greatest composer of the early Italian Baroque, but that is apparently what has happened.

My Most Illustrious Lord and Most Respected Master,

May Your Lordship forgive me if I have not managed, through my letters, to find out from Your Lordship the reply to the one I sent twenty days ago to Your Lordship (answering your kind letter which was also accompanied by the maritime fable *Le Nozze di Tetide*), in order to discover from you what I had to do about it—Your Lordship having written that before I did anything else I ought to set down on paper for you my opinion of the work.

This delay on my part came about because of the hard work that had to be done on the Mass for Christmas Eve, for what with composing it and copying it out I had to give up the entire month of December, almost without a break. Now that by the grace of God I am free of it, and everything went off respectably, I turn once again to Your Lordship with this letter asking that you honour me by letting me know what His Highness[a] wishes me to do; because being unoccupied, and through with the labours of Christmas Eve and Christmas Day, I shall have nothing to do in St Mark's for some little time. I shall therefore start to work a little on that fable if you so command, but more than that I shall not do until Your Lordship's further orders.

I have gone back to look more closely and carefully at it, and as I see it, many sopranos will be needed, and many tenors. There are very few dialogues, and those few, being in recitative,[b] do not call for attractive ensembles. There are no songs for chorus other than the Argonauts in their ship, but this will be most attractive and appealing and will be worked out eventually for six voices and six instruments. There are of course the Zephyrs and Boreals, but I do not know how these have to sing,

---

[a] Ferdinando, sixth Duke of Mantua.   [b] *parlano.*

though I do know that they blow and whistle; and it so happens that Virgil, speaking of winds, uses the word 'sibilare', which exactly imitates in its pronunciation the effect of the wind.

There are two more choruses, one of Nereids and the other of Tritons, but it seems to me that these ought to be doubled by wind instruments, so that if they were performed in this way, what pleasure—I ask Your Lordship—would they not bring to the senses! And in order that Your Lordship may carefully perceive this truth for himself, I am sending Your Lordship on this enclosed sheet the plan for the scenes as they occur in this fable, so that you may favour me by telling me your opinion.

Nevertheless everything will turn out very well, as it depends on the intelligence of His Highness, to whom I readily bow and show myself to be a most humble servant. So, I shall be looking out for Your Lordship's reply, or for whatever you will deign to command of me, and in the meanwhile I humbly kiss your hands and pray with every heartfelt emotion for the fulfilment of your every most honourable thought.

from Venice, 29 December 1616

Your Most Illustrious Lordship's

most grateful and most devoted servant

Claudio Monteverdi

21

Venice, 31 December 1616
to [Alessandro Striggio, at Mantua]

Mantua, Archivio Gonzaga, Cassetta 6, fo. 149. Folio: 2 pp.

Malipiero, 169; Paoli, 93; Lax, 53

It is clear from this letter that in spite of the Duke's decision to drop *Le Nozze di Tetide* no attempt was made to stop Monteverdi from working away at it. Agnelli's *Congiunta d'Alceste e di Ameto* was little more than a bare sketch, and Striggio knew perfectly well that by the time the poet had finished his task, sent it to the Duke, and had it read, a totally new set of circumstances could easily arise and spoil the entire plan. Better therefore to have stiff poetry set to good music than to end up with nothing at all. Monteverdi was accordingly left in blissful ignorance of the proceedings until just before the middle of January. An indication of his concern for the colour, tessitura, and quality of each individual voice is shown by the request for names. Without knowledge of the exact cast, he could not do his best, nor could he be sure of writing the most appropriate music.

My Most Illustrious Lord and Most Respected Master,

I had already sent to the post a letter of mine addressed to Your Lordship (as indeed you will see) when the Resident, Signor Sordi,[a] handed me Your Lordship's letter. I have taken note of it all, and shall set myself at once to obey His Highness's[b] commands; and I shall do all that I possibly can, with all true affection and ready desire, by trying to achieve something that would prove what a very humble and devoted servant I am to His Highness, beseeching him if by chance there should be any deficiency (as I know very well there will be, I being a most feeble creature, and through having been somewhat removed from this kind of music), that he may try always to be so kind as to compensate himself with my ready will, which shall be found ever most obedient to His Highness's commands.

[a] Camillo Sordi, the Mantuan Resident in Venice.
[b] Ferdinando Gonzaga, sixth Duke of Mantua.

You would be doing me the greatest favour, Your Lordship, by telling me the names of those who will have to play the parts as written, so that I can supply the music appropriate to the subjects. Please honour me with this—that is to say, who will play Thetis, who Proteus, who the Sirene, and so on as regards the various parts—for I shall look upon it as a very great favour. And here making a most humble reverence to Your Lordship I shall pray Our Lord for your every pleasure and true happiness.

from Venice, 31 December 1616

Your Most Illustrious Lordship's

most humble and most devoted servant

Claudio Monteverdi

22

Venice, 6 January 1617
to [Alessandro Striggio, at Mantua]

Mantua, Archivio Gonzaga, Cassetta 6, fos. 112–13. Bifolio: 4 pp.

Prunières, 248; Malipiero, 170; Paoli, 95; Fabbri 1985, 209; Lax, 54

This is the first of seven letters preserved from the year 1617, their inclusive dates being 6 January to 18 February. Thereafter no further letters are extant until 21 April of the following year, when Monteverdi began corresponding with Prince Vincenzo. It is impossible to know for certain whether Monteverdi was piqued by Ferdinando's behaviour, in commissioning a sizeable work and then calling it off, but it is perhaps significant that there are no further letters to the Duke for a period of six years.[1] The composer, who never tired of calling himself a humble servant of the Gonzaga, knew enough about courtly politics to realize that as Director of Music at St Mark's he was in fact quite independent; and that although they might need his services from time to time he could conveniently do without theirs. He wanted one thing only from them: the capital sum that would provide for him an annual income in accordance with the decree of Duke Vincenzo. But he never succeeded in obtaining it.[2]

The importance of this letter rests upon its detailed discussion of some of the problems that arise in staging a set of intermezzi, and matching the poetry with appropriate music. Monteverdi reveals his quick grasp of the situation in regard to occasional music, with which he had been concerned as performer, if not composer, since the early 1590s. Of course a work of this kind should end with a song in praise of the princely couple; and he recommends one that could be performed by two separate groups of musicians, on the stage itself and high above it.

In his suggested improvement to the song of the Sirens, Monteverdi gives us a definition of the term *cantar di garbo* (florid style of singing): 'that is, with runs (*tirate*) and *trilli*'. Such printed treatises on ornamentation as those by Bovicelli and Conforto provided singers with a remarkable choice of possibilities in 'extemporized' ornamentation,[3] and there is little doubt but that these methods or their successors were still very much in use. Monteverdi's suggestion about echo effects, to be sung by Adriana and her sisters, confirms his interest in this genre, which had been successfully exploited in the Gloria of his *Magnificat a 7* (1610), and which would find another outlet in the *Salve Regina* (with *Audi caelum* trope) in the *Selva morale* of 1641.[4]

---

[1] Letter 80, dated 4 June 1623. [2] See Letter 127.
[3] Stevens, 'Ornamentation'. [4] Malipiero edn., xv. 724.

Additional evidence of Monteverdi's practical ability as a theatre musician emerges from his comment on the effectiveness of a celestial concert heard in the space between the 'earth' and 'heaven'—*mezza la sena* as he called it. And he is reasonably sure that Adriana would have enough time to change her costume and make herself up as a Siren, after singing the role of Venus. Little did he then know of her intention to leave Mantua; and with her doubtless went Margherita and La Tolla, all of them tired of Ferdinando's strange behaviour and of the internal squabbles between various factions at court.

Artists and composers who have suffered the indignities associated with commissions which for one reason or another did not work out have often consoled themselves by salvaging some part of their work and using it on a future occasion. Perhaps Monteverdi was able to do this, for he was invited some ten years later to compose the music for a much more ambitious maritime fable, or rather a *torneo*, which made considerable use of aquatic devices: *Mercurio e Marte*, by Claudio Achillini, written for the official opening of the Teatro Farnese in Parma on 21 December 1628.[5]

My Most Illustrious Lord and Most Respected Master,

Your Lordship's most precious letter, which I have now received along with the sheet that lists the singers who are to perform in the fable about Thetis, has considerably enlightened me as regards contriving something that may be suitable to Your Lordship's taste, for I know also that it will similarly be to the taste of His Highness,[a] for whom I earnestly desire to do something that may prove agreeable.

I admit, Most Illustrious Lord, that when I wrote my first letter in reply to your first, the story which you sent me having no title on it other than this—*Le Nozze di Tetide*, a maritime fable—I must admit that it could have been something to be sung and staged with music as was *Arianna*. But, after gathering from Your Lordship's last letter that it has to serve as intermezzi for the main play, just as I believed at first that it was something of little importance, so on my second impression I consider it, on the contrary, a worthy and most noble work.

However in my opinion it does lack—at the very end after the last line which runs:

Let heaven regain its serenity, and the sea its calm

[5] Nagler, 153 ff.

[a] Ferdinando Gonzaga, sixth Duke of Mantua.

—it lacks, I would say, a canzonetta in praise of the princely bridal pair, the music of which could be heard in the heaven and earth[b] of the stage, and to which the noble dancers can dance, since a noble ending of this kind seems to me suitable to a noble scene such as I have proposed. And if at the same time you could accommodate to a dance measure the lines which the Nereids have to sing (to the tempo of which you could make expert dancers dance gracefully), it seems to me that it would be a much more suitable thing.

I have a slight objection to the three songs of the three Sirens, and it is this: if all three have to sing separately I am afraid the work will turn out to be too long for the listeners, and with little contrast; for what with one thing and another there will be need of a sinfonia to come between them, runs that can support the declamation, and *trilli*[c]—and so in general a certain similarity will emerge. So for this reason, and for overall variety, I would consider having the first two madrigals sung alternately, now by one voice, now by two together, and the third by all three voices.

As for the role of Venus (the first part, which comes after the plaint of Peleus, and the first to be heard in the florid style of singing—that is, with runs and *trilli*) I would have thought it a good idea if it could perhaps be sung also by Signora Adriana,[d] in a loud voice, and by her two other sisters, so that she is answered by an echo, in consideration of the fact that her speech has in it this line:

> And let the rocks and waves tell of love . . .

first of all preparing the minds of the audience with a sinfonia, played by instruments placed in mid-scene if possible, because after Peleus has sung his plaint these two lines appear:

> But what do I hear in the air?
> A most sweet celestial concert . . .

and I believe Signora Adriana would even have time to make herself up as one of the other three ladies.

Until now I am still thinking that there must be about 150 lines, possibly more, and I believe that before next week is over (if it please the

---

[b] *in cielo, et in terra della sena.* This refers to the highest part of the set, and the level of the stage. In between them was the 'air' (*aria*), which was sometimes called *mezza la sena*, translated above as 'mid-scene.'
[c] Vocal ornaments consisting of a rapidly repeated single note.   [d] Adriana Basile.

Lord) all the soliloquies will have been finished—that is, the ones in recitative. Afterwards I shall get down to those in florid style. Please to God that just as I have a most eager mind to do something to satisfy that Most Serene Lord's taste, so also the outcome for me may be that the results serve as true witnesses in His Highness's favour, which I so much long for and revere, and to whom in every situation and place I shall always dedicate myself as a most humble servant, remaining none the less a most grateful servant to Your Lordship, so that you may continue to be so kind as to keep me thriving in that grace, with your most gentle usage and most honourable manners. And so here making a most humble reverence to Your Lordship I pray God fervently for the fulfilment of your every true exaltation.

from Venice, 6 January 1617
Your Most Illustrious Lordship's
most grateful and most devoted servant
Claudio Monteverdi

23

Venice, 14 January 1617
to [Alessandro Striggio, at Mantua]

Mantua, Archivio Gonzaga, Cassetta 6, fo. 152. Folio: 2 pp.

Malipiero, 172; Paoli, 98; Fabbri 1985, 210; Lax, 56

Realizing at last that his work on *Le Nozze di Tetide* had been a waste of time, Monteverdi wrote this short letter to Striggio with all the external panoply of humble submission. But he undoubtedly knew that his old friend would read between the lines and understand, at least partially, his sense of outraged *amour-propre*. Perhaps Monteverdi would have been more sympathetic towards the Duke and his staff if he had known what was happening in Mantua and its environs. The anonymous writers of the Venetian *avvisi*, picking up and elaborating the more succulent pieces of scandal about the feud between Ferdinando and Vincenzo, would have circulated much of this by the end of 1616, but whether Monteverdi had the time or the inclination to read such sources of information is a matter for doubt.

Ferdinando was scared of the gossip writers, for they might make known a garbled version of the papal decree concerning the legality of Vincenzo's marriage, and this decree had so far been withheld from the Duke and his advisers.[1] They were puzzled by the decision of Pope Paul V to uphold the marriage, and chastened by his order that all Gonzaga emblems should be eradicated from Roman houses and churches. Nor did they find it particularly encouraging to learn that henceforth no Gonzaga should become a cardinal, at least for a considerable period of time.

In November of 1616 Maria de' Medici, Queen Mother of France, had sent to the Vatican an opinion written by Sorbonne lawyers in an attempt to unravel the problems surrounding the marriage question. Striggio promptly wrote to the Duke, who had left for Casale in December, complaining about the temporizing techniques of the judiciary; but Ferdinando was more concerned with the fact that his younger brother had left Goito and was moping about at court. When Vincenzo, under considerable pressure, agreed to annul the marriage, the pope at once warned the erring prince to become reconciled with his wife.[2] This made Ferdinando more furious than ever, as he had been trying his best to prove that since Ferrante Gonzaga was in the second grade of consanguinity with Duke Vincenzo I, the widow of the former could not properly marry the son of the latter.[3] But in the end he shelved the problem temporarily while he prepared for his own marriage with Caterina de' Medici.

---

[1] Errante, 'Il processo', 653.   [2] Ibid. 667.   [3] Letter to Monsignor Soardi, 16 Feb. 1617.

My Most Illustrious Lord and Most Respected Master,

I received Your Lordship's very kind letter and noted that His Highness[a] has arrived—or to put it better, returned in good health—from Casale[b] (for which may the Lord be thanked) and has decided that for the time being nothing further is to be done with regard to the fable about Thetis, preferring that another one should be worked on.

What I regret is that virtually all of this was nearly finished—the soliloquies, moreover, had already been completed—still, he is master and I look upon myself as his most obedient servant in obeying whatever His Highness may deign to command me, pointing out to Your Lordship that for setting to music a complete fable, to be sung throughout, there is little enough time from now to Easter; and for the intermezzi in the main play[c] one should not lose time if anything elaborate is to be done.

Yet I consider myself in every way a most obedient servant, and if I am to be made worthy of His Highness's commands I shall not fail to do whatever I can to show myself ready and willing at least mentally even if I were feeble physically. And here making a humble reverence to Your Lordship, I also kiss your hands and pray Our Lord for your every perfect happiness.

from Venice, 14 January 1617
Your Most Illustrious Lordship's
most humble servant
Claudio Monteverdi

[a] Ferdinando Gonzaga, sixth Duke of Mantua.
[b] Casale Monferrato, a Mantuan possession not far from Turin.
[c] de la [commedia] grande.

24

Venice, 20 January 1617
to [Alessandro Striggio, at Mantua]

Mantua, Archivio Gonzaga, Cassetta 6, fos. 154–5. Bifolio: 3 pp.

Prunières, 250; Malipiero, 173; Paoli, 100; Fabbri 1985, 139, 211; Lax, 57

Nothing could contrast more strongly with the Venetian calm in which Monteverdi received an invitation from his old friend Rinuccini to come and stay in Florence, and the Mantuan confusion surrounding the comings and goings of Ferdinando, Vincenzo, Isabella, and their various supporters. Isabella, who had already given generous proof of her fertility by the eight children she bore her late husband Ferrante Gonzaga, once more came into a position of arguable prominence when rumours went round that she was pregnant. It must all have seemed like an unfortunate recurrence of the circumstances that plagued the early years of Margherita's widowhood, just after the death of Duke Francesco in 1612.

Ferdinando thereupon had poor Isabella locked up in one of the less accessible of his many villas, where she greatly feared that she might be poisoned and put it about that she was in any event being harshly treated. Later allowed to return to Gazzuolo, she could only leave her house in a sedan chair or a two-horse carriage under guard.[1] Vincenzo, tired of constant embarrassment and political pressure, joined the Spanish troops under the Governor of Milan and managed to distinguish himself in the siege of Vercelli, thus taking away some of the fraternal weight under which he had been labouring in Mantua.[2]

Those of the select band of Mantuan virtuosi who avoided living in the city at this time were fortunate indeed. The tenor Campagnolo was one of them—he had played Silvio in the Mantuan production of *Il pastor fido* and had stayed in Monteverdi's house during his youthful years of study. As his fame grew, so did the circles of his travel widen, and he was much sought after in Rome, Florence, London, Salzburg (from which city he wrote to Striggio on 19 January),[3] and Ödenburg (Sopron) in Hungary.

Monteverdi reveals nothing of his knowledge of the state of affairs in Mantua: he is content to reassure Striggio of his willingness to write something for the wedding celebrations, and of his joy on hearing that the Florentines welcomed this new liaison between the great houses of Medici and Gonzaga. What concerns him most of all is to have enough time to produce what is asked of him.

[1] Errante, 'Il processo', 671.   [2] Coniglio, 418.   [3] Bertolotti, 101.

My Most Illustrious Lord and Most Respected Master,

Your Lordship tells me about the definite arrangement of the marriage of His Highness with Tuscany,[a] concerning which I shall now have to make a firm resolution to write some music in time for Easter, and for this purpose you will be sending me a new fable to set to music. If this regard for serving His Highness (the son of the Duke of Mantua my former master) did not keep me in Venice, I would certainly move to Florence, having received an invitation in a very warm-hearted letter from Signor Ottavio Rinuccini who advises me, on this great occasion of the Duke of Mantua's, to try and move to Florence.

For indeed I shall be seen not only by all the nobility, but also by the Most Serene Grand Duke[b] himself, and besides the Mantuan wedding we are speaking of, others too are expected, so I would therefore enjoy going; and he more or less indicated that I would be employed on some musical task, and tells me that the marriage arrangements with His Highness of Mantua were concluded to the very great satisfaction of the entire city of Florence.

May Our Lord be He who even thus makes things ever proceed to the liking of the Duke and of all his dominions, for thus do I always most heartily desire, and pray God for, the good of this Most Serene House. I shall therefore await whatever Your Lordship will command of me, reminding you that 'speed and quality do not go well together'.[c] I mean to say, if you are slow you will not complain about me if I have not done as much as—with time—I would have believed possible, sending instead to deputize for me my very devoted and willing heart, which also with like respect now makes a reverence to Your Lordship and prays God for your every exaltation and happiness.

from Venice, 20 January 1617

Your Most Illustrious Lordship's

most humble and most grateful servant

Claudio Monteverdi

---

[a] Ferdinando, sixth Duke of Mantua, was about to marry Caterina de' Medici.

[b] Cosimo II de' Medici.

[c] 'il presto con il bene/insieme non conviene'—cf. Letter 92.

25

Venice, 28 January 1617
to [Alessandro Striggio, at Mantua]

Mantua, Archivio Gonzaga, Cassetta 6, fo. 126. Folio: 2 pp.

Malipiero, 152; Paoli, 68; Lax, 58

Difficult to read because of faded ink at the right-hand edge, this short letter never-theless deserves some notice in view of the intimation that new plans were afoot in Mantua for an official celebration. It was the composer's first invitation from the Gonzaga since his departure from their midst in 1612. The visit was, as usual, to take place at the earliest possible opportunity, but in the event not only the councillor but also the Resident and later on the Duke himself were destined to gain massive experience of Monteverdi's delaying tactics.

My Most Illustrious Lord and Most Respected Master,

From the Resident, Signor Sordi,*a* I received not only Your Lordship's letter, which enjoins me in the name of His Highness*b* to come to Mantua as soon as possible, but also the entreaty of the Resident himself. Neither Your Lordship's letter nor the addition of that same entreaty has had any other effect on my ready will, than an obedient response. Tomorrow, which will be the 29th of the present month, I shall see the Procurators *de supra*,*c* all three, and shall ask for the leave Your Lordship requests, which I think I shall obtain promptly.

For this reason I think there will be no need to bring the Resident into it, for at present there is nothing going on at St Mark's; but if it should indeed be necessary to bring him in, I shall do so in order to show myself in all things most obedient to His Highness's commands. So as far as I am concerned I think I shall be in Mantua within a week at the most.

---

a Camillo Sordi, the Mantuan Resident in Venice.

b Ferdinando Gonzaga, sixth Duke of Mantua.

c *procuratori ridutti*, who were three out of nine officials, and had special charge of appointments and leaves of absence.

But even if the business should drag on, it will not go beyond the day on which the courier arrives, in whose company I shall be travelling without fail, if it please God. And so making a humble reverence to His Highness, thanking God that He has deigned to make me worthy of the commands of that Most Serene Lord, at the same time praying fervently that He may also cause me to be worthy within myself of results comparable to the favour, and finally making a humble reverence to Your Lordship, praying God for your every happiness.

from Venice, 28 January 1617
Your Most Illustrious Lordship's
most grateful servant
Claudio Monteverdi

26

Venice, 4 February 1617
to [Alessandro Striggio, at Mantua]

Mantua, Archivio Gonzaga, Cassetta 6, fos. 157–8. Bifolio: 3 pp.

Malipiero, 175; Paoli, 102; Lax, 60

If Monteverdi still had no idea of what was happening in Mantua, he must by this time have become suspicious about the information he was receiving. Urged on by Striggio, he applied for leave and obtained it at once, for the Venetians—in spite of their independence—regarded friendship with the Gonzaga as a desirable insurance for the *terra firma* that was so politically and strategically important to them. That is one reason why the Procurators acceded to Monteverdi's request; and (as he makes plain in his letter) they wanted him to tell Ferdinando that the leave had been granted immediately.

But just before the composer was about to leave, towards the end of January, he heard the disquieting news that Ferdinando planned to spend at least a month in Florence and not return to court until 7 March. It was a very strange situation indeed. Monteverdi wanted to go and stay with his friend Rinuccini in Florence and perhaps conduct one of his own compositions in the presence of the Grand Duke, Ferdinando, and their respective entourages. But Striggio apparently told him to come not to Florence, but to Mantua, and almost on the point of following these instructions Monteverdi realized that he would have arrived in a nearly empty city as far as high society was concerned, with virtually nothing for him to do for several weeks.

All this was very probably a plot on the part of Sante Orlandi and certain other Mantuan musicians, who thought that Monteverdi could be tricked into accepting a useless invitation while they could all go to Florence and shine more brightly in the Tuscan limelight.[1] What happened in fact was that on 6 February, the day prior to the weddings, a *veglia* took place at the Uffizi Theatre in which Marco da Gagliano's setting of Salvadori's *La liberazione di Tirreno e d'Arnea* was performed.[2] After the wedding ceremonies, Ferdinando and Caterina stayed on for some time enjoying the renowned hospitality and artistic delights of the Florentine court, and finally returned to Mantua in the first week of March.[3]

Monteverdi nevertheless expresses his willingness to come provided he can be sure of an audience with Striggio, whom he doubtless hoped would assist him in the running battle for the *fondo* that would guarantee his annual pension. He is even

[1] Santoro, *Monteverdi*, 85.   [2] Nagler, 131.   [3] See Portioli, *passim*.

willing to remain in Mantua until Ferdinando's return, although such a plan would cause him to overstay his leave of absence, which was limited to two weeks. His increasing distrust and annoyance can be sensed between the obsequious lines of this letter, and it was not long after writing it that he discovered the truth.

My Most Illustrious Lord and Most Respected Master,

Having been granted both by the Doge[a] and by the Most Excellent Lords Procurators[b] a very generous leave, so that I could be at His Highness's[c] command for ten to fifteen days (as Your Lordship's letter did not ask for more), with however a verbal addition from the Lords Procurators that I should let His Highness know that they had immediately granted me leave on the first request, and that moreover I should send advice of this to His Highness in the name of Their Excellencies—I had for this reason prepared myself to come as quickly as possible on this occasion of the courier's return journey, to obey His Highness's commands.

But having been advised by various gentlemen that His Highness had certainly left for Florence on the first of this month, and the very same courier having told me that throughout the city—when he left Mantua, which was the aforesaid first day of the present month—it was being said that at three in the afternoon of that day His Highness had to leave for Ferrara and then go on from there to Florence; and not being exactly reassured about all this I went to see the Resident, Signor Sordi,[d] who definitely confirmed to me that His Highness had left for Florence.

Wherefore, considering that this visit of mine could have been in vain at present, I thought it would be to the good—as much to take advantage of such leave as I now have for certain, as because I was advised by the said Resident—to write to Your Lordship about the reason why I stayed behind, and to let you know also that as long as this visit of mine allows me to see Your Lordship in person, I shall promptly set out on the journey by the very next postal coach and come to hear what Your Lordship commands me to do.

Even if you order me to stay until His Highness's return, this much shall I do and obey, beseeching you however that—if His Highness wants

[a] Giovanni Bembo (d. 19 Mar. 1618).
[b] Federico Contarini; Nicolò Sagredo; Giovanni Corner; Antonio Lando.
[c] Ferdinando Gonzaga, sixth Duke of Mantua.
[d] Camillo Sordi, the Mantuan Resident in Venice.

me to set something to music—you try not to be tardy in letting me have the words, because I hold nothing more inimical to my nature than short-ness of time in my undertakings. I shall therefore be awaiting whatever Your Lordship commands, to whom (by way of closing) I make a humble reverence and pray Our Lord with all affection for your every perfect happiness.

from Venice, 4 February 1617
Your Most Illustrious Lordship's
most grateful servant
Claudio Monteverdi

27

Venice, 11 February 1617
to [Alessandro Striggio, at Mantua]

Mantua, Archivio Gonzaga, Cassetta 6, fos. 128–9. Bifolio: 3 pp.

Prunières, 243; Malipiero, 155; Paoli, 70; Lax, 61

According to Striggio's instructions the composer should pack as quickly as possible and leave by the same boat that brought the letter. Interpreting the request as a mild one (albeit urgent), Monteverdi thinks of a few excuses—travelling conditions would be bad, undoubtedly leading to illness; the weather has been unpleasant; the Duke is said to be in Florence looking for musicians; Holy Week is not far off and there will be much to do in St Mark's. No disrespect is intended; and if the libretto is sent it will receive priority.

Apparently it was not sent and Ferdinando's enthusiasm waned, for the next letter of Monteverdi addressed to the Duke looks to him hopefully for a new commission.

My Most Illustrious Particular Lord and Most Respected Master,

Today, which is the 11th of the month, about five in the evening, Your Lordship's letter was handed to me by the postman, who is returning to Mantua at 6 p.m. this very day, so that in order to be set and ready*a* to come as you command me, it would have been necessary for me to have my boots on (as they say) to catch the courier's boat, where I would then suffer a bad night, which would later make me ill.

On top of this, the weather—having been good on the whole—has changed to rain so that one can hardly go out of the house; and besides this Your Lordship's letter makes a somewhat gentle request. For this reason and for those above-mentioned I have been so bold as not to set out so breathlessly upon my journey, as much to see what the weather will do, as to be able to go to Padua in the daytime (waiting there for the courier at my convenience), and also to seize the opportunity of trying to have my leave prolonged a little more, as indeed Your Lordship exhorts me to do.

a essere all'ordine.

[130]

So really I was no more thinking about being ready by the next post-day than (if it please the Lord) at any time, because to tell Your Lordship the truth, in view of His Highness's[b] having gone to Florence, I thought he would surely have wanted me at his command in Venice, not in Mantua; that is to say, he would have done me the kindness of sending the story here. If Your Lordship could do me this favour—inasmuch as at one and the same time I would avoid the bad roads and have nothing to fear from highwaymen[c]—I could still be serving St Mark's, for with the approach of Holy Week (at which time many functions take place in the presence of the Doge,[d] who comes to church in that week), it would indeed be much to my convenience.

I beg Your Lordship not to infer that what I have said springs from a mind unwilling to obey your commands, because I really know myself to be ever most desirous of doing something that may be to His Highness's liking, and so much the more so if it has to do with a work from the hand of His Highness. Nay, I earnestly beg you to believe that what I have said above is the pure truth.

I have set everything before Your Lordship's eyes so that if you instruct me by this next post you can be certain that I shall do whatever you tell me without any question; for if you decided to send the work, I promise Your Lordship that I would toil away at it harder than you can imagine, sending you by the courier from week to week what I would keep doing from day to day. And here making Your Lordship a most humble reverenee, from God our Lord I pray for the fulfilment of your every happiness.

from Venice, 11 February 1617
Your Most Illustrious Lordship's
most grateful servant
Claudio Monteverdi

[b] Ferdinando Gonzaga, sixth Duke of Mantua.
[c] A reference to the events of Oct. 1613.   [d] Giovanni Bembo.

28

Venice, 18 February 1617
to [Alessandro Striggio, at Mantua]

Mantua, Archivio Gonzaga, Cassetta 6, fo. 160. Folio: 1 p.

Davari, 115; Malipiero, 176; Paoli, 104; Lax, 63

Since Marco da Gagliano had assumed a role of major importance in the Florentine part of the festivities, Sante Orlandi was determined to come into his own once the bridal pair had returned to Mantua. This they did on 7 March, and four days later *Gli amori d'Aci e di Galatea* was performed for their pleasure, with music by Sante Orlandi and libretto by Gabriello Chiabrera.[1] The ever-diplomatic Striggio, uncomfortably aware that Monteverdi was not wanted, advised him to stay on in Venice and await further instructions.

The reaction was exactly as one would expect: a polite letter in which—for the first time—reference is made to the troubles and disappointments of Ferdinando,[2] followed by a protestation of loyalty and a humble bow to be transmitted by Striggio to the Duke. And then complete silence for a year. Monteverdi, once he had grasped the extent of the deceit, decided to leave Mantua to its own peculiar devices: the feud with Rome continued, Prince Vincenzo became more and more independent of his brother, Isabella was estranged and still almost a prisoner in Gazzuolo.[3]

In retrospect, it can be said that Monteverdi missed nothing of very great importance, and he certainly avoided a number of tense artistic situations. Striggio was obliged to let the Duke know that neither Adriana nor her sister Margherita could be counted on for the performance on 11 March, and this is confirmed by a letter from Margherita complaining about the length of her role and the difficulty of learning it, in addition to playing a smaller part as well.[4] Little wonder that Portioli agreed with one of those actually present, who found the festivities much inferior to those of previous Dukes.[5]

My Most Illustrious Lord and Most Respected Master,

Just as I looked forward to going over to Mantua and becoming involved

---

[1] Barblan, 'La vita', 93, 135.

[2] Paoli, uncertain as to the nature of these troubles, guesses correctly that politics are at the heart of them (Paoli, 104).   [3] Errante, 'Il processo', 671.   [4] Davari, 117.   [5] Ademollo, 224.

in this joyful occasion of His Highness's,[a] so will it be extremely disagree-
able for me to stay behind, even if it is due to the troubles and disappointments of that Most Serene Lord, for whom with all true and sincere
affection I shall always pray, that God may make him happy and contented—which I certainly hope to see, because in the last resort the just
man is protected and defended by the hand of God.

I shall therefore stay here because Your Lordship so commands, and I
shall be awaiting whatever instruction you will give, whenever it please
you; remaining both now and in the future a most devoted servant ever at
the command of His Highness, to whom (if Your Lordship will do me the
favour through your kindness) I make a most humble reverence—and to
Your Lordship, in closing, I kiss hands with every heartfelt emotion,
praying Our Lord for the fulfilment of your every well-deserved
happiness.

> from Venice, 18 February 1617
> Your Most Illustrious Lordship's
> most devoted and most affectionate servant
> Claudio Monteverdi

[a] Ferdinando Gonzaga, sixth Duke of Mantua.

29

Venice, 21 April 1618
to [Prince Vincenzo Gonzaga, at Mantua]

Mantua, Archivio Gonzaga, Cassetta 6, fos. 163–4. Enclosure: first instalment of the music for *Andromeda*

Davari, 135; Malipiero, 176; Paoli, 106; Fabbri 1985, 188, 212; Lax, 64

Malipiero assumed that this letter was intended for Striggio. De' Paoli opted for Marigliani on the grounds that he was the author of the *Andromeda* libretto mentioned here for the first time. The form of address, however, corresponds neither with the standard wording for Striggio ('Illustrissimo mio Signore . . .') nor with that for Marigliani on the first letter definitely sent to him ('Molto Illustre mio Signore');[1] and the use of 'Eccellentissimo' proves that we are dealing with a personage considerably higher in rank than a secretary such as Marigliani or even a count, as Striggio then was.

   Davari was correct in stating that Prince Vincenzo (see Pl. 5) was the recipient, and this is clear not only from the form of address, but also from the known structure of court politics in Mantua: Striggio was chief adviser to the Duke, whereas Vincenzo worked closely with Marigliani. This fact emerges also from the remark in Letter 38 about the urgent request of Vincenzo regarding the need to complete Marigliani's play.

   The year 1617 had ended quietly for Monteverdi. It is unlikely that he went to Cremona for the funeral of his father Baldassare (who died on 10 November), in view of the very heavy demands of the approaching Christmas season at St Mark's.[2] On Christmas Eve, one of the lessons at Matins was sung by Claudio's son Francesco, who was paid on 15 March of the following year.[3] In Mantua, Ferdinando kept in touch with the musical scene, hearing from Luigi Centurione in Genoa about the castrato G. B. Sacchi,[4] who was to contribute to Federico Malgarini's anthology of music by a dozen or so composers in the service of the Duke.[5] Girolamo Belli sent his condolences on the death of the Duke's aunt, Margherita, Duchess of Ferrara, on 15 January.[6]

---

[1] Letter 44, 15 Feb. 1620.   [2] Santoro, *Monteverdi*, 57.   [3] Arnold, 63.   [4] Bertolotti, 97.
[5] RISM 1618[4]. This collection was first described by Bertolotti, who throws light on the problems of runaway singers in his account of Ottavio Bargnani's visit to Padua in February 1618. One of the Mantuan singers, Lorenzo Sansci, had gone there and was most unwilling to return until Bargnani persuaded him (Bertolotti, 97).   [6] Bertolotti, 95.

5. Vincenzo II Gonzaga, seventh Duke of Mantua. Anonymous fresco. Soprintendenza alle Gallerie di Mantova. Photo: G. Giovetti, Mantua

In some ways it was unfortunate that invitations from the Gonzaga always arrived precisely when Monteverdi was preparing for some major event or religious festival in the basilica, so that he had to sidestep or delay matters in order to deal with both authorities at the same time. It is also possible that he deliberately made use of these tactics to remind his Mantuan masters of the promised capital fund; and had that fund ever been conveyed to Monteverdi along with a request to collaborate, it might have coincided with an unusual decision on the composer's part to leave at least some of the more arduous duties at St Mark's to his assistant director.

Nevertheless it was undoubtedly true that the liturgies of Holy Cross Day and Ascension Day made exceptional demands on the musical staff as a whole. The letter makes it clear that the Mass for 3 May required instruments as well as voices, even though the motets would be accompanied by organ only. Two motets with texts suitable for Inventione S. Crucis are printed in his friend Bianchi's *Libro primo de motetti* (1620), and it is therefore possible that *Adoramus te, Christe*, and *Christe, adoramus te* were written in or about 1618.[7]

Perhaps Monteverdi never set the special text for the cantata which was traditionally sung on the doge's stately vessel (called *Bucintoro*) as he officiated at the 'Sensa', an Ascension Day ceremony of the marriage of Venice and the sea, but he seems to have been obliged to rehearse it and direct the performance. Unless the cantata can be associated with one of the many occasional works written in honour of the city—such as Baldassare Donato's *Quattro Dee*[8]—it must unfortunately be presumed lost, along with a great deal of Venetian music that would have included some of Monteverdi's finest compositions.

My Most Illustrious and Most Excellent Singular Lord and Most Respected Master,

The daily round at St Mark's throughout Holy Week and Easter has kept me so busy that I have been unable before now to send Your Lordship the music for the *Andromeda* libretto. I do not know whether it will be to your liking, but I do know that it has been composed by me with a singular desire to serve Your Lordship with all affection, since I long for Your Lordship's favour, as his devoted servant. For this reason, I beg you to try and be so kind as to compensate yourself for the poverty of my music with the wealth of my affectionate good will.

I have moreover received by the present post yet more verses on the same subject of *Andromeda*. I do not know whether I shall be able to do what Your Lordship commands me, and what I long to do, before

[7] Stevens, 'Church Music', 416.   [8] Published by Faber Music, 1968.

Ascensiontide; seeing that on Thursday week[a] (which is Holy Cross Day) the Most Holy Blood will be displayed, and I shall have to be ready with a concerted mass, and motets for the entire day, inasmuch as it will also be displayed throughout that day on an altar in the middle of St Mark's, set up high especially.

Then after that I shall have to rehearse a certain cantata in praise of His Serenity,[b] which is designed to be sung[c] every year in the *Bucintoro* when, with all the Signoria, he attends the wedding of the sea on Ascension Day. And I must also rehearse a Mass and solemn Vespers, which is sung in St Mark's on such an occasion, and so—My Most Illustrious Lord—I am afraid I cannot do what I would like.

I shall however try to do all I can, so that it can be seen from the results how devoted a servant I am, to you and to him. It would be a great favour if I could find out who will be singing the part of the Messenger, so that I can give some thought to the appropriate natural voice, and whether it will be one or two who are to declaim the music, seeing that there are actually two messengers, one sad and the other bringing happiness; and to know how many there are going to be in that chorus of ladies, so that I can set it for four or more, or fewer voices. And so here making a humble reverence to Your Lordship, I pray Our Lord with all affection for the fulfilment of all your happiness.

from Venice, 21 April 1618

Your Most Illustrious and Most Excellent Lordship's

most devoted servant

Claudio Monteverdi

---

[a] *giobbia ventura* (*giobbia = giovedì*). It cannot be 'next Thursday', which would have been 26 Apr., since the day of the feast was 3 May.

[b] Nicolò Donato.   [c] *si stilla cantarsi* (*stilarsi* has the sense of 'to draw up, pen, word').

30

Venice, 21 July 1618
to [Prince Vincenzo Gonzaga, at Mantua]

Mantua, Archivio Gonzaga, Cassetta 6, fos. 166–7. Bifolio: 3 pp. Enclosure: song of the Joyful Messenger, in *Andromeda*

Davari, 137; Malipiero, 178; Paoli, 108; Fabbri 1985, 212; Lax, 65

Since Letters 29 and 30 are separated by exactly three months—a fairly long period of time in the evolution of a stage work such as *Andromeda*—some correspondence may have been lost or mislaid. In the previous letter Monteverdi asked Prince Vincenzo to tell him who would be singing the roles of the two messengers; and this news probably arrived in Venice early in May. The first part of the music for the Joyful Messenger could have been sent to Mantua towards the end of June, and the present letter accompanies the remainder of the song.

Monteverdi's extremely conscientious and professional approach to the problems of stage music emerges from a close study of the questions he asks Vincenzo. Before composing the music, he must know who is to sing the roles, how many voices, what kind of instruments, whether dancers will participate, and so forth. It would have been easy to send in a sketch and leave it to the staff at Mantua to work out details of transposition, orchestration, and the doubling of instruments and voices. But the only concession Monteverdi makes is to send the music as quickly as possible, without going over it for the sake of subtle improvements that the audience could easily miss.

Although incipits are given for two choruses and a solo, they have not so far been traced among the anonymous material in Italian libraries. Perhaps one day this particular and immense body of music will yield up at least a few choice finds.

My Most Illustrious and Most Excellent Lord and Most Respected Master,

I am sending off to Your Lordship by this post the remainder of the song for the Messenger of Joy, which was lacking in the other letter[a] already despatched. I could wish that it were as fully effective as my mind's desire would have it—a mind bent on serving Your Lordship's pleasures, that

---

[a] *l'altra* [*lettera*].

would have worked harder had it not been for a slight headache caused by the heat which suddenly occurred after the recent rains, and which kept it well away from study.

I would have delayed sending it to Your Lordship until the next post, so as to have had time to improve it, but fearing that lateness would in your eyes be a worse evil than some deficiency in the music, I wanted for this reason to send it by the present post, being content to receive praise rather for a mediocre but rapid service, than for a good but slow one, because I know to what extent rehearsal time matters to the singer.

I shall keep on setting to music those other lines I have in my possession which are not provided with notes, so that you may hear everything at an early stage, and have time to order from me—according to your wishes—whatever is not to your taste. I shall send Your Lordship the canzonetta sung by the chorus of fishermen which begins 'If the virtue of strong arms' by the next post, but you will be doing me a favour by letting me know for how many voices, and how it has to be performed, and whether any instrumental symphony will be heard beforehand, and of what kind, so that I can make it all fit together.

Similarly you will be doing me a favour by letting me know whether the canzonetta that begins 'The radiance with which they shine' (sung by the chorus of damsels) will be sung and danced—and on what instruments it will be played, and also by how many voices it will be sung—so that I can write appropriate music also for that. The Messenger of Sadness, who begins with 'It will never be true that I see . . .' will also, I hope, be with Your Lordship soon, whose hands I kiss with all reverence by way of closing, and I pray Our Lord for your every perfect happiness.

from Venice, 21 July 1618

Your Most Illustrious and Most Excellent Lordship's
most humble servant
Claudio Monteverdi

31

Venice, 9 February 1619
to [Alesssandro Striggio, at Mantua]

Mantua, Archivio Gonzaga, Cassetta 6, fos. 170–1. Bifolio: 3 pp.

Vogel, 433; Prunières, 251; Malipiero, 179; Paoli, 110; Fabbri 1985, 215; Lax, 67

This account of the journey to Bologna in January 1619 withholds almost as much information as it offers. Presumably Monteverdi and his son stayed in Venice until 28 December at least, since both were involved with special music for 'the first feast-days of Christmas'. Documentary evidence shows that Francesco sang at St Mark's during the Christmas season of 1617, and it is almost certain that he did so again in 1618. If we assume that he was admitted to the Servite convent in Bologna early in February, so that his father could be back in Venice by 7 February (when he found a letter from Striggio awaiting him), the entire journey must have taken some forty days.[1]

Since the letter tells us that fifteen days were spent in Bologna, it is not improbable that father and son devoted some time to a visit to Padua, where Monteverdi had friends and patrons, chief among them the Most Reverend Monsignor Giovanni Francesco Morosini, Abbot of Leno and Canon of Padua Cathedral. The Benedictine monastery of Leno, in the province of Brescia, was founded in the eighth century and reached the peak of its power and affluence in the late fourteenth, thanks to generous gifts of land and money. Its Abbot, *de facto* Count of Leno, enjoyed special jurisdiction both spiritual and temporal by means of a kind of episcopal court, and a civil court. Morosini fortunately chose to use part of his wealth and influence to encourage the arts, as is shown by such dedications as those of Grandi's *Motetti* of 1612 and Turini's *Madrigali a 3 con due violini*,[2] published in 1629.

Although Monteverdi expresses a decided preference for Francesco's career, he is clearly proud of the boy's progress both as singer and composer. In the years to come, he would see his son abandon the idea of a doctorate in law in order to become a brother in the Order of Discalced Carmelites; but in spite of these changes the importance of music was never forgotten. He was a regular member of the choir of St Mark's from 1624 onwards,[3] and his continuing interest in Padua is amply proved by his acceptance of an engagement at the Teatro dello Stallone in 1636, when he sang the roles of Apollo and Imeneo in *Ermiona*, with libretto by Pio Enea Obizzi and music

---

[1] See Vecchi, 80.

[2] Sartori, *Bibliografia*, 1621ᵉ; Vogel, *Bibliothek*, ii. 260.   [3] Caffi, i. 222.

by Felice Sances.[4] High praise is accorded him as a virtuoso by Matteo Caberloti in the tribute to Claudio printed in *Fiori poetici* of 1644.[5]

Mention is made here for the first time of a new stage work apparently intended for the Easter festivities at Mantua. Sometimes referred to as a ballet, sometimes as an eclogue, Striggio's libretto probably took the form of a classical idyll in which the principal character was Apollo. Subsequent discussions of this work are to be found in Letters 32, 34, 35, 38, 39, 41–3, and 45. After considerable postponement it was finally performed in February 1620 (Letter 48), but no trace of the music or libretto remains.

My Most Illustrious Lord and Most Respected Master,

I have received Your Lordship's previous letter and the present one, but with this delay however, because I went with my elder son Francesco[a] to Bologna (as the first feast-days of Christmas were over) and had the chance to remove him from Padua—to remove him from the splendid time which the Most Illustrious Lord Abbot Morosini[b] was kindly giving him so as to enjoy a little of the boy's singing. And in the long run he would have turned out to be a good singer with all the other additions[c] (as one would say—though it is better to keep quiet about that), rather than an average doctor; and yet my way of thinking would prefer him to be good in the second profession and mediocre in the first, as if it were an ornament.

So, for the sake of helping the boy (as indeed I have done) and for my own satisfaction, I went—as I said—to settle him in Bologna as a boarder with the Servite fathers, in which priory they read and debate every day. And I was there for this purpose for about fifteen days, so that what with going and coming back and stopping there, I can say that I had hardly reached Venice when Your Lordship's aforementioned first letter was handed over to me.

And even if I had not received this second one from the post a moment ago—as the debtor I was as regards replying to Your Lordship's most kind letter—I had determined to let Your Lordship know (by the courier who is returning) just what I have told you above in this letter. I hope that, as a very kind person, you will accept this my true excuse as legitimate; and

[4] Brunelli, 73.   [5] Barblan, 'La vita', 101.

[a] Francesco Monteverdi was then $17\frac{1}{2}$ years old.

[b] Monsignor Giovanni Francesco Morosini, Abbot of Leno and Canon of Padua.

[c] *li altri agionti* (= *aggiunte*), in other words the ability to play an instrument and compose. Francesco wrote many charming monodies, some of which were published by Milanuzzi in 1624.

I do assure you that if I had received the first letter in time, and had not been hindered by an urgent duty, I would already have carried into effect what you were kind enough to command me.

But since Your Lordship is pleased to have the ballet for this Easter, you may be sure of receiving it, for I would not tolerate so great a deficiency in myself (in not doing all I can to serve you) if I wanted to maintain myself, through results, as much your servant as I profess to be, both in speech and in writing. May Our Lord God grant the fulfilment of all perfect happiness to Your Lordship, to whom by way of ending I make a reverence and kiss your honoured hands.

from Venice, 9 February 1619

Your Most Illustrious Lordship's
most devoted servant
Claudio Monteverdi

32

Venice, 7 March 1619
to [Alessandro Striggio, at Mantua]

Mantua, Archivio Gonzaga, Cassetta 6, fo. 173. Folio: 1 p.

Davari, 138; Prunières, 251; Malipiero, 181; Paoli, 112; Lax, 68

Once again opinion is divided with regard to the addressee of this short letter,[1] but the salutation (which corresponds to that of Letter 31, written less than a month before) points to Striggio. Monteverdi promises the music for the eclogue *Apollo* well in time for Easter, but then begs for extra time, which Striggio grants. It is also of importance to realize that this letter is one of an otherwise unbroken sequence (nos. 21–35) mainly addressed to Striggio, the only exceptions being three to Prince Vincenzo.

My Most Illustrious Lord and Most Respected Master,

Since Your Lordship grants me the boon of a little time to write the music for Your Lordship's most beautiful words,[a] I shall accept the favour, because of the many duties I shall have at St Mark's during Holy Week, and also because of the feast-days, which are by no means few—for the Director of Music—in times like this. Besides, I would also be in a better state of health than I enjoy at present, and I am waiting for the right time to undergo something of a purge: the doctor so advised me.

From then on I shall be free and healthy, if it please God; and that will be two reasons taken away from me, that will not prevent me from receiving the favour of serving Your Lordship, which I so long for; and to whom I am so beholden and obliged that by way of ending I make a most humble reverence, praying Our Lord for your every perfect happiness.

from Venice, 7 March 1619

Your Most Illustrious Lordship's

loyal servant

Claudio Monteverdi

---

[1] Davari opts for Striggio; the others favour Marigliani, though with a shadow of doubt or uncertainty.

[a] A reference to the libretto of *Apollo*.

33

Venice, 22 March 1619
to [Prince Vincenzo Gonzaga, at Mantua]

Mantua, Archivio Gonzaga, Cassetta 6, fo. 175. Folio: 2 pp.

Davari, 139; Malipiero, 181; Paoli, 114; Fabbri 1985, 213; Lax, 69

Although the flattering phrase 'bellissime parole' appears twice—once in the previous letter and again in this one—it seems that each refers to a different text. While still working in desultory fashion on the music for Marigliani's *Andromeda*, discussed in the letters to Prince Vincenzo (nos. 29 and 30), Monteverdi had also begun the music for *Apollo*, an eclogue by Striggio. It is of course possible that communications and enclosures between 21 July 1618 and 22 March 1619 have since been lost, and that Monteverdi did in fact send music for the canzonet and the Sad Messenger's song mentioned in Letter 30.

His duties at St Mark's, along with his undoubtedly numerous contributions to the musical activities in other Venetian churches,[1] may well have caused a waning of interest in *Andromeda*; and it certainly seems that by March 1619 Marigliani had almost given up hope of receiving more music for his languishing libretto. He therefore went to Vincenzo and asked him to write a stern letter to the composer, who replied on 22 March with his usual array of excuses: work at St Mark's, concern for the well-being of his sons, minor illness, and 'mille altri acidenti'.

Monteverdi knew only too well the various political divisions at the Mantuan court,[2] thanks to his long residence in its shadow and his shrewd understanding of the Gonzaga mentality. He knew for sure that Striggio and Marigliani were in opposite camps: the former close to Ferdinando, the latter protected by Soardi and very much in the confidence of Vincenzo. What could be easier than to play off one group against another? If it is not certain that Monteverdi's classic pattern of postponement was a deliberate ploy, it is at least possible that he was still smarting under their continuing neglect of his requests for payment of the *fondo*.

My Most Illustrious and Most Excellent Lord and Most Respected Master,

It is true that Signor Marigliani,*a* whom I very much honour and like, has

---

[1] See Letter 49, where his outside earnings are stated to be 200 ducats a year.

[2] A good summary of the situation may be found in Quazza, *Diplomazia*.

a Ercole Marigliani, one of the court secretaries at Mantua, wrote librettos for carnival entertainments and special events.

not one reason to complain but rather a thousand, because in view of both my affection for His Lordship and the countless obligations I have towards him, I ought some time ago to have finished the music for those very beautiful words[b] of his. For this failure I really blush, and (by Heaven!) there is not a day, Your Lordship, when I do not rise from my bed with the firm intention of sending them to His Lordship, set to music, seeing that I am already well ahead.

But even if my work at St Mark's has proved demanding, if my sons need me to go all the way to Bologna[c] on their account, if I have had a little illness[d] and also do not find myself completely free, if a thousand other misfortunes have prevented me—so that there has been no Saturday[e] when I have not sighed to see it come so soon and then go, without having sent him the aforesaid music—I promise Your Lordship to try and pay my debt to him (inasmuch as that man is in my opinion one of the creditors whose trust I esteem the most), otherwise I would never again have the courage to appear before him.

I shall certainly pay the debt, and so much the more promptly since Your Lordship enters with that authority whose word—even if nothing at all were written down—would oblige me to hand over the capital,[f] and not just a small part like this. But let Your Lordship take note: throughout Holy Week I am at St Mark's, and the three feast-days likewise. As soon as they are over, you will not see the following Saturday without my sending satisfaction.

However I beg Your Lordship (and likewise I pray Signor Marigliani) not to discredit me, as it would do an injustice to my poor heart, which lives as your most devoted servant and is very prompt in every command. And here making a humble reverence to Your Lordship I pray Our Lord God grant you happy holidays and every other perfect happiness.

from Venice, 22 March 1619

Your Most Illustrious and Most Excellent Lordship's
most devoted and most grateful servant,
Claudio Monteverdi

---

[b] These *bellissime parole* were presumably the remaining portions of *Andromeda*.

[c] See Letter 31.   [d] See Letter 32.

[e] The usual post-day for letters directed to Mantua.

[f] Although Monteverdi uses the word *capitale* here, he may have had in mind the *fondo* for which he was still hoping, and either consciously or subconsciously made use of this figure of speech—which Vincenzo would not fail to understand.

34

Venice, 19 October 1619
to Alessandro Striggio, at Mantua

Mantua, Archivio Gonzaga, Cassetta 6, fos. 177–8. Bifolio: 3 pp. and address

Davari, 140; Malipiero, 183; Paoli, 116; Fabbri 1985, 231; Lax, 70

The seven months that separate Letters 33 and 34 witnessed a number of small but significant changes in the attitude of Duke Ferdinando and his court with regard to music. One major cause of those changes was the illness of Sante Orlandi, who had succeeded to the post left vacant by Monteverdi several years previously. The Duchess Caterina continued to correspond with composers in Florence, remaining in touch especially with Jacopo Peri, who sent her a respectful but affectionate covering letter with a composition of his based on words she had chosen.[1]

The Duke, for his part, maintained a remarkably good-humoured exchange of news and views with Adriana, who gave birth to a daughter in Rome towards the end of March.[2] Shortly thereafter the Basile family moved to Naples, her husband Mutio sending some music to the Duke as a token of his esteem. Ferdinando returned thanks in a letter that reveals his relief at the departure (for Spa) of his brother Vincenzo,[3] who at this stage was behaving in his usual ebullient manner because he thought he had regained favour.[4] It seems that Ferdinando could only tolerate certain of his friends and relatives provided they were at a safe distance, and the letters to both Adriana and Vincenzo bear this out. He even expressed the hope that the great singer would one day return to Mantua, and she finally did so in 1620.[5]

When Sante Orlandi died in July 1619, Monteverdi happened to be in Mantua as the guest of the tenor Campagnolo.[6] The question of a suitable successor immediately became a prime topic of conversation, and since there were no outstanding candidates among the other court musicians, the Duke asked Campagnolo to make an offer to Monteverdi, who not unexpectedly turned it down as being inadequate. On returning to Venice, he enquired of Magni as to the progress of *Concerto* (Seventh Book of Madrigals), whose dedicatee was none other than the Duchess. But the publication was not yet ready, and though the estimated date for completion is given as 8 to 10 November, the dedication date of 13 December shows that it probably came off the press much later.

---

[1] Ademollo, 238.   [2] Ibid. 244.   [3] Ibid. 246.   [4] Errante, 'Il processo', 672.
[5] Ademollo, 248.   [6] See Letters 49 and 50.

Monteverdi never did go to Mantua to present *Concerto* to the Duchess. He eventually sent a copy to Striggio, adding from time to time parts of the eclogue *Apollo* and sections of the ballet. More urgent demands kept him in Venice, where he took on the task of supervising another kind of publication for the Duke of Bracciano.[7]

[Address:] To my Most Illustrious Lord and Most Respected Master, the Lord Count Alessandro Striggio[8]

My Most Illustrious Lord and Most Esteemed[a] Master,

If the printer, as indeed he promised, had handed over to me my little publication,[b] I would already have presented it to Her Highness[c] (to whom it is dedicated) so as to be able to obtain through her infinite kindness and humanity that favour which was also granted to me by the Most Serene Lady Eleonora[d]—may she be in glory!—that is, her kindness in counting me among the number of her humblest, indeed, but also devoted and faithful servants: a favour which guaranteed me certain help (and genuine too, through being really deserved for once) from that small endowment or property from which I have been able to draw the income that I greatly need—little though it is—of 100 scudi given to me by His Highness Duke Vincenzo of glorious memory.

But the tardiness of that printer has been and is even now the reason why I am not in Mantua, and have not gone. I hope however it will be ready by the 8th or 10th of next month. If His Highness Duke Ferdinando has not left for Casale, as in a short time he will—so it is rumoured here— I shall then come to present it, and at the same time I shall bring you at least the greater part (if not all) of Your Lordship's eclogue,[e] set to music by me.

And I assure Your Lordship that my recollections of your singular goodness, the obligations I have, and the great desire I nourish of serving you always have ever maintained within me (and ever will) a lively and

---

[7] See Letters 36, 37, 40, 47.

[8] Cited by Davari from back of letter, using the term 'Collendissimo' (which was customary for Striggio). The salutation for the letter itself however returns to the less exalted form 'Osservandissimo', which may have been a slip of the pen.

[a] Exceptionally for Striggio, the form *Osservandissimo* is used here.

[b] Madrigals, Book VII.   [c] Caterina Medici Gonzaga.

[d] Wife of Vincenzo Gonzaga fourth Duke of Mantua. She died in 1611.   [e] *Apollo*.

earnest reminder to do whatever you may be so kind as to command me; and if I have been slow, you may rest assured that some very urgent task has distracted my attention, much to my heart's displeasure, inasmuch as God thus wishes me to be a servant, and never master of myself.

Your Lordship may therefore be sure that in a short time you will have a good part of it, and Christmas will not come without its being in your hands complete. Do not deduce from my slowness any indifference in serving you, as my mind does not proceed on a par with my physical forces, because if the latter are lame, the former takes wing; but it does not on this account yield to anyone who may wish to be a servant, and who desires from the hand of God all true happiness for you: and here with all heartfelt warmth I kiss your hands.

from Venice, 19 October 1619
Your Most Illustrious Lordship's
most devoted servant
Claudio Monteverdi

35

Venice, 13 December 1619
to [Alessandro Striggio, at Mantua]

Mantua, Archivio Gonzaga, Cassetta 6, fo. 180. Folio: 1 p.

Davari, 141; Malipiero, 184; Paoli, 118; Lax, 72

Presumably prompted by a reminder from Striggio, this short letter reassures him that the eclogue *Apollo* will truly be finished soon after Christmas. The date of the letter, 13 December, is important for other reasons: it appears at the foot of the dedication of Book VII (Monteverdi's 'little publication', as he liked to call it), and it is shared by another letter—no. 36—which opens the exchange between the composer and the Duke of Bracciano, Paolo Giordano II Orsini.

In the mean time the Duke and Duchess had left Mantua for Casale Monferrato, having given permission for some of their string-players to travel to Florence. The Grand Duke of Tuscany wrote to Duke Ferdinando on 17 November, thanking him for making the musicians available and expressing his delight in their performance.[1] Perhaps the 'casaleschi'—the Rubini brothers—were among their number. But Monteverdi was not sure whether the Duchess would return at a time that would enable him to go to Mantua with his two children, stay with his father-in-law, and arrange to make a formal presentation of a specially bound copy of his *Concerto: settimo libro de madrigali*.

Although no correspondence survives from the previous month, November, we know from Letter 48 that Duke Ferdinando's new Director of Music, Don Francesco Dognazzi,[2] had visited Venice with the express purpose of tempting Monteverdi back to Mantua. Perhaps Ferdinado had hoped that Dognazzi, a priest, would look after the music for his private chapel, freeing Monteverdi for the more attractive pursuits of secular song and stage music. The mission failed, but not before Dognazzi had let it be known that his visit was somewhat in the nature of a raid, whereupon Venetian tongues began to wag, much to Monteverdi's discomfort.

---

[1] Bertolotti, 98.

[2] Since Dognazzi began to publish music in 1607, he may have been in his thirties when he succeeded Sante Orlandi late in 1619. In the previous year he had contributed to a collection of *Motetti a una, due, tre, e quattro voci . . .* by Federico Malgarini (Vincenti, Venice). He was in Vienna in 1631 (Bertolotti, 103) and still in service at Mantua in 1643 (Davari, 117).

My Most Illustrious Lord and Most Esteemed*a* Master,

Without fail, once the feast of Christmas Eve is over, I shall devote all the time ahead of me to Your Lordship's service, though more because of my obligation than because of Your Lordship's commands, which I infinitely esteem. Neither the first nor the second post will leave without my having finished it all; and to be truthful I ask for nothing else but the outcome, for half of it is already composed—quite definitely so—and I assure Your Lordship that it will not be hindered by me.

I have in readiness a little publication of mine to present to Her Most Serene Ladyship,*b* and I am waiting for her return for this carnival; for if she were not to return, I would decide to send it rather than bring it, as indeed I shall do if she comes to Mantua. I shall however lodge with my father-in-law*c* (so as to have my sons looked after rather than for my own convenience) and shall remain infinitely grateful to you, joining with this gratitude the ardent desire which I have to serve you, since it acts as a powerful incitement to achieve all the more quickly what I must achieve. In the mean time, may you retain me as your servant, while I make a reverence to you and devotedly kiss your hands.

from Venice, 13 December 1619

Your Most Illustrious Lordship's
true-hearted servant
Claudio Monteverdi

---

a This is the second exception to the more formal *Collendissimo*.   *b* Caterina Medici Gonzaga.
c *Messere* here, though Monteverdi sometimes uses the word *suocero*. Giacomo Cattaneo was still at this time a member of the Duke's musical establishment.

36

Venice, 13 December 1619
to [the Duke of Bracciano,
at the Castello degli Orsini, Bracciano]

Rome, Archivio Storico e Notarile del Governatorato. Corrispondenza di
Paolo Giordano II Orsini, busta 163, fo. 306. Folio: 1 p.

Paoli, 120; Lax, 73

This letter, along with two others, came to light when the French literary historian,
Ferdinand Boyer, was investigating the Orsini archives shortly after 1920, in preparation for his work on Virginio Orsini. Knowing that Henry Prunières had already
completed a short study of Monteverdi and was working on a more ambitious book,[1]
he gave copies of the letters to his colleague, who included summaries of them in the
catalogue raisonné featured in the original French text and in the slightly later English
translation.[2]

Boyer subsequently discovered a fourth letter from Monteverdi to the Duke, and
discussed it briefly, with a short quotation, in his article on the Orsini and music.[3] It
constitutes an essential link in the correspondence, bridging as it does the time-gap
between 3 January and 29 February 1620.[4]

The long-standing musical and artistic interests of the Orsini family of Rome
include ceremonial works for the wedding of Paolo Giordano I, by Philippe de Monte
and Bernardo Giacomini;[5] lute songs dedicated to Leonora Orsini, Princess of
Bracciano, by Cosimo Bottegari;[6] Marenzio's *Quinto libro de madrigali a 6* dedicated to
Virginio Orsini; Cesare Zoilo's *Primo libro di madrigali a cinque voci* (1620);[7] and the
Madrigali concertati (1629) by Monteverdi's pupil and assistant, Giovanni Rovetta.[8]
The last two publications were dedicated to Virginio's eldest son, Paolo Giordano II,
who was 28 years old when he began to correspond with Monteverdi, and who
rounded out his artistic abilities—drawing, painting, engraving, poetry—with a deep

---

[1] First published in French (Paris, 1924), then in an English translation (London, 1926), both with a
supplement of 53 letters in Italian. A reprint of the London edition was issued by Dover Publications, New
York, in 1972.

[2] Prunières, 223–5; nos. 36, 37, 46. In the present edition nos. 36, 37, 40, 47.

[3] Boyer, 301 (see especially 310).

[4] I am grateful to Miss Ann Percy for obtaining photographs of these letters.

[5] Einstein, 499, 506.   [6] MacClintock, 'Songbook', 177.

[7] Vogel, *Bibliothek*, ii. 357.   [8] Ibid. 167.

interest in music which embraced both the practical and the theoretical. He had an excellent singing voice, and accompanied himself on an instrument of his own invention—the Rosidre, named after the rose in his family escutcheon.[9]

Although the Duke would doubtless have known of Monteverdi through his publications, he may also have met him personally in Florence, and was certainly aware of his reputation through his relatives the Gonzaga of Molfetta and Guastalla. Isabella Orsini, Duchess of Bracciano, had married Don Cesare Gonzaga, one of the sons of Don Ferrante (1563–1630), so that a firm link existed between the great families of Mantua and Bracciano; and when the troubles of the Mantuan succession developed, Carlo of Nevers found himself face to face with Don Cesare as a powerful and implacable rival.[10]

There is no indication that Monteverdi ever collaborated with the Duke on any other project, or that he dedicated anything to him. Perhaps the remote location of the little town of Bracciano, just twenty miles from Rome, precluded a more active association with a composer so firmly based in Venice, and there is ample evidence to show that he preferred the opportunities offered by the nearby cities of Parma, Mantua, and Padua. Nothing in the correspondence indicates that the material sent by the Duke has anything to do with music, and the speed with which it was set up in type, proofed, and printed suggests that Monteverdi would be supervising a literary rather than a musical publication.

Yet if this were so, why was he singled out for this small but apparently important task? And why did the Duke not have recourse to his own printing press at Bracciano, where Andrea Fei was perfectly able to deal with the printing and production of books?[11] Monteverdi was certainly aware of another branch of this famous printing family, for his 'Lament of Arianna' appeared in a collection published in 1623 under the title of *Il maggio fiorito*, at Orvieto, the printers being Michel'Angelo Fei and Rinaldo Ruuli.[12]

Since the first part of the letter is taken up with expressions of humble servitude that indicate a new rather than a renewed relationship, it may be that Monteverdi hoped this small beginning might develop into something more substantial and lasting. The second part deals with a printer's memorandum, originally enclosed with the letter but no longer extant. Presumably the printer had written out on a separate sheet various details concerning the type and paper to be used, together with an estimate of costs and time required for production.

Fortunately there is a clue to the nature of the publication and its author in the Bresciani notebooks at Cremona.[13] The reference in question combines several pieces of evidence, each one of which is of vital importance in the matter of identification. Bresciani's starting-point is the year 1620, the date being prompted by the publication

---

[9] Boyer, 308.   [10] Ademollo, 230; Coniglio, 490.
[11] Cosenza, s.v. Fei.   [12] RISM 1623[8].
[13] Cremona, Libreria Civica presso la Biblioteca Governativa: MSS Bresciani, no. 28. Extracts concerning music and musicians are given by Pontiroli, 'Musicisti', 149–92. The single entry on Petratti (Petracio) occurs on 167–8.

of a book of songs for one or two voices (a copy of which he may even have seen) by a young Cremonese virtuoso, Francesco Petracio, or Petratti. In accordance with his usual format for biographical sketches, Bresciani mentions certain outstanding accomplishments—playing the violin, theorbo, and other stringed instruments; previous employment—the Duke of Bracciano, to whom Petracio dedicated a printed collection of songs; and present employment—the Marchese Lodovico Barbone, president of the Accademia degli Animosi of Cremona.

Our young musician had this in common with Monteverdi: he was a native of Cremona, he was an instrumentalist (but apparently published nothing for instruments, whether solo or ensemble), and he did not disdain to write in the fashionable style for solo voice and lute. His one collection can easily be traced. It is listed by Vogel with the slightly different spelling 'Petratti',[14] but no details are given since the only extant copy formed part of the Biblioteca Borghese in Rome. In his preface to volume i, Vogel draws attention to the fact that this fine old library was dispersed shortly before 1892, and that while many of the books passed to the Accademia di Santa Cecilia, others were sold and shipped to Paris.

The copy in Rome did, in fact, find its way to Paris; and after being shelved for many years in the library of the Conservatoire it was transferred together with other rare books to the music department of the Bibliothèque Nationale, where its present shelfmark is Réserve F. 199. According to RISM[15] it still ranks as an unicum: a quarto volume of thirty-two pages, all complete and in excellent condition apart from slight discoloration here and there. The title-page confirms the year of publication as 1620, the place Venice, the printer Alessandro Vincenti; and the dedication to the Duke of Bracciano is dated 30 January 1620, which shows that this volume—*Il primo libro d'arie a una et due voci con un dialogo in fine*—was indeed the one that Monteverdi was asked to see through the press.

The reason for the Duke's request is now clear. Petratti, a court composer, wished to publish a small collection of songs, and naturally they would be dedicated to his patron, Paolo Giordano Orsini, Duke of Bracciano. He, as both patron and dedicatee, would assume the expense of publication; but more than this, he assumed the charge of sending the music to Venice and asking for an estimate of production costs. Monteverdi, a son of Cremona and the most famous musician in Venice, was the obvious man to contact; and although he might not have heard of Petratti (whose name he does not mention) he would have felt bound to assist the Duke.[16]

My Most Illustrious and Most Excellent Lord and Most Respected Master,

I am writing to express my infinite thanks for Your Excellency's infinite kindness, since you have been so good as to honour me with your com-

---

[14] Vogel, *Bibliothek*, ii. 76.   [15] RISM 1620²¹.
[16] For further details, see Stevens, 'Bracciano'.

mands—and this gives me the opportunity of being able to show Your Excellency, in writing, that I am a servant of scrupulous reverence, and of personal commitment in doing what you have been so kind as to command me. Please God that my achievement correspond to my reverent affection,[a] so that I may serve your grace in every way I can through an impassioned prayer for new commands; wherefore Your Excellency can with justification (together with my devotion) call me a not entirely useless servant.

I have received the book[b] from the postman, with Your Excellency's very kind letter. I straightway took it to the printer,[c] and he gave me the enclosed information in his own hand. I am sending it off to Your Excellency so that everything may be done to your satisfaction; and having received your reply I shall at once have him begin work, and I shall be diligent in seeing to it that you are entirely and speedily satisfied. Once again I beg you to retain me as one of your lowliest servants, while with all respectful salutations I bow to you, and pray God for your every perfect happiness.

from Venice, 13 December 1619
Your Most Illustrious Excellency's
most humble and most devoted servant
Claudio Monteverdi

---

[a] achievement . . . affection: *effetto* . . . *affetto*—a favourite zeugma of Monteverdi's.
[b] Francesco Petratti's *Primo libro d'arie*.   [c] Alessandro Vincenti.

37

Venice, 3 January 1620
to [the Duke of Bracciano,
at the Castello degli Orsini, Bracciano]

Rome, Archivio Storico e Notarile del Governatorato. Corrispondenza di Paolo Giordano II Orsini, busta 164, fo. 348. Folio: 1 p.

Paoli, 122; Lax, p. 74

The second letter to the Duke of Bracciano (see Pl. 6) tells us that Monteverdi passed on to the printer a letter from the Duke authorizing collection of an unspecified sum of money, in all probability an advance of the cost of printing and paper. As regards the time taken to set up type (text as well as music), and complete both printing and binding, Monteverdi's estimate is two weeks from the date of this letter. It actually took three weeks, the task having been started in all probability just before the end of the previous year. Letter 36 could have arrived at Bracciano about 20 December and a reply containing the letter of authorization for payment would have been in Monteverdi's hands by 28 December. The total time may therefore have been four weeks, which is short enough but still well within the bounds of possibility since Vincenti's shop had been established for many years and the expert and experienced Alessandro, son of Giacomo, had taken over as sole proprietor in 1619.[1]

My Most Illustrious and Most Excellent Lord and Most Respected Master,

I am writing to let Your Excellency know that I gave the letter to the printer[a] so that he could receive his money. As soon as he got the letter and understood Your Excellency's pleasure, he set himself to begin the work[b] with a particular desire to give Your Excellency every complete satisfaction; and in order that you may see a token of this truth, he gave me the enclosed sheet (already begun) and assured me that he will not stop work

---

[1] Vincenti published *Indici* of his production in 1621 and 1649: see Sartori, *Dizionario*, 164–7.

[a] Alessandro Vincenti.   [b] Francesco Petratti's *Primo libro d'arie*.

[155]

Illustrissimo et Eccellentissimo mio Signore et padron Collendissimo

Vengo a dar parte a .V.E. come che io diedi al stanpatore la lettera

atio potesse ricevere il suo danaro; la quale subbito hauta, et

inteso il gusto di .V.E., si mise a dar principio al opera con

particolar desiderio di dar a .V.E. ogni intero gusto, et atio

vegga segno di tal verita, egli mi ha datto il presente folio

cominciato assicuratomi che non levera la mano, sin' a tanto che

non habbia finito il tutto; et spero che fra quindeci giorni sara

alla fine; mi e parso bene mandar a .V.E. il detto folio

non tanto per la ragione detta quanto anco atio .V.E. vegga

la stanpa, atio intorno a quella ci bisognasse qualche effetto

di comando di .V.E., si possa in tenpo gustarla et servirla;

L'honor singolare che fa .V.E. alla persona mia in honorarla de co-

mandi, e tale che mi conoscero senpre obligato servitore humillissimo

all' .E.V., alla quale con ogni riverenza m'inchino, et da Dio

.N.S. li prego il colmo d'ogni felicità; Da Venetia il 3 Gienaro 1620

.D.V.E. Illustrissima

Humillissimo et Devotissimo Servitore

Claudio Monteverdi

6. Letter to the Duke of Bracciano, dated 3 January 1620 (no. 37). Rome, Archivio Storico e Notarile del Governatorato. Corrispondenza di Paolo Giordano II Orsini, busta 164, fo. 348.

until he finishes it all, and so I hope that it will be completed within a fortnight.

I thought it wise to send Your Excellency the aforementioned sheet not so much for the above reason as indeed for letting Your Excellency see the printing, so that if—regarding this—there were need of something special[c] in accordance with Your Excellency's instructions, you could be served and satisfied in good time. The special distinction which Your Excellency lends to my person in honouring me with commands is such that I shall acknowledge myself forever a grateful and humble servant to Your Excellency, to whom I bow in all reverence, and I pray Our Lord God for the fulfilment of your every happiness.

from Venice, 3 January 1620

Your Most Illustrious Excellency's

most humble and most devoted servant

Claudio Monteverdi

[c] *qualche effetto di comando.*

38

Venice, 9 January 1620
to [Alessandro Striggio, at Mantua]

Mantua, Archivio Gonzaga, Cassetta 6, fos. 183–4. Bifolio: 3 pp.
Enclosure: 'Lament of Apollo'

Davari, 141; Malipiero, 185; Paoli, 124; Fabbri 1985, 213, 234; Lax, 75

The same composers who occasionally bewail the lack of lucrative commissions are also liable to attacks of nervousness when, by way of sweet revenge, the muse demands too much of them. At the beginning of 1620, Monteverdi was tightly enmeshed in the busy counterpoint of musical life: a printing project with the Duke of Bracciano, an eclogue with ballet by Striggio, a lengthy drama by Marigliani, not to mention his usual and by no means negligible Venetian commitments.

Not unexpectedly, his first letter of the new year addressed to Striggio sets forth the Mantuan side of these complicated arrangements. No mention is made of the Duke of Bracciano, and only a hint of St Mark's creeps in—concern with ecclesiastical music has removed Monteverdi somewhat from the theatrical sphere. How can he finish off *Andromeda* when Marigliani still has 400 lines to write and deliver? How can the Mantuan musicians hope to learn and rehearse a work of such length in so little time? With only a few weeks before the onset of carnival time, such a proposition is foolhardy.

Monteverdi was, of course, perfectly justified in drawing Striggio's attention to this muddled state of affairs. He shows his musical sense in the request for extra verses at the end of Cupid's song, and his practical sense in the suggestion that *Apollo* should take preference over *Andromeda*. Striggio's role was that of author and artistic supervisor, passing on to Monteverdi the general mood and structure of the work, with details of its various sections and subdivisions.[1] Nevertheless, the composer is anxious as usual to please everyone, and to this end he asks Striggio for diplomatic assistance in arranging for an agreeable solution.

My Most Illustrious Lord and Most Respected Master,

I am sending Your Lordship the 'Lament of Apollo'. By the next post I shall send you the beginning, up to this point, since it is already almost

---

[1] For a comparable situation, see Letter 3.

finished; a little revision in passing[a] still remains to be done. At the place where Amore begins to sing, I would think it a good idea if Your Lordship were to add three more short verses of like metre and similar sentiment, so that the same tune could be repeated (hoping that this touch[b] of gladness will not produce a bad effect when it follows—by way of contrast—Apollo's previous doleful mood), and then go on as it stands, changing the manner of expression in the music, just as the text does.

I would have sent Your Lordship this song by the last post, but Signor Marigliani[c] (in a letter addressed to me) has passed on a formidable request from Signor Don Vincenzo:[d] that I finish the *Andromeda*—already begun—a fable by the aforementioned Signor Marigliani, so that it can be performed for His Highness[e] this carnival time, on his return from Casale. But just as I am having to do a bad job through being obliged to finish it in a hurry, so too I am thinking that it will be badly sung and badly played because of the acute shortage of time. I am also greatly surprised that Signor Marigliani wishes to involve himself in such a dubious enterprise, since even if it had been begun before Christmas, there would hardly be time to rehearse it, let alone learn it.

Now consider, Your Lordship: what do you think can be done when more than four hundred lines, which have to be set to music, are still lacking? I can envisage no other result than bad singing of the poetry, bad playing of the instruments, and bad musical ensemble. These are not things to be done hastily, as it were; and you know from *Arianna* that after it was finished and learnt by heart, five months of strenuous rehearsal took place.

Therefore if I could be certain that, through Your Lordship's influence, the Prince's choice[f] might fall upon Your Lordship's ballet (assuming however that this meets with your approval), I would expect this to be sufficient and would really succeed because I would have just enough time for such a short work. Then, at my convenience, I could finish off the *Andromeda*, and you could have it learnt in ample time (afterwards letting it be heard to good effect) so that I could attend with more care and thought to that ballet of yours I am talking about.

[a] *così alla sfuggita.*   [b] *coloretto.*   [c] Ercole Marigliani, court secretary and librettist.

[d] Don Vincenzo Gonzaga, younger brother of Duke Ferdinando.

[e] Ferdinando, sixth Duke of Mantua.

[f] *il gusto di S. Ecc^a*, referring to Don Vincenzo (if it were Ferdinando the abbreviation *S.A.S.* would have been used).

Otherwise, being obliged to serve Signor Don Vincenzo and Your Lordship in so little time, I continue to think that the music I send will certainly be unsuitable rather than suitable; and I know you will admit that I am right, because you will take into account the fact that my ecclesiastical service has somewhat alienated me from the^g musical style of the theatre, and so before the style has become familiar again (what with the shortage of time and the need to write much) I shall have to send mere notes rather than something appropriate.

I am however most heartily eager to serve the Prince, Your Lordship, and Signor Marigliani, and because of this I am going to beseech Your Lordship to arrange the matter so that it comes out to everybody's satisfaction, otherwise I shall do whatever I can with all my heart. You will honour me by letting me know whether this music is to your liking; and if not, send me word so that I may try and do what I can to serve you. With this warm affection I kiss Your Lordship's hands and pray God for your every perfect happiness. Please tell me also what type of ballet will have to go at the end.

from Venice, 9 January 1620
Your Most Illustrious Lordship's
devoted servant
Claudio Monteverdi

---

^{g} A redundant line appears at this point in Malipiero and Paoli.

39

Venice, 16 January 1620
to Alessandro Striggio, at Mantua

Mantua, Archivio Gonzaga, Cassetta 6, fo. 186. Folio: 1 p.

Davari, 143; Malipiero, 187; Paoli, 127; Lax, 77

Still hard at work on *Andromeda*, Monteverdi sends the beginning of Striggio's eclogue and promises to try and satisfy both Prince Vincenzo and Marigliani. The completion of these tasks by the middle of February, just in time for carnival, came about only because the threatening burden of a further 400 lines of verse was somehow lightened at the last moment. Yet there seems to be no logical explanation for the sudden desire to put on *Andromeda*. True, the legendary lady was no stranger to Mantua, for the prince's father, Duke Vincenzo, had revelled in a youthful and passionate affair with Hippolita Torelli, a noble lady of Reggio, and their letters (which have been preserved)[1] reveal that the names they used for each other were Perseus and Andromeda.

Although Jacopo Cicognini wrote to Cardinal Ferdinando Gonzaga in 1611 about an *Andromeda* of his which had apparently been weighed in the balance and found wanting,[2] there is no evidence to show that Monteverdi was in any way involved. He may, however, have witnessed the scenic wonders of Francesco Manelli's *Andromeda*, also based on this ancient Greek legend with its marvellous opportunities for ingenious stage machines, when it was given in March 1637 at the Teatro San Cassiano in Venice.[3]

[Address:] To the Lord Count Alessandro Striggio

My Most Illustrious Lord and Most Respected Master,

I am sending Your Lordship the beginning of the ballet: please to God that this may impress you favourably as did the Lament already dispatched to you, since in your very kind letter you point out that it was very welcome. I felt unusually reassured by such precious news, since I both love and revere Count Alessandro, my lord, with all the affection of my heart.

---

[1] Bellonci, 29; Reed, 277–9.   [2] Ademollo, 62.   [3] Worsthorne, 25, 168.

I do not know whether I shall be able to send you more by the next post, in view of the fact that the new commission which the Prince[a] has given me—that I send him the music for *Andromeda* as soon as possible—dictates my inability to attend to anything else, but Your Lordship will do me a very great favour by assuring the Prince that without delay, between this week and the next, I shall give him everything written out. May it please God that the shortage of time do it no harm.

I understand that Her Highness[b] will soon be in Mantua, and I too hope to be in Mantua to present certain of my little musical pieces[c] to her. In whatever way you deem it good, I shall be bound to serve you with all my heart, and here making a humble reverence I pray God for your every happiness.

from Venice, 16 January 1620
Your Most Illustrious Lordship's
most devoted servant
Claudio Monteverdi

---

[a] Prince Vincenzo Gonzaga.   [b] Caterina Medici Gonzaga.
[c] Book VII of his madrigals, entitled *Concerto*.

40

Venice, 25 January 1620
to [the Duke of Bracciano,
at the Castello degli Orsini, Bracciano]

Rome, Archivio Storico e Notarile del Governatorato. Corrispondenza di Paolo Giordano II Orsini, busta 164, fo. 532. Folio: 2 pp.

Fabbri 1985, 214, 232, 234; Lax, 78

Of the four letters written by Monteverdi to the Duke of Bracciano, three were summarized by Prunières,[1] and were later printed in full by Paoli.[2] This remaining letter, third in a sequence of four written over a period of eleven weeks, was first mentioned by Ferdinand Boyer in 1934[3] but subsequently vanished from view until I was able to obtain a photograph in 1969. The text was first printed in Stevens, 'Bracciano'.

Short as the letter is, it does reveal something of Monteverdi's persistence and industry even at a time when he admitted to Striggio that he was engaged in an impossible task—to finish *Andromeda*, and then the eclogue and ballet, all three for the court of Mantua. Yet he was simultaneously engaged in the supervision of a printing job for the Duke of Bracciano, to whom he now writes asking for further opportunities to be of service. He also explains that a copy of *Concerto* (the Seventh Book of Madrigals) has been dispatched to the Duke's major-domo, who will present it formally at some suitable time.[4]

My Most Illustrious and Most Excellent Lord and Most Respected Master,

Whereas I come to render infinite thanks to Your Excellency for the singular honour that you have been so kind as to do me (with this most courteous letter of yours just received at my house) which was to make me worthy of your longed-for grace—a favour so singular that it will forever maintain me a most grateful servant to Your Excellency—I am likewise writing to beg you to be so kind as to honour me with fresh commands.

[1] Prunières, 223–5.   [2] Paoli, 120, 122, 144.   [3] Boyer, 310.
[4] His name was Emilio Fei.

Since the printer is sending to Signor Cavaliere Fei,[a] by the present messenger,[b] four copies of the finished work[c] so that the aforesaid gentleman may present them to Your Excellency—the printer awaiting instructions as to what he has to do with the remainder he owes you, and likewise what he has to do if a few little errors have slipped through before he distributes them, which he cannot do unless he has had a quick glance through in order to put them right—I also write to beseech you kindly to accept that copy of my little madrigals[d] (now published) which I sent directly to the Signor Cavaliere by the previous post, so that he could present it to Your Excellency in my name, begging you to have regard more to my devotion than to their little merit. With this, by way of closing, I bow most respectfully to you, and at the same time I pray our Lord fervently for your every perfect happiness.

from Venice, 25 January 1620

Your Most Illustrious Excellency's

most humble and most grateful servant

Claudio Monteverdi

[a] The Duke's major-domo.   [b] *procaccio* (a term also used for a rural postman).
[c] Francesco Petratti's *Primo libro d'arie*.   [d] Book VII.

41

Venice, 1 February 1620
to [Alessandro Striggio, at Mantua]

Mantua, Archivio Gonzaga, Cassetta 6, fos. 188–9. Bifolio: 3 pp.

Davari, 144; Malipiero, 188; Paoli, 129; Fabbri 1985, 234; Lax, 79

The opening paragraph of this letter gives some indication of the degree of confusion reigning at Mantua. All manner of plans were afoot to provide a cornucopia of entertainment at carnival time. But while Striggio had conscientiously completed an eclogue, Marigliani—his junior both in bureaucracy and in the literary arts—discovered that beginning a libretto was considerably easier than finishing it, and in consequence his *Andromeda* had become bogged down in the poetical equivalent of the Mantuan marshes.

Both ventures were pressed upon Monteverdi with incessant and urgent demands that he set them to music at once and in record time. At the same time he was working on Striggio's eclogue-ballet *Apollo*, wondering whether it would have a sung text as in *Tirsi e Clori* written five years previously. In the midst of all this confusion, the chancellor probably neither knew nor cared. But since he did know that Monteverdi was under considerable stress, it seems that he willingly took the hint to recommend such drastic measures as the postponement of *Andromeda*.

Striggio, whose letter probably arrived in the last week of January, must have agreed that priority should now be given to the eclogue. Monteverdi promises to take it up again, and points out that the 'Lament of Apollo' enjoyed such success in Venice that it might be repeated on a small stage with a final ballet. There follows a further request for poetry suitable for singing and dancing.

Although the name of the Venetian family is given as Benbi, it obviously corresponds to the more familiar spelling, Bembo,[1] sometimes found in dedications. In 1606, Croce dedicated his Fourth Book of Five-part Madrigals to Agostino, Bernardo, and Benedetto Bembo. But there was a younger member of the family who enjoyed even greater fame as a musical Maecenas—Giovanni Matteo Bembo, to whom the Abbot Angelo Grillo wrote at some date after 1613, explaining why he could not leave S. Nicolò del Lido to come to Venice and enjoy the music which was heard regularly in Bembo's palace.[2] Since Grillo also corresponded with Monteverdi and sent him poems to set to music, it is very likely that the splendid house on the

---

[1] Cf. the spellings *conpita* and *tenpo*, occasionally found among the letters.

[2] Einstein, 'Grillo', 176; Grillo, 463–4 (dated [1615]).

Grand Canal, not far from the Rialto Bridge, was the one referred to by both poet and composer.

It was a far cry from the ordered and civilized musical evenings at the Palazzo Bembo to the madness and disorder at Mantua, yet Monteverdi would have liked to go there and present his latest collection of madrigals to the Duchess in the hope of persuading her to intercede for him with treasury officials so that he could at last claim the donation authorized by Vincenzo, the fourth duke. But the prospect of trying to rehearse and perform new music written in a hurry and improperly studied by the court musicians so appalled him that even the donation was set aside. Ademollo considered that much of this material was refurbished for the festivities of 1621 or 1622, the latter year being more probable.[3] The fact remains, however, that a completely new work by Marigliani was performed in 1622, as is apparent from Letter 66.

My Most Illustrious Lord and Most Respected Master,

I have received Your Lordship's very kind letter and understood the reason for the delay, and what you wish from me. I reply to Your Lordship that, believing you did not want to do anything else, I gave up work for the time being. Now that you tell me you are about to have it performed, I assure you that if you do not receive from me, by the next post, everything that is outstanding, little will remain in my hands to finish.

You have only to let me know—once the verses are finished—what more I have to do, because if you wanted the ballet to be sung as well, let Your Lordship send me the words, for which I shall try (in setting them)[a] to invent something in the metre that you give me; but should there be one metre in all the verses, I shall certainly change the tempo from time to time.

The 'Lament of Apollo' has been heard by certain gentlemen here, and since it pleased them in the manner of its invention, poetry, and music, they think—after an hour of concerted music which usually takes place these days at the house of a certain gentleman of the Bembo family,[b] where the most important ladies and gentlemen come to listen—they think (as I said) of having afterwards this fine idea of Your Lordship's put on a small stage. If I have to compose the ballet for this, would Your Lordship send me the verses as soon as possible? But if not, I shall add something of my own invention so that such a fine work of Your Lordship's can be enjoyed.

[3] Ademollo, 268.

[a] *imitando quelle.*   [b] *casa Benbi.*

[167]

I was thinking of travelling to Mantua to present my books[c]—which I have now had printed—dedicated to Her Highness[d] (to take an advantageous road that may lead me to the goal I so much desired and worked for) so as to be able, once and for all, to get possession of that small donation which His Highness Duke Vincenzo,[e] of beloved memory, was kind enough to grant me.

But remembering that Signor Marigliani's[f] play would have fallen entirely on my shoulders—and knowing that with the passage of time a feeble branch can bear a huge fruit,[g] so that in no time at all the ability to hold up without breaking would be out of the question—in order not to break myself (in my feeble state of health) I did not want to come at such short notice to sustain this impossible weight, because something other than haste is needed to do justice to such a project, and it is no small matter to make a success of it even with plenty of time.

Wherefore I have resolved to stay, and I am sorry about it because of my own interests, but in order to avoid dying I would give up whatever worldly interests you like. Your Lordship's work was a delight to me because I had already thought carefully about it beforehand. Besides this, it was very short so that I would on that account have considered it a favour to be able to serve you, just as it always will be whenever you are so kind as to command me. I kiss your hands with all the affection of my heart and pray God for your continual well-being.

from Venice, 1 February 1620
Your most Illustrious Lordship's
most devoted servant
Claudio Monteverdi

[c] *Concerto* (Madrigals, Book VII). [d] Caterina Medici Gonzaga.
[e] Vincenzo, fourth Duke of Mantua.
[f] Ercole Marigliani, at this time court secretary (see address of Letter 44).
[g] *una grossa zucca*.

42

Venice, 8 February 1620
to Alessandro Striggio, at Mantua

Mantua, Archivio Gonzaga, Cassetta 6, fos. 191–2. Bifolio: 3 pp. and address. Enclosure: further sections of *Apollo*

Davari, 145; Malipiero, 189; Paoli, 132; Lax, 81

The mention of a Mantuan basso in the opening paragraph has given rise to mild confusion as regards his name, spelt both here and in Letter 43 as Amigoni. There is no doubt about the letter 'm'. Giovanni Amigoni, possibly related to the singer Ferrando Amigone employed at Mantua in 1568,[1] was paid 1,440 lire and provisions for the year 1622 along with other soloists.[2] The news that he had been chosen to sing the role of Peneus enabled Monteverdi, who obviously knew the man and remembered his vocal capabilities, to compose the music more readily.[3]

In his list of persons cited in Monteverdi's letters, De' Paoli[4] refers to a singer named Arrigoni, a spelling apparently copied from the 'scheda Davari' in the Mantuan archives. Davari, however, gives the correct spelling Amigoni, a reading which is borne out by the autographs. This confusion may have arisen partly as a result of Monteverdi's cavalier treatment of the letter *i*, and partly because there was at that time a composer named Giovanni Giacomo Arigoni (or Arrigoni) who later contributed to Giovanni Battista Anselmi's anthology[5] and published a collection of vocal and instrumental pieces dedicated to Ferdinand III in 1635.[6]

Monteverdi reiterates his communicable reasons for not wishing to come to Mantua, but there may have been others that he preferred to conceal. He was busy with publishers in Venice, bringing out two motets in Calvo's *Symbolae*, four in his Cremonese friend Bianchi's *Libro primo de motetti*, and a Litany in his *Libro secondo*. He had also heard rumours, no doubt, of the reopening in Rome of the scandalous Vincenzo–Isabella case.[7] So he promises to send the specially bound copies of *Concerto* to his father-in-law, Giacomo Cattaneo, who will hand them over to Striggio for

---

[1] Bertolotti, 56; Canal, 76.   [2] Bertolotti, 100; Ademollo 270.

[3] See the closing paragraph of Letter 94, where Monteverdi enquires about the exact range of Margherita Basile's voice.

[4] Paoli, 348.

[5] *Madrigali del Signor Cavaliero Anselmi nobile di Treviso* (1624); Vogel, *Bibliothek*, 1624[2].

[6] Sartori, *Bibliografia*, i. 346; ii. 99; Vogel, *Bibliothek*, i. 42. Ferdinand III is referred to as Emperor on the title-page, although his investiture did not take place until 1637.

[7] Errante, 'Il processo', 672.

formal presentation to the Duchess. In this way the *fondo* may be released and his two sons will have enough money for their education.

[Address:] To my Most Illustrious and Most Respected Master, the Lord Count Alessandro Striggio, Most Worthy Councillor of His Most Serene Highness of Mantua

My Most Illustrious Lord and Most Respected Master,

I have received Your Lordship's very kind letter, and have remarked how constantly you continue to make me worthy of your grace, since you always show by your courteous expression of thanks that my service is not displeasing to you. Wherefore I am so bold as to send off to you the other remaining pieces of music for Your Lordship's very fine and beautiful eclogue.[a] The part of the River[b] is still to be done, and this—now that I know Signor Amigoni[c] will be singing it—I shall dispatch by the next post; and perhaps to my greater satisfaction too, since I shall compose it more to the mark now that I know who is going to sing it.

I further understood that you will be glad, up to this point, to give me an opportunity to serve you further at present since he has finished learning the aria already written. If you, however, are unable at present to honour me with further commands, I shall still not refrain from begging you a favour, which is that you may be so kind as to present, in my name, to Her Most Serene Ladyship,[d] those madrigals[e] dedicated to her, which I thought of presenting in person had I been able to come to Mantua; but the obvious impediments prevent me from doing so.

I shall arrange for these books (if you will so kindly do me the honour of assisting me) to be handed over personally to Your Lordship by my father-in-law.[f] More than this I was not hoping to do even if I came myself, other than to commend myself to Her Highness's favour and protection, so that one of these days I might be rewarded by His Highness the Duke[g] so as to be able to have my capital, from which I could draw my annual pension; for apart from the fact of rewarding a servant who toiled

---

[a] *Apollo.*   [b] Peneus (see Letter 43).
[c] Giovanni Amigoni was a bass singer on the court payroll.
[d] Caterina Medici Gonzaga.   [e] Book VII
[f] Giacomo Cattaneo (d. 1624).   [g] Duke Ferdinando.

hard for so many years, and is of some renown in the world, it would also relieve the Ducal Chamber of such a duty.

If Your Lordship in his kindness may be willing to lend a little help in such a matter, you know my story as well as I do; and what the prince[h] can do in such a matter, if he will be so kind, will help my two sons who are studying—sons indeed of the city of Mantua and subjects of Their Highnesses. And I am hoping that one day they will let themselves be seen by their rightful lords as not unworthy of their grace, since one is aiming at a doctorate in law, and the other in medicine.

Without the favour of Their Highnesses I cannot obtain the past half-yearly payments at the right time, and in consequence I cannot help them with these sums of money as I would do if I had them. If I am asking too much of Your Lordship's grace, blame your own kindness which has given me such a guarantee, and blame my very great need of your grace, which will ever be revered and honoured, by me no less than by my sons, and to which I—a servant—devote myself as is my wont; and kissing Your Lordship's hands I pray God for your every happiness.

from Venice, 8 February 1620
Your Most Illustrious Lordship's
most grateful servant
Claudio Monteverdi

[h] Prince Vincenzo Gonzaga.

[171]

43

Venice, 15 February 1620
to Alessandro Striggio, at Mantua

Mantua, Archivio Gonzaga, Cassetta 6, fos. 194–5. Bifolio: 1 p. and address. Enclosure: Song of Peneus and three verses for Apollo

Davari, 146; Malipiero, 191; Paoli, 135; Lax, 83

The music enclosed with this letter has been mentioned earlier—Apollo's three verses in Letter 38, and the song of Peneus in Letter 42. In Greek mythology, Peneus was the son of Oceanus and Tethys, and the father of Daphne. The name Peneus was given to a river rising on Mount Pindus, from whence it flowed across the plains of Tempe to the Thermean gulf. The aria characterizing the river seems to have been specially written with Amigoni's voice in mind, and it may well have been one of those with an unusually wide tessitura.

In his *Discorso sopra la musica*,[1] Vincenzo Giustiniani calls to mind a group of singers active in the late sixteenth century and well known in Naples and Rome for their virtuoso performances. He states that they 'all sang bass with a range of 22 notes and with a variety of passage-work new and pleasing to the ear of all'.[2] This somewhat startling three-octave range was in fact quite easily achieved by cultivating a smooth change between the natural voice and a falsetto superstruc·ure, resulting in a special kind of 'bass and countertenor' voice which apparently appealed to the connoisseurs of the *Accademie*.

The Mantuan basso Giovanni Amigoni, in all likelihood a northern and slightly later counterpart of those notable virtuosi, may also have been able to imitate the effect of a river rising high on a hillside and descending in a powerful flood of notes to a spectacular low D or C. The change of register required for such a feat may have prompted the phrase *alla bastarda*, which appears nowhere else in the letters.

[Address:] To my Most Illustrious Lord and Most Respected Master, the Lord Count Alessandro Striggio, Most Worthy Councillor of His Most Serene Highness of Mantua

[1] Lucca, Archivio dello Stato, Orsucci O 49 (*c*.1628). Translated by Carol Mac Clintock.

[2] Giustiniani, 69. In a later passage, the author tells us that the next generation of vocal virtuosi (Caccini, Rasi, and others) 'all sang bass and tenor, with a range consisting of many notes, and with exquisite style and passage-work, and with extraordinary feeling and a particular talent to make the words clearly heard'. The slight but significant change at the beginning of this translation is suggested by Hitchcock, 451.

My Most Illustrious Lord and Most Respected Master,

I am sending Your Lordship the song of Peneus and the three little verses for Apollo which had slipped my mind. This song of Peneus I have composed in such a manner—like a hybrid style[a]—because I know how effective such a style is when Signor Amigoni sings it. It will also serve to provide a change from the other songs, and the distinction will appear greater if such a deity sings only once. Please to God that it may be to Your Lordship's liking.

I shall send Your Lordship the books[b] by the next post, if it please God, in an attempt to obtain that singular favour which I so much desire, and which you with such kindness are pleased to grant me: a favour which will live in my heart for ever in this way, that even if opportunities may be lacking, because of my ill fortune in not being able to serve you, I shall never lack the fervent desire to pray God that He may always bless Your Lordship. By the next post I shall send the little symphonies, and in the meanwhile I kiss your hand and pray God for your every happiness.

from Venice, 15 February 1620

Your Most Illustrious Lordship's

most grateful servant

Claudio Monteverdi

---

[a] *alla bastarda*. A phrase relating to the wide range of the *viola bastarda*, meaning in this instance that Amigoni used his normal bass range and a falsetto.

[b] The part-books of *Concerto*.

44

Venice, 15 February 1620
to Ercole Marigliani, at Mantua

Mantua, Archivio Gonzaga, Cassetta 6, fo. 197. Folio: 1 p. and address.
Enclosure: Song for Eight Voices

Davari, 147; Malipiero, 192; Paoli, 137; Lax, 84

Of the extant correspondence between Monteverdi and Ercole Marigliani, this letter is the first; the last is Letter 107 (10 September 1627), which gives a total time-span of seven and a half years. Marigliani, whose full title appears in the address,[1] was seven years younger than Striggio, and both died away from home in 1630 as they heard the death-knell toll for the Gonzaga dynasty. Like Striggio, the young secretary aired his literary skills from time to time in the interests of courtly entertainment, and collaborated with Monteverdi's younger brother Giulio Cesare in *Il rapimento di Proserpina* as early as 1611.

The first evidence of his working with Claudio appears in the correspondence about *Andromeda*, which begins in 1618 (Letter 29) and ends as mysteriously as it began with the present message. But the earlier *Andromeda* letters are mostly to Striggio, principal intermediary between the court and Monteverdi from 1609 until 1630. The explanation lies in the political and personal factions which ranged Prince Vincenzo, Bishop Soardi,[2] and Marigliani against Duke Ferdinando and Striggio, these eventually forming two distinct camps, in each of which Monteverdi strove diligently to keep a foot.

He observes his customary care in forms of address. Striggio is 'Illustrissimo mio Signore', referred to in the body of the letter as 'Vostra Signoria Illustrissima'; but Marigliani sits on a slightly lower rung, with 'Molto Illustre mio Signore' and plain 'Vostra Signoria'. These subtle distinctions, taken into account in the present translation, help to identify the correct addressee in later letters that lack sufficient external or internal evidence.

Certain phrases indicate that Monteverdi had indeed been in contact with Marigliani at some earlier stage, and this assumption is borne out by mention of the secretary's name in Letters 33, 38, and 41. No trace remains of the eight-part vocal composition,[3] presumably part of the material referred to in the January letters as

[1] His name also appears at the bottom left-hand corner of the page.

[2] Soardi was Ambassador Extraordinary in Rome, and later in Vienna.

[3] The only secular works for eight voices occur in Book VIII, but none of the relevant texts has anything to do with the Andromeda legend.

being urgently needed in time for the entertainments at carnival, and therefore associated with *Andromeda*. This letter and the previous one were written on the same day.

[Address:] To my Very Illustrious Lord and Most Esteemed Master, Signor Ercole Marigliani, Most Worthy Secretary to His Highness of Mantua

My Very Illustrious Lord and Most Esteemed Master,

By the next post I shall send you the eight-part song,[a] and as you give me no further orders I shall continue to believe that with the enclosed compositions I am sending you, there will be no other commands. This matter in which you have been so good as to involve me has been a kind of service that bound me closer to you than ever I was before, since you commanded something much to my honour, and I consider myself too much favoured.

To you, I admit myself to be a kind of servant for whom it is worth while that the servant pay the master. But I being the servant and you the master—and in consequence very unequal in strength—at least you may be content that I acknowledge myself for ever grateful to you, whose hands I kiss as is customary, and I pray God for every true blessing upon you.

from Venice, 15 February 1620

Your Very Illustrious Lordship's
most grateful servant
Claudio Monteverdi

---

[a] From the *Andromeda*.

45

Venice, 22 February 1620
to Alessandro Striggio, at Mantua

Mantua, Archivio Gonzaga, Cassetta 6, fos. 200–1. Bifolio: 4 pp. and address. Enclosure: a Symphony for Amore, and another for the Entry (for *Apollo*)

Pruniéres, 252; Malipiero, 192; Paoli, 138; Lax, 85

From the first day of February, Monteverdi's letters to Striggio—however much they may appear to relate to festivities planned for the Mantuan carnival—play up the familiar ostinato of Duke Vincenzo's donation and the urgent need to obtain it (as a capital sum) in order to defeat once and for all the corrupt officials of the court treasury.

Striggio tried to do what he could for his friend, but was obliged to write a letter on or about 19 February explaining that he could neither force the issue nor guarantee the results. When Monteverdi received it, concerned and anxious about his plea, he hurriedly wrote the present letter in order to catch the post and make sure that Striggio received it as soon as possible. The message is perfectly clear, though cloaked in courtly language—if Duke Ferdinando cannot see his way to implement his father's instructions regarding the donation, then Monteverdi cannot journey to Mantua and supervise the music.

As usual, he has cast-iron excuses: there is insufficient time to ask for leave, and even if he obtained it there would be rumours in Venice that he might be planning to leave the city for good.[1] Worst of all, he would return from that tiresome and demonstrably perilous journey with nothing in his pocket but vague promises for the remote future. So, with a request that Striggio apologize to the Duchess, he ends on a note of reassurance—his father-in-law Giacomo Cattaneo will bring the part-books and attend on the councillor. And for good measure, two orchestral pieces for *Apollo* are enclosed.

[Address:] To my Most Illustrious Lord and Most Respected Master, the Lord Count Alessandro Striggio, Most Worthy Councillor of His Most Serene Highness of Mantua

---

[1] Another reference to these suspicions occurs in Letter 48.

My Most Illustrious Lord and Most Respected Master,

I received Your Lordship's very kind letter, but it came so late from the courier that I have hardly been able to find time to write this reply, let alone set myself in order; still less have I had time to get leave from the Doge[a] and the Most Excellent Lords Procurators my masters, as it is always necessary to do, for Your Lordship knows very well that whoever is a servant must live in obedience.

Besides this I could also be in better health, because I have been burdened with no little toil this carnival time. So my heart weeps at being unable to obey your commands, rather to give you proof that I am your obedient servant, than to hope at present for the security of consequence that I long for: that is, the ability to enjoy for certain—once and for all—those lands which the Most Serene Lord Duke Vincenzo[b] was good enough to promise me as a donation.

Now, from the singular service you have kindly done me as regards Her Highness[c] (a service, I assure you, that makes me indebted to Your Lordship as long as I live), I have seen as usual, Your Lordship, that a good expectation for the future has been obtained; but certainly not what I have always desired and still do desire—to be able to have it for the present.

For your precise words are these, namely: 'and although I did not obtain a decision there and then, I nevertheless felt very hopeful that your coming here this carnival time would achieve the object',[d] a reply, Most Illustrious Lord, which to my ill fortune I have always received from the Most Serene House of Gonzaga, since I have always obtained the future but certainly not the present.

Wherefore I am also afraid that if the ability to obey these commands of Your Lordship had been granted me by time and good health, I am certain that I would have returned with the usual hopes up my sleeve, and I would have brought back (as I also did last time) a suspicion of changing masters, since the Doge here was given to think that I had gone to Mantua in order to change employment, and I had no small difficulty in removing the aforesaid suspicion.

You would therefore do me a favour, Your Lordship, by forgiving me if I do not come at once (because of the said obstacles) to obey your

---

[a] Antonio Priuli, elected 1619.   [b] Vincenzo Gonzaga, fourth Duke of Mantua.
[c] Caterina Medici Gonzaga.
[d] The quotation comes from the letter which had arrived on 22 Feb. (Saturday, the usual post-day).

[177]

commands; and since you have kindly honoured me with a promise to present my madrigals*—in my name—to Her Ladyship, they have just been sent off to my father-in-law./ He will come and bring these to Your Lordship and will be at your service as far as Her Ladyship's residence. But I beg you to offer an apology for me, the reasons for which are the obstacles I have just mentioned, and assure her that I am her most humble and devoted servant, and that I commend myself in this business of mine to Her Highness's infinite kindness.

Here is the symphony for Amore, and another for the Entry.* If you recognize me as being competent in anything else, Your Lordship, make me worthy of your honoured commands, for God's sake, since I can receive no greater favour from my good fortune. And now kissing your hands with all heartfelt affection I pray God for the fulfilment of your every happiness.

from Venice, 22 February 1620
Your Most Illustrious Lordship's
most grateful servant
Claudio Monteverdi

e Book VII. *f* Giacomo Cattaneo. *g* Two more sections of the music for *Apollo*.

46

Venice, 29 February 1620
to [Alessandro Striggio, at Mantua]

Mantua, Archivio Gonzaga, Cassetta 6, fos. 203–4. Bifolio: 3 pp.

Malipiero, 194; Paoli, 141; Lax, 87

Monteverdi took advantage of the extra day in February[1] to write not only the following letter to Striggio, but also the subsequent one (no. 47) to the Duke of Bracciano. Dealing with two different and unrelated problems in two distant cities at the same time apparently caused him no serious worry, for he had once again achieved his principal aim, which was to avoid travelling in a season when inclement weather prevailed.

But he was slightly worried at the thought of upsetting his friend Striggio, and in view of the tone of Letter 45 he may have felt it expedient to send this one, exactly a week later, in order to smooth things over as much as possible. The trouble with Monteverdi was that he would begin a letter with an apology and then refer to the donation which would in turn induce him to write a further spate of bitter words.

There is, however, some interesting evidence concerning his reputation at Mantua in the comments he makes about the Duchess's particular regard for him and for his work. While she and Striggio seem to have been his strongest supporters, Duke Ferdinando (to whom Monteverdi wrote very infrequently)[2] definitely favoured other musicians. Hence the mildly sarcastic mention of the continual need to wait upon the Duke's pleasure with prayers and supplications—this being the only way to serve him. Since he was obviously not very interested in Monteverdi's music, it is hardly surprising to find that none of it was ever dedicated to him. On the other hand, Monteverdi did dedicate sacred and secular publications to Ferdinando's father, brother, sister, and wife,[3] which may amount to a subtle kind of snub for which the Duke himself must assume sole responsibility.

My Most Illustrious Singular Lord and Most Respected Master,

Truthfully, if I had had more time to be able to ask leave of my masters,

---

[1] 1620 was a leap year, and 29 Feb. was a Saturday (post-day to Mantua).

[2] Only seven letters are extant in sixteen years.

[3] Madrigals, Books III and V to Vincenzo; *Orfeo* and the *Scherzi musicali* of 1607 to Francesco; *Selva morale e spirituale* to Eleonora; Madrigals, Book VII to Caterina Medici Gonzaga.

and had I felt in better health, I assure Your Lordship once again that I would have come, and I would have obeyed your commands. Even if I had been sure that my hopes would have dissolved into the usual delays (for being accustomed*a* to experience them thus, I would not have thought it strange to postpone matters), I am, however, quite sure that because of her particular regard for me Her Highness*b* would have honoured me efficaciously with her favour in that aforementioned service of mine, and I am also certain that the hopes which Her Highness inspired in me were well supported.

But because of my Mantuan luck, even when they bore this name of hope—with a time-to-come somewhere in the future—they have always pointed to a conclusion quite different from the beginning. And I could cite a thousand examples of what happened to me in Mantua. But would to God I might talk about the outcome of those hopes, or (to put it better) how can I tell about hopes, for perhaps I am waiting on another Lord—as I would still be waiting on His Highness Duke Vincenzo*c*—with prayers, not being able to serve his glorious person in any other way.

So, I realize that everything comes from my ill luck, not from the generosity of princes, whom I know only too well to be magnanimous. My doubt, Most Illustrious Lord, concerning the firm hope about which you have kindly notified me, did not arise directly (as it were) from Your Lordship's person, but because it was like a hope that passes into Your Lordship's person; for he who has granted it can also take it away, and thence came my doubt, being afraid to weaken the certain by the uncertain.

If I could have from the hand of God, and from His Highness, a fund that would give me—in my time—those 100 scudi, how happy I would be! I do not wish to possess anything else, so as not to tempt Providence.*d* Yet in every way I shall always be a most humble servant of that Most Serene House, and shall always desire from God its every exaltation, every happiness, and every true good, also hoping that God will not fail me in helping my sons and myself as well. Nor shall I cease to offer proof—in so far as I can—of my devotion and my reverence.

It saddens my soul, having disturbed you so much; but may Your Lordship blame your infinite kindness which has made me so bold. There-

---

a The shortened form *suefatto* is used. *b* Caterina Medici Gonzaga.
c Vincenzo, fourth Duke of Mantua. *d* Literally, 'to tempt God'.

fore I beg you to forgive me, while I thank Your Lordship with all my heart for the honour you have done me, in having made me worthy of your honoured commands, of which I pray the Lord may make me worthy very often. In the mean time I pray God with all affection for the fulfilment of your every happiness and I make a humble reverence to you.

from Venice, 29 February 1620

Your Most Illustrious Lordship's

most grateful servant

Claudio Monteverdi

47

Venice, 29 February 1620
to [the Duke of Bracciano,
at the Castello degli Orsini, Bracciano]

Rome, Archivio Storico e Notarile del Governatorato. Corrispondenza di Paolo Giordano II Orsini, busta 164, fo. 62. Folio: 1 p.

Paoli, 144; Lax, 88

This is the last of the four letters to the Duke of Bracciano, with whom Monteverdi seems to have had no further dealings. The book has been set up, proofed, and printed; the only remaining task is to forward a certain number of copies to Bracciano or Rome (the destination is not precisely specified) and distribute the remainder through the usual channels. Presumably Monteverdi retained one copy of Petratti's *Arie*, for it seems that two of the poems caught his fancy: 'Si dolce è il tormento' and 'Più lieto il guardo'. He made good use of the former in an enchanting little song he contributed to Carlo Milanuzzi's *Quarto scherzo delle ariose vaghezze* (1624), and of the latter (omitting its fifth verse) in a monody with ritornels for strings and continuo, which appeared in the anthology *Arie de diversi* published in 1634 by the same Alessandro Vincenti whose busy presses had launched the unknown Petratti upon the stormy seas of the *seconda prattica*. He barely survived, for all we have of him is one exemplar of his one publication; but it was this modest volume that brought together, by correspondence, the Duke and the director in the winter of 1619–20.

My Most Illustrious and Most Excellent Lord and Most Respected Master,

I am writing to offer infinite thanks to Your Excellency for the singular favour Your Excellency has done me, in this most gracious letter[a] of yours, by making me a worthy servant of your grace. I shall always try, whenever I can, to keep myself worthy of so great a favour. I beg you, however, with every warm regard, to remember to warn me in advance with the favour of your instructions, so that at a suitable opportunity I may

---

[a] *queste humanissime sue.*

[182]

show myself to Your Excellency as the by no means useless servant that I desire to be.

The printer has taken note of what Your Excellency ordered in your letter. He will not fail to find a convenient opportunity to send the books[b] he owes you. Nor shall I cease prompting him, though I know it will be pointless because he is a most devoted servant to Your Excellency, to whom with all reverence I bow, and I pray God Our Saviour for the fulfilment of your every happiness.

from Venice, 29 February 1620
Your Most Illustrious Excellency's
most humble and most devoted servant
Claudio Monteverdi

---

[b] Petratti's *Primo libro d'arie*.

48

Venice, 8 March 1620
to [Alessandro Striggio, at Mantua]

Mantua, Archivio Gonzaga, Cassetta 6, fos. 206–7. Bifolio: 3 pp.

Prunières, 253; Malipiero, 196; Paoli, 145; Fabbri 1985, 232; Lax 89

At Mantua, well before the beginning of March, deliberations were in progress over the choice of works to be performed on 2 May, the Duchess's birthday, which was traditionally honoured by concerts and festivities. Inevitably, Monteverdi's name came up, and with it the certain knowledge that he would refuse to write a new work in a hurry. Perhaps it was Striggio who hit upon the idea of reusing an old Monteverdi score rather than commissioning a new one, but in any event a revival of *Arianna* soon began to receive serious consideration.

For the Gonzaga, however, this four-hour opera was decidedly insufficient, and Ferdinando began to cast longing eyes upon the Florentines whom he so much admired. On 2 March he wrote to Jacopo Peri, asking for the score of the *favola, Adone,*[1] which the composer had recently completed, based on a libretto of Jacopo Cicognini (1577–1633), with whom Peri had already collaborated as early as 1611.[2] It was perhaps on the following day, 3 March, that Striggio brought to the Duke's notice Monteverdi's letter of 29 February, with its impassioned plea for the *fondo*; and it was undoubtedly the combination of this letter and the need for *Arianna* that prompted the Duke to instruct Striggio—the one Mantuan capable of dealing with Monteverdi—to send a letter containing a firm offer of employment.

Even though Dognazzi failed in November, surely Striggio would succeed in March? The size of the bait could be slightly increased, and the persuasiveness of a councillor-diplomat would easily surpass the puny efforts of a priest-composer. But Monteverdi is careful: he makes two counter-requests, the first one a delaying action, the second a plea for the utmost secrecy and discretion.

To add weight to his words, he mentions two awesome dignitaries of St Mark's— father and son, both of an ancient and noble Venetian family, and both concerned with Monteverdi's career over a lengthy span of years—the Primicerius of the basilica, Marc'Antonio Cornaro, and his father Giovanni Cornaro, who as one of the procu-

---

[1] Davari, 123 n. 2.

[2] Davari, 183 (Peri to Cardinal Ferdinando Gonzaga). A letter to the Cardinal from Jacopo Cicognini (who was the father of Giacinto Andrea) is printed in Ademollo, 62.

rators *de supra* in 1613 had been responsible for the composer's appointment as *maestro di cappella*.

Giovanni Cornaro became Doge in 1625, 'arriving at the highest dignity of the country without having made any suit for it, and considerable not so much for his riches and the splendour of his noble family, as for his own goodness'.[3] But his brief tenure of office was by no means free from internal troubles, notably the Reniero Zeno affair[4] which exposed (among other things) the tendency towards nepotism on the part of those in power. Although one of his sons was implicated in a plot to assassinate Zeno, at the same time another son, Cardinal Federico, served as Bishop of Padua, while Marc'Antonio sustained the dignified duties of Primicerius from 1619 until 1632, in which year he went to Padua as the new bishop, his brother having been installed as Patriarch of Venice.[5]

In spite of the chiding remark of Marc'Antonio, the relationship between the Primicerius and his Director of Music must have been mainly pleasant, for at the beginning of Letter 124 Monteverdi refers to him as 'my particular Lord and most revered master'. This remark was made after many years of service, during which Monteverdi provided music for Marc'Antonio's private oratory every Wednesday, Friday, and Sunday, to the delight of many distinguished citizens.[6] None of them wanted Monteverdi to leave Venice, even for a short time. Nevertheless he expresses to Striggio his great joy on hearing that *Apollo* has been a success, thanking him in advance for the honorarium that he hopes to receive by the next post.

My Most Illustrious Lord and Most Respected Master,

I shall become so indebted to you in my lifetime, Your Lordship, that even if I were to give up my life-blood (as it were) I know for sure that I would not pay off the debt. I shall always pray God that wherever my feeble forces are powerless, His Divine Majesty may come to my aid.

Your Lordship's very kind letter came late into my hands, so you will be doing me a favour by giving me time until the next post to think about that second paragraph, though I am quite certain that (passing through Your Lordship's hands) it could not possibly have any other result than my betterment and my peace of mind. Nevertheless, the fact that you may be content to wait until the next post for my reply will be the greatest favour of all.

I implore you, however, that this proposal, made to me by His Highness's[a] infinite goodness, may in no wise (whether the outcome is successful or not) be guessed at by any singer, player, or other of His

[3] Nani, 228.   [4] Hazlitt, 463–8.   [5] Eubel, iv. 275.   [6] Letter 50.

[a] Ferdinando, sixth Duke of Mantua.

Highness's musicians whatever, for you can be sure that no sooner would they hear about it than they would straightway noise it abroad in Venice, and everything would turn out to my ruin.

And this was one of the main reasons why I did not try in any way to discuss the said business with Signor Don Francesco Dognazzi,[b] when he was here in Venice this past November to do me this outstanding favour on behalf of His Highness, which was likewise the matter of offering me employment. But he, through being in the profession, was in consequence capable of getting excited about it, and did not keep it to himself, so that not long after his departure I heard it rumoured that I was returning to Mantua.

And what is more, a month ago, when I let it be known that as soon as Their Highnesses returned from Casale I wanted to bring and present to them those books[c] of mine, the Most Illustrious Primicerius,[d] son of the Most Excellent Lord Procurator, My Lord of the House of Cornaro,[e] said to me: 'This business of your going to Mantua—they say you are going there for good!'

And this, perhaps, was one of the main reasons that kept me from bringing those books in person, because (dear Sir) the substance is bound to be dearer to me than the accident. Now that the matter is in the hands of Your Lordship, who has all the qualities one looks for in negotiating everything to my advantage and without any harm to me, I shall accordingly tell you what I think by the next post, trying to base my thoughts upon such justice that even if I were not to succeed, I hope it will do me no harm—neither to my present position nor to my relationship with His Highness, which I honour and revere as much as the greatest blessings I can possibly have in this world.

I have heard about the success that my feeble music has won—helped, protected, and raised up as it was by the great and infinite merit of Your Lordship's most beautiful words,[f] no less admired and honoured by those illustrious gentlemen than I recently predicted (and I say this with a true and sincere heart), and no less raised up to the favour of His Highness as much as by the infinite kindness of Your Lordship, so that with good

[b] Director of Music to the Duke since 1619.
[c] The part-books of *Concerto* (Madrigals, Book VII).
[d] The principal dignitary of St Mark's, at this time, Marc'Antonio Cornaro (appointed 1619).
[e] Giovanni Cornaro (elected 1609).   [f] The text of *Apollo*.

reason indeed I am still bound to be ever grateful in the manner I have already mentioned to Your Lordship, to whom I make a humble reverence and pray God with every warm affection for the fulfilment of your every happiness, and waiting to receive from your generous hand, as advised, that which you have been so kind as to promise me in your letter, by the next post.

from Venice, 8 March 1620

Your Most Illustrious Lordship's

most grateful servant

Claudio Monteverdi

49

Venice, 13 March 1620
to [Alessandro Striggio, at Mantua]

Mantua, Archivio Gonzaga, Cassetta 6, fos. 209–12. Binion: 7 pp.

Davari, 119; Prunières, 254; Malipiero, 198; Paoli, 148; Fabbri 1985, 184, 189, 239; Lax, 92

While Monteverdi was making notes, actual or mental, on the crucial second paragraph of Striggio's letter—the offer of employment from Duke Ferdinando—plans for a production of *Andromeda* were still in the air. From a letter of Alessandro Ghivizzani, written at Genoa on 12 March, it appears that his wife Settimia (a daughter of Giulio Caccini and a singer of considerable ability) had been promised the title-role.[1] But when Monteverdi signed his name on the following day, at the end of the longest letter he was ever to write, his thoughts were far removed from the petty problems of musical drama, even though he had helped solve many of them during the brilliant years spent at the court of Duke Vincenzo.

This letter, which has been translated into French[2] as well as English, grips the reader not only by its almost symphonic length but also by its sheer intensity and unassailable logic. It shows us Monteverdi at the crossroads. He has been tempted to return to the scene of his early triumphs by a persuasive letter from an old friend, and he gives the matter due consideration couched in the form of rhetoric. This is the third temptation in less than a year: at Mantua in July of 1619 he gave his answer verbally, and he did so again when Dognazzi skilfully purveyed the ducal blandishments all the way to Venice in November.

On both occasions the answer was no. This time, it is the same, but decked out with an array of evidence and proof that conjures up the atmosphere of a court of law. Mantua, which tried his patience for so many years, is now on trial, and with it the entire assembly of a corrupt court: the dukes with their lavish and uncontrolled devotion to dwarfs, alchemists, and lady singers; the courtiers whose very survival depended on their capacity for flattery and intrigue; the dishonest and inefficient men in the treasury; the sickness in the air that would break out at the end of a doomed decade and destroy the very walls of the city.

Against all this Monteverdi contrasts the security and stability of his life in Venice. It is he, the Director of Music at the great basilica of St Mark's, who approves the engagement of singers and their dismissal; he has the power to grant or withhold leave

---

[1] Ademollo, 76.   [2] Prod'homme, 112; Champigneulle, 6.

to perform elsewhere in the city; his advice is welcomed and respected by his su-
periors. Yet when they die and are followed in office by others, he has no need to fear
for his appointment because the various allowances granted him in kind, together with
his salary, are guaranteed during his lifetime. At Mantua, the death of a duke could
mean the loss of an important post—as he remembered well from the events of 1613.

Emphasizing a number of subtle points that affect the wealth and welfare of a hard-
working musician, he knows that they are not too subtle to escape the diplomatic mind
of a Striggio. At Mantua his salary (when it was paid at all) covered everything he
accomplished—composition of new works, copying parts, rehearsing, directing a
performance. In Venice, however, he is free to accept outside work, for which he
receives two fees, one for composing and the other for directing.[3]

Then there is the matter of currency. Although the Mantuan scudo and the
Venetian ducat were both gold coins, exchange time saw the latter outrank the
former.[4] That is why Monteverdi speaks of '450 [scudi] of Mantua which I am getting
from the treasury here in Venice', meaning that his salary of 400 ducats is equivalent
to 450 Mantuan scudi.[5] In other words, all the figures quoted by Striggio have to be
discounted by just over ten per cent if a proper comparison with the Venetian coinage
is to be made, and the sum total of the paragraph is designed to show that the republic
has the edge over the duchy.

Monteverdi is understandably indignant when comparing his Mantuan salary with
that of Bassano Casola (who was a mere assistant musical director), and those of
Campagnolo and Adriana Basile. He had been Casola's superior, Campagnolo's
teacher, and Adriana's accompanist; and it went against the grain to see them better
rewarded than he was. He accordingly cites the commendatory remarks made by the
procurator Antonio Landi on the occasion of his 33 per cent pay increase. He appeals
to Striggio as *paterfamilias*, knowing that the councillor has a wife and eleven children
to support, and hopes that his own two sons will enjoy a decent education so that
eventually they can bring him both credit and honour.

The final appeal, however, is for an influential word with the Duke. Monteverdi has
just heard that the Bishop of Mantua died on 11 March, and thanks to the express

---

[3] Arnold states that the Director of Music at St Mark's was forbidden by the terms of his contract to take
outside engagements ('San Rocco', 235), but the rules must have been relaxed by 1620, for there are
numerous references in the letters to outside engagements at other churches and private houses.

[4] For examples of the unstable nature of Mantuan currency, and salaries for the years 1620-1, see
Ademollo, 180, 270. At this date the scudo, a debased gold coin, was worth about 6 lire (Anthon, 116).

[5] This particular issue has been clouded by translations which introduce the word 'ducat' at the point
where Monteverdi writes of 'quattrocento et cinquanta di Mantoa'. The correct word is of course 'scudo',
which appears in all references dealing with the composer's Mantuan salary. Ducats were in use at Mantua
until approximately the end of the sixteenth century, and salaries of court musicians were often calculated
in ducats, as may be seen in the extract from treasury accounts (*c*.1567) (Bertolotti, 40). With the change in
Mantua's fortunes under the luxury-loving Vincenzo, ducats disappeared and scudi took their place. From
this time onward salaries came to be calculated mainly in lire so that the numbers looked more encouraging.
Instead of offering a musician 100 scudi, court officials would quote the sum of 600 lire in the hope of
appearing more bountiful and generous.

courier service instituted by an earlier duke, Guglielmo (father of Vincenzo and grandfather of Ferdinando), the news reached Venice in record time. The death of Mgr. Francesco Gonzaga meant that Ferdinando would almost certainly enjoy the same privileges granted by Pope Clement VIII to Vincenzo in 1593, when three rich benefices held by Cardinal Scipione Gonzaga were available for suitable and proper disposition.[6] Monteverdi clearly felt himself to be a deserving recipient, especially where his *fondo* was concerned; but the Duke had other ideas.

My Most Illustrious Lord and Most Respected Master,

I am writing to answer the second paragraph of Your Lordship's letter, about which I took time to reply until the present post. In the first place, Your Lordship, I must say that the singular honour which His Highness has accorded to my person, in doing me this particular favour of offering me employment once again, has been so heart-warming and of such kindness that I confess myself lacking in words to give expression to so remarkable a favour—inasmuch as the years of my youth spent in that Most Serene service have in such wise planted in my heart a memory of gratitude and goodwill and reverence towards that Most Serene House—so that as long as there is life in me I shall pray to God, and desire for it the greatest happiness that a servant bowed down and indebted to it can wish and long for.

And certainly if I had no other concern but for myself alone, Your Lordship may be sure that I would be compelled to fly if I could, not just run, to His Highness's commands without any other thought or expectation. But what with this Most Serene Republic, and the fact that my sons[a] oblige me to entertain second thoughts, perhaps you will allow me to run on a little about these two points, as I still believe myself to be aided by Your Lordship's kindness in this matter likewise, and know of what great worth it is in regard to prudence and brotherly love.

I shall therefore submit for Your Lordship's consideration the fact that this Most Serene Republic has never before given to any of my predecessors—whether it were Adriano or Cipriano,[b] or Zarlino,[c] or anyone else—but 200 ducats in salary, whereas to me they give 400; a favour that ought not to be so lightly set aside by me without some consideration,

---

[6] Coniglio, 359, 479.

[a] Francesco was at this time 18½, Massimiliano nearly 16.
[b] Adrian Willaert; Cipriano de Rore.   [c] Gioseffo Zarlino.

since (Most Illustrious Lord) this Most Serene Signory does not make an innovation without very careful thought.

Wherefore—I repeat—this particular favour ought to command my utmost respect. Nor, having done this for me, have they ever regretted it: on the contrary they have honoured me, and honour me continually in such manner, that no singer is accepted into the choir until they ask the opinion of the Director of Music; nor do they want any report about the affairs of singers other than that of the Director of Music; nor do they take on organists or an assistant director unless they have the opinion and the report of that same Director of Music; nor is there any gentleman who does not esteem and honour me, and when I am about to perform either chamber or church music, I swear to Your Lordship that the entire city comes running.

Next, the duties are very light since the whole choir is liable to discipline[d] except the Director of Music—in fact, it is in his hands, having a singer censured or excused[e] and giving leave or not; and if he does not go into chapel nobody says anything. Moreover, his allowance is assured until his death: neither the death of a procurator nor that of a doge interferes with it, and by always serving faithfully and with reverence he has greater expectations, not the opposite; and as regards his salary money, if he does not go at the appointed time to pick it up, it is brought round to his house. And this is the first particular, as regards basic income; then there is occasional income, which consists of whatever extra I can easily earn outside St Mark's of about 200 ducats a year (invited as I am again and again by the wardens of the guilds) because whoever can engage the director to look after their music—not to mention the payment of 30 ducats, and even 40, and up to 50 for two vespers and a mass—does not fail to take him on, and they also thank him afterwards with well-chosen words.

Now let Your Lordship weigh in the balance of your very refined judgement that amount which you have offered me in His Highness's[f] name, and see whether—on good and solid grounds—I could make the change or not; and please consider in the first place, Your Lordship, what harm it would do to my reputation with these Most Illustrious Gentlemen and the Doge[g] himself if I were to agree that these present moneys that I

----

[d] *sottoposta al ponto.*   [e] *pontare e dispontare.*
[f] Duke Ferdinando Gonzaga.   [g] Antonio Priuli.

have for life should change into those of the Mantuan treasury, which dry up on the death of a duke or at his slightest ill humour—besides abandoning 450 [scudi] of Mantua[h] (which I am getting from the treasury here in Venice) to come and pick up 300, as Signor Sante[i] had—what would these gentlemen not say about me, and with reason?

It is true that you are adding on as well, on behalf of His Highness, 150 scudi from lands that will be my freehold. But to this I reply that the Duke does not have to give me what is mine: there will not be 150 but rather 50, since His Highness already owes me the 100; wherefore what I have already acquired during an earlier period of my life with sweat and endless toil should not be taken into account. So, there would be in all but 350, and here I find myself with 450, and 200 more from extra work.

And so, Your Lordship may therefore see that the world would—without fail—have a great deal to say against me; and without mentioning others, what would Adriana[j] not say, or a brother of hers,[k] or Campagnolo,[l] or Don Bassano,[m] who up till now have been very much more recognized and rewarded! And what embarrassment would I not suffer because of them, seeing them to have been rewarded more than me! Moreover, the city of Venice—I leave it to Your Lordship's consideration! What was offered me by His Highness, through Signor Campagnolo, was of greater benefit—when on the death of Signor Sante I was in Mantua, staying at the house of the said Signor Campagnolo—which was 300 scudi income from lands, 200 of which would have been understood as mine until my death, and 100 as payment from my property rent or donation.

But because I said that I did not wish to have anything to do with the treasury he offered me a further 200 as a pension, which amounts in all to about 600 Mantuan ducats, and now His Highness would like me to settle for less by far, along with the business of going to Signor Treasurer's office every day to beg him to give me what is mine.

God forbid! I have never in my life suffered greater affliction of mind than when I had to go and ask for my pay, almost for the love of God, from Signor Treasurer. I would sooner be content to go begging than return to

[h] 450 Mantuan scudi were roughly equivalent to 400 Venetian ducats.

[i] Sante Orlandi, late Director of Music to the Gonzaga court.   [j] Adriana Basile.

[k] She had two brothers, Francesco and Giovanni Battista, and it was almost certainly the latter (a poet) to whom Monteverdi was referring.

[l] Francesco Campagnolo, the tenor.   [m] Don Bassano Casola, singer and composer.

such indignity. (I beg Your Lordship to forgive me if I speak freely; and on account of my friendship—as I am a true-hearted servant—to be pleased this once to listen to me with the ear of your infinite kindness, and not with that of your singular merits.) When the Most Excellent Lord Procurator Landi[n]—together with the other Most Excellent Lords—once again increased my salary by 100 ducats, this gentleman said these precise words: 'Most Excellent Lords and Colleagues:[o] whoever wishes a servant to be honoured must also deal with him honourably.'

So, if the Duke has a mind that I should live honourably it is right and proper that he treat me in such a manner, but if not I beg him not to trouble me, since I live honourably as Your Lordship can ascertain. I say nothing about the point concerning my sons because I am speaking to Your Lordship, who is also the father of a family;[p] you know very well what consideration a father needs, who desires (and who ought by the laws of nature to desire) honour for himself and for the family he leaves behind him.

My conclusion, Most Illustrious Sir, is this: that in regard to Claudio, he already submits himself completely to the will and command of His Highness; in regard, however, to his having considered the aforementioned points, he cannot—with the honour he has—change employment unless he changes for the better, so that he could take leave of these Most Excellent Lords to his genuine satisfaction (having been so honoured and favoured by these Lords) through not being laughed at even by those who have earned much through little merit, and not censured either by society or by his sons.

Indeed, His Highness—now that the Lord Bishop of Mantua[q] has passed to a better life—would easily be able to give satisfaction with stipends and with a little more land, without delivering up Monteverdi to the vexations of the treasury, and to its uncertainty. In short, 400 Mantuan scudi as salary, and 300 from lands would mean little to His Highness, but to Claudio it would mean true and undisputed quiet. But is this perhaps

---

[n] Antonio Landi, one of the four procurators who had appointed Monteverdi in 1613. Landi was made a procurator in 1612, and died in 1618; there is a bust and an inscription in the family chapel in the church of San Antonio (Sansovino, 32).

[o] *Collega* (Venetian plural).   [p] Striggio had eleven children.

[q] Mgr. Francesco Gonzaga, who died on 11 Mar. 1620. As in the case of Pallavicino (Letter 1), Monteverdi lost no time in applying for whatever might become available.

[193]

asking the impossible? In a word, he asks for even less than Adriana used to get, and perhaps Settimia;^r but he asks only for what he gets now.

I see no other disagreement but that bit of property, since it is really my duty to leave a little something to my sons, and if I leave something given by the Most Serene House of Gonzaga it will also be to the everlasting honour of that house, for having helped a servant of so many years' standing; nor indeed was he disdained by rulers. But if this were to seem too much to His Highness, let him do me the honour of assigning to me my little bit of land, as I shall be content with the capital since the 400 ducats I have here are like a pension. And His Highness will have paid his servant well and truly, for if he will be pleased to command me he will see that in order to serve him, that servant will get out of bed in the middle of the night to render greater obedience.

Forgive me, Your Lordship, if I have gone on for too long. There remains nothing for me to do at present other than to thank Your Lordship from the bottom of my heart for the singular favour done to me in having presented my madrigals^s to Her Highness, and I am sure that through the most honourable medium of Your Lordship they will have been much more acceptable and welcome. May God assist me, where I cannot, in making Your Lordship's most honourable person happy, to whom with all the affection of my heart I bow and kiss hands.

from Venice, 13 March 1620
Your Most Illustrious Lordship's
most grateful servant
Claudio Monteverdi

---

^r Settimia Caccini, wife of Alessandro Ghivizzani. She had sung the role of Venus in *Arianna*, and was to collaborate with Monteverdi again in 1627, singing the part of Aurora in the *torneo*, *Mercurio e Marte*.
^s *Concerto* (Book VII).

50

Venice, 17 March 1620
to [Alessandro Striggio, at Mantua]

Mantua, Archivio Gonzaga, Cassetta 6, fos. 214–15. Bifolio: 3 pp.

Davari, 147; Malipiero, 203; Paoli, 155; Lax, 97

This letter, taken to Mantua by hand instead of by the usual courier route, is the first of six (all written in 1620) concerning a new production of *Arianna*.[1] This was to have been the artistic high point of the Duchess's birthday celebrations on 2 May, but after Monteverdi had gone to the trouble of revising the opera and having it recopied, the Gonzaga—playing the role of Theseus—abandoned *Arianna* and substituted another work.[2]

Once again the composer displays his uncommon abilities in the gentle art of postponement, and by referring to the long letter of 13 March he hints at his unwillingness to come near the court until his suit has been settled. But it is clear that the Mantuans too are anxious, for instead of relying on the normal post they send their wily factotum Antonio Callegari to collect the music in person. 'Il Bergamaschino', as he was called, had reported from Graz and Prague as early as 1602 on the imperial situation,[3] and he was certainly known to the Venetian Resident, Camillo Sordi, in 1613 as a professional carrier of information.[4] In 1623 he was connected in some way with the state visit of the Mantuan court to Venice,[5] and came under suspicion for espionage five years later.[6]

Monteverdi mentions here a regular weekly assignment which is rarely discussed in the standard biographies: his involvement in the music for the private oratory of Marc'Antonio Cornaro, Primicerius of St Mark's, who would most certainly have had the right to ask of the *maestro di cappella* some favours in the matter of arranging for suitable compositions to be performed when needed. Indeed, many of Monteverdi's

---

[1] Letters 50, 51, 52, 53, 55, 56.

[2] The occasion had nothing to do with the election of the Holy Roman Emperor, as suggested in *Monteverdi Companion*, 56. Ferdinand II of Austria, nephew of Maximilian II, had already been elected on 28 Aug. 1619; and it is hardly necessary to add that he should not be confused with Duke Ferdinando Gonzaga of Mantua.

[3] Quazza, *Diplomazia*, 42. [4] Paoli, 350; after Davari's notes in the Archivio Gonzaga.

[5] Ademollo, 280.

[6] 'Era sospettato di spionaggio a danno del Nevers anche il Bergamaschino, che tentava introdursi presso tutti gli ambasciatori' (Parma to Striggio, 6 May 1628; from document E/XLV/3/1559 in the Archivio Gonzaga, quoted in Quazza, *La guerra*, i. 135).

small-scale liturgical works, such as his motets for one or two voices, perhaps with violins and continuo, could have been written expressly for this oratory.

My Most Illustrious Lord and Most Respected Master,

I am sending this (by the hand of Don Vincenzo[a] here, a Mantuan who is just now going to Mantua) to let you know that I have received a letter of Your Lordship's from Signor Bergamaschino,[b] who commands me in the name of His Highness to have *Arianna* recopied as soon as possible, and then send it without delay to Your Lordship. I straightway gave it out to a copyist, so I hope that within a week or ten days Your Lordship will have it without fail. I would have written by the last post if the said Signor Bergamaschino had handed the letter over in time for the courier.

I also gathered that His Highness[c] entrusted him to tell me that I should come over to Mantua for a week or ten days, with the certainty that he would not keep me from these Most Excellent Lords[d] for longer than the stated time, so that I would indeed be back in time for Holy Week and the performance of my duty. I shall do everything within my power to obey with deeds the commands of His Highness, but in truth whenever I say a word about wanting to come to Mantua, there is not a soul who refrains from putting sinister thoughts into the heads of these Most Excellent Lords, and all to my disadvantage through the suspicions which they put into their minds. Besides which there is the Most Illustrious Primicerius[e] for whom—every Wednesday, Friday, and Sunday—I make music in a certain oratory of his, to which half the nobility come; and if I speak of leave, they at once chalk it up[f] against me.

Yet if it were possible to delay my coming, the first three feasts of Easter[g] being past, I could in the meanwhile arrange everything, and so

---

[a] Not identified, but he was probably a musician and a priest. A likely candidate is Vincenzo Zampoli, a singer at the chapel of S. Barbara, but there is no proof that he was in minor orders. See Tagmann, 387.

[b] The real name of 'the little man from Bergamo'—who served as a scribe and reporter, a runner of minor errands and an expert in espionage—was Antonio Callegari. On the day following that on which Letter 50 was written, he confirms that 'Monteverdi is having *Arianna* copied, and I shall bring it on Saturday' (Paoli, 350). This is substantiated by Letter 51, in which 'Il Bergamaschino' is mentioned again.

[c] Ferdinando, sixth Duke of Mantua.   [d] The three procurators *de supra*.

[e] Marc'Antonio Cornaro.

[f] *mi fanno conti adosso* (the implication being that gossips would make impertinent conjectures about the extra income Monteverdi would earn).

[g] Presumably a loose liturgical reference meaning Easter Sunday, Monday, and Tuesday, for all three of which Monteverdi would have had to supply special music.

would have the freedom to obey. But if not, I shall in the last resort do what Your Lordship commands me, hoping that Your Lordship's prudence will never order me to do anything that is not to my betterment.

I have written by way of reply to the second paragraph of Your Lordship's letter by the previous post and shall therefore be awaiting your advice, praying you for the love of God to maintain me in your favour, which I hope will be not less than what I promise myself, because I know how full you are of boundless humanity and courtesy. And here making a humble bow to Your Lordship, I pray God for your every contentment.

from Venice, 17 March 1620

Your Most Illustrious Lordship's

most grateful servant

Claudio Monteverdi

51

Venice, 21 March 1620
to [Alessandro Striggio, at Mantua]

Mantua, Archivio Gonzaga, Cassetta 6, fo. 217. Folio: 2 pp. Enclosure:
part of *Arianna*

Davari, 148; Malipiero, 204; Paoli, 157; Fabbri 1985, 236; Lax, 98

Antonio Callegari, otherwise known as 'Il Bergamaschino', had brought a letter
from Striggio to Monteverdi in mid-March with instructions to bring back a
score of *Arianna*. Not having a duplicate score, Monteverdi—after making a few
hasty revisions—sent the bulk of the work to be copied, reserving for himself
the copying of the 'Lament', which he describes as 'the most essential part of the
work'. He clearly wished to avoid letting the manuscript of the 'Lament' go out
of his hands, and since no solo version was at that time in print,[1] he may have met
the demand for this justly popular excerpt by selling individual copies. The latter
part of the communication refers to Striggio's reply to the lengthy letter dated 13
March.

My Most Illustrious Lord and Most Respected Master,

In order to show you that as soon as I received Your Lordship's command
(in the name of His Highness)[a] I did not fail to act upon it, here I am
already sending you four quires, recopied. I could have sent[b] five of them,
but I wanted to keep the last one by me so as to improve on it. This quire,
along with the others, I shall send off to Your Lordship by the next post.
I would even have held on to the ones enclosed, had I not persuaded
myself that every bit of time gained is to the good, inasmuch as a month (or
a little more) for rehearsal is by no means too long. In the mean time,
however, this opening section can be learnt.

   I am also sending the first part of the 'Lament', which I had already
copied at home on a different sheet of paper, so you will also gain time with

---

[1] Two separate editions came out in 1623 (Magni, Venice; Fei & Ruuli, Orvieto).

[a] Ferdinando, sixth Duke of Mantua.   [b] *potrei mandar.*

this item, being as it is the most essential part of the work.[c] Signor Bergamaschino,[d] bearer of this letter, will be able to certify to Your Lordship how busy I am at the moment; and at the same time he will also render the service of begging Your Lordship on my behalf to secure for me an extension of time until Low Sunday is past, for then I shall be able to come over to Mantua and have the pleasure of directing[e] *Arianna* and anything else that might be required.

Further, I have taken note of all that Your Lordship has been so kind as to write to me by this post. To which I reply by begging you to take all the time you need to negotiate with His Highness, because it does not inconvenience me in the least; on the contrary, I want to implore you—if by starting with my donation it might be possible to obtain the desired result—to try and be so kind as to negotiate this before anything else, because every subsequent new topic could bring with it unforeseen mishaps. And that I dread.

I know how very careful you are; I know from your infinite goodness how much you honour me, and how fond you are of me, and for this reason I submit myself in all respects to Your Lordship, whose hands I kiss with all reverence, and for whose every perfect happiness I pray God.

from Venice, 21 March[f] 1620

Your Most Illustrious Lordship's

most grateful servant

Claudio Monteverdi

[c] *opera*. This word was still used in a general sense in the first quarter of the 17th c. Individual compositions for the stage were referred to as *intermezzo, dramma, favola*, and so on.

[d] Real name, Antonio Callegari (see Letter 50).   [e] *concertare*.

[f] Originally 20 Mar., but altered by Monteverdi.

52

Venice, 28 March 1620
to [Alessandro Striggio, at Mantua]

Mantua, Archivio Gonzaga, Cassetta 6, fo. 219. Folio: 1 p. Enclosure: part of *Arianna*

Davari, 149; Malipiero, 205; Paoli, 159; Fabbri 1985, 236; Lax, 100

Like the previous letter, this one deals with two topics only—the ongoing revision of *Arianna* (of which further quinternions are enclosed), and the discussion of the Duke's offer of employment at Mantua, which is to be negotiated by Striggio. For it is to Striggio that this letter is addressed, although the covering has not survived and the salutation is that usually reserved for Marigliani. Monteverdi gives the impression of keeping an open mind with regard to the offer, since his main purpose is to secure payment of the donation granted to him by Duke Vincenzo.

Even if a satisfactory settlement had been made, it is very doubtful whether Monteverdi would have resigned his post at St Mark's, because Venice offered him much more than a secure and dignified position. Apart from his own publications in 1620, he had the pleasure of seeing in print a book of motets by his brother Giulio Cesare[1] and two volumes by his new assistant, Alessandro Grandi.[2] Mantua could not offer so much.

My Most Illustrious Lord and Most Esteemed[a] Master,

I am sending Your Lordship the enclosed quires of *Arianna*. I was thinking of sending you everything, but the man who is copying it for me lags behind—not indeed because he does not work hard, but because it is turning out to be longer than was believed. I shall, however, send it to you for sure, all complete, by the next post; nay, even sooner if I had someone

---

[1] *Affetti musicali ne quali si contengono motetti a 1–6 voci.* For his later career, see Sartori, 'Salò'.

[2] *Cantade et arie a voce sola . . . nuovamente ristampate; Motetti a 5 voci con le Letanie . . . nuovamente ristampate.*

[a] Instead of the usual *collendissimo* (respected), Monteverdi uses *osservandissimo*, which ranks very slightly lower. This minor lapse in the matter of honorifics is one of the very few committed by the composer in a collection of letters ranging over a period of more than forty years.

to give it to for special delivery,[b] since the music is finished—all that is lacking is part of the words. Had I been warned, or (to put it better) informed, before now, I would have sent it considerably more improved; because I know what I am talking about.

Your Lordship will do me a favour by making my excuses to His Highness[c] should he perhaps in some way not be satisfied with me; but believe me, Your Lordship, time is the good and the bad element in works such as this. Nevertheless I am trying to fall in with His Highness's liking, which indeed I must do, being his reverent servant.

Now, about the other business—when I come to Mantua we can talk about it, for I am absolutely certain and assured that Your Lordship's favour is going to help me in everything, just as I know for sure that it will not be wanting even at this juncture; wherefore I am and always shall be your most grateful servant. With this I pray God for your every happiness, while with all reverence I kiss your hands.

from Venice, 28 March 1620
Your Most Illustrious Lordship's
most grateful servant
Claudio Monteverdi

[b] *per straordinario.*   [c] Ferdinando, sixth Duke of Mantua.

53

Venice, 4 April 1620
to [Alessandro Striggio, at Mantua]

Mantua, Archivio Gonzaga, Cassetta 6, fos. 221–2. Bifolio: 3 pp. Enclosure: final section of *Arianna*, and a letter to the Duchess (no. 54)

Davari, 150; Prunières, 257; Malipiero, 207; Paoli, 163; Fabbri 1985, 236; Lax, 101

The usual order of the two letters dated 4 April is here reversed in accordance with the folio numbers in Cassetta 6 and the sense of the letters. Striggio is the first recipient, and his task is to read through Monteverdi's letter to the Duchess, expressing his approval or disapproval as the case may be. The letters and music were presumably made up into a single package, as with the two previous consignments.

Arianna was copied in its entirety, by Monteverdi and another unnamed person, during the last two weeks of March. The score was sent in three packages to Mantua, on 21 and 28 March and 4 April. Since it was never used, as far as we know, for a Mantuan production in 1620 or in any subsequent year, the eventual disappearance of this particular score may be attributed to the sack of the city by imperial troops in 1630.

The Mantuan court possessed an earlier copy of the opera until December 1613, when it was sent to Don Francesco de' Medici.[1] As Monteverdi had already left for Venice in October it is unlikely that he was ever consulted by the court official responsible for sending what might even have been the original autograph. In view of the lack of evidence that the Medici ever gave it back to the Gonzaga, Striggio's request for a new copy suggests that the earlier score was not returned.

In addition to the scores known to have existed in Florence (December 1613), Mantua (April 1620), and Venice—for the revival of 1639—there were almost certainly others: but every single one has disappeared.

Monteverdi's request to Striggio regarding the offer of thanks to the Duke and Duchess indicates that he is still very much in favour of maintaining polite diplomatic relations with the House of Gonzaga, and he mentions in particular his appreciation of the necklace, a topic that has given rise to some confusion in Monteverdi literature.[2] Although he expresses a hope that he might, in future years, set more of Striggio's

---

[1] Davari, 123.   [2] Stevens, 'Necklace'.

poetry to music, this renewal of an old association apparently never came to pass. Striggio became more and more preoccupied with the increasing complexity of both local and external politics as well as with the rapidly deteriorating position of the Gonzaga court, while Monteverdi, for his part, found Venice (and later Parma) even more demanding than he had ever dreamed. There was no successor to *Apollo* in the sense of a Monteverdi–Striggio collaboration.[3]

My Most Illustrious Lord and Most Respected Master,

I do not know whether I have done well or not in having written the enclosed letter to Her Ladyship[a] by way of thanks for being so kind as to grant me such an outstanding favour (through the medium of Your Lordship's special protection), she having sent me by courier that beautiful necklace as a gift. Your Lordship will do me a favour by giving it a glance, and if you consider it suitable I entreat Your Lordship to have it sealed and to present it to her.

If otherwise, I beg you to be so kind as to make good[b] what is necessary in your accomplished manner, thanking Her Highness on my behalf with the greatest possible warmth. I also beg Your Lordship to perform the same office towards the Most Serene Lord Duke,[c] my Singular Lord, as principal mover of such an outstanding favour.

I am sending off to Your Lordship the remainder of *Arianna*. If I had had more time, I would have revised it more thoroughly, and even perhaps greatly improved it. I shall not let a day go by without composing something in this theatrical style of song—and all the more willingly if you will make me worthy of it to a greater extent with your beautiful verses, so that I can give you some indication of how much this heart of mine longs to be kept in His Highness's favour, and how much it longs to be favoured by Your Lordship's singular worth.

I cannot be more grateful than I am to Your Lordship for the special favours that I keep receiving daily from your noble hand; and because these favours greatly exceed my merit, I therefore pray God that he accomplish[b] on my behalf that which I cannot do, by rewarding Your

---

[3] He subsequently worked with Marigliani, Strozzi, Achillini, Ascanio Pio, Vendramin, Badoaro, Morando, and Busenello.

[a] Caterina Medici Gonzaga, Duchess of Mantua.

[b] make good (see also 'accomplish', last paragraph): *complire* for *compire*.

[c] Ferdinando Gonzaga.

Lordship (whose hands I kiss with all reverence) with every perfect happiness.

from Venice, 4 April 1620

Your Most Illustrious Lordship's

most grateful servant

Claudio Monteverdi

54

Venice, 4 April 1620
to [Caterina Medici Gonzaga,
Duchess of Mantua]

Mantua, Archivio Gonzaga, Cassetta 6, fo. 224. Folio: 2 pp.

Malipiero, 206; Paoli, 161; Lax, 102

In this autograph, Monteverdi's handwriting aspires to a neater and more readable form of the chancery cursive than is usual in his correspondence, where there are sometimes problems in transliteration due to his corrections of words or phrases. He was clearly making a special effort to ensure that his patroness, Caterina Medici Gonzaga (see Pl. 7), understood the points at issue.

They were three in number, and each was an expression of thanks for favours granted: her willingness to accept his excuse for not coming to Mantua, her acceptance of the dedication of *Concerto*, and her gift of a necklace (which he kept by him as an investment until circumstances forced him to sell it). See Letter 116. The present letter was, of course, enclosed with the message to Striggio of the same date, which in turn was sent in the package containing the final pages of *Arianna*.

Most Serene Lady and Most Respected Patroness,

It was my bounden duty this carnival time, Most Serene Madam, to appear promptly before you and to lay at Your Highness's feet these poor songs[a] of mine; but some illness having stricken me in the meantime, I was therefore compelled to ask—as indeed I did most earnestly—the Most Illustrious Lord, Count Alessandro Striggio,[b] my special protector as regards the favour of Your Most Serene Highnesses, to be so kind as to present them to Your Highness in my stead, begging you to be so good as to accept them favourably as a sign that Your Highness did not disdain my admittedly poor but genuinely devoted and reverent service, since it had also been deemed worthy by the entire Most Serene House of Gonzaga.

[a] *Concerto* (Seventh Book of Madrigals).
[b] Alessandro Striggio, ducal councillor, was Count of Corticelli.

7. Caterina Medici Gonzaga, wife of Ferdinando, sixth Duke of Mantua. Oil painting, Florentine school. Florence, Galleria degli Uffizi

But Your Highness, who cannot favour the very least of her servants (as I am indeed) in any other way than in lofty proportion to your great mind—for this reason Your Highness has not only been so kind as to consider me excused for my failing, and indeed to receive this feeble token of my devoted service with a happy countenance, but (more than all this) has wished to honour me with a gift of a fine necklace.

Wherefore, being so overcome with grace, I have not been able to refrain from coming to Your Highness's feet with this letter of mine, to offer you the best thanks of which a humble, devoted, and grateful servant of Your Highness is capable, to whom I pray God with all my heart that He grant every perfect happiness; and so I bow to you most humbly.

from Venice, 4 April 1620[c]

Your Most Serene Highness's

most humble and most grateful servant

Claudio Monteverdi

[c] This letter, bearing the same date as no. 53, was enclosed with it.

55

Venice, 18 April 1620
to [Alessandro Striggio, at Mantua]

Mantua, Archivio Gonzaga, Cassetta 6, fos. 226–7. Bifolio: 3 pp.

Malipiero, 208; Paoli, 165; Lax, 103

This letter is of interest for several reasons, not least among them being the evidence of a continuing state of cold war between Monteverdi and Mantua. The composer's inner desire to associate in some way his personal anguish and suffering with that of Petrarch in the *Rime* must have surfaced on countless occasions,[1] even though the circumstances were not exactly analogous; and if his feelings for Mantua were still troubled by frustration, hurt, and suspicion, he may often have recalled affectionately that time of uneasy happiness when he was married to Claudia Cattaneo. One of his most vivid realizations of mental war and peace occurs in *Hor che 'l ciel e la terra*:[2]

> Guerra è il mio stato, d'ira e di duol piena;
> E sol di lei pensando ho qualche pace.

But the peace was now a faint memory, while the war raged on. Once more he experienced trouble in obtaining from the treasury due payment of the interest from his donation or *fondo*. He quotes to Striggio the exact words of the document in question, and the point is well made even though the legal wording differs slightly here and there.[3]

If Striggio were unable to extract the money, Monteverdi would have to travel all the way from Venice to Mantua, at a cost of 25 ducats, and waste time trying to persuade the corrupt and unhelpful officials to give him what was his due. If he requested assistance from the Duke (as he did in the summer of 1619),[4] a polite reply would assure him that everything would be taken care of, but nothing would subsequently be done. Either the Duke never gave instructions, or those instructions were ignored by his staff. Being a weak ruler, Ferdinando probably did what he conceived to be his duty, but neglected to find out what, if any, were the results.

Nevertheless Monteverdi shows himself willing to come and direct *Arianna*, and apologizes to Striggio for continuing to bother him with personal troubles and trials. He almost begs him to give up the struggle, but within a month a further letter on the

---

[1] Pirrotta, 62.   [2] *Madrigali guerrieri et amorosi* (1638)
[3] The full text, taken from the Libro mandati of 1609, is quoted in Pontiroli, *Monteverdi*, 79–80.
[4] See Letter 49.

subject of the voucher turns up on Striggio's desk. The Count was also in touch with Peri at this time, receiving two letters from the Florentine composer and singer on 7 and 12 April about his setting of Jacopo Cicognini's *Adone* and a separate ballet. Unlike Monteverdi, Peri has no axe to grind: he discusses the music only, and his concern for its acceptance. He must have pleased Striggio by recalling to mind the honour in which his father, the madrigalist and viola da braccio player, was held in Florence in former days.[5]

My Most Illustrious Lord and Most Respected Master,

I am writing to beg Your Lordship not to exert yourself, please, if you have to go to some trouble in getting the money from that voucher, for I know how tiresome a business it is, coping with extraction of money from the Treasury. But I so much value that Prince's[a] good will and your own peace of mind that the money would almost be unimportant to me, or rather definitely so, if any trouble or vexation might ensue.

But, Your Lordship, it seems to me very strange that in my donation these precise words are to be found: 'We command the President of Our Magistracy that he execute this our donation and obligation without any other mandate or commission, this being our well-considered wish.'

And yet I have always been obliged—and am now to a greater extent even more obliged—either to come and ask His Highness to grant me the favour of an order that they be given to me (always with travelling expenses of 25 ducats), or that I beg the likes of you to be so kind as to put themselves out for me in asking, on my behalf, for something that should not have to be requested. For truly, Your Lordship, I sometimes cannot decide what causes the greater suffering in my heart: the dislike of wholly giving up such sums of money to them, or (because of a claim) seeing troubles of this kind for the like of you, and expenses and inconvenience for me if I try to come and take possession of it.

And as for me, Your Lordship, if in future the affair goes on in this way, I wish to renounce the said donation for my sons;[b] for if they do receive it, well and good; but if not, it may also be to their detriment. It will be better for the mind to calm down once and for all, than try to hold on continually, with all the expenses, the fatigue, the inconvenience and the obligations, to a hope which may only come to an end after my death.

[5] Ademollo, 239.

[a] Ferdinando, sixth Duke of Mantua.   [b] Francesco and Massimiliano.

I begged His Highness when I was at Mantua last year that he might be so good as to arrange for these moneys to reach me as quickly as possible, for the maintenance of my children in their studies. I certainly had a reply, full of kindness and benevolence, but nevertheless I am worse off than before. That is the way my luck goes in Mantua. And because I know it to be thus, I once again beg Your Lordship to simply give the task to someone else,*c* since your infinite humanity and kindness so ordains—for if it were not thus I could never have been so bold.

If it is possible, well and good; if not, however, let us leave it to whatsoever time may be pleasing to God. With regard to my promptness in obeying the orders of His Highness and, at the same time, of Your Lordship—whenever you may be so good as to give me the slightest hint about my helping with *Arianna* or anything else, you will see and know from the results my genuine willingness, and the great desire I have, to show myself no less a very humble servant of His Highness than I desire to be an affectionate and grateful servant to Your Lordship.

As for the future, Your Lordship, do not bother yourself further about setting to rights the troubles of the likes of me, for they are numerous because of the constant necessity that besets me, and if one of them is taken care of today, another comes up tomorrow—just as it happens to a poor man who has old clothes: as soon as one hole is repaired he discovers another that has to be mended. Allow yourself to reckon it up, and you will discover the truth. First there was the inconvenience to Your Lordship over the books;*d* now the voucher has suddenly turned up; after this comes the request for money, with all that inconvenience—and so I never cease troubling you with it all.

Do it then as I say, I beg you, by not taking on troubles like these, and be content that I am your servant because of past favours, for so maintaining myself always I shall not fail to pray God that He grant Your Lordship the grace of every happiness, and here I make a most humble reverence to you.

from Venice, 18 April 1620
Your Most Illustrious Lordship's
most grateful servant
Claudio Monteverdi

---

c *farne una senplice passatella.* The term is borrowed from the game of bowls (*bocce*).
d The part-books of *Concerto.*

56

Venice, 10 May 1620
to [Alessandro Striggio, at Mantua]

Mantua, Archivio Gonzaga, Cassetta 6, fos. 229–30. Bifolio: 3 pp.

Prunières, 258; Malipiero, 210; Paoli, 168; Fabbri 1985, 237; Lax, 105

Having received a reply to his letter of 4 April to the Duchess, Monteverdi wrote soon after Easter (which fell on 19 April) thanking Striggio for his kindness in acting as intermediary, adding that the Duchess in turn would prove to be useful as an intermediary with the Duke. Granted the need for third-party influence at court, this approach was more necessary than ever in Monteverdi's case because of the awkward and protracted nature of his negotiations with his former employers.

That they were difficult to deal with one can scarcely doubt, and the flexibility of their plans must often have given an impression of wildly speculative improvisation to those who had the good fortune to live beyond the Mantuan marshes. The frenzied reworking and copying of *Arianna*, the goading of Peri in Florence to finish off *Adone* and a ballet—all in time for the Duchess's birthday celebrations on 2 May—show the Gonzaga in their true light, as does their sudden decision to cancel everything except the ballet.

In vain were Monteverdi's protests about the hurrying along of a production that would normally require many months of rehearsal; in vain the pleadings of Peri, who urged Striggio not to think of *Adone* as a work that could be prepared in a fortnight.[1] Their advice was ignored until the last possible minute; for on 30 April the town council of Brescia wrote to the Duchess thanking her for the honour done them by engaging their wind band.[2] This was almost certainly an attempt to fill the gaps in the entertainment quickly and inexpensively: instead of two stage works, the court had to make do with a band and a ballet.

It has more than once been suggested that the ballet was none other than Monteverdi's *Tirsi e Clori*, and its inclusion in the *Concerto* volume recently presented to Madama Serenissima would appear to confirm such a theory. But Monteverdi does not say that the Duchess, in her letter, has done well to decide on *his* ballet; he merely says *the* ballet, which must refer to Peri's, because in the following paragraph he says how pleased he is that Peri may be given a chance to show his worth, and that the element of rivalry thereby introduced will enable the others—the local composers—to contribute something of their own in a different vein or genre.

[1] Ademollo, 238.   [2] Bertolotti, 98.

Peri's *Adone* has not survived, nor, apparently, has the ballet. Since this contained at least one scene about the moon, it might have been a reworking of the *Endimione* written by the Duke in 1616 as a *favola*.[3] But however uncertain this may be, the existence of three musical scores at Mantua in 1620—each one of them a stage work of major importance—cannot be denied. Posterity can only regret that the Gonzaga took less care of the music entrusted to them than of their own voluminous archives.

My Most Illustrious Lord and Most Respected Master,

At every moment I keep receiving infinite favours from Your Lordship's generous hand; and so, every day, I keep considering myself so much the more indebted to Your Lordship's noble ways. Would that I could make the outcome equal to my devotion, so that I might perhaps be more worthy than I am of Your Lordship's commands! But fortune goes on tormenting me in this delightful manner, while it makes me worthy of favours and not of merit.

I received a most gracious reply to my letter, through Her Ladyship's infinite kindness, and this singular favour alone was (without any other recognition) sufficient to make me perforce her lifelong servant. But I am not so modest a connoisseur of the truth as not to realize that the greater part of my credit as regards Her Highness's[a] favour springs from Your Lordship's special protection, so that I must therefore remain no less obliged to Your Lordship in recognition of your assistance than I must to Her Highness in recognition of her patronage.

I shall try and entertain much greater hopes for the future (aided by the favour of Her Highness and that of Your Lordship) than I had for the past, in the belief that I shall be made worthy of that little bit of capital which I claim for myself, by favour (not by merit) of the generous hand of the Most Serene Lord Duke of Mantua,[b] as much a kind master as he is a just one. And I shall hope to be able, before I die, to enjoy once and for all that favour which the kindness of the Most Serene Lord Duke Vincenzo[c] (may he be in glory!) granted to me.

It was a good decision that the Most Serene Lord Duke made, in not letting *Arianna* (and also that other composition by Signor Zazzerino[d]) be

---

[3] Ademollo, 233.

[a] *S.A.S.*, which could refer either to the Duke or to the Duchess, but refers here (as in the following paragraph) to the latter.

[b] Ferdinando Gonzaga, sixth Duke of Mantua.   [c] Duke Vincenzo, fourth Duke of Mantua.

[d] Jacopo Peri, whose tousled, reddish-blonde hair earned him this nickname. The 'other work' was his *Adone*.

put on the stage at such short notice, because really and truly haste is far too harmful to such projects, inasmuch as the sense of hearing is too general and too delicate—all the more so in company where the presence of great princes such as himself has to be taken into account. And Her Ladyship has shown great prudence by deciding on the ballet,[e] for the presence of great subject-matter[f] is enough to provide what is needful for festivals like this, but in others it does not work out in this way.

For then Signor Zazzerino may be given a chance to show that he too is a servant worthy of Her Highness's favour. Not only does he possess all the qualities about which you write to me, but the gentle and healthy rivalry will give the others a better chance to do something else in order to gain favour for themselves; for without knowledge of the way one cannot arrive at the place decided upon. I assure you, however, that Your Lordship's affection, which you continue to show me in every way, goes on binding me immeasurably closer in the knot of service.

If I am also presumptuous in accepting that favour (so much more necessary now for looking after my sons, than for myself) which through your spontaneous goodwill you offer me in this very kind letter of yours—which is that my father-in-law[g] may put in an appearance at Your Lordship's, who will see to it that the voucher of mine which he now has in his hands will be paid—blame my very great need and your kind nature (since the former has made me bold and the latter has led me on) and not my temerity, for indeed I knew only too well that it had inconvenienced you.

You will therefore be seeing my father-in-law at your house; and do forgive him the intrusion. And so with this, making a humble reverence to Your Lordship, I pray God heartily for your every true contentment.

from Venice, 10 May 1620

Your Most Illustrious Lordship's

most grateful servant

Claudio Monteverdi

[e] Peri's ballet (title unknown), mentioned in his letter of 7 Apr. to Striggio.
[f] *sogetto.*   [g] Giacomo Cattaneo.

57

Venice, 11 July 1620
to [Alessandro Striggio, at Mantua]

Mantua, Archivio Gonzaga, Cassetta 6, fos. 232–3. Bifolio: 3 pp.

Prunières, 259; Malipiero, 212; Paoli, 171; Lax, 107

If the learned city of Bologna, in the early years of the seventeenth century, harboured one of Monteverdi's most implacable enemies—Giovanni Maria Artusi, canon of S. Salvatore—its monastery of S. Michele in Bosco was from 1608 until 1634 the home of a good and loyal friend: Adriano Banchieri, a most versatile musician and writer whose personality dominated Bolognese musical life and animated the two organizations that rank as forerunners of the famous Accademia Filarmonica.

Shortly after Artusi's *Discorso secondo* of 1608, in which the rationale of the *seconda prattica* was once more attacked, Banchieri leapt to the defence of Monteverdi by praising his music in a frequently quoted passage from the *Conclusioni nel suono dell'organo*, published in 1609: 'I must not neglect to mention the most noble of composers, Claudio Monteverdi, in speaking of modern music, since his expressive qualities are truly deserving of the highest commendation, and we find in them countless examples of matchless declamation, carefully set out and enhanced by comparable harmonies.'

In 1614, one year after Artusi's death, the ever-optimistic and forward-looking Banchieri founded the Accademia dei Floridi (sometimes called 'dei Fioriti') within his own monastery. Its pleasant location, only half a mile from the Porta S. Mamolo at the southern end of the city, made it a convenient meeting-place for those interested in music and literature. Although the rooms that once resounded to the music of the Olivetan monk and his friends now form part of an orthopaedic institute, the building itself still remains as an impressive example of ecclesiastical architecture, while the organ (originally built in 1524–6 by Giovanni Battista Facchetti) is regarded as one of the most important in that part of Italy.

The rules and regulations of the Accademia were set forth in Banchieri's *Cartella musicale nel canto figurato fermo e contrapunto* (Venice, 1614), and apart from naming the usual day of the weekly meeting—Monday—and the hour (between Vespers and Compline), they also specified the kind of music that should be performed. The opening music took the form of a 'concerto di voci alla spinetta', in other words a composition in the more modern style, with continuo. After the first allocution, the assembly listened to a solemn motet or spiritual madrigal by Lassus or Palestrina, 'it

[214]

being possible also to perform one of those madrigals by that most noble of composers, Claudio Monteverdi, at present the most worthy Director of Music at St Mark's, Venice, which have been changed into motets by Aquilino Coppini, by request of the Most Illustrious Cardinal Federico Borromeo; and these are to be sung at the small table without an instrument'. After the second allocution came the final music, which was open to choice.[1]

Banchieri's growing admiration for Monteverdi is proved by his willingness to link his name with that of two of the greatest composers of the sixteenth century. It comes as no surprise, therefore, to learn that on the Feast of St Anthony of Padua (13 June), in the year 1620, Monteverdi was given a warm and solemn welcome at S. Michele in Bosco not only by Banchieri, but by Girolamo Giacobbi (then organist of San Petronio) and by numerous other Bolognese singers and instrumentalists. The event is referred to in a letter of congratulation on Monteverdi's formal admission as an honorary member of the Accademia dei Filomusi—which had succeeded that of the Floridi—probably in 1624.[2]

The speeches in honour of Monteverdi have not survived, and there is no way of knowing what music was performed on that notable occasion in 1620. It is possible, however, that his son Francesco was among the musicians, for he was still studying law at Bologna and singing in his spare time.[3] The meeting between father and son turned out to be more than a mere family reunion accompanied by music and festivities, for it was surely at this juncture that Francesco intimated his wish to become a monk. This news is first conveyed in the letter of 11 July, which by a strange coincidence is the last time Monteverdi mentions his musically gifted son in his surviving correspondence.

Although we do not know which of Monteverdi's compositions were performed on 13 June, there is one that would have been perfectly appropriate for the day in question: the hymn *En gratulemur hodie*, for tenor voice, two violins, and continuo, in honour of St Anthony of Padua. Francesco could have sung the tenor part, which at that time would hopefully have been supplied with more than the non-committal selection of alternate verses later published in the *Selva morale e spirituale*.[4] When the full text of the hymn is studied in *Analecta hymnica* (iv. 90), it becomes clear that the name omitted at the end of stanza 1 is that of 'Antonius', while the beginning of the second stanza—'Francisci patris aemulus'—demonstrates that the particular saint referred to is indeed the Franciscan, St Anthony of Padua.

By 24 June he was back in Venice to fulfil one of his numerous freelance engagements—supplying and directing music for the feast of St John the Baptist at the church of San Giovanni Elemosinario near the Rialto Bridge. We owe the following

---

[1] Vecchi, 139.

[2] Vogel, 373; Vecchi, 82. The letter of congratulation was published in the 1628 edition of Banchieri's *Lettere armoniche*.

[3] Vecchi, 91 n. 88 suggests that the Monteverdi who sang at San Petronio in 1619 was probably Francesco.

[4] *Collected Works*, xvi. 517.

description to a diary kept in French by the 24-year-old Dutch diplomat and composer, Constantijn Huygens.[5]

> On [June] 24th, the feast of St John Baptist, I was taken to the church of [San Giovanni Elemosinario]—(Huygens writes 'Saint Jean et Lucie')—where I heard the most excellent music that I think I shall ever hear in my life. The renowned Claudio Monteverdi, who composed it, supervised and conducted it on this occasion, with the accompaniment of four theorbos, two cornetti, two bassoons, two violins, a bass viol of enormous size, organs, and other instruments all of which were managed and played superbly well, with ten or twelve voices in addition. I was quite beside myself with delight.

As it happened, Monteverdi had already written a motet for this feast-day, *Fuge anima mea, fuge mundum: ecce Iohannes qui docuit populos*, published that same year in Don Lorenzo Calvo's *Symbolae diversorum musicorum*.[6] The psalms, hymn, and Magnificat would have caused no problem, since there were so many of his own settings on which to draw.

In the meanwhile, at nearby Modena, Adriana Basile was preparing for the last stage of her long journey from Naples to Mantua. Her voice was no longer at its best, and the Princess Giulia Felice d'Este admitted as much in two of her letters, while yet maintaining that if Hippolita Marotta was endowed with superior vocal powers, Adriana far excelled her in beauty.[7] She arrived at Mantua about 26 June and immediately began a musical correspondence with the Infanta Isabella of Savoy, wife of Alfonso III d'Este, Prince of Modena.

My Most Illustrious Lord and Most Respected Master,

Now that my hectic days[a] at St Mark's are over (nor will they recur until All Saints' Day) and I find myself not only somewhat at liberty but also impelled by the crisis that chanced upon me—which was that my son Francesco (aged twenty and thinking of becoming a Doctor of Law in a year or just over) unexpectedly decided in Bologna to become a friar of the reformed order of Discalced Carmelite Fathers, wherefore what with the journey (going to Milan) and the friar's habit, he has saddled me with a debt of more than 50 scudi—I therefore decided, because of the opportunity and the need, to come over to Mantua and see whether (through His Highness's[b] inherent goodness) I can get hold of that little bit of money due to me.

---

[5] Stevens, '1993', 574; original in Worp, 128.
[6] *Collected Works*, xvi. 444.   [7] Ademollo, 264.

[a] 1 July (Feast of the Most Precious Blood); 2 July (Visitation of the Blessed Virgin Mary). There would be four months of relative calm until 1 Nov. (All Saints' Day).
[b] Ferdinando, sixth Duke of Mantua.

But before coming over I first of all sent word, a week ago, to my father-in-law.[c] And he told me by this post about being at Your Lordship's, and your informing him that since there is now an order from His Highness to pay for the music, you would have honoured me by seeing to it that my voucher was also paid, without my having to inconvenience myself and put up with the journey these hot days.

So, tending to think that my father-in-law[d] had said this because he knows that Massimiliano is here with me (and I fear he bears him little love, for the boy knows his own mind) and because he is worried that I might bring my son[e] along, causing him displeasure, I could not refrain—being forced by the above-mentioned need—from writing the present letter to Your Lordship, begging you to honour me by letting me know whether, without my coming to Mantua, it will be possible to favour me with such moneys this month.

For if it so turns out, I shall stay here; otherwise, in order not to lose the chance of being able to come, I would seize the opportunity of this free time to come and beg His Highness (so compelled, in truth, by my great need) in the hope that having to persuade him to help the one son who has turned to such a holy life, and the other in his studies—both of them his subjects—he would not deprive me of such a well-deserved favour.

I know that I am a nuisance to Your Lordship (and have been even more so) because of the many tiresome tasks I have given you; but I assure Your Lordship that my being ashamed of all this will remove the urge to importune you, although I am quite sure that your kindness would of its nature never fail anyone, especially me, since you have given me, Your Lordship, so many indications that convince me of your honoured grace—in which I pray that God maintain me always, and that He also bless and preserve Your Lordship's person, to whom by way of ending I make a humble reverence and kiss your hands.

from Venice, 11 July 1620
Your Most Illustrious Lordship's
most devoted and most grateful servant
Claudio Monteverdi

[c] Giacomo Cattaneo.   [d] *messere* is used here instead of *suocero* (father-in-law).
[e] Added to clarify the slightly confused personal pronouns. Massimiliano was at this time just over 16 years old.

58

Venice, 19 July 1620
to [Alessandro Striggio, at Mantua]

Mantua, Archivio Gonzaga, Cassetta 6, fo. 235. Folio: 2 pp.

Prunières, 260; Malipiero, 214; Paoli, 174; Lax, 109

Still recovering from his journeys to Milan and Bologna in June, Monteverdi was not over-anxious to visit Mantua although he wanted to collect two important sums that were overdue: the voucher for his pension and the honorarium for preparing a copy of *Arianna*. By appealing to Striggio, who had so often given proof of his ability to persuade the Duke, and by writing to Giacomo Cattaneo, the composer made plans for obtaining the money and having it sent on to Venice. The successful outcome is described in the present letter.

He had another reason for wishing to remain in Venice, this time a valid professional one: on the third Sunday of July, it was customary for the Doge and the Signoria, attended by vast crowds of citizens and visitors, to hear Low Mass at the Chiesa del Redentore, Palladio's masterpiece on the Giudecca. Motets were sung by the choir of St Mark's, directed by their *maestro di cappella*, at the Offertory and the Elevation. When the service was over, dignitaries and populace returned to the main island for a solemn procession to the basilica, where High Mass was celebrated by one of the canons and adorned by more music of an appropriately festive kind.[1]

This notable event, which is still observed (though with less pomp than in former times), marked the anniversary of the vow made by the Doge to build a church in commemoration of the deliverance of Venice from the plague, which destroyed one-fourth of the population in 1576. The first stone was laid in the presence of the Doge and Patriarch on 3 May of the following year, and the construction of a temporary church at this site enabled the July *andata*, or solemn procession, to take place for the first time. A predecessor of Monteverdi, Gioseffo Zarlino, composed and conducted the music for that occasion, and ever since then music has played an important part in the ceremony.[2]

---

[1] Sansovino, 255, 513.

[2] Hazlitt, ii. 129. The Redentore was a Capuchin house, and a treatise on the origins of that order was included in the fourth (non-musical) volume of Zarlino's works published in 1589, the year before his death. For the harmonic proportions of the church, see Honour, 116. Sir Henry Wotton, British Ambassador to Venice at the time when this letter was written, was well aware of Palladio's sense of order when he wrote (in his *Elements of Architecture*, 1624), 'In truth, a sound piece of good Art, where the *Materials* being but

Writing as usual under pressure to catch the Saturday courier to Mantua, Monteverdi made two small errors in connection with the name of the church and the date of the festival. Aware of a by no means illogical mental connection between the Saviour and the Redeemer, he called the church 'Salvatore' instead of 'Redentore', and indeed a Chiesa San Salvatore does exist in Venice. With regard to the date of his letter, which is given as 19 July, he must have meant 18 July, which fell on a Saturday in 1620, a leap year. The third Sunday of July, when the festival took place, was the 19th.

My Most Illustrious Lord and Most Respected Master,

Even if Your Lordship is not the man who honours me with the commands I so much desire, I must confess myself, inevitably, to be ever bound to you by an indissoluble bond of infinite gratitude for the favour— so outstanding and so important to me—which you have obtained for me of His Highness's[a] grace. But how then could I even feel myself other than bound[b] when Your Lordship's commands bring me both favours and honours? Excuse my poor mind, Your Lordship, which would like to do more than it can; yet nobody will ever make it lose the consciousness of being your true-hearted servant.

If I had any idea that I would meet with His Highness's approval—and with Your Lordship's—in the smallest way, believe me truly: I would already have come flying to Mantua two weeks ago. But my good fortune did not wish to accompany me in this manner. I shall be staying here not so much because the occasion (as indeed you hint) is not now so urgent, but because the task has been given me of serving this Most Serene Republic tomorrow, which will be the 20th of this month, at the Church of Our Redeemer,[c] a day celebrated by this Most Serene Republic in memory of a favour received from the hand of God, which was the liberation of the city from a terrible plague.

I mentioned[d] to my father-in-law[e] the particular favour Your Lordship did for me as regards His Highness. I do not know whether he will be able to refrain from coming to see you, to be directed as to what he will have to

ordinary Stone, without any garnishment of Sculpture, do yet ravish the beholder (and he knows not how) by a secret *Harmony* in the *Proportions*.'

  [a] Ferdinando, sixth Duke of Mantua.   [b] *slegato*.

  [c] *chiesa del Salvatore* (one of Monteverdi's rare lapses of memory in regard to the buildings and topography of Venice).

  [d] *ho tocco* (apocopated participle of *toccare*).   [e] Giacomo Cattaneo.

do in order to enjoy the longed-for favour; but please excuse my need, and the great desire which the poor man has to do me a service, if perhaps through his appearance before Your Lordship he should cause some annoyance.

For all of this I shall feel even more boundless gratitude to Your Lordship's courteous nature; and now with heartfelt affection I pray God for your every perfect happiness, while I bow to you and kiss your hands.

from Venice, 19 July 1620

Your Most Illustrious Lordship's
most grateful servant
Claudio Monteverdi

59

Venice, 24 July 1620
to [Alessandro Striggio, at Mantua]

Mantua, Archivio Gonzaga, Cassetta 6, fo. 237. Folio: 2 pp.

Prunières, 261; Malipiero, 215; Paoli, 176; Lax, 110

This relatively cheerful letter deals with the successful payment of Monteverdi's pension and the news of a further performance of *Apollo* at Mantua. The money, to be paid via his father-in-law, is to be set aside especially for Francesco and Massimiliano, studying religion and medicine respectively.

My Most Illustrious Lord, and Most Respected Master,

Thanks be to God that I was born a servant of that merit in serving you, as you were born a master to me, ever favouring me and honouring me! Even when I think I have received so much from your most gracious hand, in having received the payment order (so much desired by me) for those small sums of money enabling me to meet my sons'[a] urgent need, which—with time at a premium—does not fail to give me constant and diligent reminders of its existence, lo and behold! Your Lordship adds new information about a new favour; namely that my poor music—which served with great courage, it is true, but little strength, for Your Lordship's most beautiful eclogue[b]—has once more been doubly honoured and praised: by His Highness[c] and by Your Lordship.

But even if I can do nothing else, I shall try to pray God most fervently that he come to my aid in granting every favour and happiness to Your Lordship's most honoured and most noble person, to whom I make a most humble bow. I have written to Signor Giacomo,[d] my father-in-law, that he may appear[e] before Your Lordship as you have instructed me, and if by chance Your Lordship should perhaps be somewhat annoyed by his solici-

---

[a] Francesco and Massimiliano.
[b] *Apollo* (this is the last of eleven references to the Striggio–Monteverdi collaboration).
[c] Duke Ferdinando Gonzaga.   [d] Giacomo Cattaneo.   [e] *che si lassi vedere.*

tude, blame both your kindness for so ordering it, and the great need which urges me on in this way.

from Venice, 24 July 1620
Your Most Illustrious Lordship's
most grateful servant
·   Claudio Monteverdi

60

Mantua, 22 September 1620
to [Alessandro Striggio, at ?Casale Monferrato]

Mantua, Archivio Gonzaga, Cassetta 6, fo. 239. Folio: 2 pp.

Malipiero, 216; Paoli, 178; Lax, 111

Three months elapse without a communication from Monteverdi to Striggio, and that is just sufficient time for the quarterly payment to fall due. But on this occasion the composer has come to Mantua, only to find that Striggio is away (probably at Casale Monferrato) and the Duke has departed for Goito, a country seat of the Gonzaga built on the Mincio by his grandfather Guglielmo, the third Duke. This quiet and attractive resort was famous for its heraldic paintings, notably a series by Tintoretto on the family's military exploits. The old hunting lodge dating from the time of the marquisate had slowly been transformed into a *delizioso soggiorno*, and it was here that the Duke gave audience to his former music teacher, on 20 September.

The request seems to agree with what one might expect in the circumstances: to avoid troubling Striggio and Cattaneo every three months, the money should be paid directly to Monteverdi in Venice. The Duke concurs, the composer is delighted; but he is experienced enough to know that an order given from on high can lose a considerable amount of its striking power by the time it has descended to the level of the Mantuan treasury officials. He therefore begs Striggio to superintend personally the first stage of this transaction, perhaps in the hope that later instalments will arrive automatically.

Just before leaving Venice, Monteverdi may have seen a copy of Claudio Saracini's *Le seconde musiche*,[1] in which he is named as the dedicatee of the very first song— *Udite, lagrimosi spirti*, Mirtillo's complaint from Guarini's *Il pastor fido* (Act III, Scene vi). Nothing is known of the relationship between the two composers, yet they must have met in Venice, for the position of the dedicatory piece implies that Saracini held his elder colleague in great esteem.[2]

My Most Illustrious Lord and Most Respected Master,

The Most Serene Lord Duke,[a] full of infinite humanity, deigning to listen

---

[1] The main dedication, to the Grand Duke of Tuscany, is dated 26 Aug.

[2] 'Intitolato Al Molto Illustre Sig. Claudio Monteverde Maestro di Capella della Serenissima Signoria di Venetia in San Marco.'

[a] Ferdinando, sixth Duke of Mantua.

to me only the day before yesterday at Goito[b]—while I begged him that if he wanted to be so good as to give an order[c] that the sums due should be paid to me, since I have in my hand vouchers from my donation—was pleased to answer me in well-chosen words that he was ready to give me every satisfaction: a reply really far too worthy for my feeble merits. It therefore remains, in order for me to receive this favour duly implemented, for His Highness to kindly direct that they be paid to me so that I can help my sons[d] in their studies.

And so, to receive this outstanding favour, I hasten back to Your Lordship as my particular master, beseeching you to try and be so good as to remind His Highness about it at an opportune moment, take the payment order yourself, and then refer it either to Signor Paolo Anselmi[e] or to some other gentleman who hands out these moneys to me; wherefore beyond the infinite obligation to Your Lordship that I shall always have, I shall not fail to pray Our Lord with all my heart that he bless and prosper Your Lordship, whose hands I kiss with all reverence.

from Mantua, 22 September 1620
Your Most Illustrious Lordship's
most grateful servant
Claudio Monteverdi

[b] The Gonzaga hunting lodge and castle, about ten miles to the north-west of Mantua.
[c] *commissione*, here an order for payment of pension money.
[d] Francesco and Massimiliano.   [e] Presumably one of the court treasurers.

61

Venice, 9 October 1620
to [Alessandro Striggio, at Mantua]

Mantua, Archivio Gonzaga, Cassetta 6, fo. 241. Folio: 1 p.

Malipiero, 217; Paoli, 180; Lax, 112

This short letter explains that lack of time prevented Monteverdi from meeting Striggio, who had been away from Mantua, then returned to attend the Duke at Goito, and finally retreated for a short time to his own country estate. Striggio was at this time one of the Duke's most trusted advisers, so he could not avoid being closely and continuously involved in the wretched affair of Prince Vincenzo's clandestine marriage to Isabella Gonzaga di Novellara. Vincenzo and Ferdinando were again on speaking terms, but the case brought by Isabella (with the aid of her brother Count Camillo) had just reopened in Rome,[1] where there were rumours that the Gonzaga might run into serious trouble with the papacy.

My Most Illustrious Lord and Most Respected Master,

I come before Your Lordship with this letter of mine to perform that duty which lack of time prevented me from doing[a] (since I heard that no sooner had Your Lordship arrived in Mantua, on returning from Goito,[b] than you were taken out to your country estate), which duty was to write and thank you for the great favour I received of your infinite kindness, and to inform you that I received promptly from Signor Anselmi[c] those moneys due to me; and at the same time to beg you to honour me with commissions in order to make me a worthy servant of your grace.

Not having been able, however, to do so by word of mouth—for the above reason—I beg Your Lordship to accept my good intent on this sheet of paper[d] which with heartfelt sincerity offers you infinite thanks and begs

---

[1] Errante, 'Il processo', 680.

[a] *che non mi fu concesso dal tempo.*
[b] The Gonzaga hunting lodge and castle, about ten miles to the north-west of Mantua.
[c] Presumably one of the court treasurers.   [d] The subject of this peroration is *questo foglio.*

you with warm entreaty to be so kind as to keep me in your good grace, while with all affection it prays for every perfect happiness and contentment for Your Lordship, and with all reverence kisses your hand.

from Venice, 9 October 1620

Your Most Illustrious Lordship's

most grateful servant

Claudio Monteverdi

62

Venice, 21 October 1620
to Alessandro Striggio, at Mantua

Mantua, Archivio Gonzaga, Cassetta 6, fo. 256. Folio: 1 p.

Prunières, 261; Malipiero, 223; Paoli, 182; Fabbri, 239; Lax, 113

Such was the cosmopolitan nature of the city of Venice, and such the renown of its senior *maestro di cappella*, that it would be difficult to believe in any kind of isolation or non-involvement during the last thirty years of his life. In fact, the interplay of music and politics proved to be a constant and colourful feature of Venetian life as Monteverdi knew it. This letter mentions the Milanese colony and their desire to celebrate the feast of San Carlo Borromeo on 4 November, with special music directed by Monteverdi.

In 1621 his artistry would be placed at the service of the Florentines for the obsequies of the Grand Duke of Tuscany, and two years later to the month his secular muse would shine upon the visit of the Duke of Mantua and his court. Two more years, and the Polish King Sigismund III would invite Monteverdi to direct music both for his court and his chapel while they were lodged in Venice, in March 1625.[1] He would be summoned to the residence of Sir Isaac Wake, the English Ambassador, in 1627,[2] where he would meet Duke Wolfgang Wilhelm, Count Palatine of the Rhine, and other eminent visitors. It goes without saying that the list of his achievements in this field of endeavour could be considerably augmented.

Dognazzi's talents were well known to Monteverdi and keenly appreciated by him, for the composer-priest had been active in Mantuan music since about 1603.[3] He was also appreciated by other courts and confraternities, as we know from the letter of Antonio Possevino concerning special Whitsuntide music at Ferrara in 1622.[4] Both Dognazzi and Monteverdi had served under Vincenzo, fourth duke of Mantua, whose early marriage to Margherita Farnese had been dissolved by Cardinal Borromeo because of the girl's apparent inability to have children. Although he acted against his better judgement, and behaved throughout the unpleasant negotiations with consideration, sympathy, and tact, he was certainly swayed by medical evidence as well as by his brief from Rome. Related to both the Gonzaga and the Farnese, Borromeo was certainly venerated by them, yet it was the Milanese who felt closest to him as their

[1] See Letters 82, 106. [2] See Letter 101.
[3] See the preface to his *Musiche varie da camera a cinque voci* (Magni, Venice, 1643).
[4] Bertolotti, 100.

protector and comforter in their darkest hour, when the plague struck the city in 1576. Thus it was that the Milanese living in Venice wished to honour the feast of their new saint with the best possible music, and Monteverdi desired as his chief assistant a man whom he knew and could trust.

[Address:] To the Most Illustrious Lord Count Alessandro Striggio

My Most Illustrious Lord and Most Respected Master,

The Milanese gentlemen very much want to engage Signor Don Francesco Dognazzi,[a] the better to celebrate their Feast of San Carlo[b] which will take place on the 4th of next month, but I want him more than they do because they have asked me to be in charge; and so, desiring to do ample justice to this, over and above the request of these gentlemen I add mine most affectionately, begging Your Lordship (should the opportunity arise in His Highness's[c] presence for an earnest request of that sort to allow him to come) to try and oblige me also—if I can be even more grateful for the infinite favours received from Your Lordship—in this matter of smoothing the way so that this Signor Don Francesco can come to Venice for a week, not more, and lodge in my house.

Dear and Most Illustrious Sir, forgive me for being such a nuisance,[d] for if it were not a pressing matter I would certainly not be so bold; because if I were to make a bundle of all the troubles I have given Your Lordship, and then look carefully at them, I would blush with shame. But necessity does not let me see this much at present, only that I know for sure I am Your Lordship's perpetually grateful servant, who with all reverence kisses your hands and prays God for your every happiness.

from Venice, 21 October [1620][e]
Your Most Illustrious Lordship's
most grateful servant
Claudio Monteverdi

[a] A priest-musician who had been appointed as Director of Music to Duke Ferdinando in 1619. See also Letters 19, 48, 63.

[b] San Carlo Borromeo, Bishop and Confessor, who had endeared himself to the Milanese through his courage and fortitude during the plague of 1576. He was canonized in 1610.

[c] Ferdinando, sixth Duke of Mantua.   [d] *mi perdoni per tanto incomodo.*

[e] The date has frequently been misread as 1621, but the autograph has *il 21 ottobre* only. That it belongs to 1620 is proved by Letter 63. Striggio's name is written in the bottom left-hand corner.

63

Venice, 31 October 1620
to Alessandro Striggio, at Mantua

Mantua, Archivio Gonzaga, Cassetta 6, fo. 243. Folio: 2 pp.

Malipiero, 218; Paoli, 184; Lax, 114

Monteverdi admits that ten days prior to writing the present letter, he had sent a request for Dognazzi's services not only to Striggio, but also to the man himself so that all concerned should be informed. Second thoughts on the matter have now convinced him that those requests were ill-timed, in view of the close proximity of All Saints' Day and All Souls' Day (1 and 2 November) to the Feast of S. Carlo Borromeo (4 November). He thanks Striggio and hopes to receive further commissions from him in the future. In the bottom left-hand corner of the letter, the inscription 'Sig. Ill. Conte Striggio' can still be seen.

[Address:] The Most Illustrious Lord Count Striggio

My Most Illustrious Lord, and Most Respected Master,

I wrote to Signor Don Francesco Dognazzi,[a] by the way, concerning the very same period of time about which I begged Your Lordship to help me in the presence of His Highness[b]—that he be so kind as to grant leave for a week to the said Signor Don Francesco in order that he might come over to Venice to assist[c] me on a feast-day, and I had a reply from Signor Don Francesco that it was impossible to get leave because of his responsibility for personally supervising His Highness's music; and since he has to perform music on All Saints' Day and All Souls' Day[d] it was (I repeat) impossible for him to leave such duty. After the letters were written and (truth to tell, Your Lordship) after having considered the fact that there

---

[a] Francesco Dognazzi was Director of Music at the court of Mantua.

[b] Ferdinando, sixth Duke of Mantua.

[c] *honorarmi* (in the sense of helping as well as honouring, since this was not a personal anniversary but a religious feast—that of S. Carlo Borromeo, 4 Nov.).

[d] These feasts are celebrated on 1 and 2 Nov.

were these two feast-days to be attended to, I suddenly became repentant, but I had already posted the letters.

I come, however, to offer the best thanks that I know, and of which I am capable, to Your Lordship's most gracious solicitude, through which you have shown that you are most ready and willing to honour me with the favour; and just as Blessèd God grants me the grace of so many obligations towards Your Lordship's person, so shall I pray Him that He may make me worthy of the possibility of deserving Your Lordship's commands.

These too I shall hope to receive when you know, by the results, that I am worthy of the opportunity to serve you, giving you my absolute assurance, however, that my good intent will never be surpassed by any other person who professes to love, honour, and serve you, with which intent also I pray God that He may long bless Your Lordship, whose hand I kiss.

from Venice, 31 October 1620

Your Most Illustrious Lordship's
most grateful servant
Claudio Monteverdi

64

Venice, 26 February 1621
to [Alessandro Striggio, at Mantua]

Mantua, Archivio Gonzaga, Cassetta 6, fo. 246. Folio: 1 p.

Malipiero, 219; Paoli, 186; Lax, 116

No letters survive from November and December of 1620, nor do the first eight weeks of the new year provide any correspondence containing details of carnival preparations. Quite possibly one or more of Monteverdi's letters to Striggio could have been mislaid or lost, for the present communication seems to refer to a work discussed at some previous date. It was a composition intended for carnival, in which the performers (like most of the audience) would wear masks. Some slight misunderstanding as regards the purpose of the work apparently prompted the composer's reassuring words, and with these his contact with Striggio comes to an end for a year and eight months. The explanation for this gap in their correspondence is almost certainly bound up with Striggio's frequent absences from Mantua in connection with the reopening in Rome of the Vincenzo–Isabella case. His place was ably taken by the younger but equally enthusiastic Ercole Marigliani.[1]

Although Ademollo dismisses the possibility of theatrical entertainments at Mantua during the carnival of 1621 because of the death of Pope Paul V on 28 January, he draws attention to the important role of music in the festivities that took place early in March.[2] These were intended to celebrate the election of Gregory V on 9 February, and the enthronement of Philip IV of Spain, who succeeded his father on 31 March. If the Gonzaga were a little late in paying joyful homage to the papacy, and somewhat anticipatory in their deference to Spain, they nevertheless found what they wanted in a new eclogue, *Licori, ovvero L'incanto d'amore*, specially written for them by Alessandro, the son of Battista Guarini.[3] Adriana Basile took part in it, together with the Duke's sisters Margherita and Eleonora. There is no proof that the music for this eclogue was Monteverdi's, although the reference to a carnival piece indicates that he might have been involved in something else planned for the same general occasion.

My Most Illustrious Lord and Most Respected Master,

I have taken note of what Your Lordship asked me to do in this matter;

---

[1] See Letters 66 and 68.　　[2] Ademollo, 270.　　[3] Ibid. 267.

that much I shall do. Your Lordship knows that I wrote the piece for carnival time so that you could, at your pleasure, have the whole thing in masks;[a] for I intended nothing other than what arose from Your Lordship's considerable prudence and will.

I beg you, with eager heart, to be so kind as to maintain me in that grace which (through your generosity) you have been so good as to offer me,[b] and to believe that I am Your Lordship's most devoted and most indebted servant of heartfelt loyalty, while with all true affection I pray God for Your Lordship's every perfect happiness and kiss your hands with all reverence.

from Venice, 26 February 1621
Your Most Illustrious Lordship's
most grateful servant
Claudio Monteverdi

[a] *mandar il tutto in maschera* (a reference to the festivals planned for the papal election and the enthronement of Philip IV of Spain).

[b] *condonarmi* (intensified from *donare*).

65

Venice, 5 March 1621
to [Caterina Medici Gonzaga,
Duchess of Mantua]

Mantua, Archivio Gonzaga, Cassetta 6, fo. 248. Folio: 1 p.

Malipiero, 219; Paoli, 187; Fabbri 1985, 241; Lax, 116

This is the second of Monteverdi's extant letters to Caterina Medici Gonzaga, Duchess of Mantua. Nearly a year had passed since her acceptance of a presentation copy of his Seventh Book of Madrigals, and during that time she probably listened to a number of them in performances by her court musicians.[1] More and more under the spell of Monteverdi's music, she began to take an almost personal interest in his career, even to the extent of helping his children with their education. But her husband, never a wholehearted supporter of Monteverdi (due to the tensions generated by the *fondo*), tended to seek new music from Florentine composers, and on at least one occasion went so far as to commission a Requiem Mass from the Flemish composer Guglielmo Dillen, Director of Music to the rival court of Parma.[2]

The brevity of the letter disguises its importance. Monteverdi thanks the Duchess for a new commission, hopes to prove himself worthy of it, and promises to send the music to Marigliani. The nature of the music is not mentioned until Letter 66, in which he tells Marigliani that certain scenic arias demand attention. Other arias have been allocated to Mantuan composers, and this fact suggests that we have a situation not unlike that of 1608 when Monteverdi was one of six composers whose task it was to set the prologue, intermezzi, and *licenza* written by Chiabrera to frame Guarini's play *L'Idropica*.

The term intermezzo is mentioned in Letter 68, and *licenza* in Letter 69; but no title is given, nor is there any direct reference to the author. No biography or critical study of Monteverdi has identified the work, although several go so far as to mention it in passing.[3] Yet the answer to the riddle was published as long ago as 1905, in the first volume of Angelo Solerti's *Gli albori del melodramma* (p. 120 n. 1), where reference is made to a printed account by Gabriel Bertazzolo of the wedding

---

[1] Ademollo, 270 n. 1, lists names and salaries.

[2] Bertolotti, 99. The Requiem was for Cosimo II de' Medici, who died on 28 Feb.

[3] Davari, 124, Schneider, 156; Prunières, 138 (who finds no proof of Ademollo's supposition that Monteverdi's music was used in the celebrations of 1620 [*recte* 1622], though in this case Ademollo's theory is supported by Solerti); Paoli, 240; Barblan, 'La vita', 103.

ceremonies in Mantua and Innsbruck for Eleonora Gonzaga and the Emperor Ferdinand II.

According to this description, the evening of 18 July 1622 was given up to a performance of Marigliani's play *Le tre costanti*, the text of which was published by the ducal printers Aurelio and Lodovico Osanna in the same year. Solerti adds that Marigliani also wrote a prologue, four intermezzi, and a *licenza*, all of which were set to music ('andavano tutti cantati') in order to provide contrast to the spoken dialogue of the play itself. The theme of this extra material deals with the disagreements between heavenly love, represented by Reason, and earthly love, portrayed as Sentiment.

The prologue concerns itself with a struggle between Love and Cupid, presumably in the sense of lofty emotion versus blind passion, and the four intermezzi introduce four different couples from mythology: *Alcide e Onfale*; *Nettuno e Amfitrite*; *Borea e Orizia*; *Plutone e Proserpina*. The *licenza* begins with the Triumph of Cupid (soon to be struck by a shaft of lightning hurled by Jove) and continues with the triumph of Love, which leads to a ballet culminating in an allegorical finale in praise of the Habsburgs. This was exactly the kind of entertainment required for such an occasion, and the musicians would have had little or no difficulty in doing justice to it.

Monteverdi's part in this elaborate stage work is nowhere clearly defined, for his letters mention only the third intermezzo and the *licenza*. Perhaps the other four sections were allocated to Dognazzi and his colleagues, as is suggested by the reference to 'those gentlemen composers who are on hand'. And in any event the music seems not to have survived, so that these newly identified works of the master can only be added to the growing list of lost music.

Most Serene Lady and Most Respected Patroness,

I received Your Highness's command with such solace that I admit to not having words capable of expressing the happiness within me, being the recipient of so remarkable a favour. I come in all humility to offer Your Highness the greatest thanks I can utter, praying God that He make me as worthy of the undertaking in Your Highness's estimation, as He has made me worthy of the command.

I shall be sending the music to Signor Marigliani,[a] Your Highness's most worthy secretary, from whom also I shall continue to hear what Your Highness will command. Making a most humble reverence to you with

---

[a] Ercole Marigliani, court secretary, ducal councillor, and librettist of *Le tre costanti* (the work referred to here, for the first time, though without designation).

deepest humility, I pray God with all my heart for your every true happiness.

from Venice, 5 March 1621
Your Most Serene Highness's
most humble and most grateful servant
Claudio Monteverdi

66

Venice, 17 April 1621
to Ercole Marigliani, at Mantua

Mantua, Archivio Gonzaga, Cassetta 6, fo. 250. Folio: 2 pp.

Malipiero, 220; Paoli, 188; Fabbri 1985, 241; Lax, 117

Monteverdi's first extant letter to Ercole Marigliani is dated 15 February 1620 (no.44); this is his second, and a third follows in September 1621, after which the correspondence lapses for four years. He still remains closer to Striggio, although he now sets not his libretti but those of the younger secretary. Marigliani has assigned certain arias to Monteverdi, keeping others for the Mantuan composers because careful timing is necessary in view of the important role played by the stage-machines. The word *machine* in this letter has been usually misread as *maschere*, thus obscuring the point of this logical division of labour. But the music for these intermezzi was set aside for a much more urgent task—Monteverdi's contribution to the memorial service for Cosimo II, Grand Duke of Tuscany, who died on 28 February.

[Address:] My Lord Ercole Marigliani

My Very Illustrious*ᵃ* Lord and Most Esteemed Master,

I had a communication from Your Very Illustrious Lordship to the effect that it would be sufficient if I worked only on certain scenic arias,*ᵇ* since with regard to certain others (which ought to have a definite order and duration for as long as the machines*ᶜ* are operating) you have been pleased to give this task to those gentlemen composers who are on hand; besides which you also told me that you felt that I could have until September of this year.

Because of this I sent nothing by the last post, nor indeed (on account of there being such pressure on my time) am I sending anything at the moment, as I am holding over the special tasks until twenty or more days

---

ᵃ The abbreviation *Illʳᵉ* is accidentally repeated.   *ᵇ* *canti rapresentativi* (for *Le tre costanti*).

ᶜ The autograph clearly has *machine*, referring to the stage-machines whose noises the music was expected to cover.

from now, due to the pressure I am now under because of the Requiem Mass*d* for the Most Serene Grand Duke,*e* which has to take place soon for the colony of Florentine gentlemen in Venice, who are preparing worthy and well-thought-out ceremonies.

Dear Sir, please see if you can obtain this concession from His Highness,*f* for I promise you that I shall do perhaps more than you think I can, because a free and willing mind can achieve much in a short time. And believe me, you will certainly not have to wait for me in vain: it is enough if I know the deadline, for then I can go on planning absolutely to time.*g*

Forgive me, for the love of God, and continue to maintain me in His Highness's good books, and you will find and see from the results that neither shall I have too much time, nor shall I have held up the project for nothing. I know you wish me well, and I know that you will be rewarded by my trust and my promise, which I shall carry out within the agreed time-limit. I remain Signor Marigliani's servant and pray for him every true happiness, while I kiss his hands.

from Venice, 17 April*h* 1621

Your Very Illustrious Lordship's

most grateful servant

Claudio Monteverdi

---

d This took place on 25 May, at SS. Giovanni e Paolo.   *e* Cosimo II de' Medici.

f Ferdinando Gonzaga, sixth Duke of Mantua.   *g* a ponto a tempo.

h The date has been changed from 27 to 17, and the right-hand corner of the letter is heavily discoloured. The addressee's name is, however, clearly visible at the bottom left.

67

Venice, 7 August 1621
to [Caterina Medici Gonzaga,
Duchess of Mantua]

Mantua, Archivio Gonzaga, Cassetta 6, fo. 252. Folio: 2 pp.

Vogel, 434; Prunières, 262; Malipiero, 221; Paoli, 190; Fabbri 1985, 244; Lax, 119

Monteverdi was nothing if not a conscientious father, but he seems to have been subject to mild confusion, from time to time, in the matter of the age of his two sons. This letter to the Duchess of Mantua gives Massimiliano's age as $16\frac{1}{2}$, whereas in fact it was 17 years and 3 months. The boy was ready to proceed to a course of higher education, and a suitable path had to be prepared with the aid of influential assistance. By this time, Monteverdi had met Cardinal Montalto on several occasions—when he was in Rome in 1610, probably in Florence where dignitaries and musicians came together for festive and artistic events, and in Bologna, where the Cardinal served as papal legate. Although a direct application for a place in the Cardinal's college might have been in order, Monteverdi preferred to approach the matter through his new patroness, whose recommendation would naturally carry considerable weight.

Alessandro Peretti Damascene, who rose to the highest degree of affluence on his appointment as Vice-Chancellor of the Roman Curia in 1589, was born in modest if not humble circumstances in 1560, his father being Fabio Damascene and his mother Maria Felice Peretti-Mignucci. She was the daughter of Camilla, sister of Pope Sixtus V, whose accession in 1585 guaranteed (as was customary) high offices for his relatives. Alessandro, a mere 25 years of age, was created Cardinal *in prima promotione* on 13 May 1585, and from then onwards his career was assured.

Generous almost to a fault, Cardinal Montalto gained fame throughout Italy as an enlightened patron of the arts and an unsurpassed paragon of hospitality. Ottavio Gentile, the Mantuan agent entrusted with the safe conduct of Adriana Basile on her northbound journey in 1610, wrote to Cardinal Ferdinando Gonzaga from Bracciano about the hospitality lavished upon the party by the Orsini—it was, he said, up to the standard of Cardinal Montalto.[1] His patronage of composers was rewarded in the traditional manner by dedications, including those of Felice Anerio (1590), Sebastian

---

[1] Ademollo, 134.

[238]

Raval (1593), Massimiano Gabbiani (1604), G. B. Nanino (1612), Carlo Fiorillo (1616), Pietro Pace (1617), and G. C. Bianchi (1620).

Doubtless Monteverdi would have dedicated something to him, if only as a gesture of appreciation for so graciously granting Massimiliano a place in his college, but not long after this event—on 2 June 1623—the Cardinal died from a surfeit of cold beverages and ice-cream, much to the sorrow of all who knew him.[2] His passing deprived the world of a generous patron who was more than an amateur, for he enjoyed performing music as singer and harpsichordist. Vincenzo Giustiniani mentions him twice in his *Discorso sopra la musica*,[3] listing first of all some of the virtuosi whom he supported in his splendid palazzo at the Chancellery:

> he played the Cembalo excellently and sang in a sweet and sensitive manner; and he had in his house many professional musicians who were far from mediocre. Among them were the Cavaliere del Leuto and Scipione Dentici del Cembalo, both excellent players and composers; and then also Orazio [Michi], a rare performer on the Double Harp; and for singers he had Onofrio Gualfreducci, a eunuch, Ippolita [Marotta] Napoletana, and Melchior [Palantrotti] Basso, and many others for whom he provided generously.

Giustiniani adds a further brief mention of the Cardinal's musical abilities in his discussion of 'singing with grace', which he defines as the close observation of the styles and rules of singing, resulting in pleasure and delight for the listener: 'Cardinal Montalto . . . played and sang with much grace and feeling, even though his appearance was more Martial than Apollonian, and who had a scratchy voice, as we say'. In other words, he did not possess a suave and beautiful voice, but he made excellent use of what he had. Such a man could not fail to take an interest in Monteverdi, and if circumstances precluded his helping the composer in Rome, he more than made up for this in Bologna.[4] And it was as well that Monteverdi asked for assistance when he did.

It will be noted that this letter contains no reference to the composition of the intermezzi, which had been put on one side because of the urgent task of writing, rehearsing, and performing the Requiem Mass for Cosimo II, Grand Duke of Tuscany, who had died on 28 February.[5] The ceremony took place on Tuesday, 25 May, at SS. Giovanni e Paolo, and the Florentine poet Giulio Strozzi, who was later to collaborate with Monteverdi, wrote and delivered the funeral oration. This and his description of the entire event appears in a small volume printed by Ciotti (Venice, 1621) with the title *Esequie fatte in Venetia della Natione Fiorentina al Serenissimo Don Cosimo II, Quarto Gran Duca di Toscana*. As usual in such cases, the printed word survives, but the music is lost.

The ceremony must have been a lengthy one, since it comprised numerous polyphonic works, some plainchant, various liturgical prayers, and the funeral oration. Strozzi mentions ten categories of music, either by genre or by incipit; and since these

---

[2] See Briccio, *passim*.   [3] Giustiniani, 71, 74.
[4] Vecchi, 82.   [5] Not April, as in Vogel, 376.

have not hitherto been discussed in any detail, the following account may clarify matters to some extent.

ORDER OF SERVICE

Sinfonia (in the Mixolydian mode)	Monteverdi
Motet, *O vos omnes*	Monteverdi
Introit, *Requiem aeternam*	Monteverdi
Kyrie	Grillo
Graduale, *Requiem aeternam*	Usper
Tract, *Absolve Domine*	Usper
Sequence, *Dies irae*	Monteverdi
Psalm-motet, *De profundis*	Monteverdi
Offertory, *Domine Jesu*	Grillo
Sanctus and Benedictus	? Monteverdi
Agnus Dei	? Monteverdi
Communion, *Lux aeterna*	? Monteverdi
Responsory 1, *Subvenite Sancti Dei*	Monteverdi
2, *Qui Lazarum*	Monteverdi
3, *Domine quando veneris*	Monteverdi
4, *Ne recorderis*	Monteverdi
5, *Libera me Domine*	Monteverdi

The first three items appear to have formed a unit, for Strozzi tells us that the sorrowful and pathetic mood of the Sinfonia recurred as the instruments played again during the Introit. Monteverdi took part in this ensemble as one of the viola da braccio players.[6] His son Francesco, recently returned from the Carmelite House in Milan, sang the introductory motet and the Introit. The form could have been as follows:

Sinfonia; *O vos omnes*; Sinfonia; *Requiem aeternam*; Sinfonia; *Te decet hymnus*; Sinfonia; *Requiem aeternam*.

The repeats of the Sinfonia may have been shortened versions of the opening statement, depending on the structure of the piece and the time available. *O vos omnes* can be classified as an occasional motet, taking as its point of departure the Holy Saturday antiphon beginning with the same words. Monteverdi's motet follows a slightly different course from that of its well-known model:

(a) Holy Saturday antiphon: *O vos omnes, qui transitis per viam,*
(b) Text of solo motet: *O vos omnes,*
(a) *attendite, et videte si est dolor sicut dolor meus.*
(b) *attendite et videte   dolorem nostrum.*

Whereas the antiphon leads directly into the psalm *Laudate Dominum*, the motet continues with a text that is not liturgical at all, though nothing could more appropriately express the emotions of those in attendance: *Pupilli facti sumus absque patre* ('We are orphans and fatherless') from Lam. 5:3.

---

[6] Barblan, 'La vita', 103 (but compare Vogel, 377 n. 2).

The two contributions by Giovanni Battista Grillo, who is mentioned obliquely in Letter 76, and the two by Usper appear to have suffered the same fate as the music specially written by Monteverdi. As regards *De profundis*, this psalm is traditionally not said on the day of death or of burial; but since the service ranked as a memorial, there would be no reason to exclude it.[7] It is not clear as to who wrote the Sanctus and Benedictus, Agnus Dei, and Communion, but these items too may have been Monteverdi's, since he is named as the principal composer of the Requiem. Additional proof of the fact that he had a possibly new polyphonic mass available later in the year may be gathered from Letter 69, in which he offers the Duchess of Mantua 'una messa sollenne in musica', but whether parts of this originally belonged to the Requiem is a matter for conjecture.

On the subject of the responsories (Strozzi definitely uses the plural form) there seems to be some divergence from the normal custom at an Absolution when the body of the deceased is not present. At such a service, the responsory *Libera me Domine* is sung after Mass, when the celebrant has approached the catafalque. No further responsory occurs, although there are brief responses to the verses sung by the priest; for instance—V. *Requiescat in pace.* R. *Amen.* Could Strozzi have confused responsory and response? And would such short phrases have been considered worthy of setting to music? It is surely more likely that the form for a solemn funeral service was adopted, with five responsories, since the memorial concerned a grand duke; and if this were the case, the five compositions would have been based on the texts indicated above, in the Order of Service.

If Monteverdi really had to compose thirteen works for the Requiem Mass, his concern as shown in Letter 66 can easily be understood, for over and above the creative aspect of the undertaking, he was deeply involved as an executant and as director. But the finer details may never be known. All we do know is that a considerable amount of apparently remarkable music was written, only to be relegated to the archive of the basilica or the apartment in the canonry where Monteverdi lived; and after his death the music disappeared without trace.

Most Serene Lady and Most Respected Patroness,

Most Serene Lady, I have a son[a] aged 16 and a half years—a subject and most humble servant of Your Highness—who has now left the seminary at Bologna, having completed there the course in humanistic studies and rhetoric. I would like him to go on to the other sciences in order to obtain a Doctorate in Medicine. He has always been under the discipline of tutors who have kept him in the fear of God and on the right lines of study.

[7] Paoli, *Monteverdi*, 242.

[a] Massimiliano, who later practised medicine in Mantua.

Considering his liveliness and the licentious freedom of students (because of which fact they fall oftentimes into bad company, which diverts them from the rightful path, causing great sorrow to their fathers and tremendous loss to themselves), and in order to ward off the great harm that could come about, I thought that a place in the college of the Most Illustrious Lord Cardinal Montalto[b]—which he has in Bologna—would be a real boon to me, and the salvation of my son; but without a royal hand to aid me in so great a need it would not be possible for me to obtain such an outstanding favour.

Knowing therefore that Your Highness is by nature a princess full of infinite kindness towards everyone, in particular towards her respectful subjects, as is this poor boy, and to servants (though lowly) like myself, I have on this account been so bold as to beg Your Highness with most heartfelt sincerity (as I am doing) and with the most humble respect of which I am capable, that you may be so kind as to write to the said Cardinal Montalto in recommendation of such a place for the afore-mentioned son in the aforesaid college in Bologna, so that he may receive so lofty a favour.

But if at present all the places are filled, the first vacancy would still be in time. I beg Your Highness to forgive me for being too bold, while with deepest reverence I bow to you and pray with all my heart for your perfect happiness.

from Venice, 7 August 1621

Your Most Serene Highness's

most humble and most grateful servant

Claudio Monteverdi

[b] Grand-nephew of Pope Sixtus V, and a patron of music.

68

Venice, 10 September 1621
to Ercole Marigliani, at Mantua

Mantua, Archivio Gonzaga, Cassetta 6, fo. 254. Folio: 2 pp. Enclosure: part of intermezzo *Borea e Orizia*

Prunières, 263; Malipiero, 222; Paoli, 192; Lax, 120

The form of the opening salutation, suggesting Marigliani as the recipient of this letter, is confirmed by the appearance of his name in the lower left-hand corner. Composition of the intermezzi had apparently been delayed by unspecified commitments during the previous ten days. One of them may have been the rehearsal and performance of special music for the Feast of the Nativity of the B.V.M. on 8 September. The other was a domestic matter discussed but not defined— Massimiliano went down with a serious fever on 3 or 4 September, and two days later *varole* (pockmarks or spots) began to break out. If the fever was bad enough to send the boy to bed, he could have been suffering from an attack of measles, which often happened (and still does) to young people in the autumn or winter. The appearance of a rash after a few days would seem to confirm this condition, which seems to have been made slightly more bearable by the good news from Bologna about the strong likelihood of a place in Cardinal Montalto's college.

Monteverdi somehow managed to send, with this letter, the first part of the third intermezzo for *Le tre costanti*. Its title, *Borea e Orizia*, indicates that the tale as told by Marigliani leaned heavily upon the old legend of Boreas, the north wind, carrying off Orithyia (daughter of Erechtheus, king of Athens) as she was crossing the river Ilissus. Although at first she rejected his advances, her resistance gradually weakened and she became the mother of Cleopatra, Chione, Zetus, and Calais. The second instalment is promised by the next post (18 September) but no letter survives with this date. On 23 September Massimiliano recovered sufficiently to be able to compose a poem by way of thanks to Alessandro Striggio for using his influence—presumably in the matter of the place at Bologna, where the persuasive pen of the Duchess had already made its mark. The expectation of an early reply from the Cardinal proved to be mere wishful thinking, but the certificate of entrance did finally arrive in February of the following year.

[Address:] My Lord Ercole Marigliani

My Very Illustrious Lord and Most Esteemed Master,

By the present post I am sending off to you part of the third musical intermezzo.[a] The remainder (if it please God) I hope to send you by the next post. My commitments over the past week and part of the present week have hindered my ability—but certainly not my most ready willingness—to serve you, for which I beg you to consider me worthy of an excuse.

I heard from Bologna that Cardinal Montalto[b] has already received Her Highness's[c] request with especial pleasure, and I am told they regard it as certain that I shall be granted this favour. The reply, it is thought, will be received either by this post, or by the next, without fail. When it arrives, I pray you let me know of His Eminence's good disposition, so that I may be comforted.

I have passed on to the boy the news that I received and he felt very happy about it. He is still in a state of having to cheer himself up a little, because a week ago he went to bed with a very high fever, and two days later spots began to break out, and now it is at its worst. Nevertheless, we hope for good results in a short time, if it please God, because they have come to the surface very nicely[d] so that inside he feels all right; and I hope they may act as a really good purge for him.

Nothing remains but for me to kiss your hands with heartfelt sincerity and pray God for your every happiness.

from Venice, 10 September 1621
Your Very Illustrious Lordship's
most grateful servant
Claudio Monteverdi

---

[a] *Borea e Orizia*, from *Le tre costanti*.

[b] Grand-nephew of Pope Sixtus V, and a patron of music.

[c] Caterina Medici Gonzaga.

[d] *molto bene* (*molto* is almost illegible, near the right-hand edge of the page). Monteverdi must have written the letter on a folded sheet, of which he later tore off the right-hand part. The name of the addressee is in the lower left-hand corner.

69

Venice, 27 November 1621
to [Caterina Medici Gonzaga,
Duchess of Mantua]

Mantua, Archivio Gonzaga, Cassetta 6, fo. 258. Folio: 1 p.

Prunières, 263; Malipiero, 224; Paoli, 194; Fabbri 1985, 241; Lax, 121

Monteverdi, having heard nothing from the Duchess about the place for his son Massimiliano in Cardinal Montalto's college, writes to remind her of his constant concern for the musical needs of the House of Gonzaga, the most recent evidence of which has been the dispatch of the final item (*licenza*) for *Le tre costanti*. The function of a *licenza*, besides serving as an epilogue to a stage work, was to make special reference to some ceremonial event such as a patron's birthday or wedding. In this case it was the marriage of Eleonora Gonzaga (sister of the reigning Duke) to the Emperor Ferdinand II, and accordingly the grand finale culminated in an allegorical *gloria* celebrating the Habsburgs.[1] Presumably Monteverdi's task was to compose recitatives and arias for Cupid, Jove, and Amore, followed by a ballet, all of which perished in the sack of Mantua decreed by the weak-minded Emperor in whose honour this expensive entertainment had been devised.[2]

The music, sent to Marigliani on 20 November, may have been accompanied by a covering letter, but this seems not to have survived. No further materials being required, Monteverdi offered the Duchess a mass, the archives being silent with regard to her acceptance or rejection.

Most Serene Lady, and Most Respected Patroness,

By the previous post I sent off to Signor Marigliani the musical

[1] The published version of the play contains no intermezzi; but the following stanza, which appears at the very end, may have been set to music:

> Lodi si dieno a Ciel
> e gioiscano i cuori;
> non sia chi de prima
> l'animo per colpi di fortuna contraria
> confidi, speri, nè si confonda
> perchè e virtù nell'avversità esse costante.

[2] A proxy marriage took place in Mantua on 21 Nov., according to a letter written by the Duke to his mother on that day (Ademollo, 268).

licenza[a] for the intermezzi which Your Highness was good enough to commission from me, and I asked for a further chance to be able to busy myself. His Lordship answered that he wanted nothing more at the moment. However I come with this letter of mine to Your Highness's feet, to thank you from the bottom of my heart for the honour received from this Your Highness's commission, offering myself to you as a most humble servant were it to happen that these intermezzi might be performed for you, both in the matter of scoring[b] for the instruments in symphonies and in the various vocal dispositions.[c]

Nor should I neglect to offer at the same time to Your Highness's infinite humanity a solemn mass set to music, if perhaps it might please you to accept it. But even if Your Highness commands nothing more, I beg you—with the most humble respect of which I am aware and capable[d]—to be so kind as to keep me among the number of those very humble, indeed, but genuinely devoted and respectful servants of Your Highness, to whom with the deepest possible respect I bow most humbly, and pray God with all my heart for your every perfect happiness.

from Venice, 27 November 1621

Your Most Serene Highness's

most humble and most grateful servant

Claudio Monteverdi

[a] A musical epilogue to a stage work, usually referring to the celebration of some special event.
[b] *nella variatione de istrumenti.*   [c] *proprietate de voci.*   [d] *ch'io so et posso.*

70

Venice, 26 February 1622
to [Caterina Medici Gonzaga,
Duchess of Mantua]

Mantua, Archivio Gonzaga, Cassetta 6, fo. 261. Folio: 1 p.

Malipiero, 225; Paoli, 195; Lax, 122

Massimiliano, having secured a place at Cardinal Montalto's college in Bologna, began a four-year course of medical study which ended early in 1626. On 19 March of that year he received from his father a letter of recommendation to Striggio (Letter 88), and took it with him to Mantua together with other letters whose purpose it was to introduce him to courtly circles. Monteverdi's gratitude is expressed not only in the present letter, but also in the next one, enclosed with an unusual gift.

In the mean time, *Le tre costanti* had been performed, presumably under the direction of Dognazzi, the new *maestro di cappella*. Although Monteverdi had offered his services in this regard, there is no indication that he travelled to Mantua either to direct the music or to listen to it. Music for the carnival had already been commissioned from Marco da Gagliano in Florence: on 31 January he sent two acts of his *Medoro* to the Duchess, the remainder following on 7 February.[1]

Most Serene Lady and Most Respected Patroness,

I have finally received, Most Serene Lady, through the supreme kindness of Your Highness, that blessing from God which my heart has so long desired and sought after with such passion—the certificate allowing Massimiliano, my son and Your Highness's most humble subject, to enter the college of His Eminence Cardinal Montalto in Bologna.

If I wanted to rely on words, Most Serene Lady, to render those due thanks which so great a favour deserves, I confess that I could not find within myself a support fit for such a weight; and even if I wanted to display my talents (which I know to be most feeble) at Your Highness's feet, it would be in vain to offer anything to Your Highness.

[1] Davari, 125.

All that I shall do is to offer prayers to God on high with a true and thankful heart, that He may always be so good as to ensure that the Most Serene House of Gonzaga, my fair sponsor,[a] is protected and blessed by His divine grace, and in particular Your Highness, to whom with the deepest respect I bow to the ground.

from Venice, 26 February 1622

Your Most Serene Highness's

most humble and most grateful servant

Claudio Monteverdi

[a] *mia padrona et signora*. These words are the same as those used for the Duchess, but they refer here to the House of Gonzaga.

71

Venice, 15 April 1622
to [Caterina Medici Gonzaga,
Duchess of Mantua]

Mantua, Archivio Gonzaga, Cassetta 6, fo. 263. Folio: 1 p.

Prunières, 264; Malipiero, 225; Paoli, 197; Lax, 123

With this brief but touching letter, Monteverdi's extant correspondence with Caterina Medici Gonzaga comes to an end. She had accepted the dedication of *Concerto*, sent him a valuable necklace by way of thanks, commissioned music for Marigliani's intermezzi, and helped to obtain a place at Bologna for Massimiliano. But there is no evidence that she displayed any interest in the *messa solenne* offered to her in November 1621. No further commissions materialized, and in consequence Monteverdi was hard put to it to express his gratitude for her generous intercession with Cardinal Montalto.

If music, which was never wanting at the Gonzaga court, now seemed inappropriate or superfluous, what would please her most? If she were a Gonzaga, she might have evinced a partiality for dwarfs; but she came from a princely house of somewhat more wholesome tastes. The answer came from Alexandria, where Monteverdi's brother-in-law had been engaged in missionary work for the Capuchin order. Friar Cesare, doubtless a formidable advocate of proselytization among the crowds that thronged the multi-national Egyptian seaport, nevertheless found time to acquire a small monkey whose fur was remarkable for its colour and texture.

On his return to Venice, he handed over this charming creature to Monteverdi, who presumably had to find room for it in the canonry of St Mark's, where he lived. The incongruity of this arrangement must have convinced others besides the composer that it might be better to give the monkey to someone capable of looking after it in larger premises. But how it reached Mantua, together with the letter, is nowhere explained. Perhaps the good friar took it with him on a visit to his father, Giacomo Cattaneo, one or the other of them being responsible for appearing at court with this unusual gift. One hopes that the Duchess enjoyed its company.

Most Serene Lady and Most Respected Patroness,

The Reverend Father Friar Cesare (my brother-in-law)[a] having given

---

[a] In Letters 15 and 18 he is simply mentioned as 'my brother-in-law the Capuchin'. He was the brother of Monteverdi's wife Claudia and the son of Giacomo Cattaneo.

me—on his return from Alexandria in Egypt—a small young monkey[b] which has been praised by gentlemen for the unusual appearance of its fur, I have therefore been encouraged to come to Your Highness's feet with all reverent affection, begging you that you may deign to be so kind as to accept it.

I know that it ought to be much more beautiful, the more to satisfy Your Highness's most noble taste, but trusting in your infinite humanity, I likewise hope that you will honour me by accepting (in lieu of this)[c] my respectful intent, which with the greatest possible warmth of emotion prays God that He may always bless Your Highness, and with the very greatest respect bows to you.

from Venice, 15 April 1622
Your Most Serene Highness's
most humble and most grateful servant
Claudio Monteverdi

[b] *simiottino.*   [c] In lieu of this greater beauty.

72

Venice, 21 October 1622
to [Alessandro Striggio, at Mantua]

Mantua, Archivio Gonzaga, Cassetta 6, fos. 265–6. Bifolio: 4 pp.

Prunières, 264; Malipiero, 226; Paoli, 198; Fabbri 1985, 245; Lax, 124

On the whole, the year 1622 proved to be an unusually pleasant one for the Duke and Duchess of Mantua, thanks to the imperial boost given to the reputation of their House, and this feeling of buoyancy and success can be felt even in the correspondence that reached the court from musicians in Modena, Ferrara, and Vienna. Everybody suddenly wanted to compose music in praise of the Duke, or dedicate to him any songs and madrigals that happened to be available. Erasmus de Sayve, a member of the chapel of Ferdinand II, wrote from Vienna offering two compositions in honour of the Emperor and Empress that might not displease so near a relative of the recently married couple.[1] And a more illustrious member of the same chapel, Giovanni Valentini (a former pupil of Giovanni Gabrieli), sent a letter to the Duke from Vienna[2] with a copy of his latest publication—the *Musiche a doi voci* of 1622, complete with a flowery dedication.

From Ferrara came a request to borrow the services of Don Francesco Dognazzi for the consecration of a new church built at the instance of the confraternity of the Holy Spirit,[3] while from Modena a book of theorbo music was sent for the Duke's delectation by Bellerofonte Castaldi.[4] Yet another musical offering from Vienna, duly dedicated to the Duke, was the *Musiche concertate* of Giovanni de Prioli, who—because he was detained at Ödenburg (now Sopron, in Hungary)—entrusted its delivery to the singer Francesco Campagnolo, one of Monteverdi's former students.[5]

Domestic affairs were also looking a little brighter for the Gonzaga, in spite of the long drawn-out affair between Vincenzo and Isabella.[6] Camilla Fàa, whose clandestine marriage to the Duke had been dissolved five years previously, took the veil at Ferrara and vanished from the scene, although her insistence on signing herself as Sister Camilla Gonzaga produced occasional stings of remorse and annoyance.[7]

As for Monteverdi, he decided (or was persuaded) to take a purge in the early part of October, but the illness or side-effects of the cure remained with him until the following February, as may be gathered from Letter 78. He was certainly unwell on Tuesday, 18 October, when Lorenzo Giustiniani and several of his friends came to

---

[1] Bertolotti, 100.   [2] Ibid. 99.   [3] Ibid. 100.   [4] Ibid. 99.
[5] Ibid. 101.   [6] Errante, 'Il processo', 680.   [7] Ademollo, 228.

visit him, hoping to obtain assistance—with the cooperation of Alessandro Striggio—
in the matter of arranging a series of plays to be given by a company of actors known
as I Fedeli.[8]

Giustiniani's interests lay more in the theatre than in music, but since the two
arts—already so closely connected—were soon to become even more entwined and
interdependent, he felt a great admiration for Monteverdi, who was later to compose
the music for Strozzi's *Proserpina rapita*, performed in 1630 on the occasion of
Guistiniani's marriage to Giustiniana, daughter of Girolamo Mocenigo. Who better
than the Director of Music at St Mark's and the composer of *Orfeo* to intercede with
the librettist of that opera, now a count and a highly placed official at the court of
Mantua?

Giovanni Battista Andreini's company, I Fedeli, had last appeared in Venice in
1619.[9] Their subsequent career had taken them to Paris and Fontainebleau (6–28
April 1621) where they reaped both artistic success and financial rewards. But the
jealousies and rivalries that split the company as long ago as 1609, when trouble had
arisen at Turin between Andreini's wife, 'Florinda', and Pier Maria Cecchini's wife,
'Flaminia', proved to be needless thorns in the side of their leader, who as an author
and actor had better things to do than attend to what Monteverdi describes as 'sinistri
acadere et disturbi'.

A typical crisis occurred just after the success at Fontainebleau, when Louis XIII
requested the entire company to stay on for another year. All agreed except for
Tristano Martinelli.[10] After joining the company in 1612 he had brought to perfection
the role of Arlecchino, one of the two *zanni* characters whose task it was to provide
witty and amorous intrigue. Unlike the others, he wanted to return to his home in
Mantua and take a well-earned rest. The King granted him leave of absence, and the
queen gave him a necklace worth 200 scudi.

An application to the Duke of Mantua for a year's leave so that the company could
remain in Paris was also granted, but it was at this juncture that trouble began. An
incriminatory report, seven pages long, was laboriously drawn up, signed by the entire
company, and sent to the Duke with the object of discrediting Martinelli, accusing
him of disloyalty, and proving that he used the same tactics when he was a member of
the rival company headed by Pier Maria Cecchini, whose stage name was 'Fritellino'.

A few days later, on 12 July 1621, Andreini wrote a personal letter to the Duke
begging him to disregard the report and have it destroyed. He emphasized the point
that since Martinelli had been working for forty years, he had a right to enjoy a little
peace and quiet. But he did not in fact retire. After visiting Lyons and Turin (where
the company followed him for the Easter festivities of 1623) he appeared later in
Padua, Verona, and Venice.

---

[8] See Baschet, 285 ff.; Rasi, 117 ff. The best summary of the activities, travels, and troubles of I Fedeli
is still that of Kathleen M. Lea, i. 281–92.

[9] Santoro, *Iconografia*, 27.

[10] A famous portrait of Martinelli by Feti was mistaken in 1966 for a likeness of Monteverdi. The
confusion is discussed in Askew, 60–3.

The result of all this was that the company was in poor shape when it returned to Italy in the summer of 1622, at the end of the year's leave. An attempt to replace Martinelli and another member of the troupe by a pair of Spanish actors met with no success. Without Martinelli they were demoralized; with him they were unable to stop fighting each other. And it was at this point that Lorenzo Giustiniani, faced with a confusing and seemingly irreconcilable situation, turned to Monteverdi for assistance.

He should have guessed that it would take more than diplomacy to solve the problem. Andreini would come only if Martinelli also agreed to join him. Martinelli would come only if a certain actor[11] specializing in the role of Dr Gratiano, the Bolognese lawyer, agreed to join him. Virginia Andreini did not wish to act at all, because of the discord within the company. But Giustiniani's plan was to offer special inducements to the Andreinis, and if necessary supply the missing roles of Arlecchino (Zanni) and the Doctor (Gratiano).

One possible way of solving this theatrical puzzle was to engage, or if necessary kidnap, the elusive 'Dr Gratiano' who was then wandering through Savoy into Italy. If he consented to come and act in Venice, Martinelli would also consent, and in turn Andreini, who might even persuade his wife to change her mind. Nevertheless the operation promised to be tricky and subtle. Monteverdi's excitement is betrayed not only by his phrasing of the request but by his obvious concern to please Giustiniani, and the difficulties encountered in understanding the letter have been increased by two of the standard transcriptions.[12] But as this particular series of letters unfolds, the situation gradually becomes more clear, offering the reader a glimpse (from the wings) of a *commedia* not without its own peculiar brand of cloak-and-dagger intrigue.[13]

My Most Illustrious Lord and Most Respected Master,

Three days ago the Most Illustrious Signor Giustiniani,[a] a gentleman of great authority in this Most Serene Republic and a very good patron of mine, paid a special visit to my house in company with many other very distinguished gentlemen, to tell me how only a few days previously he

---

[11] Almost certainly Francesco Scattolone, who was met at Padua by a Mantuan factotum about the third week in November, and returned with him to the Gonzaga court (Bertolotti, 101). He is also identified by Rasi, ii. 525; and by Lea, i. 483.

[12] Both Malipiero and Paoli read the phrase *che Arlichino dicesse di sì* as if it were *che Arlichino non . . .* , due to the slight separation of *Arlichi* and *no* in the autograph.

[13] Giustiniani was certainly not unacquainted with the trials and frustrations of dealing with actors and their rival companies. In 1619 he attempted to engage Flaminio Scala, but soon found that a counter-offer had been made by a member of the Troni family. In the following year he seems to have been in negotiation with Cecchini and Aurelio, sworn enemies of the Andreini group (Lea, i. 289, 308).

[a] Lorenzo Giustiniani, who in 1630 married the daughter of Monteverdi's patron and benefactor, Girolamo Mocenigo.

arranged for an invitation to be written to Signor Lelio Andreini[b] the actor, so that he might make himself available—together with Signora Florinda and all his company—to come to Venice and produce plays for the general public;[c] provided however that the Duke[d] did not wish to make use of him, for in such a case he would in no wise wish to negotiate.

He received a reply to the effect that Andreini was as ready as could be; all the more so because the Lord Duke had already let it be known that he would not wish to make use of him. The only thing lacking was for Arlecchino[e] to say yes, for without this—to avoid loss of reputation through having to act in the place where Fritellino[f] was also acting (even though in another hall)—he could not agree to come. So, this most illustrious gentleman had a letter sent to the said Arlecchino, and received a reply saying that if His Highness were not making use of him, and would grant him official leave also, he would come on the understanding that a certain Doctor Gratiano,[g] who is now in Savoy, were to come.

But while this gentleman is trying by negotiation to set everything straight, lo and behold Signor Lelio writes him a letter, saying that as far as he is concerned personally he stands in complete readiness to be of service, and that he offers himself as a most humble servant, but neverthe-less makes it known to His Lordship that Signora Florinda does not wish to act, and that he has got it into his head to perform as a buffoon on his own (even in other companies) for two years, and no longer as head of a company, in view of the fact that so many unpleasant things happen and there are so many problems in trying to run a company.

This gentleman, having gathered from the letter that the negotiation had almost collapsed, and knowing how very humble a servant I am of His Highness and of Your Lordship, begged me (as also did those other gentlemen who were with him) that I try with a letter of mine—still assuming His Highness is not about to make use of him—to ask Your Lordship most urgently to persuade this Signor Lelio to oblige the gentle-man, and if Signor Lelio should insist on making excuses because of the

---

[b] Giovanni Battista Andreini, actor, author, and head of a theatrical company known as I Fedeli, at this time attached to the court of Mantua. 'Florinda' was his wife, Virginia Andreini.

[c] *nel suo loco publico*, referring to the theatre owned by the Giustiniani family in the district of San Moisè.

[d] Ferdinando Gonzaga, sixth Duke of Mantua.   [e] The role created by Tristano Martinelli.

[f] The actor Pier Maria Cecchini, head of a rival troupe.

[g] Another *commedia dell'arte* character, whose role generally emphasized the pompous and the pedantic.

shortage of actors in his company, this gentleman offers him Gratiano and Zanni[h] and Doctor, and any other part that might be lacking.

I am therefore writing to beg Your Lordship, or rather (to put it better) I am writing to entreat Your Lordship's infinite kindness to honour me by asking Your Lordship to try and be so kind as to perform this service of requesting the said Signor Lelio to place himself at the disposal of this most illustrious gentleman, for he will show himself full of kindness towards Signor Lelio's person, both with gifts and with payment of travel costs and so on; and also to bring Signora Florinda, and others of whom he approves.

But if he does not want to, Signor Giustiniani[i] asks Signor Lelio to consider that as a result of the expectations already raised by his letters, he will not only be hindered in his search for another company, but his theatre will be prevented (because of Lelio)[j] from giving performances— a disappointment which he can well imagine.

Your Lordship's authority will, I know, be such as can take care of everything perfectly, and I shall always be most grateful to Your Lordship for a favour I have so long desired, and which I know will make it clear to these most distinguished gentlemen how much you hold my servitude dear to Your Grace. Do not look, I beg you, upon my modest worth, but marvel rather at your own kindness in deigning to have a request made to Signor Lelio, persuading him with the gentleness of your favour. And here making a humble bow to you, I pray God with all affection for your every most longed-for happiness.

from Venice, 21 October 1622

Your Most Illustrious Lordship's

most devoted and most grateful servant

Claudio Monteverdi

---

[h] Gianni (or Arlecchino). By adding the names of 'Doctor' and 'Gratiano' Monteverdi accidentally divides one character into two.

[i] Giustiniani (name supplied to avoid confusion between the various personal pronouns referring to different men).

[j] Lelio (supplied).

73

Venice, 19 November 1622
to [Alessandro Striggio, at Mantua]

Mantua, Archivio Gonzaga, Cassetta 6, fo. 268. Folio: 2 pp.

Malipiero, 228; Paoli, 201; Lax, 126

Striggio having sent Monteverdi an encouraging reply about the situation of the *commedia dell'arte* players, the present letter combines the composer's thanks with those of Giustiniani. This gentleman, determined above all else to secure the services of the elusive 'Dr Gratiano' (whose agreement to act would make everything else fall into place), had probably left for Padua by the time Monteverdi had sent off the letter to Mantua. Indeed, it was between Mantua and Padua that certain negotiations were under way for the future of the troupe in its reconstituted form.

Letter 72 clearly states that 'Dr Gratiano' was in Savoy on or about 21 October. By 29 October he had arrived at Brescia where he met the Prince de Condé, then en route for Mantua to choose actors for the next season in Paris. The actor also intended to travel to Mantua, but had to spend some time in Padua; and because of this the prince gave him a letter addressed to Duke Ferdinando, asking formal permission to invite the troupe to Paris and so satisfy the wishes of Louis XIII.[1]

The identity of 'Dr Gratiano' is revealed in a Mantuan treasury document dated 15 November, authorizing advance payment for travelling expenses to Sante Morandi (presumably a court factotum) enabling him to go to Padua and bring back one 'M. Francesco, detto Scattolone e Graziano di Comedia'.[2] But before he could do so, Giustiniani had arrived in Padua to seek out Francesco Scattolone and invite him to play the role of the pompous Bolognese lawyer in the performances planned for Venice. The results of Giustiniani's attempt are summarized by Monteverdi in Letter 74, dated 3 December, by which time Scattolone had left for Mantua in the company of the factotum.

My Most Illustrious Lord and Most Respected Master,

I received Your Lordship's most courteous and kind letter, full of especially warm feelings towards me, poor as I am yet rich from an inner feeling of reverence and love which desires nothing but to be worthy of

---

[1] Baschet, 313.   [2] Bertolotti, 101.

Your Lordship's commands so that I can prove myself your by no means useless servant.

I have shown Your Lordship's letter to the Most Illustrious Signor Giustiniani,[a] and he having seen that you did not disdain to favour my entreaties, believed me to be in Your Lordship's good books. For the outstanding favour that Your Lordship so kindly granted me, I write now to offer the best thanks I know and am capable of, and Your Lordship may be sure that I would have added to them an obligation if any part of me had known that it was not previously obliged to you in some other way.

The aforementioned Most Illustrious Signor Giustiniani has instructed me to give you, in his name, a thousand thanks. May God our Saviour grant Your Lordship the summit of greatest happiness, and to me the merit of being your servant both by results and by intention; and with this I humbly kiss your hands in all reverence.

from Venice, 19 November 1622

Your Most Illustrious Lordship's

most devoted and most grateful servant

Claudio Monteverdi

---

[a] Lorenzo Giustiniani, at this time a youthful scion of an ancient Venetian family.

74

Venice, 3 December 1622
to [Alessandro Striggio, at Mantua]

Mantua, Archivio Gonzaga, Cassetta 6, fos. 270–1. Bifolio: 4 pp.

Prunières, 265; Malipiero, 229; Paoli, 202; Lax, 127

Although this letter is obviously intended for Striggio since its subject-matter, like that of the surrounding correspondence, concerns the *commedia dell'arte* actors, Monteverdi—in one of his rare lapses—uses the honorific 'osservandissimo', usually reserved at this time for Marigliani.[1] The cause of this lapse may have been his continuing illness, which once again necessitated a personal visit from Giustiniani, for in normal circumstances Monteverdi would have gone to see his patron.

Giustiniani, evidently upset about the non-arrival of the actors and the lack of any communication from them, was also apprehensive about Pier Maria Cecchini's plot to keep them out of Venice at all costs so that he could continue to bask in solitary glory. There was certainly no love lost between Cecchinis and Andreinis, the wives being on worse terms than the men. But to what extent the breakdown in plans can be attributed to this fact is open to question. If Striggio assumed that the company would be able to spend a few days in Venice on their way to Paris, he nevertheless knew that such a route could hardly be described as direct. A group of actors in a hurry would have chosen to travel via Milan and Turin, then over the Col de Montgenèvre into France. Venice would be too far to the east. Nevertheless, the presence of Cecchini in Venice may have deterred them as much as considerations of topography and travel.

They had in fact already left for France when Monteverdi sent his request to Striggio for further help or information. In vain had Giustiniani travelled to Padua, in vain had he spoken to Scattolone, used threats when entreaties failed, and finally told him that he would be forced into a gondola and brought to Lizza Fusina—the disembarcation point for Venice. Perhaps the full implications of Giustiniani's act have been obscured because of the mystery surrounding the 'word' *Zaffutine*. What Monteverdi actually wrote was *a leZaffusine*, a bizarre portmanteau word whose true meaning has only recently become clear.[2]

---

[1] Prunières reads 'Coll^mo'.

[2] I am grateful to Dr Maria Teresa Muraro, of the Fondazione Giorgio Cini, for her letter of explanation dated 7 May 1971. For further references to Lizza Fusina (including various confused spellings) see Hazlitt (index).

An aside of sociological interest appears in the final paragraph, where the composer mentions that Giustiniani would have liked to express his indebtedness to Striggio by writing a letter, but that gentlemen such as he do not write to ministers of state without special permission. The fact that the composer could write directly to Striggio was due to his long acquaintance with the man and his collaboration with him in artistic affairs; for as regards rank Giustiniani was certainly above Monteverdi.

My Most Illustrious Lord and Most Esteemed[a] Master,

This morning (which is the 3rd of the present month) the Most Illustrious Signor Giustiniani,[b] my lord, came expressly to call on me in my own room and tell me about a certain ticklish situation, which has come about through fear that Fritellino[c] has been busy[d] with some of his intrigues in order to remain supreme[e] in Venice (although little appreciated), so that the arrival of the Mantuan actors—very much looked forward to by the entire city—can be thwarted, inasmuch as they are late; and all the more so through having heard that Dr Gratiano[f] was so much to His Highness's[g] liking as to be rewarded with a present of 100 scudi, living expenses, and other secure maintenance, but Signor Giustiniani (this approval being what it is) would not want the skill of the said Fritellino to have been able to prevail.

As regards the other matter: having already seen Your Lordship's letter (which you were so kind as to send me in reply) confirming the arrival of the aforementioned actors with the Duke's full approval, but not so far having seen letters brought by the courier from any of those actors— which, however, gives us hope that they may come—it is nevertheless assumed that the desired favour will be received. This most illustrious gentleman certainly deserves to have his mind set at rest about the matter by His Highness, for (believe me, Your Lordship) he has not failed to apply himself to it with all diligence and affection, so that His Highness also might be pleased by having actors sent to fill the company's need.

Not only did he go to the trouble of arranging for these leading actors to come, and still more, of making Franceschina[h] decide; but as regards the

---

[a] One of Monteverdi's rare lapses into *osservandissimo*, usually reserved for the younger and less exalted Marigliani.

[b] Lorenzo Giustiniani, a Venetian gentleman.   [c] The actor Pier Maria Cecchini.

[d] *non si sij affaticato* (the *non* being pleonastic).   [e] *solo* (alone in the sense of unchallenged).

[f] A *commedia dell'arte* character.   [g] Ferdinando Gonzaga, sixth Duke of Mantua.

[h] The name usually given to the wife of Zanni.

Doctor—who would not answer 'yes' to mild but insistent entreaties—he decided on the opposite approach, changing entreaties into threats, whereby the said Doctor would have to get into a gondola with him and be taken to Lizza Fusina,*i* with the idea of forcing him to come. But the Doctor having sworn to His Lordship that he would come, he was content just to have someone accompany him.

On account of His Lordship's having exerted himself with such enthusiasm—both because of the promise which Your Lordship made to him in your letter by way of reply to mine, and because of not having seen letters to the contrary in the present delivery—he lives in greatest hopes; but since he so much desires this favour he has again instructed me to write and ask Your Lordship, so that in case of need you may be so kind as to assist him. But even if (as he believes) they would have come without any further inconvenience to Your Lordship, he still asks you to try and set his mind at rest with the latest news of their certain arrival, which would still be in time if it were (as he hopes) within ten or fifteen days.

That most illustrious lord also added that if he could have written to Your Lordship—since he knows very well that gentlemen such as he cannot write to ministers of princes without leave—he would already have demonstrated the obligation that he owes to Your Lordship. So, once again asking Your Lordship's kindness for the long-desired favour, the Most Illustrious Signor Giustiniani being very much my lord, I am and always shall be your most grateful servant. And here making a bow to Your Lordship I pray God our Saviour for the fulfilment of every supreme joy.

from Venice, 3 December 1622

Your Most Illustrious Lordship's

most devoted and most grateful servant

Claudio Monteverdi

i The original has *a leZaffusine* (the embarcation point on the mainland for the journey to Padua).

75

Venice, 10 December 1622
to [Alessandro Striggio, at Mantua]

Mantua, Archivio Gonzaga, Cassetta 6, fo. 273. Folio: 1 p.

Malipiero, 231; Paoli, 205; Lax, 129

Although Striggio's much-delayed letter still held out some hope of the actors appearing in Venice under the sponsorship of Giustiniani, the lack of direct communication from the troupe must have brought a feeling of dejection both to him and to Monteverdi. Over-optimistically perhaps, they had looked forward to a few performances before the Christmas festivities began, but the beckonings of the King of France[1] and the intrigues of Pier Maria Cecchini were to thwart their desires. Perhaps Andreini, an old friend of Monteverdi, had sent an explanation or apology as he hastened to Paris; but his letter (like the present one) would have been held up by the December weather and difficult road conditions.

Most Illustrious Lord and Most Respected Master,[a]

The letters are arriving so late at present that there is hardly time to send replies, for which reason I have so far not been able to show Your Lordship's most courteous letter to the Most Illustrious Signor Giustiniani.[b] But I know that when he sees it he will be most obliged to Your Lordship, and at the same time most relieved, because he desired beyond all belief to receive that particular favour.

Furthermore, as regards myself, I shall always be infinitely grateful to Your Lordship. May Our Lord grant you a Merry Christmas and a Happy New Year, and allow me to be made worthy of your desired commands; and here making a humble bow to Your Lordship I pray God our Saviour for your every happiness.

from Venice, 10 December 1622
Your Most Illustrious Lordship's
most grateful servant
Claudio Monteverdi

[1] Letter from Henri de Bourbon, 29 Oct. 1622 (Archivio Gonzaga, E.xv.628) cited by Lea, i. 290.

[a] The usual *mio* is omitted.   [b] Lorenzo Giustiniani, a Venetian gentleman.

76

Venice, 31 December 1622
to [Alessandro Striggio, at Mantua]

Mantua, Archivio Gonzaga, Cassetta 6, fos. 275–6. Bifolio: 4 pp.

Prunières, 267; Malipiero, 231; Paoli, 206; Lax, 130

Both Giustiniani and Monteverdi would have realized, by the middle of December, that the actors they had hoped to entice to Venice were already on their way to Paris. And after Christmas, two explanatory letters arrived from Striggio, one of them offering to do Giustiniani 'a favour', which is mentioned but not defined by the composer. In all probability Striggio, embarrassed by having to disappoint an old friend and his patron, offered to find other actors and inform them of the opportunity available in Venice. Monteverdi then speaks of the Spanish actors, who could be helped out by some Italians, for he must have been well aware of the continual and confusing flow of talent from one company to another, and the consequent possibility of building a small company from the remnants of larger ones.[1]

The second topic provides us with a fascinating glimpse of the way in which subsidiary posts were filled.[2] Giovanni Battista Grillo, who played the first organ at St Mark's, died about the middle of November—Monteverdi writes that this was 'already a month and a half ago'. A former colleague of his at Mantua, Ottavio Bargnani, lost no time in writing to find out whether he might be considered for the vacancy; what is more, he seems to have been slightly upset because he had to contact Monteverdi rather than the other way about. Within the context of his letter to Striggio, Monteverdi quotes verbatim the letter which he felt bound to write to Bargnani, in view of possible reprisals for alleged poaching on ducal preserves.

Notwithstanding the professed affection for Bargnani, and a certain willingness to admit that he was talented (when asked by the Procurators), there was undoubtedly a modicum of reserve on Monteverdi's part. He had been a colleague of Bargnani's at Mantua, but never seems to have felt particularly drawn to him. The Brescian organist, said to be of a noble family, had come to Mantua in 1610 as the successor of Giacomo Bongiannino. As a member of the musical establishment at S. Barbara,[3] he

---

[1] Lea, i. 257.

[2] A detailed account of a large-scale appointment can be studied in Arnold, 'Succession', 205–11.

[3] Tagmann, 394–5. Canal, summarizing without citing a document of the Procurators, indicates that Bargnani actually went to Venice for an audition in 1623, and that he mentioned his previous employment with the Emperor Rudolf II (presumably in Graz or Vienna), and at Rome. He is known to have exercised

would have been involved more deeply in sacred than in secular music, yet by 1618 (when he contributed three motets to Malgarini's collection)[4] his duties appear to have been modified, for he is described as being 'organista di camera del Serenissimo'. In the same anthology, Simpliciano Mazzuchi is designated as 'organista di S. Barbara'. Perhaps there was an exchange of offices at some point in their careers, even though thus far the documents provide no evidence.

Apart from the three motets of 1618, Bargnani appears to have written comparatively little. In 1599 the Venetian publisher Amadino issued a volume of his *Canzonette, Arie, et Madrigali a tre et a quattro voci* (Nuovo Vogel, no. 248). In 1601 Angelo Gardano published his *Primo Libro de Madrigali a cinque voci* (Nuovo Vogel, no. 249). A little before this there probably appeared a *Primo Libro di Canzoni da suonare*, of which no copy has survived, and to this succeeded in 1611 (Erede di Tini e Filippo Lomazzi, Milan, 1611) a *Secondo Libro delle Canzoni da suonare a quattro, cinque e otto voci* (19 canzoni), dedicated to Vincenzo Gonzaga.[5] Concerning the *Primo Libro di Canzoni*, the only reference is that of G. M. Artusi to the readers in the book of *Canzoni da suonare a quattro et otto voci* by Floriano Canale,[6] published at Venice in 1600 by Giacomo Vincenti. From this it appears that Bargnani was a pupil of Floriano Canale, presumably at Brescia. The last notice of him is in 1627, when he received a pension of 26 scudi from the Mantuan Treasury.[7]

My Most Illustrious Lord, and Most Respected Master,

At the time when I received Your Lordship's two letters by the most recent post, a man was waiting here for what you were so kind as to write—the messenger of the Most Illustrious Signor Giustiniani.[a] After I had read them and given them to the messenger so that he could take them for his master to see, he returned to my room with the letters and requested that I write to Your Lordship in the name of the Most Illustrious Signor Giustiniani, to the effect that he acknowledges himself to be as much obliged to you as if he himself in fact had received the favour.

And he begs you to command him if you consider him in any way suitable for serving Your Lordship, both with his person and with his

his profession at Salò in 1595, at Brescia in 1605, and at Treviso (1606–7); besides which he is said to have taken a Mantuan choirbook to Udine. (See Canal, 745; MacClintock, Communication.)

[4] *Motetti a una, due, tre e quattro voci* (Venice, Vincenti). Canal (745) looked only at the Cantus II part-book, where he found the composer's Christian name given erroneously as 'Orazio', and where only two motets are listed. A collation of the entire set of books shows that Bargnani contributed three motets and that his name appears in its proper form.

[5] Sartori, *Bibliografia*, ii. 1611f.   [6] Ibid. i. 107.   [7] Communicated by Claudio Sartori.

[a] Lorenzo Giustiniani, a Venetian gentleman who later married the daughter of Monteverdi's patron, Girolamo Mocenigo.

possessions, inasmuch as he is again enquiring of Your Lordship's kindness (having heard that there is a company of Spanish actors in Mantua) and whether with such a favourable situation and with that diplomatic manner[b] Your Lordship can adopt, our aim might be achieved—His Highness[c] being perhaps more pleased with the said Spaniards than with the Italians—for the favour would always be welcome. Nevertheless he wants everything to be done with Your Lordship's approval.

Aside from this, I am even more grateful to Your Lordship since you have been so kind as to show in writing that you are not ashamed of your fondness for me, weak as I am in this world of ours; therefore I shall always feel bound to pray God that He bless and preserve Your Lordship, and that He make me worthy to deserve Your Lordship's commands, so that I may prove myself a worthy servant of yours by the results.

My Lord, already a month and a half ago an organist[d] of St Mark's passed to a better life, and a little while after his death Signor Ottavio Bargnani[e] wrote to me complaining that I did not let him know about this vacancy, so that he could apply for the post. I replied to him: 'Dear Signor Bargnani—I am very fond of you, but since you are a servant of that Prince who is as much my master and lord, I would never have considered (let alone risked) writing such a thing to you, for it would have amounted to a desire that you leave that service which I so much revere and honour. You will therefore do me a kindness by discussing with me any matter other than that one.'

So the affair quietened down, and when I thought it had been dropped, lo and behold only the other day I was summoned to the Procurazia[f] by the chief representatives of the procurators; and when I arrived, they immediately had a letter read out from Signor Bargnani (I do not know where they got it), who is trying to obtain the aforementioned post, which is still not filled. The letter having been read, they asked me whether this person would be acceptable, and I answered yes. They then asked me to write him a letter on behalf of Their Excellencies to the effect that he should come for an audition[g] at his convenience, for they assure him that

---

[b] *destro modo.*   [c] Ferdinando Gonzaga, sixth Duke of Mantua.

[d] Giovanni Battista Grillo (died *c.*15 Nov. 1622).

[e] An organist from Brescia who served at S. Barbara, Mantua.

[f] This account of Monteverdi's interview with the procurators is all in the present tense, here modified to a narrative imperfect tense.

[g] *che li farà apiacere lasciarsi udire.*

if he is the kind of man he says he is, they would not seek to harm his reputation, although there are still five others who are interested in the post, so that a competition will be necessary.

Thinking to myself that such a letter (without first letting Your Lordship know about it, so that you may in turn tell His Highness) would greatly injure me in His Highness's grace—which I esteem and shall esteem as long as I live, in boundless respects—I have for this reason told Your Lordship about the matter, begging you to let me know by the next post as to what I can do, with His Highness's approval, in the event that Signor Bargnani hints in his letter that he would be able (also with His Highness's approval) to come and serve at St Mark's. I wanted to place the matter in Your Lordship's hands, because I know that everything will be done discreetly, and without embarrassment to me. And here making a humble bow to Your Lordship, I pray God our Saviour grant you a Happy New Year.

from Venice, 31 December 1622
Your Most Illustrious Lordship's
most grateful servant
Claudio Monteverdi

77

Venice, 23 January 1623
to [Alessandro Striggio, at Mantua]

Mantua, Archivio Gonzaga, Cassetta 6, fo. 279. Folio: 1 p.

Malipiero, 233; Paoli, 210; Lax, 132

Monteverdi, feeling unwell, forgot the proper salutation for Striggio and wrote 'osservandissimo' instead, as he had done in the letter of 3 December. There seems to be no doubt that his health was in a poor state, for he kept to his rooms if not to his bed and received visitors only when absolutely necessary. The attempt on the part of Ottavio Bargnani to replace Grillo came to nothing, and on 1 May Carlo Fillago was appointed first organist.[1]

My Most Illustrious Lord and Most Esteemed[a] Master,

Due to my having been sufficiently indisposed to have gone to bed for a rest, I was obliged by this circumstance to delay until the present post my thanks to Your Lordship, with the sincerest affection I know and of which I am capable, for your letter full of infinite kindness. I followed His Highness's[b] suggestions, and accordingly wrote nothing further to Signor Ottavio;[c] and for the trouble Your Lordship has taken in telling His Highness what I requested of you, I offer infinite thanks to Your Lordship (as I said before) with a special obligation.

I beg you to maintain me in your good grace, praying God that he grant me merits worthy of your commands; and here making a humble bow to Your Lordship I pray God our Saviour for your every greatest happiness.

from Venice, 23 January 1623
Your Most Illustrious Lordship's
most grateful servant,
Claudio Monteverdi

[1] S. Dalla Libera, 'Chronologia musicale della basilica di S. Marco in Venezia', *Musica Sacra*, 85 (1961), 90.

[a] *osservandissimo* (in place of the usual *collendissimo*).   [b] Ferdinando, sixth Duke of Mantua.
[c] Ottavio Bargnani, at this time an organist of the ducal basilica in Mantua.

78

Venice, 10 February 1623
to [Alessandro Striggio, at Mantua]

Mantua, Archivio Gonzaga, Cassetta 6, fos. 281–2. Bifolio: 3 pp.

Prunières, 268; Malipiero, 234; Paoli, 211; Fabbri 1985, 246, 247; Lax, 133

Carnival in Venice, carnival in Mantua. The 56-year-old composer, hardly a perfervid devotee of those latter-day lupercalia at the best of times, must have looked upon them with particular loathing in 1623, for he had been unpleasantly and painfully ill for nearly twenty weeks. Yet the carnival spirit, mindless of suffering humanity, brushed him closely in the person of the Gonzagan agent Callegari, otherwise known as Signor Bergamaschino,[1] who brought an urgent message from Duke Ferdinando to the effect that Monteverdi was to seek out two castrati and two chitarrone-players capable of realizing their harmonic accompaniments from a bass part, and then travel back with them to Mantua as soon as possible.

This typical Gonzaga command, with its overt assumption that the luckless recipient could, and would, drop everything and come running, was no different from innumerable previous ones. Over the years, the wary composer had built up an arsenal of excuses which he had no hesitation about using as a legitimate means of self-defence. But this time the excuse was genuine. At the beginning of October 1622 he had taken a purge, the effects of which would normally be expected to improve his health almost immediately. Instead, they made it much worse, producing a secondary illness which crept like a slow poison through his entire body, leaving him weak, listless, and yet unable to rest.

The cause of all this has not so far engaged the attention of Monteverdi's biographers, although the illness was undoubtedly one of the worst he had ever endured. He would have known from his father, a respected medical doctor in Cremona until the time of his death in 1617, that the use of cathartics could be dangerous if not supervised by a competent authority. Yet his nascent interest in alchemy may have made him bold, and as the son of a doctor he would be able to avoid the worst mistakes at least. If he could look forward in matters musical, then why not in matters medical?

At that time the most widely accepted medicine for a purge was senna, a substance known and used for that purpose by the Arabs as long ago as the ninth century. But a more fashionable and recent discovery was calomel or mercurous chloride, found in nature as horn mercury or manufacturable by subliming pure mercury with mercuric

---

[1] See Letter 50.

chloride.[2] Calomel was certainly efficacious, and it rapidly became popular; its toxic properties nevertheless tended to play unfortunate tricks on careless users, unaware that exposure to light or being subjected to poor storage caused the chemical properties to change. In other words, it was comparatively easy for a purge to become a poison.

This is almost certainly what happened in Monteverdi's case. He chose the most up-to-date medicine, purchased unknowingly a defective sample, swallowed it, and lived to regret it for a quite considerable time. When he recovered, probably by the early spring of 1623, his first action was to try and discover what had gone wrong, for shortly after this time he began writing to Ercole Marigliani, the Mantuan court secretary, not about a libretto but about alchemy, and in particular about mercury. Between August 1625 and March 1626 he writes of experiments, jars, bottles, and wires. Letter 83 describes an experiment with mercury, which is mentioned mysteriously and namelessly in Letters 84 and 86. Pure and 'very pure' mercury are discussed in Letters 87 and 89, while it is perfectly clear that Letters 83 and 86 were sent to Mantua with mercury which had been obtained in Venice. Thereafter alchemy is dropped in favour of music.

With a genuine illness to contend with, Monteverdi could write with a clear conscience to Striggio and decline the invitation, or rather command, to go to Mantua. As an additional safeguard, he tells Striggio that there are no good castrati or theorbo-players in Venice (a statement that the Count must have found hard to swallow) and goes on to offer help in finding wind-players, in which the Mantuan court was clearly not interested. Verona, with its famous Accademia, could supply better and cheaper players on the theorbo.[3]

Thus did Mantua's carnival pass the composer by, and each could well manage without the other.

My Most Illustrious Lord and Most Respected Master,

His Most Serene Lordship the Duke,[a] my particular lord, has kindly informed me verbally—through Signor Bergamaschino[b] who has now returned from Mantua to Venice—that he would like me to be in Mantua by the next courier and to bring with me two soprani and two theorbo-players. I am writing this letter to beg you to try and be so kind as to let His Highness know that really I am so badly affected by an illness which (as a

---

[2] Other methods of preparation include the heating of mercurous sulphate with common salt, or precipitation from a mercurous salt solution by the addition of hydrochloric acid.

[3] Monteverdi's knowledge of Verona's musical activities went back for at least thirty-five years, for he had dedicated his First Book of Madrigals to Count Marco Verità, a well-known musical patron of that city. For this particular type of chitarrone-player, see Letter 11.

[a] Ferdinando Gonzaga, sixth Duke of Mantua.

[b] His real name was Antonio Callegari (see Letters 50 and 51).

result of a purge I gave myself at the beginning of October last year) has made its way down from my head to my shoulders and the whole of my waist, that it is necessary for me to have myself dressed, for I am hardly able to help myself because of the pain in my hands, arms, and feet.

It is true that there seems to be some indication of the beginnings of a recovery, but I am nevertheless more on the bad side than the good, apart from which I have experienced for about the past three days a weakening of the body which does not allow me any repose. Adding to all this the disappointment running through my mind at not being able to come because of the aforementioned illness, this inability upsets me more than the disease itself.

I am so eager, however, that if only my illness would leave me alone until the next-but-one post,^{c} I shall be so encouraged (and helped by my desire to serve His Highness) as to expect to be on my way. But if I do not come, believe me Your Lordship I shall have been constrained by my illness to stay here entirely against my will. And therefore I beg Your Lordship for the love of God to offer His Highness my true and genuine apologies, if this should come about—and I consider it more likely than not.

As for the soprani, believe me Your Lordship there is nobody suitable, nor is there anyone who can play continuo^d on the theorbo other than moderately well, therefore in my opinion it would not be worth the expense of getting ordinary players from here. But there are certainly good wind instrumentalists, and if Your Lordship will let me know about these, I would hope to send you someone reasonably good. Regarding the need for rank-and-file theorbo-players, I believe His Highness would find satisfactory ones at Verona, and much less expensive.

Excuse me, Your Lordship and my dear master, for causing you so much trouble, and forgive me. I am and always shall be your most grateful servant, praying God that He may always bless and preserve Your Lordship, whose hands I kiss in all affection.

from Venice, 10 February 1623

Your Most Illustrious Lordship's

most grateful servant

Claudio Monteverdi

---

^{c} Here the word for a rural postman is used (*procaccio*).

^{d} *sopra alla parte* (realizing the bass from a part-book, as opposed to playing from tablature).

79

Venice, 11 March 1623
to [Alessandro Striggio, at Mantua]

Mantua, Archivio Gonzaga, Cassetta 6, fo. 284. Folio: 2 pp.

Malipiero, 236; Paoli, 214; Lax, 135

Striggio, as usual, took pains to placate the Duke, while Monteverdi's slow return to health coincided with the end of winter in Venice. Among the more pleasant occurrences were two publications of the monodic version of the 'Lament of Arianna': a Venetian fascicle, without dedication (and therefore with no day or month) but containing in addition the *Lettera amorosa* and *Partenza amorosa*, reprinted from Book VII; and a collection entitled *Il maggio fiorito* issued in Orvieto, again lacking an exact date, and without any credit to Monteverdi for having composed the work. Perhaps by that time it was so well known that Monteverdi's name would have been automatically associated with it; on the other hand Rinuccini's text attracted four composers[1]—two chose solo settings, while the other two preferred polyphony—and a new 'Lament of Arianna' by Giambattista Marini drew forth another monodic essay from Pelegrino Possenti, a fervent admirer of Monteverdi.[2]

A by-product of Monteverdi's convalescence was his music for Modena. In December 1622 Prince Alfonso II d'Este had contacted his Venetian agent, the medical doctor Alberto Colombo, requesting the purchase of secular works by Monteverdi and his contemporaries. In January 1623 came another request, this time for original compositions, and by 11 March two madrigals by Monteverdi were despatched from Venice. The archives at Modena contain a draft letter from the prince thanking the composer and commenting on the 'leggiadra e finezza della compositione'.[3]

---

[1] A setting for five voices by Giulio Cesare Antonelli, a canon of S. Andrea in Mantua, appears in a set of manuscript part-books dated 1606 in the library of Milan Conservatory, see Barblan, 'Lamento'. Severo Bonini, a monk of Vallombrosa near Florence, produced a solo version of Rinuccini's text in 1613 (Venice, Gardano), which is discussed by Luisi, 573–82. Another polyphonic setting appears in Book Fifteen of the five-part madrigals of Antonio il Verso (Palermo, 1619). The fourth setting is one by Francesco Antonio Costa included in a volume of his monodies published in 1626 (Venice, Vincenti). Pellegrino Possenti's setting of Marini's poem, 'Misera è chi m'ha tolto', is the final solo in his *Canora sampogna* of 1623 (Venice, B. Magni).

[2] The preface to his *Canora sampogna* (dated 28 Oct. 1623) singles out Monteverdi for special praise. See commentary to letter 81.

[3] Fabbri, 'Inediti', 74–7; Prunières, 209, 217.

[270]

Is there a madrigal published subsequent to 1623 that seems full of prettiness and finesse? No indication of the titles has survived, and if subsequently published they could only have appeared in Book VIII. In this collection there are only two madrigals so described—the two Guarini settings, *Dolcissimo uscignolo* and *Chi vol haver felice*. Now Book VIII is dominated by settings of Rinuccini and Petrarch; the Guarini madrigals clearly belong to an earlier period, and 1623 would not be out of the question because Monteverdi was still setting poetry by Guarini shortly before that time. A further point in support of this theory is that they are the only two five-voice madrigals in the late collection. It should also be borne in mind that in 1629, one year after his father's death, Alfonso retired to a monastery and to all intents and purposes bade the world of music a fond farewell.

My Most Illustrious Lord and Most Respected Master,

Your Lordship will forgive me if I did not thank you most affectionately (as was my duty) by the previous post for having so graciously aided me in offering His Highness[a] my excuses for being unable to come to Mantua and obey his instructions, since actually I am still rather ill—much more so just recently—yet at present (thank God) I feel better and hope for further improvement at the first purge. I am, and shall be as long as I live, a most grateful servant to Your Lordship.

Please God that I may be worthy of your commands so that I can make myself known as a not unproductive servant of Your Lordship, whose hands I kiss with all reverence; and I pray God for your every perfect happiness.

from Venice, 11 March 1623
Your Most Illustrious Lordship's
most grateful servant
Claudio Monteverdi

[a] Ferdinando Gonzaga, sixth Duke of Mantua.

80

Venice, 4 June 1623
to [Duke Ferdinando Gonzaga, at Mantua]

Mantua, Archivio Gonzaga, Cassetta 6, fo. 286. Folio: 1 p.

Malipiero, 236; Paoli, 216; Lax, 136

The twelve weeks between Letters 79 and 80 witnessed plans and events ranging from an attempted murder in Rome to a regatta in Venice, from confessions extracted by torture in Mantua to the musical interests of the ruling family of Modena. In all of these Monteverdi was involved to the extent that he knew personally some or all of the leading figures, and heard either officially or through the spicy medium of the Venetian *avvisi* a great deal of what was going on, without, however, being able to influence the course of events. Throughout his life and to its very end he remained first and foremost a musician, shunning politics and double-dealing even though he was well aware of its existence at certain levels of his profession.[1]

Cesare I d'Este, who had married Virginia, daughter of Cosimo I, Grand Duke of Tuscany, at the Florentine church of S. Spirito, in 1586, was no stranger to music. During the course of a splendid entertainment planned as an adornment of that festive occasion, the designer Buontalenti had invented a stage-machine simulating a huge cloud, which opened to reveal a choir of angels. They sang, in suitably exalted harmony, a chorus beginning with the words 'O benedetto giorno', the words and melody then being taken up as a solo by Giulio Caccini.[2] Cesare maintained and developed his musical establishment even after his disinheritance by Clement VIII in 1597, when Ferrara was claimed as a papal fief and the Este court had to move to Modena.

On 7 April 1623 his son Alfonso wrote again to Alberto Colombo, enquiring about various musicians—Monteverdi, Luca Salvadori (a castrato from Pistoia), and the Brescian madrigalist Francesco Turrini.[3] A reply came back, undated, but with all the necessary information. In the form of a memorandum, it was dictated by Monteverdi to Colombo, who then passed it to Modena, and like the earlier letters about the alto from Modena (no. 9) and the lady singers (no. 10) this one shows us Monteverdi as a

---

[1] His young Cremonese colleague and friend, Tarquinio Merula, left the service of S. Maria Maggiore, Bergamo, in 1633 because of a very clear case of persecution conducted with extraordinary malevolence. For a transcript of the original document, see Padoan, 297.

[2] Ademollo, 136–7.

[3] Fabbri, 'Inediti', 77; Prunières, 217 n. 159. See also commentary to Letter 79.

much respected critic. He is fairly complimentary about the castrato and quite enthusiastic about Turrini. A few weeks later his own work was praised to the skies by the prince in a letter to the Modenese lutenist and poet Bellerofonte Castaldi, then living in Venice.[4] Castaldi needed no encouragement, for he too was a great admirer of Monteverdi, referring to him as 'a new Apollo and musical Orfeo'.[5] In the following year, the ducal archives show that there was direct contact with Monteverdi and receipt of musical manuscripts from him.[6] By the mid-1620s secular vocal music was an indispensable adjunct to Alfonso's leisure, and among the outstanding singer-composers who had performed before him in Modena was Sigismondo d'India. This gifted but sometimes eccentric genius dedicated to the prince his *Musiche . . . Libro Terzo*, published in Milan on 3 January 1618 by Filippo Lomazzi, whose preface hints that the extraction of the music from the composer had proved no easy matter. He too was a distant member of Monteverdi's circle.

That circle, while Monteverdi was at Mantua in the service of the Gonzaga, included a number of eminent men and women, some of them close relatives of his brilliant patron, Vincenzo I. At a concert he gave in 1611, one of the guests was Isabella Gonzaga da Novellara, also known as Isabella di San Martino, after her principal place of residence. At this juncture she was imprisoned in Castel S. Angelo, Rome, on charges of treason against the Gonzaga. In the spring of 1623, fresh accusations were being brought against her, in the hope of proving that she had somehow bewitched or drugged Don Vincenzo, later seventh Duke of Mantua, into falling in love with her.[7] Her servants at the villa in San Martino dell'Argine were also suspect, and 'confessions' were duly extracted from them by means of torture.

Ferdinando tried to involve the Mantuan Inquisitor, but much to his disappointment the matter was referred to Rome because the charges concerned abuse of the Holy Sacrament. Informers had made such bold use of their imagination as to persuade the Duke's advisers that the love elixir which resulted in the clandestine marriage of Isabella and Don Vincenzo had been carefully concocted from powdered human skulls and shredded holy wafer. The sheer stupidity of such an accusation could only be matched by the credibility of those who collected the evidence. Among the highly placed officials who became increasingly involved was Monteverdi's friend Alessandro Striggio, who reluctantly began to agree that the only way out of the impasse was to have Isabella done away with.

Discussions and correspondence relating to attempts on the life of this wretched and deeply wronged woman go back until at least May of 1623, and not long after this Striggio was in touch with the Marchese Tassoni in Rome about the possibility of hiring a Neapolitan assassin who specialized in poisons. It would be a comparatively simple matter for such a man to mingle with the staff of Castel S. Angelo, awaiting the chance to administer the fatal dose. But the plot came to nothing, and by the early part of the following year Isabella was released. It may have been due to a desire to escape from this oppressive atmosphere of intrigue that Ferdinando decided to pay a visit to Venice.

[4] Prunières, 217.   [5] Canal, 108.   [6] See Letter 81.   [7] Errante, 'Il processo', 686.

Arriving in the city, apparently incognito, on 28 April, he lost no time in communicating to the Doge, Antonio Priuli, that his main purpose was to fulfil a vow to St Lucy of Syracuse, by whose gracious intercession one of his eyes had regained its sight.[8] The Doge probably guessed that there were other reasons for the Duke's sudden descent upon the lagoon city, and not long after appointing Pietro Foscari as Ferdinando's official escort he learned of the impending arrival of the Duchess, her ladies-in-waiting, and of Vittoria Doria, wife of Don Ferrante Gonzaga of Guastalla.[9] What had at first appeared to be an unofficial call now took on the proportions of a state visit, and by 4 May the Senate had decided to make thorough and detailed arrangements.

The major problem facing them was to find a large and suitable property in which the Duke, the Duchess, and their extensive retinue could find lodging not too far distant from the Doge's palace and the basilica. Their choice fell upon a fine house situated near the eastern tip of the Giudecca, formerly the property of Andrea Dandolo but at that time belonging to the procurator Antonio Barbarigo.[10] It was a dignified and spacious residence, generously provided with elegant courtyards and quiet gardens, and the Molo but a short distance away by boat.

On hearing from Valerio Crova, the Mantuan Resident, that the cortège would arrive at the Venetian border near the little town of Loreo, those in charge of ceremonies appointed six noble youths, with the title of 'ambassadors', to go there and meet the Mantuans and bring them to Chioggia by boat, where they would be greeted by the Podestà (mayor) of that city and by a contingent of sixty Venetian senators in five small vessels. At Chioggia there would be a grand reception, after which the party would proceed across the lagoon to Venice. Monteverdi could not have failed to hear of all these preparations, nor could he have entertained any doubt that he, as the uncrowned head of music in the Republic and the former servant of the Gonzaga, would be called upon to provide suitable musical entertainment. By great good fortune, his health was steadily improving.

The Duchess and her retinue were met, as planned, on 21 May, and there followed a splendid succession of formal and informal events, of which the most memorable was the Sensa. Easily the most colourful and spectacular of Venetian festivals, Ascension Day naturally attracted by far the greatest number of tourists and visitors, who crowded into boats of all kinds and sizes in order to witness the ceremony of the Wedding of the Sea. This took place on Wednesday, 25 May, and the Mantuan party, after enjoying the event from the comfortable vantage-point of the Gradenigo galley, visited Murano after dinner and returned to the Giudecca late at night. The balm of

---

[8] The body of St Lucy, formerly in the church of that name, was translated to the north transept of S. Geremia when Palladio's building was removed to make way for the railway station which now in turn bears the name of the Sicilian virgin and martyr. One of the reasons for Ferdinando's homage in 1623 was the fact that the church was then quite new: it had been consecrated on 17 November 1617 by Cardinal Francesco Vendramin (Sansovino, 140–4).

[9] Extracts from the *Cerimoniali* (Archivio di Stato, Filza Collegio 1603–23) are in Ademollo, 271–9. A more recent and exceptionally thorough account appears in Whenham, 'Gonzagas'.

[10] Sansovino, 389.

the evening and the still waters of the canal lent enchantment to a concert they heard, with the sweetest music, both vocal and instrumental.[11]

Earlier in the day they had been entertained at the Arsenal, which at that time was more than a vast repository of naval and military power: its famous banqueting hall could accommodate large numbers of guests and still leave room for a stage whereon singers and players might gather to perform *concerti musicali* by the greatest composers of the day. It was there, five years later, that Monteverdi directed music in honour of the Grand Duke of Tuscany, Ferdinando II.[12] Surely he was present both as conductor and composer when his patroness Caterina Medici Gonzaga, Duke Ferdinando, and the cream of the Mantuan court came to hear the best that Venice could offer? Who more appropriate than Monteverdi to arrange such a concert? And who more perfect as soloist than Adriana Basile, formerly an honoured guest of the Gonzagas, and now a diva of universal renown?

The impression she made on the Venetians on this particular occasion and frequently thereafter was such that Domizio Bombarda wrote a book about her, with the title *Teatro delle glorie della S^ra Adriana Basile*,[13] but it is only fair to assume that a great interpreter (as she undoubtedly was) derived some part of her magnetism from the music she sang; and because of her long-standing acquaintance with Monteverdi it is almost certain that she would have chosen at least one of his compositions. In view of the fact that the dedicatee of the Seventh Book of Madrigals was present, she could have chosen the wonderful setting of Guarini's *Con che soavità*—the only soprano solo in the entire book, unless one includes the *Lettera amorosa*, which Doni thought more appropriate for a male singer on account of the sentiments expressed in Achillini's poem.[14]

Five days later, the court left Venice with the same display of pomp and circumnavigation that had given such a distinguished touch to the arrival, with its homage to the churches of S. Giorgio in Alga and S. Spirito. The homeward journey was more direct, but once again the youthful ambassadors accompanied the ducal pair and their retinue as far as Loreo, after which the route led overland through Rovigo and Legnago to Mantua. Before leaving, however, Ferdinando made arrangements for Adriana and her husband Mutio to spend some time in Mantua, the only undecided question being the date of departure. Perhaps he hoped that they would all travel westwards together, but there was audible opposition from Adriana's Venetian host, Girolamo Mocenigo, whose noble palace had come to be regarded as a mecca for artists of all kinds, and especially for musicians.[15]

Monteverdi referred to Mocenigo as his special patron and protector in the preface to *Madrigali guerrieri et amorosi*, when introducing the subject of the *Combattimento di Tancredi e Clorinda*, which was given its first performance in 1624 in one of the great rooms of Mocenigo's palace. Composer and patron would certainly have been in

---

[11] Ademollo, 277.   [12] See Strozzi, *Fratelli* (Deuchino, Venice, 1628).
[13] Deuchino, Venice, 1623 (reprinted with many additions in Naples, 1628).
[14] Doni, ii (App.), 26. See also Gallico, 'Lettera', 287.
[15] For further information on Mocenigo, see below, pp. 280–81.

contact with each other in 1623, and the presence of Adriana in the patrician's household and Monteverdi in the nearby canonry must have resulted in several public or private concerts in addition to the elaborate one at the Arsenal. In a letter to the Duke, dated 2 June, Antonio Callegari reported on the situation, making it quite clear that the reason for Adriana's delayed departure was the urgent request on the part of Mocenigo that she should stay as long as possible.[16]

   She planned to leave once Whit Sunday was over, and this fell on 4 June—the day on which Monteverdi answered the Duke's letter concerning travel arrangements for Adriana, her husband, and a musician named Donati.[17] The only suitable candidate for this otherwise unknown person is Ignazio Donati, a composer and organist who was at that time between appointments at Casalmaggiore and Novara. An almost exact contemporary of Monteverdi, he was also a countryman of his, having been born at Casalmaggiore near Cremona about the year 1570. Between 1612 and 1636 he published numerous volumes of church music and a few secular works, one of which was dedicated to Carlo Milanuzzi, a friend of Monteverdi's. When Donati applied for the vacant post of organist at Milan Cathedral in 1631, he may well have done so on the recommendation of Monteverdi, whose opinion the Chapter habitually sought whenever a major appointment had to be made. He was successful, and (as Sartori points out) 'perhaps the authoritative recommendation for his appointment carried the signature of Claudio Monteverdi'.[18] Although Donati's name appears nowhere else in Monteverdi's extant correspondence, the two musicians could certainly have known each other; and Monteverdi's friendship with the Basiles made it a comparatively easy matter for him to ask them if they would allow Donati to travel with them 'without his having to spend any money'—in other words to avoid bothering the already overcommitted Mantuan treasury with a request for travel funds.

My Most Serene Lord and Most Respected Master,

Your Highness's letter having been shown to Signor Donati,[a] he at once—without demur—offered to obey your commands, and so he is coming together with Signora Adriana and Signor Mutio,[b] who is bringing him without his having to spend any money. I am writing to render Your Highness a thousand thanks for the honour you have so kindly done by commanding me. I beg to be maintained in Your Highness's good grace, while with every most humble reverence I bow to the ground, and

   [16] Ademollo, 280.

   [17] Paoli, 216, links 'Signor Mutio' with Muzio Effrem, who was indeed connected with the musical establishment in Mantua at that time. But it may be safer to assume that Adriana would travel in the company of her husband.

   [18] Sartori, 'Monteverdiana', 413.

   [a] Probably Ignazio Donati, a composer and organist.   [b] Adriana Basile and her husband.

pray God with the most earnest affection for your greatest possible happiness.

from Venice, 4 June 1623
Your Most Serene Highness's
most humble and most grateful servant
Claudio Monteverdi

81

Venice, 2 March 1624
to [Duke Ferdinando Gonzaga, at Mantua]

Mantua, Archivio Gonzaga, Cassetta 6, fos. 289–90. Bifolio: 4 pp.

Prunières, 269; Malipiero, 237; Paoli, 217; Lax, 136

Although no correspondence with Mantuan court officials survives between 11 March 1623 and 15 March 1625, Monteverdi may have kept in touch with both Marigliani and Striggio after his illness. A two-year gap in an otherwise flourishing correspondence stretches credibility too far, unless we assume that some letters have been mysteriously lost, or that the officials were too busy dealing with the political subtleties of the Isabella–Vincenzo case. The two letters addressed to Duke Ferdinando (80 and 81) nevertheless provide some evidence of a desire to maintain contact with Mantua, and the nine-month gap that separates them coincides with a particularly active period in Monteverdi's life.

Venice on the other hand was becoming slightly sinister. Shortly after 15 June 1623 an anonymous accusation was dropped into the *bocca del leone* outside the Doge's palace. It mentioned only one date, that of SS. Vito e Modesto (15 June), and took Monteverdi severely to task for upholding the Holy Roman Empire and the King of Spain against the Republic of Venice. He was also censured for insisting on his rights as Director of Music, and for making a mistake during Vespers in St Mark's on the day of the 'Sensa', that most colourful of Venetian festivals when the Ascensiontide liturgy received additional impetus from the ceremony of the Wedding of the Sea.

The composer, for good measure, was also accused of blasphemy.

Seeking out the trouble-maker is not too difficult, for Domenico Aldegati had shown his mettle shortly after Monteverdi's arrival in Venice in 1613, and although ejected from the basilica's group of musicians he would return to further mischief-making in 1637, as Letter 126 shows. The irascible singer was almost certainly behind this attempt to discredit the composer, who in 1631 received two testimonials as to his honesty and good behaviour from two colleagues: Zuanne Arzignan and Stefano Rinieri.

The accusations, whether true or not, are of little consequence now, and probably belong to that class of *ad hominem* attack which all eminent people have to suffer. It was true that between 1623 and 1627 Monteverdi explored artistic links with Salzburg and the Emperor Ferdinand II, but there is no evidence of disloyalty to Venice. As for the mistake at Vespers, who in the musical profession today has not noticed a conductor forget some vital point in the score?[1]

On 13 August Monteverdi was by duty bound to supervise the music for the funeral of the Doge, Antonio Priuli, who was succeeded by one of the senior men among the procurators *de citra*, Francesco Contarini. Outside and beyond St Mark's, the confraternity of San Rocco were planning their annual festival (16 August), in which music usually played an important part. Because its standards had slipped so badly in the previous year that Sir Henry Wotton, English ambassador to Venice, drew attention to the matter,[2] the elders of the Scuola di San Rocco decided that only the best would suffice for the festival of 1623. Monteverdi was therefore invited to take charge, receiving for his team of musicians and for his own services the sum of 620 lire.[3] Presumably he once again made use of a two-voice motet, *O beatae viae*, the text of which describes the miraculous life of San Rocco and the efficacy of his powers in warding off the plague.[4]

A generous tribute to him appeared in a volume of solos, duets, and trios by Pellegrino Possenti, a composer then living in Venice, and possibly a priest, for the title 'Don' precedes his name in the anthology of G. B. Anselmi. Possenti's collection, fancifully entitled *Canora sampogna*,[5] begins with a dedication to Don Virginio Dina, visitor to the monastic community of San Salvatore. Decrying as is usual in such contexts his own feeble invention, the composer goes on to praise the many fine works by greater men than he, especially those of Monteverdi, 'who by his loftiness being near to heaven, has learned harmonious song from the angels'.

Two months later, Anselmi's poems (or *madrigali*, as he called them) emerged from the same publishing house of Magni in a series of settings by various composers, among them several Venetian citizens or residents.[6] Monteverdi contributed the duet *O come vaghi* and the trio *Taci Armelin*.[7] This ermine-clad canine, with its inopportune bark, appears with Monteverdi and three musical associates in a little-known Mantuan portrait.[8] Grandi and Fillago from St Mark's were also represented, along with the countertenor Bartolomeo Barbarino, who sang at the San Rocco festivals under the name of 'Il Pesarino'.

The autumn of 1623 saw Monteverdi engrossed in what was to become one of his most original and impressive compositions: *Il combattimento di Tancredi e Clorinda*, based on part of the twelfth canto of *Gerusalemme liberata*. It is quite possible that the work was specially commissioned by Girolamo Mocenigo, in whose magnificent house it was first performed during the 1624 carnival, which began on Quinquagesima

[1] Glixon, 404–6; Vio, 348–9.   [2] Smith, ii. 245.

[3] Arnold ('San Rocco') discusses the confraternity and its musical associations. The document concerning Monteverdi, however, appears in the same author's monograph on the composer (1963 ed., p. 202).

[4] First published by Calvo in the *Symbolae diversorum musicorum* (Venice, 1620). Modern edition in *Collected Works*, ed. Malipiero, xvi. 454.

[5] Vogel, *Bibliothek*, ii. 97. Date of dedication, 28 Oct. 1623.

[6] Ibid. 512. Date of dedication, 23 Dec. 1623.

[7] Modern editions in *Collected Works*, ed. Malipiero, ix. 102 and 106.

[8] Santoro, 'Iconografia', pl. 18.

Sunday (18 February) and continued until Shrove Tuesday (20 February). Monteverdi's artistic contributions to his patron's musical evenings at the time of Adriana Basile's sojourn in Venice may well have given rise to the commission, but whether or not this was the case, the emotional impact of the *Combattimento* cannot be denied.

In common with many forward-looking scores, it aroused opposition among the performers, some of whom took a particular dislike to the vigorous reiteration of one note within a single bar, in a measured non-tremolando intended to convey with pointed accuracy the composer's idea of anger and aggression. It was typical of Monteverdi's practical outlook to compose and perform music before writing a theoretical treatise about it; and the steady pace at which he developed his theories may be observed in the lapse of time between the première in 1624, his first mention of the treatise (Letter 124 of 1633), and the discussion of his ideas—as they affected the *Combattimento*—in the preface to the Eighth Book, in 1638.

Mocenigo, who lived from 1581 to 1658, belonged to a small circle of wealthy and distinguished Venetians who encouraged the arts out of a genuine desire to make them more widely known. One of four children born to Andrea Mocenigo and Giustiniana di Giovanni Giustiniani, he was brought up as a potential servant of the republic and lost no time in fulfilling his duties to it. At the age of 33 he was elected *capitano* of Vicenza, and six years later in 1620 he became a member of the Venetian senate, as *provveditor*. Concern with the commissariat did not, however, seriously interfere with his devotion to music, which was acknowledged by an echo canzona, *La Moceniga*, in Giovanni Battista Riccio's third book of *Divine lodi musicali* (1620).[9]

At this time he acquired part of the old palazzo Dandolo, which he renovated and refurnished at great expense.[10] In 1624, the year of the *Combattimento*, he was appointed adviser for inland affairs (*savio di terraferma*), a position that he held with distinction for ten years, during which time he received as dedicatee a set of madrigals by the 15-year-old Domenico Obizzi.[11] Much as he favoured established musicians, he did not neglect the younger generation. Mocenigo moved up the official ladder in 1634 as *sindaco* (mayor being a near equivalent), and two years later was elected a member of the Doge's *consiglio*. Later honours included a year as *capitano* of Padua (1637–8) followed by high office in his native city: senior adviser, head of the Council of Ten, and *consigliere ducale*. He was twice married: in 1606 to Elisa di Alvise Pisani, by whom he had a daughter Giustiniana, who married Lorenzo Giustiniani in 1629; and in 1612 to Cecilia di Giambattista Foscarini.[12]

This then was the man whom Monteverdi claimed as his special patron, and in whose house many of his mature compositions were undoubtedly performed. The

---

[9] Although named after Mocenigo, the dedicatee is Alessandro Grandi. See Selfridge-Field, 111.

[10] It is now better known as the Hotel Danieli, whose unusually distinguished list of visitors has included George Sand, Alfred de Musset, Dickens, Ruskin, Wagner, and Proust. For an illustration of the *salone*, see *Musica II* (1943), pl. XIX.

[11] Vogel, *Bibliothek*, ii. 26.   [12] Litta: Dispensa 157.

success and sympathy evoked by the form and content of the *Combattimento* were such that Monteverdi tried to follow it up a year or so later with a setting of the scene between Armida and Rinaldo, from Tasso's epic,[13] but the music has not survived. The copy made for Mantua probably disappeared in the holocaust of 1630. And in 1624 the Mantuan carnival went its own way, as we know from letters received in Modena. Preparations for a musical entertainment were being planned for Quinquagesima Sunday, but the Duke was in a melancholy mood, and had weightier things on his mind.[14] What they were becomes painfully clear from the dramatic change in the situation at Rome, for on 5 January Isabella Gonzaga had finally been released from Castel S. Angelo. The general joy and relief of her many supporters found outlet in a Te Deum sung in the Chiesa della Pace.[15]

By a strange coincidence, the Duchess authorized another official departure on that same day in January, giving leave to Adriana Basile and offering best wishes for her journey back to Naples.[16] Adriana cannot therefore have taken part in the intermezzi given on 18 February: *La favola delle Arpie*, *Il canto delle Sirene*, and *Perseo taglia il capo a Medusa*, well supplied as they were with lively music. The great singer must have sensed that Mantua was deteriorating, and although she allowed her sons to remain, she herself never returned.

Gradually Ferdinando recovered from the departure of Adriana and the release of Isabella, for he appears to have written to Monteverdi about the possibility of finding a singer in Venice. On Saturday, 2 March, Monteverdi had gone early to St Mark's, in all probability for a rehearsal, and one of his singers had told him that a letter had already been sent to a brother at Salzburg Cathedral, advising him that better musical opportunities could be found in Venice. The Salzburg man was a young castrato; and if Monteverdi thought that he might be a suitable candidate for the Duke of Mantua, should it be inferred that Ferdinando, in despair at losing Adriana and incapable of believing that she could ever be replaced, turned his attention to the only alternative in that particular tessitura?

In any event Monteverdi found, on returning to the canonry, that a letter had just arrived from the Duke, and he sat down to answer it without delay. He seems to have understood the situation perfectly: the Duke, having lost a peerless prima donna who was also very expensive, needed a young castrato willing to study with Monteverdi for a suitable period of time. After this there would be an offer from Mantua, and the gap would be filled at minimum cost. The desirability of a sojourn in Venice is confirmed by Monteverdi, who assures the Duke that everything possible will be done to find the candidate suitable employment. Ferdinando cannot have failed to notice the subtle flattery inherent in the composer's reference to the Duke of Modena: an enthusiast, but not yet a connoisseur.

---

[13] This work is mentioned as having already been completed before May 1627 (see Letter 92).
[14] Solerti, *Albori*, i. 120 n. 2.   [15] Errante, 'Il processo', 713.   [16] Ademollo, 287.

My Most Serene and Particular Lord and Most Respected Master,

I am writing to offer Your Highness the greatest thanks I most reverently and possibly can, with all my heart and mind, for the special honour which you have deigned to do me, namely by honouring me with your commands, which I shall always look upon as sent by the hand of God, and the greatest honour and good fortune I could receive.

At present, Most Serene Lord, there is no suitable individual here in Venice; however I heard of the following possibility through a monk attached to[a] San Stefano, in Venice (a singer at St Mark's), who told me ten days ago that he has a brother—a young castrato with a very good voice, ready ornamentation, and a *trillo*—in the service of the Most Illustrious Lord Bishop of Salzburg.[b] But because nobody in that establishment is capable of improving his talent, this monk would be glad for him to come and stay in Venice if there were an opportunity to do something useful.

I replied that he should have him come here, for I would not fail to help him as regards employers and with a little advice too. This very morning (as it so happened) before I received Your Highness's command, he told me in chapel that he had written and asked him to come. Now that I know what I have to attend to, in regard to Your Highness's pleasure, I shall not be neglectful in keeping myself most carefully informed about it, and should it be appropriate I shall not fail to press the matter so that I can show by the results—over and beyond my most ready intent—how I long to be a servant of Your Highness.

Nor shall I limit myself merely to this—indeed I shall not forget to look elsewhere for further possibilities about which I shall at once inform Your Highness if they come to my notice. I believe that Signor Campagnolo,[c] as one who has been in those parts, would perhaps be able to give Your Highness a report.

During the past few days I heard that in Ferrara, in the service of the community of Santo Spirito,[d] there is a man with a very fine voice and

---

[a] *dell'ordine*. He was almost certainly not a member of the order founded by St Stephen of Grandmont, but served at San Stefano.

[b] Count Paris Lodron (installed 3 Mar. 1621; died 15 Dec. 1653). His *maestro di cappella* at this time was Peter Gutfreund (otherwise known as Bonamico), and at least half of the court musicians were Italians.

[c] A former pupil of Monteverdi, the tenor Francesco Campagnolo had been in Salzburg in 1617–18 at the invitation of the Duke of Bavaria.

[d] The Accademia di Santo Spirito enjoyed a notable musical establishment and reputation: Monteverdi's

good vocal graces who has been giving by no means ordinary satisfaction. Since the Most Serene Lord Prince of Modena*e* is beginning to enjoy music the way he does, and since he is not slow in hiring the best (yet finds them only with difficulty), for this very reason I do not entirely believe those who have told me about this man from Ferrara.

Nevertheless I did not wish to refrain from mentioning it to Your Highness, so that (if it please God) you would be served as I desire. And here making a very low and humble bow to Your Highness, I beg you with every affectionate entreaty to preserve me in that part of your grace which you are accustomed to give to the least (indeed) but truest and most genuine of Your Highness's servants. I pray God with all my heart for the fulfilment of every supreme joy.

from Venice, 2 March 1624

Your Most Serene Highness's

most humble and most grateful servant

Claudio Monteverdi

assistant, Alessandro Grandi, was in charge of the music there from 1610 until 1616, and this news may even have come to his notice through Grandi's contacts.

e Alfonso III, Prince of Modena (1591–1644).

82

Venice, 15 March 1625
to [Alessandro Striggio, at Mantua]

Mantua, Archivio Gonzaga, Cassetta 6, fo. 293. Folio: 1 p.

Prunières, 270; Malipiero, 238; Paoli, 220; Lax, 138

Venice, Mantua, Modena, Bologna, Milan—these cities certainly, and others very possibly, engaged Monteverdi's attention during the period of just over a year that separates this letter from the previous one. His involvements were for the most part of a pleasant and artistic nature, except with Mantua: for some strange reason, the wretched treatment he received there prior to 1613 seemed to generate an aftermath of problems and intrigues. His complaints, incessant and tiresome as they may sound nowadays, were in many ways justified, for the Duke could have treated him decently if not as generously as he did Adriana Basile.

The letters that passed so frequently between Ferdinando and Adriana in 1624 and 1625 demonstrate the degree of his infatuation, and the lengths to which he was prepared to go in order to tempt her back to his court. On 17 April, he informed her that income from lands was at her disposal, and a later missive from her husband to Marigliani makes it clear that the figure ran into several hundreds of ducats.[1] Poor Monteverdi, never hoping for one-tenth of what Adriana received, was always being put off and cheated of his due reward. Yet her art perished at her death, while his lives on, still providing pleasure and inspiration to all who come into contact with it.

By the end of May, Ferdinando had taken himself off to a country retreat near Florence, as he was in very poor health due to a combination of physical and mental causes, among the latter being his virtual defeat in the Vincenzo–Isabella case. As the summer months dragged on, his condition—instead of improving—gradually became worse. Adriana stopped writing, but when Ferdinando complained, a bread-and-butter letter came almost by return. Far from pleasing the Duke, this attempt at pacification prompted another complaint, the burden of which was that Adriana must have written out of a sense of duty rather than affection. By the middle of August, his health and spirits improved, as did the tone of his subsequent correspondence.

The death of Annibale Chieppio in 1623 had the expected result of improving the rank and fortune of Alessandro Striggio, so that his importance in the political affairs

---

[1] Ademollo, 289 ff., gives a sequence of letters written by or to the Duke, Duchess, Adriana, and her husband Mutio. See also the letter from the Duke to Striggio (13 June 1624) regarding the near-completion of the organ in S. Barbara (Bertolotti, 100).

of Mantua removed him from those areas of entertainment and diversion which he formerly enjoyed as an active participant. Monteverdi apparently wrote no letters to him between 11 March 1623 and 15 March 1625 (nos. 79 and 82), and after five in succession to Marigliani, the next letter to Striggio was not written until a year later, on 19 March 1626. The complete lack of correspondence between them in 1624 is explained by the fact that Striggio's time was almost totally absorbed by a series of complex negotiations with the House of Savoy, a treaty being finally drawn up in Turin thanks to the efforts of the councillor's younger colleague, Giulio Cesare Faccipecora Pavesi.[2]

Monteverdi's main concern at this time was not with the court, but with the law. When his father-in-law Giacomo Cattaneo died on 24 April, trouble began almost immediately because of a 13-year-old agreement regarding his right to have lived in a certain house in the Mastino district of Mantua. The origins of the case go back as far as 1605, when a widow named Cassandra Ventuna gave her house and possessions 'titulo donationis inter vivos' to Giacomo Cattaneo,[3] an arrangement which worked very nicely for a few years until the widow's grandniece, Barbara Berini, decided to marry Ippolito de Belli, a local gentleman of substance and property.

The bride's father, Alessandro Berini, had already made one attempt to contest the donation, and faced now with the prospect of providing his daughter with a generous dowry, which was to include three houses, he set his sights once more on the Mastino property. All this took place in 1609, dragging on into the following year (when the widow Ventuna passed to a less litigious life), and almost to the end of 1611. On 15 November Berini dropped his suit against Cattaneo, agreeing to permit him the use of the property for the remainder of his life, after which it would revert to Berini's daughter and her husband, Ippolito de Belli.

On 6 May 1624—less than two weeks after Cattaneo's death—Monteverdi appointed Dr Giulio Bagozzi as his lawyer. Perhaps Belli was at first reluctant to enter into legal proceedings, because he waited until 11 July before appointing, as his lawyer, Paolo Camellino. Two days later, the case opened at the palazzo of Judge Filippo Brandolo, and on 15 July Monteverdi appeared in court. The documents record no further appearance, the matter being presumably left in what turned out to be the incapable hands of Bagozzi.

The available evidence suggests that in actual fact Monteverdi had no claims on the house or its contents. Cattaneo's will had made no provision whatever for him and hardly anything for the two grandsons born of Monteverdi's union with Claudia Cattaneo. Nevertheless Monteverdi may have believed for some reason or other that he would be required to challenge the situation, and his promptness in retaining the services of a lawyer bears out this attitude. An additional factor may have been his disappointment over the donation granted him by Duke Vincenzo I: a house in Mantua would have yielded a rent that might to some extent make up for what he kept losing through the wide mesh of the Mantuan treasury.

---

[2] Quazza, *Diplomazia*, 45.
[3] A detailed account of the lawsuit appears in Gallico, 'Contra C. M.', 346–59.

Whatever the rights and wrongs of the case, it seems that the two lawyers enjoyed themselves for at least eighteen months. Camellino even went so far as to object to Monteverdi's appearing in court on the grounds that he was not a citizen of Mantua, but of Cremona, even though documents existed to prove the contrary.[4] When Bagozzi tried to annul the Cattaneo–Berini agreement of 1611, Camellino threatened to claim rent, damages, and interest from 1610 until 1624, since Cattaneo could be considered as a paying tenant rather than one enjoying merely the usufruct.

Both sides eventually reached the point of an appeal to the Duke, who had returned to Mantua with the Duchess towards the end of August, neither of them in the frame of mind to deal with a lawsuit. Moreover, by this time the situation had become almost violent, with an order for sequestration being resisted physically at the disputed house by agents appointed either by Bagozzi or by Monteverdi. From Venice, the composer sent a plea to the Duke on 2 October, and this was transcribed by Giuseppe Colorno three days later, when the Duke and Duchess were thinking of little else but tempting Adriana to return and sing for them.

Monteverdi recounted, in his plea, the whole story about the house, pretended (perhaps on the advice of Bagozzi) that the agreement of 1611 was invalid and that the house in dispute might not even be the same one that Belli wanted; he maintained his rights as a Mantuan citizen, and asked that the judge might be directed to 'grant justice summarily to the contending parties, without suit or process, treating in such case the petitioner and his sons as citizens and servants of His Highness, being sons born in the city (although they no longer live in the state of Mantua), one of whom is a student at Padua, giving back immediately those few pieces of furniture which have been sequestrated, among which are a number of musical instruments going to rack and ruin'.[5]

Ferdinando's reply to all this was curt and to the point—'let justice be done without delay'—after which he went back to the more pressing business of providing Adriana with a safe-conduct for her return to Mantua. But she never came back. Ferdinando had only two years to live, and Mantua was foredoomed by the mounting crisis of the succession. The judge, in no mood to be ordered what to do by Monteverdi, interpreted the Duke's instructions as confirmation of the sequestration order, given on 11 December. Camellino then asked that the costs of the case should be met by Monteverdi, who immediately appealed again to the Duke for permission to have the case debated before the Senate. This was duly granted, Colorno drew up the document of appeal on 19 December, and everyone withdrew for the Christmas holidays.

The appeal being approved by Duke Ferdinando on 15 January 1625, the entire case was reopened, with witnesses appearing for both parties and copious transcripts being made, as was customary. Monteverdi remained in Venice, and must have written to Striggio for assistance (as was his custom whenever anything went wrong in his relationships with Mantua) towards the end of February or the early part of

[4] Davari, 84.   [5] Gallico, 'Contra C. M.', 353.

March. Although that letter seems not to have survived, Striggio replied favourably and Monteverdi's delayed answer of 15 March—the present letter—expresses his gratitude. Malipiero, Paoli, Prunières, and Gallico all assume that the letter was sent to Marigliani, but the form of address—'Illustrissimo mio Signore et padron collendissimo'—is the correct one for Striggio.

By 4 July 1624 Prince Alfonso had received the second of the promised madrigals by Monteverdi (presumably *Chi vol haver felice*) and promptly requested two more, perhaps with some three-part canzonette.[6] The madrigals may never have been written, but there is a canzonetta in the Biblioteca Estense at Modena: a manuscript copy of *Ahi che si parti*, which was never published in the composer's lifetime and had to wait until the appearance of Malipiero's vol. xvi (p. 542) before coming even faintly to the notice of the musical world at large.

If there were later dealings with Modena, concrete evidence is lacking. But this is not quite true of Bologna, although some of the details of Monteverdi's visit to that city could appear in better focus. Vogel guessed that membership in the Accademia dei Filomusi was offered 'about 1624' in view of a passage from Banchieri's *Discorso della lingua bolognese*, first published in 1626.[7] But the evidence suggests that Monteverdi and Agostino Facchi were elected to the Academy as outside (or visiting) members—*forestieri*—in the same year; and since Facchi did not leave his post in Bologna until late in 1624 (he became organist of the cathedral at Vicenza in December) he could not really be classified as a non-resident until 1625. Although Monteverdi could have travelled on to Bologna after his brief appearance in Mantua on 15 July 1624, it is just as likely that the visit took place in 1625.[8] Until documents relating to the history of the Filomusi become available, the matter must rest undecided.

In Venice, a census of inhabitants for the year 1624 reveals the name of Claudio Monteverdi as head of the 'family' then residing in the apartment set aside in the canonry for the Director of Music. The names of the other two residents are not given, but from the various categories and definitions into which the census is divided, it is clear that one was his son Francesco (at that time a tenor in the choir of St Mark's), and the other a female servant.[9] Massimiliano was still a student at Bologna.

---

[6] Fabbri, 'Inediti', 77.   [7] Vogel, 373.

[8] Vecchi (184) states that the Accademia dei Filomusi was inaugurated in 1625, but the facsimile (150)—showing the official motto and device of the Academy—prints a date exactly three years earlier: Accademia de Filomusi | nell | Anno. 1622. Instituita dal Sig:re | Do: Girolamo Giacobbi. He also suggests (82) the date of 1627 for Monteverdi's reception, though without evidence other than the assumption that it took place one year prior to the appearance of a congratulatory letter in the 1628 edition of Banchieri's *Lettere armoniche*. Vecchi considers *La sampogna* as a homage to Monteverdi, who might have attended the *serata* at which the music was performed (88). But the facsimile of the title-page of this edition shows that is was certainly not dedicated to Monteverdi, but to a Padre D. Angiolo Maria Cantoni. The date of the gathering, 14 Nov. 1625, would have been too late in the year to tempt Monteverdi away from Venice: there were Advent and Christmas ceremonies to prepare, and the roads were not exactly at their best in the winter months.

[9] Damerini, 105–20.

Two short compositions by Francesco appear with three by his father and several songs by other composers of the time in the 1624 reprint of Carlo Milanuzzi's *Quarto scherzo delle ariose vaghezze*,[10] a charming collection of light and amorous music by a broad-minded Augustinian monk who was the capable organist of San Stefano in Venice. Another admirer of Monteverdi, Don Lorenzo Calvo, Director of Music at Pavia Cathedral, included three of his motets in a *Seconda raccolta de' canti sacri*.

As Monteverdi hints in his letter to Striggio, a 'Polish monarch' constantly kept him busy with sacred and secular music. This was Sigismund III (1566–1632), brother-in-law of the Emperor Ferdinand II, and a considerable though unpopular figure in the political life both within and without his domain. His Catholic upbringing and his alliance with the Habsburgs led him to appreciate, as they did, the actual and potential contribution of Italian musicians to ceremony and entertainment, to the furtherance of which he sought unceasingly for the very best in the way of composers and singers. Visiting Venice in the spring of 1624 with his retinue, he attended on 9 March a Mass at the basilica with music by Monteverdi. This pleased Sigismund not only by its excellence but by its brevity.[11]

He tempted Monteverdi but failed to entice him to Warsaw; he also wrote to Mutio Barone offering travelling expenses at once if he and Adriana would agree to serve him.[12] For some time his musical factotum was Antonio Tarroni, whom Monteverdi had known in Mantua, but neither Tarroni nor the King himself could lure the singer from her Neapolitan *otium cum dignitate*. Monteverdi, as usual, was perfectly willing to assist as long as he could remain in Venice, for his dislike of travel increased as the years went by. And he was not afraid to ask for assistance when he needed it, or thought he needed it, when it was a small matter of a benefice in Cremona towards the end of 1627.[13]

Otherwise life in Venice continued on its peaceful way. When the Doge Francesco Contarini died in December, Monteverdi was presumably called upon to provide and direct the funeral music, and when in January Giovanni Cornaro succeeded to the highest office, there was music of a more joyful kind.[14] The man who had shared in the processing of Monteverdi's appointment to St Mark's in 1613, as one of the four procurators responsible for the basilica, came to the Doge's Palace in solemn triumph.

Far off in Milan, the cathedral chapter took a long and hard look at its musical establishment, wishing perhaps that it might one day measure up to that of Venice. But the choir contained almost as many bad singers as good, and the Director of

---

[10] Vogel, *Bibliothek*, i. 465. The sole surviving copy at Hamburg was destroyed in World War II, but a handwritten copy of the entire collection was made by Alfred Einstein and is bound in with other transcriptions by him in vol. 34 of the Einstein Collection at Smith College, Northampton, Mass.

[11] Fabbri 1994, 192.

[12] Ademollo, 299 (Vienna, 18 Apr. 1625). See also 144, 145, 301, 309. Sigismund's patronage of other Italian musicians may be seen in the dedications of Tarquinio Merula's two books of madrigals published in 1624 (Vogel, *Bibliothek*, i. 454, 455) and Francesco Rognoni Taeggio's *Selva di varii passaggi* of 1620 (Sartori, *Bibliografia*, 262). See also F. de Daugnan, *Gli italiani in Polonia* (Crema, 1905–7), and Padoan, 232.

[13] see Letter 106.   [14] For Cornaro, see Letter 48.

Music, Vincenzo Pellegrini, lacked many of the qualities of a true leader. The members of the chapter therefore met together and decided upon a five-point plan for improvement which was duly drawn up on 12 March 1625. The third point concerned Pellegrini: his standards of discipline and performance being below par, consideration should be given to a replacement, and to this end the Rector should speak with someone able to contact Monteverdi in Venice and find out his opinion. Whether this meant that he would be offered the post if Pellegrini were pensioned off, or whether it was simply a case of a professional opinion regarding improvement or replacement, is not completely clear in the original document.[15] But Monteverdi's name was on everybody's lips, whether in Milan, Mantua, Modena, Bologna, or Venice.

My Most Illustrious Lord and Most Respected Master,

I was unable, by the previous post, to thank Your Lordship's infinite goodness (as was my duty) for being so kind as to assure me—beyond what I deserve—of your favour in the matter of a certain problem I have in Mantua, due to a lawsuit that I neither thought of nor wanted. But the multitude of tasks I have had, and still have to do, in serving this Polish monarch[a] both in his chapel and at his court has done away with my ability to repay (at least partially) the great debt which I owe and always shall owe to Your Lordship.

I beg you to forgive me, just as I beg you also to do me the kindness of letting me explain the aforesaid business of mine the next time I write, in order to beseech you—having considered my reasons—at least to calm the matter down without any harm to me, since the other party has obtained all he wanted. And with this ending, making a most humble bow to Your Lordship I pray God Our Saviour for your every perfect good.

from Venice, 15 March 1625
Your Most Illustrious Lordship's
most grateful servant
Claudio Monteverdi

[15] For Monteverdi's Milanese contacts, see postscript to Letter 93, and also Sartori, 'Monteverdiana', 411–13.

[a] Sigismund III.

83

Venice, 23 August 1625
to [Ercole Marigliani, at Mantua]

Mantua, Archivio Gonzaga, Cassetta 6, fos. 295–7. Bifolio + folio: 5 pp.

Prunières, 270; Malipiero, 239; Paoli, 222; Lax, 139

Striggio, burdened by the increasing complexity of political affairs and worried by the failing health of Duke Ferdinando, passed the problem of Monteverdi's lawsuit over to a younger colleague, Ercole Marigliani, who proceeded to unravel as best he could the tangled threads of a situation that everybody—except the lawyers Bagozzi and Camellino—had begun to find exceedingly tiresome and boring. On 18 June and again on 23 July Ippolito de Belli appealed to the Duke for payment of arrears and costs, and at last his plea was answered—in the affirmative.[1] Bagozzi's inept handling of the case in August 1624, when he tried to annul the Cattaneo–Berini agreement, had caused the lawsuit to drag on well into the next year, and it would not end until December 1625.

Marigliani's part in the matter was to see that Cattaneo's personal goods were sold, with the exception of some of the musical instruments, and presumably the proceeds of that sale were used to pay costs. Since the entire affair had given Monteverdi more trouble than he had bargained for, he must have felt a sense of relief when handing over the local arrangements to Marigliani. Formerly collaborators in musical affairs, they were now concerned with questions of law and finance, and in this atmosphere of mutual trust they moved on to a new kind of collaboration, the first hint of which is discovered in the present letter.

In the collection of tributes, both prose and poetry, assembled and published by G. B. Marinoni in the year following Monteverdi's death, there is a sonnet by the Venetian priest and musician Paolo Piazza, prefaced by these words: 'In morte di Claudio Monteverdi, Gran professor della Chimica'.[2] Yet the only evidence of Monteverdi's interest in alchemy, apart from this reference and a poetical nod to precious metals in the sonnet, occurs in Letters 83, 84, 86, 87, and 89. Nevertheless it should be borne in mind not only that his father had been a doctor and his son was about to become one, but also that a more than casual relationship then existed between medical science and alchemy, so that a man who mistrusted the one might easily find consolation in the other.

---

[1] Gallico, 'Contra C. M.', 356.   [2] *Fiori poetici* (Venice, 1644), 22.

[290]

Monteverdi had passed his formative years as a musician at the court of Vincenzo Gonzaga, a luxury-loving prince whose stranger quirks included a somewhat unhealthy enthusiasm for the pseudo-sciences, among which alchemy took pride of place. His considerable team of test-tube manipulators were kept constantly at work in distant corners of the Palazzo del Tè, brewing bizarre concoctions whose uses ranged from the provision of poison gas during battle to the arrangement of aphrodisiacs in the ducal bedchamber.[3] Vincenzo was of course well aware that research of this kind consumed vast sums of money, but since the élite among his alchemists were normally employed in attempting to transmute base metals into gold, the problem of financing them was at least theoretically solved in advance.

Quite possibly this particular ducal mania so impressed the young Monteverdi that, many years later when comfortably established in Venice, he decided to take it up as a hobby and help out his friend Marigliani, equally well established in Mantua, for there were certain basic materials for experiments that could be obtained more easily in the great seaport than in any other Italian town or city. Nevertheless the real attraction of alchemy, as far as Monteverdi was concerned, lay not so much in its scientific aspect as in its symbolism and its pretence towards a search for perfection.

Long before his own interest was aroused, theorists and practitioners of alchemy had gone deeply into questions of numerology, astrology, medicine, and music—not to mention the magic of colours. In a manuscript copy of Salomon Trismosin's *Splendor Solis*,[4] the fifth in a series of twenty-two illuminated pages depicts a Peacock in the Vase of Hermes, with the chariot of Venus above and an instrumental consort in the lower right. Monteverdi could easily have read works of this kind, even if not so finely illuminated, and indeed the manuscript collection of the Biblioteca Marciana in Venice still contains numerous treatises on alchemy. In addition there were many printed books dealing with the same topic: from Basel came the *Artis Auriferae quam Chemiam vocant*, and from Strasburg the later volumes of the *Theatrum Chemicum praecipuos selectorum auctorum tractatus*.

Yet the essentially light-hearted nature of the correspondence seems to indicate that Monteverdi's involvement could not have been all that deep, and perhaps for Marigliani too the experiments were rather in the nature of a pastime. Since it is hardly likely that a composer would go to the trouble of sending wine to an affluent court secretary, the 'beverages' to which Letter 83 was attached were in all probability chemicals, a view which is confirmed by later requests for pure mercury. The bottles, beakers, and *bevande* were all part and parcel of an amusing diversion, which was exactly what Monteverdi needed in the midst of an unwanted and troublesome lawsuit.

As this agreeable interlude pursued its course, a relationship of long standing and deep complexity came to its inevitable end. Adriana Basile, who for fifteen years had served Ferdinando's ends as mistress, musician, and protégée, found herself invent-

---

[3] Bellonci, 190, 249.

[4] British Library, Harley MS 3469 (dated 1582). A colour facsimile of the page appears in Read (frontispiece).

ing excuse after excuse in order not to make the journey back to Mantua. A stillborn child, rumours of war, and the interference of the Duke of Alba all contributed to her unabashed reluctance, and on top of all this she was being pressed by the former Mantuan musician Antonio Tarroni, now in the service of Sigismund III of Poland, to leave her beloved Bay of Naples for the rigours and rituals of court life in Warsaw.[5] Remorse took the upper hand briefly, but her protestations of eternal loyalty to Ferdinando brought no reply from him. In March 1625 his old ailment of the eyes returned, and with it a disintegration of general health that betokened the fateful end. Although the Duchess attempted to continue the correspondence for a while, this too eventually petered out amidst unsuccessful attempts at cajolement.

One wonders whether Monteverdi and Nicholas Lanier met in Venice during the month of July, for this versatile Englishman of French descent visited the city on his way to Verona and Mantua, there to begin negotiations on behalf of His Majesty Charles I of England to purchase art treasures from the financially embarrassed Gonzaga family.[6] Lanier, an able painter and a competent dealer, was also a professional musician who sang well, composed somewhat, and excelled in playing the lute and viola da gamba. His prowess in the subtle art of improvised variations on the latter instrument is singled out for praise in a letter that Daniel Nys sent to Mantua on 2 August, just after Lanier's departure.[7] Since Monteverdi too was known as a player of stringed instruments, notably the viola bastarda, a meeting could have been arranged by the recently appointed English ambassador Sir Isaac Wake, with whom Monteverdi became acquainted in 1627, as is proved by Letter 101. In any event, Lanier was given a splendid welcome in Mantua, returning to Venice in quasi-triumph just before Monteverdi sat down to write his alchemical missive to Marigliani.

My Very Illustrious Lord and Most Esteemed Master,

I received Your Lordship's very kind letter (full of a special regard for me of which I am in no way worthy) promising me that you will be so good as to speak with Belli[a] in order to put an end—once and for all, and with friendly agreement—to what has been troubling me; and indeed it has, because I repent a thousand times of ever having let it begin, for no greater reason than to have done with litigation, which is so distasteful to me that even if I were in the right I do not think that I would ever again want to initiate such intrigues.

Your Lordship wrote to me by the last post of your having spoken to Signor Doctor[b] about the other party, and that he said I had in fact been

---

[5] Ademollo, 297–300.   [6] Luzio, *passim*.   [7] Bertolotti, 102.

[a] Ippolito de Belli, who claimed the house formerly occupied by Giacomo Cattaneo as part of his dowry from Barbara Berini.

[b] Presumably Paolo Camellino, solicitor for de Belli, but not apparently a doctor of laws (as Bagozzi was).

agreeable to annulling that instrument of transaction. I do not know whether I said that, but if I did, I would have had to be drunk at the very least, for the Lord Prince[c] ordered that in three days everything had to be settled; and how could I have judged it proper to make a lengthy case out of something which I desired only to finish off so that I might leave for Venice? Moreover I did nothing beyond what my solicitor[d] asked, yet having advised me to litigate he did so to my detriment—all the more so through having advised me to do something against my better judgement, and in what followed he was either indifferent to me or else corrupt.

Well, let the matter be as he wishes it: I beg Signor Marigliani, my lord, to do me the favour of arranging the matter conveniently, which he can accomplish better than I can describe. And forgive me—I beg you whole-heartedly to forgive me—for I assure you that everything will be bound up in my heart by an everlasting knot of obligation.

The present beverages have been given to me and I am sending them to Your Lordship in the basket you know of. You will be doing me a favour by accepting it all as an expression of my love, or at least as a token of the debt that I owe you. I know that so little does not bear comparison to so much, but let me rely on your accustomed kindness and everything will go along perfectly.

About the vessel for calcinating gold with lead—Signor Piscina[e] and Signor de Santi the doctor,[f] both great men in this field, have told me that you take a vessel like an earthenware chamber-pot, or a small pot, and they have to be well luted so that they stand firmly on the fire. At the bottom of one of these vessels you put a reasonable amount of lead, tending rather to more than less, so that enough fumes are given off. Then you take some thin iron wire and beat a gold coin[g] so as to make it rather thin, and you perforate the vessel towards the neck, in four places, and there in the middle you place the said coin, hung up from four sides, arranged as a square, in the air.

Then you place on the said vessel its earthenware lid, and you lute it with the vessel so that it remains firm and completely closes the mouth of the vessel, and in the top of the lid you make a little hole. Then you light a fire below the vessel making the aforementioned lead boil, and thus the

---

[c] Vincenzo II, younger brother of Duke Ferdinando.
[d] Dr Giulio Bagozzi.   [e] An unidentified Venetian alchemist.
[f] Presumably a medical doctor in Venice and an acquaintance of Monteverdi.
[g] *cechino* (*zechino*).

fumes go circulating around the coin and they calcinate it in such a manner that you can pound it, and it becomes so thin that you can hardly feel it.

You may also attach a single wire to the top of the lid, and on this copper wire you put the said coin, or two or more, as you please but nevertheless somewhat separated from each other, and so in this way gold is calcined with lead, and in no other way better than this. The vessel will be like this, for example:

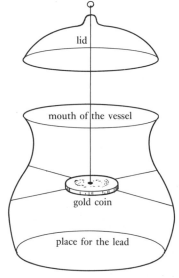

lid

mouth of the vessel

The wire that goes the middle of the without the four attach it with the one that hangs.

gold coin

perpendicularly through coin can be on its own, wires, or you can four wires without Let's draw it for you.

place for the lead

I must then tell you how I shall be able to make mercury from unrefined matter which changes into clear water, and although it will be in water it will not however lose its identity as mercury, or its weight; because I have tested it by taking a drop, and have put it on a brass spoon and rubbed it, and it became all tinged with silver colour. From this purified water I shall hope to make something worth while, inasmuch as it is a powerful solvent of silver. And here making an affectionate bow to Your Lordship, I pray God for the fulfilment of every supreme joy.

from Venice, 23 August 1625
Your Very Illustrious Lordship's
most grateful servant
Claudio Monteverdi

84

Venice, 19 September 1625
to [Ercole Marigliani, at Mantua]

Mantua, Archivio Gonzaga, Cassetta 6, fo. 299. Folio: 2 pp.

Malipiero, 242; Paoli, 226; Lax, 142

Marigliani, working away at alchemy in his spare time, and keeping closely in touch with Don Vincenzo Gonzaga during official hours, was fortunately able to offer help to Monteverdi when he most needed it. The lawsuit had been lost: the salvage little more than a few pieces of old furniture and a small collection of musical instruments. But there were costs to settle—and at this point the composer desired nothing more than to have done with the whole wretched business. At least partly responsible for his father's house in Cremona, he might also have had charge of his father-in-law's residence in Mantua; and between the two of them he would soon have found that the efficient management of property demanded more time than he had to spare for such matters. In many ways the loss of the house in Mantua was a blessing.

By way of repaying Marigliani for his assistance, Monteverdi put in hand a special order for a retort to be used in connection with further experiments, and he naturally turned to the craftsmen of Murano, from whose well-established workshops one could expect products of great beauty and utility. The glass-blowers, thanks to their guarded formulas of Syrian seaweed ash, crushed white flints from Pavia, and the finest white sand, were able to create innumerable vessels of unparalleled excellence, so that they too could almost be considered alchemists of a kind.

Although music is not mentioned, it could hardly have been far from the composer's mind, for if there were no major publications in 1625, he had the satisfaction of seeing a duet of his, *Ego dormio*, in Sammarucco's anthology of *Sacri affetti* (L. A. Soldi, Rome), and four tenor solos—perhaps for his son Francesco—in the *Ghirlanda sacra* proudly put together from musical blossoms, mainly Venetian, by one of the musicians of St Mark's, Leonardo Simonetti. All four are perfectly suited to a youthful, smooth, and agile voice: the movingly beautiful *Salve Regina, Currite populi* with its lively refrain, the expressive *O quam pulchra es*, and the unusual text of *Ecce sacrum paratum* to round off the group.

My Very Illustrious Lord and Most Esteemed Master,

I have heard how Your Lordship continues with infinite kindness to look after my interests, and I have heard of the goodwill of the Most Serene

Lord Prince[a] (which he is so kind as to maintain, through his innate goodness, towards my poor self), and for all this I shall always be bound to pray God for his perfect happiness, and remain forever most obliged to Your Lordship.

I am looking forward to the favour of the settlement so that I can say I am finally free from intrigues, for I don't think those ancient writers understood 'labyrinth' to mean anything other than litigation. Forgive me, for the love of God, for the great inconvenience and bother you are putting up with on my account, and rest assured that I shall never forget such a favour, hoping that all will be arranged with the greatest possible advantage to myself.

Within a week the furnaces at Murano will be at work, and mine will certainly be among their first major tasks. As soon as the vessel is received, the aforesaid work will be put in hand, and when this is finished (which I think will be in a week's time) I shall send—God willing—a small jar of it[b] to Your Lordship, to whom I do all reverence while with all my heart I pray for your every happiness.

from Venice, 19 September 1625
Your Very Illustrious Lordship's
most grateful servant
Claudio Monteverdi

[a] Vincenzo II Gonzaga, who (like his elder brother) enjoyed the right to be addressed as 'Serenissimo'.
[b] probably mercury.

85

Venice, 22 November 1625
to [Ercole Marigliani, at Mantua]

Mantua, Archivio Gonzaga, Cassetta 6, fos. 301–2. Bifolio: 3 pp. Enclosure: letter from Dr Giulio Bagozzi

Malipiero, 243; Paoli, 228; Lax, 143

In spite of Marigliani's sincere attempt to settle matters in a reasonable and practical way, further legal quibbles on 8 October were followed by Camellino's demand dated 12 November for payment of overdue rent. On or about 17 November Bagozzi sent news of this to Monteverdi, who promptly penned this letter to Marigliani in the hope that he would try once more to calm things down.

Whatever the rights or wrongs of the case, it certainly appears from the documents that Ippolito de Belli and his lawyer Camellino[1] were determined to make themselves as unpleasant as possible once they were sure of victory. Monteverdi's point of view, however, was one of resignation. He wished to forget about the lawsuit, and accordingly told his friend that all he really wanted from Mantua was the *provigione* first allotted to his wife Claudia and later promised to him, though always the subject of dispute—as also was the infamous donation.[2]

The costs of the lawsuit amounted to some 400 scudi, or slightly less than Monteverdi's annual salary from St Mark's, but the sale of some of his father-in-law's musical instruments and furniture seems to have realized enough to defray these expenses, as is shown by a letter from Marigliani to Bagozzi dated 24 December—one day after the case was closed:

> As I have arranged Monteverdi's affairs with de Belli, you may release the money from the sequestered goods, sold at my request, and together with it those musical instruments which have not been sold, since this is all being done with Signor Claudio's approval.[3]

So ended an unfortunate episode, which in Monteverdi's opinion might have taken a very different course had he remained in Mantua and taken a more active part in the lawsuit. On the other hand, his reluctance to leave Venice is only too well known, and his presence in Mantua during the long period in which the case unfolded would have been as impractical as it would have been ineffective. He was after all a musician, and demonstrably unsympathetic to litigation.

---

[1] Gallico, 'Contra C. M.', 357.   [2] See Letter 6.   [3] Gallico, 'Contra C. M.', 358.

My Very Illustrious Lord and Most Esteemed Master,

Having received from the Most Excellent Signor Bagozzi,[a] my solicitor, the present letter in which—as Your Lordship can see—he notifies me as to how Signor Belli[b] uses all manner of means to take action against me in every way he wishes and finds possible (which is something I did not believe, in view of the words you were good enough to write to me in your previous letters; namely, my goods being sold, he would have gone about it in such a way that everything would have been settled), I turn to you once again and beg you to make him calm down and wait for the result of what you are trying to accomplish through the one party or the other.

I know it will be better for you to act than for me to speak, therefore I entrust myself in every respect to your love and great prudence, putting it to you that what I have been trying to get hold of is an endowment of Signora Claudia's,[c] given to me by the Lord Duke,[d] of which I have had little or nothing; and that if I have been trying to get hold of that house, and it could not rightly be mine, the other party has lost nothing of his own because of this, since he possessed it anyway.

If now from my nothing I were to have to pay 200 or more scudi beyond the expenses—another 200—and, it seems to me, Signor Belli[e] having given me nothing of his own except tyranny and ill will, past injuries would be quite enough without adding more. If only I had been in Mantua, the affair that went off in one way would certainly have gone off in another. You can help me, and I know you will use your influence to free me from such unimaginable and unthinkable vexation.

Dear Signor Marigliani, my lord, may you honour my request and make that man of little conscience keep quiet so that (by God) you will add merit to your soul. And I earnestly request your reply about this matter, so that I may know in what state of mind I should be. I believe that if you so wish, you will see that I am satisfied, and I hope for everything through your precious grace, to which in all affection I surrender myself as a true

---

[a] Dr Giulio Bagozzi, a Mantuan lawyer.
[b] Ippolito de Belli, Monteverdi's adversary in the lawsuit.
[c] Monteverdi's wife, who had died in 1607.
[d] Vincenzo I Gonzaga, fourth Duke of Mantua.
[e] Belli's name has been added here for clarity.

[298]

servant; and here doing reverence to you I pray God for your every greater happiness.

from Venice, 22 November 1625
Your Very Illustrious Lordship's
most grateful servant
Claudio Monteverdi

86

Venice, 15 February 1626
to [Ercole Marigliani, at Mantua]

Mantua, Archivio Gonzaga, Cassetta 6, fo. 305. Folio: 1 p. Enclosure: half a pound of pure mercury

Malipiero, 245; Paoli, 230; Lax, 144

The lawsuit over and done with, Monteverdi and Marigliani returned to their work and, whenever time permitted, to their leisure pursuit of alchemy. For some reason, mercury was hard to find in Mantua, and in consequence Marigliani turned to his friend in Venice, who obligingly sent him—with suitable apologies—half a pound to be going on with.

Although the letter is damaged, a tolerable reconstruction presents no serious problem. This closing sentence, with its brief reference to carnival time, serves to remind us that no works were commissioned from Monteverdi in this particular year. The general gloom in Mantua had become noticeably deeper as the Duke's health declined, and the only notice of an entertainment appears to concern a play, *Europa*, by Balduino di Monte Simoncelli.[1]

But there was no lack of good music in Venice. On 1 January, Monteverdi's capable young assistant Giovanni Rovetta signed the dedication of an impressive anthology of psalms and hymns for Vespers, rounded off by four canzone,[2] and in making the customary genuflection to his patron he also acknowledged his indebtedness to Monteverdi, whose example he had tried to follow.[3] His words were eventually to come true, for in 1643 he became the next *maestro di cappella* of St Mark's in the long succession that had begun at least a century and a half before.

My Very Illustrious Lord and Most Esteemed Master,

I thought I would be able to send at least a pound of it, but since my friend has very little he has only been able to give me this half-pound. He has given it to me, so no further payment will be necessary. I shall be on the

[1] Solerti, *Albori*, i. 120.

[2] *Salmi concertati a cinque et sei voci* (Bartolomeo Magni, Venice, 1626).

[3] 'E di questo, oltre al suo benigno patrocinio, mi assicura l'haver nel comporli cercato di seguir l'orme d'un nuovo vivente Apollo, sovra 'l cui verde Monte le vere Muse cercan di ricovrarsi per apprendere i tuoni de gli esquisiti concenti.'

lookout, and if I can get hold of some I shall at once send it to Your Lordship. I am deeply sorrowful not to have been able to satisfy you entirely, because I have and always shall have a great obligation and great desire to carry out whatever you deign to command me.

Once carnival is over I shall give [my mind] to a certain something, and I shall then [inform Your Lordship] to whom I am and always [shall be] most grateful, and I kiss [your hands] wholeheartedly.[a]

from Venice, 15 February 1626

Your Very Illustrious Lordship's

most grateful servant

Claudio Monteverdi

---

[a] The left-hand edge of the page is damaged from the eighth line of the original down to the end of the letter. The final sentence probably read as follows: '*Passato carnevale darò* [*la mente*] *ad un non so che, et ne darò poi*[*haviso a V.S.*] *Molto Ill^{re} alla quale vivo et vive* [*rò per*] *sempre obbliga^{mo} et gli bacio di vivo core* [*le mani*].'

87

Venice, 24 February 1626
to [Ercole Marigliani, at Mantua]

Mantua, Archivio Gonzaga, Cassetta 6, fo. 307. Folio: 1 p.

Prunières, 272; Malipiero, 245; Paoli, 231; Lax, 145

Something of the tense and uneasy atmosphere at court can be sensed in the conciliatory yet cautious tones of Adriana Basile's letter to the Duchess, dated 20 February.[1] Family duties being fulfilled for the time being, the great singer offers to return to Mantua but begs that the Duke write to Dr Pompeo Grasso, who will then convince the Viceroy of Naples that Adriana's journey northwards is indeed justified. The political wisdom of such an approach is borne out by the fact that the Viceroy himself seems to be the source of a rumour that Duke Ferdinando cares very little whether Adriana returns or not. Once official objections are silenced with a letter of authority, the plan will proceed.

   Probably the Duke did care little, in spite of his love for music and his adulation of Adriana. Poor health is not the best incentive towards playing an active part in courtly life and entertainment. Marigliani, as one of the principal secretaries, must have felt the pressure and tension, and found relaxation mainly in the fitful development of experiments that became more and more bizarre as time went on. Instructing Monteverdi to find out all he could about a certain kind of 'frozen mercury', he appears to have reached the limits of alchemy as it was then known. Only one further letter mentions the topic: after that, music assumes its former place of importance.

My Very Illustrious Lord and Most Esteemed Master,

I felt very happy about the pleasure you derived from receiving the pure mercury, sent as requested. I shall keep an eye open and try to find some more, in order to comply fully with your wish, should you still need a further supply. Next, I took note of the task you set me, which is that I work with some Signor Doctor in such a way as to get from him the method—as he practises it—of making a certain kind of frozen mercury.

---

[1] Ademollo, 302.

I shall set to work enquiring diligently which Signor Doctor this can be, and shall perform any task to serve Your Lordship. I know a certain Signor Doctor de Santi,[a] with red hair, who greatly enjoys investigating the philosopher's stone. If he is not the one, I know of no other who can teach me what Your Lordship wishes. By the next post I shall perhaps be able to satisfy you better than at present, therefore you will excuse me for the time being. And here making reverence to you with all affection I pray God our Saviour for your every happiness.

from Venice, 24 February 1626
Your Very Illustrious Lordship's
most grateful servant
Claudio Monteverdi

[a] The Venetian doctor mentioned in Letter 83.

88

Venice, 19 March 1626
to [Alessandro Striggio, at Mantua]

Mantua, Archivio Gonzaga, Cassetta 6, fo. 309. Folio: 2 pp.

Malipiero, 245; Paoli, 233; Lax, 146

Massimiliano did not receive his Doctorate in Medicine until 17 May,[1] but being free from his various obligations in Bologna by the early part of March, he was at once able to arrange a visit to his father in Venice. His elder brother Francesco, still a member of the choir of St Mark's, would also have been in Venice at this time, so that the visit provided a rare opportunity for a family reunion in the canonry apartment where Monteverdi lived.

A new and youthful member of the medical profession, the 22-year-old Massimiliano had set his heart on returning to the city of his birth where he could count on the patronage and encouragement of those who had followed his career from its outset. His father had many friends in Mantua, both at court and in the city, and the present letter (which Massimiliano took with him on his journey) was one of five written to introduce a new doctor to old friends. Letter 89 (to Marigliani) was sent a few days later not as a formal letter of introduction but rather as a reminder that Massimiliano might need a little extra help. As it turned out, he did need help towards the end of the following year, and both Striggio and Marigliani came to the rescue of an innocent victim of the Inquisition.[2]

Although Malipiero gives the addressee as Marigliani, three separate pieces of evidence prove that this letter was intended for Striggio. First, the salutation 'Illustrissimo mio . . .' is the one normally associated with him; second, the reference to 'all Your Lordship's Illustrious House' is particularly apt in view of the fact that Striggio had eleven children; third, Letter 89 mentions that a letter had already been written to 'Count Alessandro Striggio, my lord'.

My Most Illustrious Lord and Most Respected Master,

The bearer of this letter is a son[a] of mine, who as many as four years ago

---

[1] This date is cited from *Notitia Doctorum*, ed. G. Bronzino (Bologna, 1962), 132; in Vecchi, 91 n. 91.

[2] See Letters 115–19.

[a] Massimiliano, now nearly 22 years old.

(thanks to the Lady Duchess)[b] gained a place in Montalto College at Bologna, in order to study. Now, with a Doctorate in Medicine, he has come to Mantua purposely to express those very great thanks that he owes to his Most Serene Patrons, and at the same time to make himself known as their most humble servant and vassal. He also comes, most appropriately, to offer himself with the greatest humility as Your Lordship's servant.

Therefore I beg Your Lordship's good grace—just as you have deigned to honour me with that very favour—to make him worthy of what he and I desire of your infinite humanity, for he will not fail to seize any and every opportunity of showing himself appreciative of the longed-for favour that you may be so good as to grant him. And adding these to the other great debts which I owe in perpetuity to Your Lordship's kindness, even if I can go no further in my ability to serve you, I shall at least never fail to pray the Lord that He ever bless and prosper from good to better all Your Lordship's Illustrious House, and here bowing to you with all reverent affection I kiss your hands wholeheartedly.

from Venice, 19 March 1626
Your Most Illustrious Lordship's
most humble and grateful servant
Claudio Monteverdi

[b] Caterina Medici Gonzaga.

89

Venice, 28 March 1626
to [Ercole Marigliani, at Mantua]

Mantua, Archivio Gonzaga, Cassetta 6, fos. 311–12. Bifolio: 3 pp.

Prunières, 272; Malipiero, 246; Paoli, 235; Lax, 147

This is the last of an almost uninterrupted batch of letters to Marigliani, going back to no. 83; and it is also the last to discuss alchemy. The events of 1627, of which the most pressing and important was the commission from Parma, turned Monteverdi away from this pastime and back to the essential thing in his life—music, of whose elements, properties, and general alchemy he was by general acknowledgement a consummate master.

Of the four letters he wrote on behalf of Massimiliano, the three addressed to the Duke, the Duchess, and Prince Vincenzo appear to have been lost. The one intended for Striggio is no. 88. In writing to Marigliani, the composer makes it clear that rather than have his son back in Venice he would prefer to see him settle down in Mantua and develop a medical practice. This, in fact, is what happened: and Massimiliano seems to have continued his theoretical studies in addition to helping two Mantuan doctors, Bertoletti and Count Bruschi.[1]

My Very Illustrious Lord and Most Esteemed Master,

I keep asking a very intelligent fellow for the purest mercury in order to send it to Your Lordship as soon as possible, but as yet he has not been able to give it to me. I hope to send it to you by the next post. I wanted to tell you all about this to let you know that Your Lordship's commands live in my heart.

I have written four letters: one to the Lord Duke, another to the Lady Duchess,[a] a third to Prince Vincenzo, and the fourth to Count Alessandro

---

[1] Count Francesco Bruschi, who had served Vincenzo, fourth Duke of Mantua, as a philosopher as well as a doctor (he was *protomedico* of Monferrato), was praised for his excellence by Eugenio Cagnani in the *Lettera cronologica* addressed to Duke Francesco in 1612. (*Mantova—Le lettere*, ii. 621). A member of the Accademia degli Invaghiti, Bruschi gave an oration there on the 'Cielo d'Amore', and in 1623 published his *Promacomachia latro chimica*.

[a] Ferdinando and Caterina.

Striggio,[b] my lord. Signor Marigliani, my lord, if my son[c] should need an introduction, I beg you to honour him with your favour, and I shall always have a perpetual obligation to Your Lordship for this kindness, as I do for countless others.

He writes to me in his letters that he is now asking admission to study circles, and is attending the astrology lectures of a certain Jesuit father, as well as applying himself to consultations. He still continues to work for the Most Excellent Signor Bertoletti,[d] and at the same time works for Count Bruschi,[e] my lord.

At the same time I am still waiting for Massimiliano to let me know that he has received three vouchers owed to me by the ducal treasury, and what hope he has of getting the said money, 50 scudi of which I am content that he should use for his victuals; and I am wholeheartedly determined not to consent to his returning to Venice until he has settled down to a different life and career from what he has pursued previously. However, I hope to God that he will do me honour, for I know he possesses honour and judgement.

I would also hope that one day when the Duke realizes the extent[f] of my son's knowledge, he will not perhaps disdain to grant him his good grace, for I desire deep in my soul that God may make him worthy of this. And here doing reverence to my Very Illustrious Lord Signor Marigliani, I also pray God with all my heart for the peak of your every perfect happiness, sending you news as to how I am at present engaged in making a fire under a glass beaker,[g] with its cover on, to extract something from it and then make something of it, so that (please God) I may then cheerfully explain this something to My Lord Marigliani.

from Venice, 28 March 1626

Your Very Illustrious Lordship's

ever most grateful servant

Claudio Monteverdi

[b] The letter written to him is no. 88.   [c] Massimiliano.

[d] A Mantuan doctor, probably attached to the court.

[e] Francesco Bruschi, *protomedico* of Monferrato.

[f] Literally, 'When the Duke gets to know what my son knows'.

[g] *orinale* (lit. 'urinal').

90

Venice, 2 January 1627
to [Alessandro Striggio, at Mantua]

Mantua, Archivio Gonzaga, Cassetta 6, fo. 315. Folio: 2 pp.

Malipiero, 248; Paoli, 238; Lax, 148

Venice, whose vigorous and variegated musical life attracted composers and performers from the four corners of Europe, held a special fascination for singers
because of the opportunities offered by countless churches and private patrons, and as
time went on those chances for employment were increased and improved by the
growth of opera. During his thirty years in the city, Monteverdi must have met
and worked with a considerable number of singers ranging from basses to castrati, and
in addition a group of lady singers on the topmost rung of their profession. Since, as
a connoisseur of vocal art, he possessed a talent for training young voices and perfecting mature ones, it undoubtedly gave him great pleasure when his former pupil
Francesco Campagnolo arrived from Mantua one day with a verbal message from
Striggio.

He had heard little of court affairs for several months, due most probably to the
death of Duke Ferdinando, who was barely 40, on 29 October 1626. Pilgrimage and
penance had done nothing to help the ailing ruler of a doomed principality, and there
were many, including Monteverdi, who must have shuddered for the future of
Mantua when Ferdinando, a reliable leader both in government and in the arts, finally
met his end. There being no legitimate sons, the dukedom would pass to his younger
brother Vincenzo, who if he shared the same name as his illustrious father could
hardly be said to take after him in character and resolution.

There is no evidence that Monteverdi tried to contact the new Duke, although he
had formerly written to him about musical matters in 1618 and 1619 (Letters 29, 30,
33). Yet others in the world of music and theatre lost no time in writing: Adriana
Basile, skilfully combining condolences and congratulations, sent him a few lines from
Naples on 24 November 1626,[1] and a month later the actress Maria Malloni (Clelia)
offered Christmas greetings.[2]

The investiture of Vincenzo II was to take place at Mantua on 8 February 1627, and
would presumably be marked by the customary succession of new entertainments for
carnival. But Monteverdi had received no hint of a commission for either event. The
welcome but unexpected appearance of Campagnolo, with news that Striggio had

---

[1] Ademollo, 305.   [2] Bertolotti, 102.

some poetry to be set to music, must have meant a great deal to the 60-year-old composer, and he expresses his feelings in a blithely optimistic fashion as he sends his thanks to Striggio. The nature of this poetry is never revealed, for when the correspondence continues in Letter 92 the all-pervading subject turns out to be music for the theatre.

Campagnolo's career was typical of the more fortunate among male virtuoso singers who grew up in an atmosphere of princely patronage and entertainment on a lavish scale. According to Doni, he was a born actor-singer,[3] fulfilling in excellent fashion all the qualities expected of such a figure. The date of his birth is not known, but it may have been about 1580, in the city of Mantua. When Guarini's *Il pastor fido* was being rehearsed there in 1591 (for a performance that was eventually postponed for seven years) the court secretary Chieppio recalled Campagnolo from Ferrara to take over the role of Silvio, and after hearing him in Acts I and II he duly signified his approval.[4] By 1594 the young singer was taking lessons with Monteverdi, whose salary was increased about this time, only to be effectively cut because he was made responsible for his pupil's board and lodging.[5]

After a visit to Rome in 1607 for further study, Campagnolo returned to Mantua in the following year, passing through Florence, where he attended several musical events, noting, however, in a letter to the Cardinal Prince Ferdinando that they were somewhat inferior to those of the Gonzaga.[6] In 1609 he travelled through the northern territories of Belgium and Holland on his way to London, which he intended to visit for a short time only. But before long he was invited to stay as an honoured guest with Henry, Prince of Wales. In all probability a pupil of Giovanni Coperario (John Cooper), the Prince possessed a highly developed musical taste and expressed his warm appreciation of Campagnolo's vocal virtuosity. There was even an audience with Queen Anne, which gave the singer high hopes of being entertained at court until Christmas.[7]

In fact he stayed on until the following summer, and when he finally crossed the Italian border on his way back to Mantua it was clear that the long journey and its consequences had greatly enhanced his reputation at home. The musical Abbot Angelo Grillo wrote about him in glowing terms,[8] and from then onwards his reputation was firmly assured. He corresponded with Striggio about a spiteful rumour that had been spread abroad concerning Monteverdi's conduct at Milan, and must have been glad to receive confirmation of his old master's innocence.[9] The next ten years saw him active in Mantua and in musical centres throughout Europe: Rome in 1612, Salzburg in 1617, and Ödenburg (Sopron) in Hungary, where in 1622 he joined forces with Giovanni Priuli, at that time Director of Music to the Emperor Ferdinand II.[10] Campagnolo had been given the title 'Cavaliere' in recognition of his services to music, and it is in this letter that Monteverdi uses the title for the first time.

[3] Doni, ii. 135.   [4] Canal, 86 n. 1.   [5] Letter 6.   [6] Davari, 93.
[7] Bertolotti, 101.   [8] Einstein, 'Grillo', 176; Grillo, 458.   [9] Davari, 104.
[10] Bertolotti, 101; Federhofer, 189.

My Most Illustrious Lord and Most Respected Master,

Signor Cavalier Campagnolo,[a] having arrived in Venice, came expressly to visit me and tell me of the continual and special affection which Your Lordship deigns to bestow upon me, and he added that you have in mind the desire to honour me with a commission to set to music some poetry which you would be so kind as to send me. I therefore write these lines to acknowledge this particular favour by praying that Your Lordship may see from the results how much I long to be a by no means useless servant.

Please therefore rest assured that your commands will be to me as favours and graces; and should you specify anything else, this letter will at any rate serve to assure you of my great affection and devotion, which I shall maintain as long as I live, if in no other way then at least by praying God that he may always bless and comfort Your Lordship, whose hands, by way of a close, I kiss with all reverence.

from Venice, 2 January 1627

Your Most Illustrious Lordship's

most devoted and most grateful servant

Claudio Monteverdi

[a] Francesco Campagnolo, the tenor.

91

Venice, 20 March 1627
to [Alessandro Striggio, at Mantua]

Mantua, Archivio Gonzaga, Cassetta 6, fo. 317. Folio: 1 p.

Malipiero, 248; Paoli, 239; Lax, 149

The new Duke, Vincenzo II, probably had no more idea than did his two brothers or his father of the time that a court secretary could waste in trying to pry open the reluctant coffers of the Mantuan treasury. But the present letter indicates that Striggio had once again exerted himself on behalf of Monteverdi, in order to retrieve half-a-year's pay, which was to be divided equally between the composer and his son Massimiliano. This brief success, however, could only be described as superficial, for the treasury was in such a disastrous state that Striggio would soon be in correspondence with Daniel Nys regarding the sale of paintings, sculpture, jewellery, and other *objets d'art* to shore up the tottering finances of the Gonzaga.[1]

Vincenzo's unstable health, both mental and physical, was precisely on a par with the state of the family fortune. All that Duke Guglielmo had so painstakingly built up, his sons and grandsons scattered to the four winds of pride, sensuality, caprice, and wastefulness. But it was the hand of Vincenzo II that would sign away those art treasures to the King of England, Charles I, 'condemning to exile the Mantegnas, the Raphaels, Titians, Tintorettos and Rubens, which had belonged to Francesco and Isabella, to Federico and to Vincenzo I, pictures for which they had accumulated debts, paid pensions, granted fiefs and created apartments and galleries'.[2]

If there was trouble in Mantua, a storm was brewing in Rome, where the irrepressible Isabella of Novellara (Vincenzo's rejected wife) had begun to demand heavy damages for the ills and wrongs she had suffered. At the same time, Pope Urban VIII entrusted to the Sacred Rota the annulment of the marriage; and the House of Gonzaga, already denied the cardinalate for all time, prepared to face further shame destined to lead to ultimate ruin.

My Most Illustrious Lord and Most Respected Master,

Having heard from Massimiliano, my son and your servant, about the special favour from Your Lordship's kindly hand, by the good grace and

---

[1] See Luzio, *passim.*   [2] Bellonci, 304.

infinite goodness of His Highness,[a] of helping him to get a semester's salary owed him by the treasury, half of which money is going to pay his expenses and keep up his medical studies, I wanted to write this letter and offer you my deepest thanks, both he and I being infinitely grateful to Your Lordship.

He no less than I will always long for God to grant him the opportunity to be worthy of the precious commands of Your Lordship, for whose every perfect happiness I pray God with all reverence, and with the same reverence I kiss your hands.

from Venice, 20 March 1627

Your Most Illustrious Lordship's

most humble, most grateful, and most devoted servant
Claudio Monteverdi

[a] Vincenzo, seventh Duke of Mantua.

92

Venice, 1 May 1627
to [Alessandro Striggio, at Mantua]

Mantua, Archivio Gonzaga, Cassetta 6, fos. 319–20. Bifolio: 4 pp.

Davari, 150; Malipiero, 249; Paoli, 240; Fabbri 1985, 261; Lax, 150

Despite Campagnolo's hint of verses to come in January,[1] not so much as a single line arrived, yet when Monteverdi wrote to Striggio on 20 March he phrased his letter in such a way as to enquire what was happening without seeming to appear too eager. The long-awaited commission finally came on 24 April,[2] and in this delayed letter of 1 May the composer expresses his willingness to accept it with the proviso that he is not rushed and that the play (whose title is as yet unknown) is well written. There had been previous attempts to palm off substandard librettos on the luckless Monteverdi, notably Agnelli's *Le nozze di Tetide*, which he adversely criticized in Letter 19. Striggio, a literary man of considerable intelligence, saw the defects of these librettos no less clearly, yet he too was a servant of the reigning Duke, and probably felt it advisable not to interfere.

Recalling the confusion over *Le nozze de Tetide*, which he first thought to be an opera but later found was no more than an intermezzo,[3] Monteverdi asks cautiously about the form and function of the unnamed play. Then, barely concealing his fear of the possibility of working extremely hard for several months, only to find the results bogged down for ever in the Mantuan marshes of indecision and whimsy, he puts in a plea for Striggio to persuade the new Duke to make use of music that was already available. How much easier to send out a score to be copied, than to sit down and write a new one! Venetian musical life was quite demanding enough, without the prospect of having to deal with frantic or frivolous assignments from outside.

The plea is cleverly thought out, for it brings in the name of Tasso, whose imprisonment was the talk of Ferrara in 1584 when Striggio, in the company of his father, visited the city to make music and listen to it. Later, the Striggio family settled in Mantua, just before Tasso—a free man at last—made his way there in 1586; and when he paid his last fleeting visit in 1591 the younger Striggio was already 18 years

[1] See Letter 90.

[2] Vigil of St Mark's Day (25 Apr.). No extant composition by Monteverdi celebrates this feast, although his illustrious predecessor Giovanni Gabrieli wrote such motets as *Deus qui beatum Marcum* and *Virtute magna* in honour of the saint. The former text was used for the blessing of the standard of St Mark's and the coronation of a doge.

[3] See Letter 22.

old, and could have met the poet. But even if he were a stranger to the man, he would certainly have known his epic poems and his love lyrics; and Monteverdi's mention of the celebrated name would have touched a responsive chord.

He had indeed set to music many stanzas of Tasso, that is to say many *ottave* from *La Gerusalemme liberata* and from its later recension, *La Gerusalemme conquistata*. The following list shows the order in which these excerpts occur in relation to the epic as a whole:

Piagne e sospira (*a 5*), Book IV (1603)	*G.C.* VIII, 6 (*G.L.* VII, 19)
Combattimento (composed 1623), Book VIII (1638)	*G.L.* XII, 52–62; 64–8[4]
Vivrò fra i miei tormenti (*a 5*), Book III (1592)	*G.L.* XII, 77–9
Armida (?composed 1626), unpublished; lost	*G.L.* XVI, 41–55
Vattene pur, crudel (*a 5*), Book III (1592)	*G.L.* XVI, 58, 59, 63

He was almost certainly thinking in terms of a performance of *Armida*, which is usually referred to in Monteverdian literature as 'an opera', though in all probability it was a parergon to the famous *Combattimento di Tancredi e Clorinda*.

At least two scores of *Armida* were extant in 1627, for Monteverdi states that the one in Venice is being specially recopied for Mantua.[5] Both disappeared without trace, like so many other manuscripts formerly in the possession of the composer or his acquaintances, yet it is possible to guess at the nature of the work from a handful of isolated references in his correspondence. The first reference, in the present letter, gives us the incipit in an almost exact quotation from Tasso—two words have been transposed, but nothing is misspelt:[6] 'O tu che porte parte teco di me, parte ne lassi.' Cauto XVI, stanza 40 of *La Gerusalemme Liberata* begins:

> Forsennata gridava: — O tu, che porte
> teco parte di me, parte ne lassi,

the lament and anger of Armida following at stanza 44, with Rinaldo's reply at 53. These are the sections specifically referred to by Monteverdi, and together they would make up a miniature dramatic cantata of the same type as the *Combattimento*.

In view of the success of that work in the house of his patron Mocenigo, what more likely than an attempt to follow it up with another composition based on Tasso's epic, using similar vocal and instrumental resources, and of approximately the same length? There are sixteen stanzas in the *Combattimento*, and if the same number of stanzas are taken from canto xvi, beginning at 40, the work would close most appropriately at 55, where Rinaldo speaks these lines:

> Deh! non voler che segni ignobil fregio
> tua beltà, tuo valor, tuo sangue regio.

There is one final piece of evidence that *Armida* was a cantata rather than an opera. Letter 118 tells us that in February 1628 the composer's score was at Mocenigo's

---

[4] Variants from *La Gerusalemme conquistata* in Pirrotta, 23 n. 37.
[5] See Letter 115.   [6] *La Gerusalemme liberata*, canto XVI, stanza 40.

house, a fairly certain indication that it had recently been performed there, perhaps in the very room where the *Combattimento* had first been given. Thus it was that an enlightened patron gave Monteverdi the necessary encouragement to compose two works, both based on Tasso and both scored for similar resources.

Although Monteverdi's artistic relationship with Giulio Strozzi seems to date from 1627, it may go back as far as 1622, when the poet gave a funeral oration at the Requiem for Cosimo II, Grand Duke of Tuscany, on which occasion Monteverdi was in charge of the music.[7] However, the year 1627 was a particularly fruitful one with regard to their collaboration, and it was followed by further productions in 1628 (*I cinque fratelli*) and in 1630 (*Proserpina rapita*). There would also have been chances for collaboration at the accademia founded by Strozzi under the patronage of the Marquis Martinenghi Malpaga, or at the later one which had its meetings in the poet's own house. Many of these reunions were graced by the singing of his adopted daughter Barbara, who became an accomplished composer and set to music many of Giulio's lighter verses.[8]

His easy fluency in both verse and prose may be judged by the large list of his works (by no means complete) given in *Le Glorie degli Incogniti*,[9] while his willing amiability in the matter of cooperation emerges from Letters 92–102, most of which give some hint or other of his deference to Monteverdi's ideas about the libretto of *La finta pazza Licori*. This projected comic opera—never completed—began as a comparatively brief poetic essay of 400 lines, later spreading over three acts, and finally five.[10] Modification and expansion of this nature would have given Strozzi little or no trouble thanks to the ease with which he wrote occasional verse, to which category *I cinque fratelli* and *Proserpina rapita* belong, not to mention the Serenade which he wrote at great speed for the election of Giovanni da Pesaro as a procurator of St Mark's in 1641.

My Most Illustrious Lord and Most Respected Master,

Your Lordship will forgive me for not being in time to respond by the previous post to your very kind and precious letter, inasmuch as time was not available—partly through late receipt of the letter, and partly because of the many tasks I still had at that juncture—for it was the Vigil of St Mark,[a] a day which kept me extremely busy looking after the music.

Be so kind, therefore, Your Lordship, as to accept this letter of mine in lieu of the previous post, and by way of an addition to the present one; and please rest assured that I shall never receive a greater boon from my good fortune than being made worthy of His Highness's[b] commands. Indeed I

---

[7] See the commentary to Letter 67.   [8] Vogel, *Bibliothek*, ii. 234–5; Rosand.
[9] Venice, 1647. The entry is reprinted in Ademollo, 282–5.   [10] Tomlinson, 303–11.

[a] 24 April.   [b] Vincenzo, seventh Duke of Mantua.

shall pray to God that He grant me to an even greater extent the power of being able (with better results than I alone could achieve) to show myself that much more worthy of such conspicuous favours, ever rendering infinite thanks and obligations to Your Lordship for such honour received.

I would wish, however, to pray and beseech Your Lordship that His Highness, graciously allowing me to set to music the play which you mention, might deign to take two points into consideration: one, that I should have ample time to compose it; the other, that it should be written in an excellent style. For I would no less have put up with considerable worry and little peace of mind (indeed, very great distress) by setting tawdry verses to music, than I would if I had to compose in a hurry—this lack of time being the reason why I almost killed myself when writing *Arianna*.

I know that it could be done quickly, but speed and quality do not go together. So, if there were time, and again if I were to have the work of production from your most noble intellect, you may be very sure that my joy would be boundless, because I know what facility and propriety Your Lordship would bring to it. If the project related to intermezzi for a full-length play, its birth would be neither so tiring nor so long drawn out, but a sung play which says as much as an epic poem, to be set in a short time—believe me, Your Lordship, it cannot be done without falling into one of two dangers: either doing it badly or making oneself ill.

However, I happen to have set many stanzas of Tasso—where Armida begins 'O tu, che porte parte teco di me, parte ne lassi',[c] continuing with all her lament and anger, with Rinaldo's[d] reply; and these perhaps would not be displeasing. I also happen to have set to music the fight between Tancredi and Clorinda. Again, I have carefully considered a little play by Signor Giulio Strozzi,[e] very beautiful and unusual, which runs to some 400 lines, called *Licori finta pazza innamorata d'Aminta*, and this—after a thousand comical situations—ends up with a wedding, by a nice touch of stratagem.

Both these and similar things can serve as short episodes between other pieces of music. They do not come off too badly, and I know they would not displease Your Lordship. Then, if church music were needed, either for Vespers or for Mass, I rather think I might have something of this kind

[c] The quotation is from *Gerusalemme liberata*, XVI, 40.
[d] The original letter has 'Ruggiero' in error.   [e] Venetian poet and librettist.

that would be to His Highness's liking.*ʄ* Your Lordship will honour me by running through such work of mine as I have briefly mentioned, and in whatever you know me to be good at, you may rest assured that I shall do everything to fall in with His Highness's liking and with Your Lordship's special favours; to whom being perpetually grateful, now bowing I kiss your hands with true and lively heart and pray for the fulfilment of your every supreme joy.

from Venice, 1 May 1627

Your Most Illustrious Lordship's

most humble and most grateful servant

Claudio Monteverdi

ʄ Works later to be published in the *Selva morale* (1641).

93

Venice, 7 May 1627
to Alessandro Striggio, at Mantua

Mantua, Archivio Gonzaga, Cassetta 6, fos. 322–4. Bifolio + folio: 5 pp. Enclosure: manuscript copies of librettos of *La finta pazza Licori* by Strozzi and *Narcisso* by Rinuccini

Davari, 152; Vogel, 435 (partial copy); Prunières, 273; Malipiero, 251; Paoli, 243; Fabbri 1985, 262; Lax, 152

The generous span of Monteverdi's life and career brought him into contact not only with musicians of all kinds, but also with poets whose range of artistry and renown encompassed the great, the good, and the competent. He would doubtless have preferred not to deal at all with those of the last category, but such were the terms and demands of occasional music that composers, even of his stature, often had to put up with poetry which even a fully stretched imagination would fail to find inspiring.

Yet, in his youth, he had met and collaborated with such giants of the literary world as Tasso, Guarini, and Rinuccini, each of them his senior in age; and as he grew up in Mantua he came to know the talents of Striggio, the charms of Chiabrera, and the brilliance of Marini. Poets of adequate powers were never lacking, and many of them cheerfully compensated for the weakness of their verse by the strength of their friendship—Cherubino Ferrari, Angelo Grillo,[1] Claudio Achillini, Scipione Agnelli, and the noble Giovanni Battista Anselmi of Treviso. Later on the composer enjoyed ample opportunity to work with Ascanio Pio di Savoia, Giulio Strozzi, Giacomo Badoaro, and G. F. Busenello. He admired their genius, prized their friendship, enhanced their creations, and never ceased to rewrite, rearrange, and refurbish what they so willingly gave him. No mean judge of literary talent, he was for that very reason rarely afraid to criticize—with intent to improve—whatever came to hand; and the results invariably justified the means.

His skilful manipulation of Strozzi's verse shines brilliantly through this series of letters about *La finta pazza Licori*. Yet at first he is not certain whether the work will be suitable, and sends by the same post a manuscript copy of Rinuccini's *Narcisso*,[2] about which he also entertains some doubt with regard to its suitability for musical setting. At the same time he is conscious of the need for first-rate casting, and his knowledge of the musical and dramatic capabilities of singers such as Margherita

---

[1] When writing as himself, not as his *alter ego* Livio Celiano.

[2] Printed in Solerti, *Albori*, ii. 189–239.

Basile and Giacomo Rapallino stamps him as a reliable connoisseur of vocal art to whom many besides Striggio turned for advice.

[Address:] To my Most Illustrious Lord and Most Respected Master, Count Alessandro Striggio, Grand Chancellor of His Most Serene Highness of Mantua, with a small packet

My Most Illustrious Lord and Most Respected Master,

I am sending off to Your Lordship *La finta pazza Licori* by Signor Strozzi[a] (as you stipulated in your very kind letter), so far neither set to music, nor printed, nor ever acted on the stage; for as soon as the author had completed it he himself straightway gave me, with his own hands, a copy of it, which was in fact this one.

If the aforementioned Signor Giulio gets to know that it might be to His Highness's[b] taste, I am quite sure that with extreme promptness of thought and deed he will put it in order—divided into three acts, or however His Highness wishes—desiring beyond all measure to see it set to music by me, and rejoicing to see his most honoured literary works clothed with my modest music. For truly both in the beauty of its verse, and in its ideas, I have found it indeed a most worthy subject, absolutely ready for setting, so that if such a story were to Your Lordship's taste, you need pay no attention to its present form,[c] because I know for sure that the author will arrange it to your complete satisfaction in a very short space of time.

In my opinion, the story is not bad, nor indeed is the way it unfolds; nevertheless the part of Lycoris, because of its variety of moods, must not fall into the hands of a woman who cannot play first a man and then a woman, with lively gestures and different emotions. Therefore the imitation of this feigned madness must take into consideration only the present, not the past or the future, and consequently must emphasize the word, not the sense of the phrase. So when she speaks of war she will have to imitate war; when of peace, peace; when of death, death, and so forth.

And since the transformations take place in the shortest possible time, and the imitations as well—then whoever has to play this leading role, which moves us to laughter and to compassion, must be a woman capable

---

[a] Giulio Strozzi, the Venetian poet and librettist.
[b] Vincenzo, seventh Duke of Mantua.   [c] *divisione*.

[319]

of leaving aside all other imitations except the immediate one, which the word she utters will suggest to her. All the same, I believe that Signora Margherita*d* will be best of all.

But to give further proof of my heartfelt affection (even though I know for sure that the task would be more difficult for me) I am sending you the enclosed *Narcisso*, a play by Signor Ottavio Rinuccini,*e* which has never been set to music, or actually produced. This gentleman, when he was alive (how fervently I pray that he is now in heaven!) did me the favour not only of giving me a copy but also of asking me to take it on, for he liked the work very much, and hoped that I might have to set it to music.

I have had a go at it several times, and turned it over to some extent in my mind, but to tell Your Lordship the truth it would not, in my opinion, succeed so powerfully as I would wish for, because of the numerous sopranos we would have to employ for so many nymphs, and the numerous tenors for so many shepherds, and nothing else by way of variety. And then a sad and tragic ending! However I did not want to neglect sending it so that Your Lordship could look it over and give it the benefit of your fine judgement.

I have no copy of either work other than the present ones I am sending off to Your Lordship. When you have read everything please do me the favour of sending back the aforementioned originals so that I can make use of them should some occasion arouse my interest, for as you may know they are very precious to me. And here making a most humble reverence to Your Lordship, and awaiting your longed-for commands, I pray God for your every perfect happiness.

from Venice, 7 May 1627

Your Most Illustrious Lordship's

most grateful and most humble servant

Claudio Monteverdi

[PS] As regards reminding Your Lordship of some bass singer who might be suitable and to His Highness's taste; and of the need for excellent singers—about which His Highness is particular—for the sopranos assigned to those female roles, I must say I would not know whom to mention. I have heard, however, by chance (as it were) that there is somebody-or-other good in Milan, in the cathedral. Here, for chamber

---

d The younger sister of Adriana Basile.   *e* Florentine poet and librettist.

music, we have nobody better than Rapallino the Mantuan,*ƒ* whose name is Don Giacomo; he is a priest, but a baritone and not a bass. Nevertheless he lets his words be heard clearly, he has something of a *trillo*, some graces, and he sings boldly. I shall, however, be on the lookout for a better one, and here make another bow to Your Lordship.

ƒ Don Giacomo Rapallino, chaplain to Girolamo Mocenigo.

94

Venice, 22 May 1627
to [Alessandro Striggio, at Mantua]

Mantua, Archivio Gonzaga, Cassetta 6, fos. 326–7. Bifolio: 4 pp.

Davari, 154; Malipiero, 254; Paoli, 247; Fabbri 1985, 263; Lax, 155

Two weeks after sending for Striggio's consideration the two librettos—*La finta pazza Licori* and *Narcisso*—of which he possessed manuscript copies, Monteverdi had them back from Mantua with a positive decision in favour of the former. The Grand Chancellor's involvement in intrigue and administration had not completely blunted his sense of theatre, and he found the play about the supposedly crazy girl much to his liking. In his reply, Monteverdi assures him that the libretto will soon begin to look even better, once the author (prompted by an ever-concerned composer) has had time to work on it.

It is pleasant to think that Strozzi's dramatic trifle may have helped to cheer up the gout-ridden Striggio, with whom Monteverdi is quick to sympathize. It was apparently a bad enough attack to keep Striggio in bed, for he recalls his discomfiture in a letter to Vincenzo II written late in July.[1]

The end of the letter returns to the subject of Rapallino, the priest-baritone who is being sounded out for possible employment in Mantua. Monteverdi's confidential asides to Striggio display not only a shrewd interest in the salaries of Venetian musicians,[2] especially those who worked under him, but also an ability to give an accurate breakdown of the amount and sources of a singer's income. The grand total seems to be 280 ducats a year, which is roughly equivalent to two-thirds of Monteverdi's salary as Director of Music at St Mark's. On the whole, Rapallino seems to have worked fairly hard for his comfort and security, except in the matter of his small sinecure from the procurator Foscarini.

My Most Illustrious Lord and Most Respected Master,

I read with sorrow, in Your Lordship's most kind and courteous letter, of the painful unpleasantness of the gout which has given you considerable

---

[1] Quazza, *Mantova*, 288.

[2] As Letter 6 shows, his knowledge of the financial circumstances of composers ranged far in time and wide in area.

trouble. Nature requires some way of getting rid of the catarrh, and so much the better if it goes to the feet and hands, those extremities of the body, allowing good health to be enjoyed by other and better parts.

Therefore I pray the Lord that these parts may maintain their strength and vigour for many years, so that they may be well preserved, besides banishing the afflictions which harm the extremities. Just as I hope that up to the present they have functioned so well that Your Lordship is now out of bed and in good health (which, please God, may be granted and given to you!) so do I heartily desire it thus, and with true affection and perpetual obligation I wish and pray for you.

I have received from the courier not only Your Lordship's most welcome letter, but also both *Narciso* and *La finta pazza*. I have also received Your Lordship's opinion and instructions regarding *La finta pazza*, and I truly agree with Your Lordship's verdict that a supposedly crazy girl like that will—on stage—turn out to be even more novel, versatile, and amusing. But now that I have come to know your mind, I have no intention of failing, when Signor Strozzi[a] arrives from Florence in three or four days' time—I repeat, I have no intention of failing—to confer with him and (as is my habit) to see that this gentleman enriches it to an even greater extent with varied, novel, and diverse scenes.

This I shall explain according to my judgement, in order to see whether he can improve it with other novelties, such as additional characters, so that the crazy girl is not seen so frequently in action. In this way, each time she comes on stage she can always produce new moods and fresh changes of music, as indeed of gestures, and I shall give a most detailed report of all this to Your Lordship.

In my opinion she has very good speeches in two or three places, but in two others it seems to me that she could have better material—not so much on account of the poetry, as of the originality. And I must also insist on his rearranging the discourse of Amyntas, when the girl is fast asleep, for I would like him to speak as if he had not enough voice to be able to wake her up. This consideration—the need to speak in a low voice—will give me a chance to introduce to the senses a new kind of music, different from what has gone before. And likewise I shall insist that he decides, with special reason and consideration, on the ballet inserted

---

[a] Venetian poet and librettist.

in the middle; and then, as I have said, I shall give Your Lordship a detailed account of it all.

As yet I have not been able to negotiate with Signor Giacomo Rapallino,[b] as he has been in Padua for two days. However, as is my custom, I have already had a word with him about it, and he answered that he was a most humble servant and subject of His Highness,[c] and that he would have gloried in being made worthy of His Highness's commands; hoping that if the occasion should arise, His Highness would deign to grant him such a post that, by means of some ecclesiastical benefice, he would be able to enjoy a secure livelihood for as long as he lived.

Here he gets about 80 ducats from the chapel, he is free to say Mass elsewhere, and he gets 40 ducats as chaplain to the Most Excellent Procurator Foscarini,[d] for whom he has not yet said Mass, so that you could say he is paid for doing nothing. It is true that if this gentleman dies, the said money automatically dries up. Beyond this he earns another 100 ducats by singing for religious festivals in the city, but the guaranteed fees are those from the chapel of St Mark, and those from his daily Mass, which may amount to a further 60, and if he takes care of himself, the additional fees from the city; and that is about the lot.

I shall not fail to consider doing what Your Lordship has commanded me, for up till now I have already assimilated the ideas fairly well, and soon hope to send something to Signora Margherita,[e] as principal singer; but I would like to know about the actual range of her voice, as regards her highest and lowest notes. And here making a humble reverence to Your Lordship, I pray God for your every happiness.

from Venice, 22 May 1627

Your Most Illustrious Lordship's

most devoted and most grateful servant,

Claudio Monteverdi

---

[b] Mantuan priest and singer.   [c] Vincenzo, seventh Duke of Mantua.
[d] The procurator *de citra* Giovanni Battista Foscarini.
[e] The younger sister of Adriana Basile.

95

Venice, 24 May 1627
to [Alessandro Striggio, at Mantua]

Mantua, Archivio Gonzaga, Cassetta 6, fos. 329–30. Bifolio: 3 pp.

Davari, 155; Malipiero, 256; Paoli, 251; Fabbri 1985, 264; Lax, 157

Although Strozzi has not yet returned from Florence, Monteverdi is rapidly develop-ing plans for improving the libretto of *La finta pazza Licori*. He is much taken by the idea of matching certain words with off-stage noises, and suggests that where such correspondences do not exist, they should be written in. He clearly looks forward to composing the music that will accompany the scene in which Lycoris pretends to be asleep; and if that music were extant it would be fascinating to compare it with similar scenes in later operas. Monteverdi's growing enthusiasm for the opera can be sensed in the urgency of his prose, and in the brief interval of two days between this letter and the previous one. Striggio probably did not write immediately because of the after-math of the celebrations on 16 May, when Vincenzo II was crowned as seventh Duke of Mantua.

My Most Illustrious Lord and Most Respected Master,

As yet, Signor Giulio Strozzi[a] has not returned from Florence, but I keep looking out for him anxiously because of the great longing in my heart to do what Your Lordship has ordered with regard to *La finta pazza*. I would have written about it already, at some length, had I not been waiting for the author to improve it to a very considerable extent; for according to letters received from him recently he ought surely to be in Venice within two or three days (God willing), and I hope it will then be rearranged in such a state of acceptability to Your Lordship that you will be well and truly satisfied.

I have already assimilated it so that the entire work is in such shape that I know I could set it to music in a very short while; but my aim is that whenever she[b] is about to come on stage, she has to introduce fresh

---

[a] Venetian poet and librettist.   [b] Lycoris, the girl who feigns madness.

delights and new inventions. In three places I certainly think the effects will come off well: first, when the camp is being set up, the sounds and noises heard behind the scenes and exactly echoing her words should (it seems to me) prove quite successful; secondly, when she pretends to be dead; and thirdly, when she pretends to be asleep, for here it is necessary to bring in music suggesting sleep. In some other places, however, because the words cannot mimic either gestures or noises or any other kind of imitative idea that might suggest itself, I am afraid the previous and following passages might seem weak.

For these results I must wait for Signor Strozzi, and as soon as he arrives I shall let Your Lordship know; but I would like you (with God's good grace) to receive my news without any bother from the gout and without being bedridden, since pleasure and pain go ill together. I pray and shall always pray the Lord that He may grant Your Lordship with all affection a return to your pristine state of health, and at the same time I pray and shall always pray God that He may make me worthy of Your Lordship's commands, as He has made me worthy to call myself your most grateful servant. And here making a most humble reverence to Your Lordship I devotedly kiss your hands. If, later on, you will kindly let me know a little about Signor Rapallinoᶜ I shall do all I can in the most appropriate manner.

from Venice, 24 May 1627

Your Most Illustrious Lordship's

most devoted and most grateful servant

Claudio Monteverdi

ᶜ Mantuan priest and singer.

96

Venice, 5 June 1627
to [Alessandro Striggio, at Mantua]

Mantua, Archivio Gonzaga, Cassetta 6, fos. 332–3. Bifolio: 3 pp.

Davari, 156; Malipiero, 257; Paoli, 253; Fabbri 1985, 264; Lax, 158

The generous documentation of musical activities in the churches of Venice unfortunately has no comparable counterpart in entertainments devised for the Doge or for members of the nobility. Occasional and casual references can never rank as true substitutes for well-kept records such as we have for St Mark's, for the Scuola di San Rocco, and for S. Giovanni Evangelista. If Girolamo Mocenigo's secretary for household affairs had kept a diary of the plays and music performed at the palazzo that is now the Hotel Danieli, the history of music in Venice would have been incontestably enriched; and if some musical member of his family had retained and preserved for posterity one copy of every score written especially for this worthy Maecenas, the history of opera—at least as regards its earlier chapters—would have to be rewritten.

Apparently Strozzi's play, or dialogue, was intended for an evening entertainment at the Palazzo Mocenigo. It may even have been performed as such, without music, but Monteverdi claims to have looked at it previously, weighed it in his sensitive artistic balance, and found it lacking in certain elements that a really successful opera ought to possess. Now he is ready to persuade the author to improve it, augment it, and make it fit for princes. As a genuine connoisseur of music and of vocal virtuosity, he realized at once the possibilities of a large-scale work planned with such singers as Margherita Basile in mind. And there were others still in Mantua to match her, as Monteverdi was quick to point out.

In Florence, the musical fort was held by Marco da Gagliano, already at work on a new opera, *La Flora*, with a libretto by Andrea Salvadori. Gagliano, like Monteverdi, preferred to work slowly and steadily, with the result that the première did not take place until 14 October 1628, in which year both words and music were published.[1] The occasion was the wedding of Duke Odoardo Farnese and Margherita of Tuscany, for whom Monteverdi was soon to write a series of intermezzi and a *torneo*.

My Most Illustrious Lord and Most Respected Master,

Three days ago Signor Giulio Strozzi[a] arrived in Venice, and having been

---

[1] Vogel, *Bibliothek*, i. 267.

[a] Venetian poet and librettist.

urged by me very insistently to do me the honour of adapting *La finta pazza Licori* to my way of thinking, so that I could make use of it for the entertainment of great princes, he willingly offered his services, confessing that in writing this play he did not achieve the degree of perfection he had in mind, but wrote it in dialogue to provide entertainment at a musical evening which a certain Most Illustrious Signor Mocenigo,[b] my lord, had arranged to give. I, visualizing its presentation with some by no means straightforward rearrangement, did not want to set it to music.

I told him that I would like to make use of it to present to His Highness[c] of Mantua on some occasion, and he (knowing that besides Signora Margherita[d] there are also two other very fine lady singers) told me that he would take care of each one as regards letting them be heard, as likewise with the other virtuoso singers in His Highness's service. He also admits that as far as the part of Lycoris is concerned, he will make her come in later, and not in almost every scene, yet he will see to it that she always expresses new ideas and actions.

And so, with the help of this most excellent poet, who is beside me here and wishes to please me, being very much my lord and friend, I hope to create something that will disappoint neither His Highness nor Your Lordship, for I want very much to obey your orders with all my heart. If Your Lordship approves the outline as mentioned, let me know so that I can set to work without delay.

I shall negotiate no further with Signor Rapallino[e] until Your Lordship advises me by letter. By the way, I am pleased and genuinely moved to hear of the vigorous recovery you have made from that importunate attack of gout. May Our Lord long preserve Your Lordship in good health, and bless you, while I kiss your hands with all reverence.

from Venice, 5 June 1627
Your Most Illustrious Lordship's

[PS] I heard from the aforementioned Signor Giulio Strozzi, on his arrival from Florence, that His Most Serene Highness there wanted to send me something of a theatrical nature (as it so happens) for setting to music, but

---

[b] Girolamo Mocenigo (1581–1658), ducal councillor and patron of the arts (see commentary to Letter 81).

[c] Vincenzo, seventh Duke of Mantua.   [d] Younger sister of Adriana Basile.

[e] Mantuan priest and singer, chaplain to Girolamo Mocenigo.

since Signor Gagliano*f* has worked hard on his own account, it seems that His Highness is well content. Signor Giulio adds that they are preparing beautiful things without knowing the whys and wherefores.*g*

most humble and most obedient servant,
Claudio Monteverdi

f Marco da Gagliano, Florentine composer and canon of S. Lorenzo.

g This final paragraph was added as an afterthought in the space which Monteverdi habitually left between his two closing lines.

97

Venice, 13 June 1627
to [Alessandro Striggio, at Mantua]

Mantua, Archivio Gonzaga, Cassetta 6, fos, 335–6, Bifolio: 3 pp.

Davari, 157; Malipiero, 259; Paoli, 256; Lax, 160

Although this letter belongs to the series in which the composition of *La finta pazza Licori* occupies centre stage, Monteverdi can offer little news to Striggio because Strozzi has gone to Padua for the feast of St Anthony, whose only connection with the city is his being buried there after his death at nearby Arcella in 1231. Monteverdi's respect for the Franciscan saint and doctor of the church may be judged from his simple but moving hymn for solo tenor, strings, and continuo—*En gratulemur hodie*—posthumously published in a collection of motets by 'diverse most excellent composers'.[1]

Nevertheless Monteverdi was at this moment more concerned with a new arrival from Bologna, a young and fairly capable bass singer who could be just the man for Mantua, in view of Rapallino's seeming reluctance to leave his Venetian sinecure and musical pleasures for the trouble-laden atmosphere of the Gonzaga court. Further references to 'the young bass from Bologna' occur in Letters 98, 99, 100, 101, and 103, the last-mentioned letter having been brought personally by this man to Striggio in Mantua. Ten years later, Letter 126 provides us with the name of a 'Bolognese cantor of the chapel' whose initials are G.B., and it is tempting to link the young bass of 1627 with the cantor of St Mark's in 1637.

Monteverdi's consistent omission of the man's name is somewhat unusual in view of the frequent discussions in his letters concerning singers, composers, and instrumentalists, all of whom are referred to either by their Christian name (Signora Margherita) or their surname (Campagnolo), and sometimes by both names (Ottavio Bargnani). One reason may have been Monteverdi's reluctance to burden Striggio with yet another name to remember, especially when the singer was on the lower rungs of the ladder and, comparatively speaking, without experience.

Yet there is no lack of detailed description, both personal and musical. He goes 'vestito alla lunga', which means that he wears the kind of long breeches that were then coming into fashion.[2] Men's trousers, in the early seventeenth century, had for

---

[1] Music reprinted in *Collected Works*, ed. Malipiero, xvi. 517. The text for the omitted verses is given in *Analecta Hymnica*, iv. 90.

[2] In *Monteverdi Companion* (69) the meaning of the term is said to be unknown; and in Paoli (257) the

so long been baggy and loose that a reverse trend set in and they soon became long and narrow, with exposed buttons fastening them in front. What is more, they reached below the knee, where they sometimes fitted into high-heeled leather boots so as to present an ensemble that has recognizable parallels with masculine clothes fashions in recent times.

At first, Monteverdi declines to call him either a baritone or a bass, and previous letters show that he always made a careful distinction between the two types of voice and their range.[3] Instead, he uses the diminutive term 'bassetto', suggesting that the sound is not big or heavy, and therefore eminently suitable for chamber music ('da camera'). When he comments on the young man's prowess in vocal ornaments, he again resorts to diminutives—'tiradinette per entro' and 'garbetti'.[4] Unusual words, these, but their derivation is perfectly clear: the normal word for a run is *tirata*, and the general (as well as the specific) term for grace, or harmony of line, is *garbo*. In a more generous summing-up, however, the singer is praised for his range, reliability, and clear diction.

After some of this information has been repeated in Letter 98, we learn further that the young man is of good height, and consequently might be useful in theatrical as well as in chamber music. Moreover, he seems to be well connected, in view of the letter of recommendation from the Emperor Ferdinand II to the Imperial Resident, Nicolò Rossi.[5] By the middle of July Monteverdi was in the very centre of these negotiations, trying to strike a careful balance between Rapallino on the one hand—a fellow Mantuan and chaplain to their joint patron Mocenigo—and the young man from Bologna on the other. Rapallino may have appealed to Monteverdi for assistance, thinking perhaps that he would do well to leave Venice for a short time and appear as a guest artist in Mantua, thereby earning some fame if little fortune, because in Letter 101 Monteverdi's enthusiasm for the young man begins to falter—his singing is somewhat melancholy, his ornaments not well projected, his head and chest voice at odds.

This is exactly the opposite of Monteverdi's first opinion. But the volte-face is surely due neither to a poor memory on his part, nor to a drastic and sudden change in the voice of the young Bolognese: it is simply the result of a demand for money which Monteverdi found exorbitant. He remembered only too well the pittance grudgingly paid to him by the Gonzaga during his many years of faithful service. Why should a younger and less experienced musician demand—and obtain—more than that? But if Letter 101 sees the pendulum of his musical opinion swinging sharply away from the 'bassetto', Letter 103 slightly restores the balance by referring to him, at long last, as a 'basso'; after all, the man had kindly agreed to take one of Monteverdi's letters to Mantua.

garment is referred to as a cloak. Detailed explanations appear in the standard books on costume and fashion. See e.g. Hansen; Levi Pisetzky.

[3] As in the postscript to Letter 93.
[4] For a careful discussion of vocal techniques in Monteverdi's time, see Wistreich.
[5] For Rossi, see the commentary to Letter 98.

Who was this singer, whose nature Monteverdi describes as 'calm, modest, and humble'? If he was indeed the same man as the 'Bolognese cantor' of 1637, and if (like many other church singers in Venice) he also sang in opera when the opportunity presented itself, he could well be the 'Signor Giovanni Battista Bisucci from Bologna' who interpreted the roles of Proteus and Jove in Manelli's *Andromeda*, first produced at the Teatro San Cassiano in March 1637.[6] He was a bass singer, and had been a member of the choir at St Mark's for ten years,[7] so his appointment began in 1627, the year in which Letters 97–103 were written. What probably happened was that he went to Mantua in mid-August and remained there for a short time, returning to Venice before the end of the year. For it was in Venice, according to Monteverdi, that the young man really wanted to live; and he even resisted the blandishments of Tarroni, who was busily engaged at this time in finding singers for the court of Sigismund III of Poland.

Although this is the only reference to Antonio Tarroni in these letters, Monteverdi must have known him in Mantua, where he was temporary Director of Music at the ducal chapel of S. Barbara from January until April 1609, and then again from August until September 1612. On the first of these two occasions, it was rumoured that Tarroni would succeed Gastoldi (who died on 4 January 1609)[8] on a permanent basis, which would oblige him to give up his canonry; and almost immediately three priests applied to the Duke for the benefice which they thought would soon become vacant.[9] Tarroni's First Book of Madrigals, reprinted in Venice in 1612,[10] reveals that he set a number of texts by Guarini which had previously appeared in Monteverdi's earlier books. Apart from these and a collection of masses, there is little evidence of Tarroni's creative talents, and his name does not recur until 1625, when he was in Vienna with Sigismund III. This artistically inclined monarch,[11] being anxious to engage Adriana Basile and her husband as members of an ambitious musical establishment looked to Tarroni, as his Director of Music, to make the first approach. But Adriana, who must also have remembered Tarroni from Mantuan days, did not reply immediately: indeed she waited until Sigismund himself wrote to her, adding a postscript in his own hand.[12] Nothing came of this lofty overture, however, and the Basile family continued to live in Naples. When Sigismund and his entourage visited Venice, Tarroni was still busily seeking out singers, as is clear from the present letter.

My Most Illustrious Lord and Most Respected Master,

Six days have already elapsed since I gave *La finta pazza* to Signor Giulio Strozzi,[a] who promised to adapt it at once to your liking; but today,

---

[6] Worsthorne, 28.   [7] Arnold, 'Singers', 983.   [8] Jeppesen, 319.   [9] Tagmann, 398 n. 28.
[10] Madrigals sent with a letter from G. B. Sacchi to Cardinal Ferdinando Gonzaga in 1610 could have been either manuscript copies or a set of the original edition printed in that year or shortly before.
[11] See the commentary to Letter 82.   [12] Ademollo, 299.

[a] Venetian poet and librettist.

Saturday, when I paid a special visit to his house to see the adaptation and let Your Lordship know about it in detail, and at the same time to get hold of it myself in order to start sending the music to Your Lordship, I found that he had gone to Padua for two or three days for the feast of the saint[b] which is being celebrated tomorrow, and for this reason I cannot inform you properly before the next post, I know for certain, however, that he is in the process of touching it up and adding to it with great enthusiasm, because he very much wants the other lady singers to take part, as indeed I told Your Lordship in my other letter.

Just now a certain young man[c] has arrived here in Venice from Bologna. He is about 24 years old, wears long breeches,[d] composes a little, and professes to sing light bass[e] parts in chamber music. I have heard him sing a motet of his in church, with a few short runs here and there,[f] and little ornaments, with a decent *trillo*: the voice is very pleasing but not too deep. He articulates the words very clearly, his voice goes up into the tenor range very smoothly indeed, and as a singer he is very reliable.

A certain Tarroni,[g] who entices[h] musicians to Poland, is after him with offers of employment, but he would like to stay on at St Mark's in order to continue living in Venice. He is not aware that I am telling Your Lordship about him, and this I swear to you by God. As a most reverent and (as I profess to that Most Serene Highness) most grateful servant, I thought it a good idea to point him out to Your Lordship, so that if anything were asked of me, I would know what to do about it.

And even if Your Lordship does not instruct me, it will matter very little because—as I said to Your Lordship—he has no idea of this report of mine. And now with most singular affection, praying for Your Lordship's complete recovery of health, I kiss your hands with all reverence.

from Venice, 13 June 1627

Your Most Illustrious Lordship's

most grateful and most affectionate servant

Claudio Monteverdi

---

[b] St Anthony of Padua (13 June).   [c] Giovanni Battista Bisucci.   [d] *va vestito alla lunga.*

[e] *bassetto*, which defines the quality rather than the range of the voice. For baritone, Monteverdi uses the word *baritono*.

[f] *alquante tiradinette per entro.* The unusual term *tiradinette* is derived from *tirare* in its normal musical sense.

[g] Antonio Tarroni, priest and musician.

[h] *conduce*, from *condurre* meaning 'to conduct' (lead away).

[333]

98

Venice, 20 June 1627
to [Alessandro Striggio, at Mantua]

Mantua, Archivio Gonzaga, Cassetta 6, fos. 338–9. Bifolio: 4 pp.

Davari, 158; Malipiero, 260; Paoli, 259; Lax, 162

The negotiations over bass singers continue, Rapallino's financial situation is once more summed up in Monteverdi's typically shrewd and succinct manner, and the young bass Bisucci is praised for his vocal technique. In a month's time, praise will turn into sharp criticism when fees come to the fore. But even at the age of 24 Bisucci had a realistic idea of his own worth, for among his letters of recommendation was one from the emperor Ferdinand II, addressed to Nicolò Rossi, the Imperial Resident in Venice at that time. It is not unlikely that the young singer travelled to Graz or Vienna on leaving Bologna, so that he could collect testimonials before trying his luck in Venice; and if he did in fact sing at the imperial court (where Italian musicians were always given a generous welcome)[1] his sense of pride can be understood and applauded. When it came to music, the Habsburgs were no fools.[2]

Neither, for that matter, were their secretaries, envoys, and residents: in them a fondness and feeling for music counted almost as a branch of diplomatic skill, and Nicolò Rossi was no exception. Before being promoted to the rank of Resident, he served the imperial cause in Venice as a secretary, and displayed an interest in music and musicians in 1613 and 1614, when Monteverdi was still a comparatively new arrival. Among other things, Rossi was entrusted with disbursements to a bass singer, Michelangelo Rizzio,[3] who later contributed two motets to the *Parnassus Musicus Ferdinandaeus* of 1615.

In 1621 he invited the blind harpsichordist and composer Martino Pesenti to put into working order a rare and unusual archicembalo made some twenty years previously by Vido Trasentino (or Trasuntino), who appears to have specialized in instruments of this kind. Pesenti, in the foreword to his *Correnti, gagliarde e balletti* of 1645,[4] recounts at some length his interest in Rossi's prize possession, which he describes as 'diatonic, chromatic, and enharmonic'. He also compares it with a much

---

[1] Federhofer, 167–244.

[2] Ferdinand II is referred to as 'einer der begeistertsten Musikfreunde seiner Zeit' in Adler (introduction to vol. i).

[3] Federhofer, 239 (Docs. 62 and 63).   [4] Sartori, *Bibliografia*, 392.

earlier instrument which came into his hands in 1641—a prototype archicembalo made in 1548 by Domenico da Pesaro at the instance of Zarlino.

Although Pesenti admits his preference for the instrument made by Domenico da Pesaro, he evidently enjoyed tuning and playing the other one until 1634, when Rossi's death brought about its removal from Venice. Although the intention was to send it to Vienna for the imperial collection of musical instruments, it got only as far as Trieste and was still there (according to Pesenti) in 1645. Trasentino made another archicembalo in 1606, and this—unlike the Trieste instrument—is still preserved: it can be seen in the Civico Museo at Bologna.[5] Different in range, the two instruments were probably similar in construction and mechanism.

Monteverdi, in all likelihood Pesenti's teacher, may occasionally have heard and watched him unravel the intricacies of the archicembalo that Rossi owned, for he seems to have known the Resident well enough to enlist his help when Massimiliano was imprisoned by the Inquisition in Mantua later in the year.[6] Rossi was certainly an influential man, and his position would have given him ample opportunity to cultivate social and diplomatic connections on a high level. He was well acquainted in 1622 with the Earl and Countess of Arundel, the Tuscan Resident Sachetti, and the English ambassador, Sir Henry Wotton.[7] His patronage of music brought him at least one dedication: the *Arie, libro terzo* published by an Augustinian monk named Guglielmo Miniscalchi in 1630, where he is described as 'Consigliere & Residente in Venetia della Cesarea Maesta'.[8]

My Most Illustrious Lord and Most Respected Master,

I shall let Your Lordship know, by the next post, the results of what you have deigned to command me regarding the negotiations for basses, since I have been unable in so short a time to find the opportunity to speak tactfully to the person you asked about, a service I must perform myself and not through someone else. But I can tell Your Lordship (as I also mentioned in another of my letters, submitting it for your consideration) that Rapallino[a] gets, I believe, 80 ducats from the chapel, 60 or 70 from masses, and 40 for being chaplain to a Most Excellent Lord Procurator,[b] without counting the unknown sums for singing around the city in performances that take place there.

The young man[c] who has come to Venice—the Bolognese—does not have anything certain as yet; but he does manage, by asking frequently, to

---

[5] *MGG* xiii, col. 626 (with illustration showing keyboard).
[6] Paoli, 295.   [7] Hazlitt, ii. 191.   [8] Vogel, *Bibliothek*, i. 470.

[a] Mantuan priest and singer (baritone).   [b] Giovanni Battista Foscarini.
[c] Giovanni Battista Bisucci.

come into chapel. He is not a priest: he is a young man of good stature, but dresses in long breeches; he sings with more charm of voice than Rapallino, and more reliably, since he composes a little. Not only does he pronounce his words extremely well, he sings ornaments very nicely, and has something of a *trillo*.

He does not go down too far, nevertheless for chamber and theatrical music he would not, I hope, displease His Highness.[d] This young man came to Venice with letters of recommendation so that he could be helped in his various plans; among them there was even one addressed to the Most Illustrious Resident Rossi,[e] from His Majesty[f]—that is, the Emperor. If you were to entrust such a negotiation as this to the said Signor Rossi, it would seem to me very good, for then these singers could not say that I was turning other singers away, and I tend to think that Your Lordship will approve of this.

Signor Giulio Strozzi[g] has returned from Padua, but even though he was absent, he has not on that account forgotten to improve *La finta pazza Licori*, which he has rearranged in five acts. Within four days he will either give it to me completely finished, or give me about two or three completed acts by way of a beginning, so that by Saturday week at the latest I hope to send some of it to Your Lordship with the music added. And I hope you will see something to please you greatly, because Signor Giulio is a worthy subject, courteously and willingly following my ideas, a convenience which makes it very much easier for me to set it to music. And here making a most humble reverence to Your Lordship, I wish from Our Lord God your every perfect happiness.

from Venice, 20 June 1627

Your Most Illustrious Lordship's

most grateful and most devoted servant

Claudio Monteverdi

[d] Vincenzo II, seventh Duke of Mantua.
[e] Nicolò Rossi, Venetian Resident of the Imperial Court.
[f] The Emperor Ferdinand II.   [g] Venetian poet and librettist.

99

Venice, 3 July 1627
to [Alessandro Striggio, at Mantua]

Mantua, Archivio Gonzaga, Cassetta 6, fo. 341. Folio: 2 pp.

Davari, 159; Malipiero, 262; Paoli, 262; Fabbri 1985, 265; Lax, 163

La finta pazza, now expanded to five acts, is no longer a dialogue designed to while away an hour at an evening party: it is a full-length libretto for a comic opera, perhaps the first in the history of that genre. But progress with the music is held up temporarily because of a catarrh affecting Monteverdi's right eye. It must have become a recurring problem at this time of his life, for he mentions it again, this time near the left eye, in Letter 125.

As far as the search for a bass is concerned, Monteverdi still has nothing definite to report, except that Bisucci—who had only just joined the choir at St Mark's—was apparently asking for an official release, or possibly a short leave of absence. Striggio seems to have taken note of Monteverdi's recommendation, in his previous letter, to contact the Imperial Resident Nicolò Rossi: the negotiation has now reached a diplomatic level.

My Most Illustrious Lord and Most Respected Master,

As long as a week ago I had the first act of *La finta pazza* from Signor Giulio Strozzi,[a] and spent a day working at it, when suddenly three evenings ago I began to feel a catarrh coming on—with much pain—by the side of the right eye, together with a swelling[b] and a weakening of the body, which I thought would make no little progress. But, God be praised, it has already begun to give way somewhat, and now permits me to write this to Your Lordship, which it would not have done yesterday or the day before yesterday.

By the next post I hope to send Your Lordship a good piece of the said act set to music, and at the same time I shall send the text of the entire act so that you can enjoy reading it. The young bass[c] continues to petition the

---

[a] Venetian poet and librettist.   [b] *infiagione* (= *enfiagione*).
[c] Giovanni Battista Bisucci, of Bologna.

[337]

Lords Procurators for his release, and I think that you will be further informed about this negotiation by the man to whom Your Lordship has written,[d] because I know that he has been to dine at least twice with that gentleman. And here making a most humble reverence to Your Lordship, with all my heart I wish you perfect happiness from Our Lord God and at the same time I kiss your hand.

from Venice, 3 July 1627

Your Most Illustrious Lordship's

most humble and most grateful servant

Claudio Monteverdi

[d] Nicolò Rossi, the Imperial Resident in Venice.

100

Venice, 10 July 1627
to [Alessandro Striggio, at Mantua]

Mantua, Archivio Gonzaga, Cassetta 6, fos. 343–4. Bifolio: 3 pp. Enclosure: libretto of Act I of *La finta pazza Licori*

Davari, 160; Malipiero, 262; Paoli, 264; Fabbri 1985, 265; Lax, 165

Strozzi's revision of his libretto as a five-act comic opera brought in various new ideas, among them a separate ballet and a new topic for each act. It had become an ambitious work, full of musical possibilities which Monteverdi was ready to seize upon and develop, especially in view of his knowledge of the vocal range and aptitude of Margherita Basile.

This talented singer, who had been invited to Mantua in 1615 after the remarkable success and popularity of her elder sister Adriana, was at first unwilling to accept, and Duke Ferdinando was therefore obliged to send letter after letter to her parents and to her two brothers.[1] Eventually, however, she agreed to leave her beloved Naples for Mantua, where she arrived towards the end of April 1615. The overjoyed Duke immediately sent off letters of thanks to her family, assuring them of his high regard for her artistry and his indebtedness to all who had made the journey possible.[2] To her brother Lelio, who had gone to fetch her and act as chaperone, he gave the income from certain import taxes formerly enjoyed by the poet Eugenio Cagnani.[3]

Within two months of Margherita's arrival in Mantua, a strange turn of events occurred. The Duke took it into his head to give her in marriage at somewhat short notice to Ettore Cattaneo Dadi, who may have been distantly related to Monteverdi's father-in-law. No reason for this unexpected decision appears in the document defining the terms of the dowry,[4] other than the fact that the services of Margherita and other members of her family were deserving of ample reward. The dowry amounted to 5,000 scudi, of which one-fifth was in gold and jewels (to be chosen by the bridegroom), while the other four-fifths were to be paid within two years.

So much for outward appearances. Margherita had no sooner settled down in Mantua than she was married off, virtually at the order of the Duke, by way of appreciation of her 'services'. But the court gossips thought otherwise, as did Lelio Arrivabene in one of his letters to the Duke of Urbino: 'this young singer, so recently arrived from Naples, met by His Highness, honoured by him, and treated like a deity,

---

[1] Ademollo, 209.   [2] Ibid. 210.   [3] Ibid. 213.   [4] Ibid. 211.

is now deprived of his favour and of all else that is useful; it is believed, however, that she deserved it'.[5]

Nevertheless, Margherita survived the scandal, whatever it might have been. She was duly praised to the skies, along with her sister Adriana, by the singer and poet Francesco Rasi in his anthology *La cetra delle sette corde*: for him they were 'the two fair Sirens', or 'Love's two sweetest Sirens'. Like most singers, however, they were not without temperament, and they could on occasion make it quite clear to the Duke that they would not he put upon. When *La Galatea* of Sante Orlandi and Chiabrera was being rehearsed for the carnival of 1617, a sudden change of cast obliged Margherita to study a lengthy and strenuous role that would have kept her on her feet for an uncomfortable stretch of time, and she immediately appealed to the Duke to be relieved of it.[6]

When Monteverdi finally found out what kind of fee the young bass, Giovanni Battista Bisucci, had in mind, he almost went out of his own mind. Bisucci asked for an annual salary considerably higher than that of the Director of Music at St Mark's, and according to Monteverdi's cautious opinion he would have been overpaid were he given half that amount. Once more the ball was in Striggio's court.

My Most Illustrious Lord and Most Respected Master,

I am sending off to Your Lordship the first act of *La finta pazza* by Signor Giulio Strozzi,[a] as you ordered. I wanted to send his original copy so that Your Lordship could look not so much at the verses as at the plot of the fable and the characters in the author's own hand. Two of the middle acts, which the author will give me tomorrow or the day after, have been completed; and he says that the feigned madness will begin in the third act, which I shall also send off to you as soon as I have received it. There will be a ballet in every act, each one different from the other, and in a fantastical style.

I beg Your Lordship, as soon as you have read each act, to try and be so kind as to send it back to me, as I have not been able to finish making a copy because of my eye trouble, which I told Your Lordship about in my last letter; which illness (God be praised) has almost entirely gone away. And Signor Giulio has told me that each act will present a new subject, so I rather think that nothing bad can possibly come of it.

It will now be up to Signora Margherita[b] to become a brave soldier, timid and bold by turns, mastering perfectly the appropriate gestures

---

[5] Ademollo, 214 (letter dated 1 Aug. 1615).   [6] Ibid. 235 (letter dated 18 Feb. 1617).

[a] Venetian poet and librettist.   [b] Margherita Basile, sister of Adriana.

herself, without fear or favour, because I am constantly aiming to have lively imitations of the music, gestures, and tempi take place behind the scene.^{c} And I believe it will not displease Your Lordship because the changes between the vigorous, noisy harmonies and the gentle, suave ones will take place suddenly so that the words will really come through well.

I shall not therefore say anything further about the role which the light bass is to sing, since Your Lordship is awaiting a reply from the other party.^{d} That gentleman, however, told me that the singer had made an exorbitant demand of 500 Mantuan scudi. My reply was that he could inform the youth that I considered him well paid at 20 scudi a month (even if His Highness^e too had wanted him to come), because he would not have been able to obtain more here, even with extra fees. So I think I have already told you everything, and here making a most humble reverence to Your Lordship I pray with all my heart for your every perfect happiness.

from Venice, 10 July 1627

Your Most Illustrious Lordship's

most humble and most grateful servant

Claudio Monteverdi

---

^{c} Presumably by a concealed stage band. ^{d} Giacomo Rapallino. ^{e} Duke Vincenzo II.

IOI

Venice, 24 July 1627
to [Alessandro Striggio, at Mantua]

Mantua, Archivio Gonzaga, Cassetta 6, fos. 346–7. Bifolio: 4 pp.

Davari, 161; Malipiero, 264; Paoli, 266; Fabbri 1985, 267; Lax, 166

In several of his letters Monteverdi mentions the musical opportunities offered by churches, confraternities, and private patrons in Venice, implying that he was rarely if ever short of extra-basilican work with which to fill his spare time. Of this agreeable commodity there was often a generous amount, especially at those times in the church year when major festivals were few and far between; for then the daily round could with some justification be looked after by his assistant. From 1620 until the spring of 1626, when he moved to Bergamo, Alessandro Grandi discharged these duties with commendable efficiency, and his successor was chosen in a leisurely manner. Undoubtedly there were several among the senior members of the musical establishment who would have liked the appointment for its useful if modest salary of 120 ducats a year. Eventually the choice fell upon the bass singer Giovanni Rovetta, just over 30 years old, and he officially took up his new post on 22 November 1627, watched over no doubt by St Cecilia.

Perhaps Rovetta was allowed, in the intervening time, to function as 'acting assistant to the Director' in order to give proof of his capabilities. He, or some other energetic musician, must surely have shouldered some part of the burden of rehearsals and services in July, for when the present letter was written Monteverdi was dealing with Striggio and Strozzi over *La finta pazza Licori*, with Sir Isaac Wake (the English ambassador) over a programme of chamber music, and with the prior of the Carmelite Church about their festival of Our lady of Mount Carmel.

Through one of those fortunate (or unfortunate) overlappings of engagements known to all professional musicians, the chamber concert and the vigil of the feast took place on the same evening, Saturday, 17 July, which was the usual post-day for Mantua. Not surprisingly, Monteverdi had more to think about than writing letters on that particular Saturday, yet he somehow managed to rehearse with the secular and the sacred group—certain musicians could have been common to both—in time for the start of the concert at 11 a.m. By great good fortune the house of the ambassador and the Church of the Carmelites were less than a quarter of a mile apart, well within the limits of the Sestiero di Dorsoduro.

Sir Isaac Wake, following the illustrious Sir Henry Wotton who finally left Venice for England in 1623, combined political shrewdness with a lively interest in the arts.

His term of office ran from 1624 until 1630, being interrupted only by comparatively brief visits to other cities, notably Zürich and Berne in 1626.[1] In that year he rented a house on the Zattere opposite the Church of San Baseggio (San Basilio),[2] not far from the old Guild of Water-Carriers who—if they knew and recognized him— referred to him as 'Il Vaccher' (Wake), as did many other Venetians. His instructions from London included a strong recommendation to try and gain the assistance of Savoy and Venice in the recovery of the Palatinate, which, having suffered not a little from its share in the Thirty Years' War, was dominated by Spain and the Habsburgs.

Wake's political involvement can be sufficiently gauged by the names dropped in a letter to London dated 16 July, the day before the concert directed by Monteverdi: among those mentioned are the Prince of Brandenburg, the Administrator of Magdeburg, and the King of Denmark.[3] Little wonder that he invited the most famous musician in Venice to supervise the music, for it seems that the 'Prince of Brandenburg'—the Elector George William (1595–1640), who in that same year attacked the invading army of King Gustavus II Adolphus of Sweden—was actually present in Venice from 9 July until the end of the month, as a guest in the ambassa-dor's house.[4]

The Elector's plan was to enlist the aid of England, France, Holland, and Venice in the campaign to free German Protestants from the Habsburg yoke. In this matter, one of his most powerful rivals was his father John Sigismund's cousin, Wolfgang Wilhelm, Count Palatine of the Rhine. The problems of succession and of territorial division in the Palatinate were such that these two 'possessing princes', as they were called, at first enjoyed little real power and later gambled even with that in the interests of so-called independence. John Sigismund adopted Calvinism in 1613; but when Wolfgang Wilhelm became Duke of Neuburg in 1614 he embraced the Church of Rome, thus placing the two branches of that ancient family in opposite camps.

Monteverdi was obviously delighted to be able to point out to the arch-diplomat Striggio that a Bavarian Duke was the guest of honour at one of his concerts. Yet he gives the name as 'the Prince of Neuburg', spelling it 'Noimburgh' which some have misread as 'Norimburgh'. But there were no princes of Nuremberg, so that the intended name must have been Neuburg, a town on the Danube some five miles from Ingolstadt. Monteverdi's friend Biagio Marini, composer and violinist, was in the service of the Duke of Neuburg in the early 1620s and dedicated an anthology to him.[5] This knowledge may have caused the confusion between Neuburg and Brandenburg, though Monteverdi generally kept family names clear in his head, and his letters as a whole show great care and reliability whenever he mentions them.

A more likely explanation is that Sir Isaac Wake, intent on helping his noble guest to preserve as far as possible the desired state of incognito, put it about that the visitor

---

[1] Soon after 1625 he wrote an essay 'Of the State of Italy', later published in his *Threefold Help to Political Observations* (London, 1655). His despatches, few of which have been published, are in the Public Record Office, while his letter-books are preserved in the British Library (Add. MSS 18639–42; 34310–11).

[2] *Calendar of State Papers, Venetian*, xix. 369.   [3] British Library, Add. MS 34311, fo. 100ᵛ.

[4] Paoli, 268.   [5] *Concerti per le Musiche di Camera* (1636); Vogel, *Bibliothek*, i. 416.

was the Duke of Neuburg. Venice, after all, was a city to which political rivals could repair with impunity and immunity, so that there would be nothing unusual in the brief sojourn of a Catholic prince, more especially one who was known for his patronage of music and of Italian musicians.

The concert over, Monteverdi hastened from the house on the Zattere, following the Fondamenta San Sebastiano to the Calle Avogaria, along the Calle Lunga San Barnaba for a few yards and then left to the east door of the Carmini. In his day, the interior of this impressive fourteenth-century edifice was considerably less light and spacious, for the choir lofts and organ now placed behind the main altar were situated, until 1653, in the middle of the building.[6] Music would have sounded acoustically different when Monteverdi directed the choir for First Vespers of the feast of Our Lady of Mount Carmel on that Saturday in July 1627, for it floated above rather than before the congregation.

Of the works he performed we have no record, nor do we know who took part in the ceremony. His son Francesco might have been there, a member of the Discalced Carmelites in a church adhering to the older branch of that order, which split into two after the papal bull of 20 December 1593. But the feast grew in popularity and importance towards the end of the sixteenth century, so that the liberal policies prevailing throughout Venetian religious life, combined with the persistent petitions of the general chapters for an Octave (which was authorized by the pope in 1628), could have had a beneficial effect on music too.[7]

Among the richness and variety of Monteverdi's church music, there is in fact one composition whose text indubitably belongs to the feast: *Sancta Maria, succurre miseris*.[8] This antiphon to the Magnificat at First Vespers is set with great sensitivity for treble voices (or two-part boys' choir) with organ continuo, and it might well have been especially composed for the occasion described in this letter, for it appeared in print in the same year, 1627, as part of the *Promptuarium Musicum III* issued by the Strasburg music publisher, Johannes Donfrid. It ranks as a miniature musical offering to the Carmelites from a man who must have helped them at many such feasts during his years in Venice.

In the meantime, *Licori* was by no means forgotten or neglected, and Act I was nearly finished. The cautious Monteverdi arranged to have the libretto copied in his own apartments so that no unauthorized versions of the revised text could be passed from hand to hand. But the problem of the young bass was still not solved, for even though Striggio had agreed to the fee that Monteverdi thought excessive, nobody really knew at this stage how well he would fit into the scheme of things. Certain aspects of Bisucci's vocal technique now come under the withering fire of Monteverdi's criticism, which as usual possesses an inherent interest through its revelation of the principles to which most teachers then subscribed.

He emphasizes the need for a singer to join together, as smoothly and elegantly as possible, the lower and middle registers of the voice, which he calls *la vocale del petto*

[6] Sansovino, 265.   [7] King, 273–4.

[8] Monteverdi, *Collected Works*, ed. Malipiero, xvi. 511. For text see Stevens, Communication, 503.

[344]

and *la vocale della gola*. These terms belong to an old and venerable tradition discussed as early as the middle of the thirteenth century by Jerome of Moravia,[9] who distinguishes three types of voice—*vox pectoris*, *vox gutturis*, and *vox capitis*, the first two being equivalent to Monteverdi's terms. It was understood that the different registers could sometimes be controlled by a single voice, especially when it had undergone the proper training. Giulio Caccini and Francesco Rasi, both of whom were known to Monteverdi, enjoyed the gift of a wide vocal range, extending from bass to tenor, and presumably Bisucci—in spite of his youth and lack of experience— was well on the way to joining their ranks, though he never became quite as famous as they did.[10]

My Most Illustrious Lord and Most Respected Master,

I beg you to forgive me for missing the previous post, not having replied to Your Lordship's most kind and courteous letter; because the many tasks I had last Saturday (the post-day) were the reason for my failure. There were two tasks: one was having to provide chamber music from 11 a.m. until 2 p.m. for the Most Serene Prince of Neuburg,[a] who is staying incognito in the House of the English Ambassador;[b] and this music being over, I then had to go—pressed by the entreaties of many friends—to the Carmelite Church, as it was the day of First Vespers[c] of the Most Holy Madonna of that Order, and stay there fully occupied until almost 7 p.m.

I am writing this now to let Your Lordship know what great delight I had on reading, in your very kind letter, of the pleasure you received from the first act of the brave *Lycoris* of Signor Giulio Strozzi.[d] I now have it all in my hands, given me by the same Signor Giulio, and full of many beautiful variations. At present I am having it written out at home, so that no copies, either partial or complete, can be taken.

I have already completed practically all the first act, and would be even further ahead if I had not had that little trouble with my eyes that I told Your Lordship about, and if I had not had some church music to write. From now on I shall work harder at it, and if you would like to see it, that is to read the whole of it, I shall send it off to Your Lordship when I have

[9] *Tractatus de musica* (Coussemaker, *Scriptores de musica*, i. 90).   [10] Hitchcock, 451–2.

[a] Wolfgang Wilhelm, Count Palatine of the Rhine.   [b] Sir Isaac Wake.
[c] The Commemoration of Our Lady of Mount Carmel (16 July) was celebrated on the nearest Sunday, which was two days later (18 July). First Vespers took place on Saturday 17 July.
[d] Venetian poet and librettist.

[345]

copied it, so that you can give it a glance, and you will see that Signora Margherita*e* will have a great deal to do on her own.

I took note of what Your Lordship proposed for the young bass,*f* and it seems to me that he has firmly decided to enter His Highness's*g* service, but I really think that the allowance is more generous than he deserves, because although it is true that he performs with assurance, he sings nevertheless in a somewhat melancholy manner; and regarding the ornaments, he does not separate them too well, because he fails most of the time to join the chest voice to the middle voice,*h* for if the middle fails the chest voice, the ornamentation becomes harsh and hard and offensive; if the chest voice fails that of the middle, the ornamentation becomes unctuous, as it were, and almost continuous in the voice, but when both function, the ornamentation comes off both sweetly and separated, and is most natural.

Although he is not in the chapel,*i* this going around earning fees here and there (since both major and minor feasts are celebrated a great deal in this city, especially at this time) pleases him, seeing a few small coins coming into his purse, as they do come in this delightful kind of liberty. Otherwise I can give no explanation. The young man's nature is very calm, modest, and humble. And here making a most humble reverence to Your Lordship I pray Our Lord God for the fulfilment of every supreme joy.

from Venice, 24 July 1627
Your Most Illustrious Lordship's
most humble and most grateful servant
Claudio Monteverdi

e Margherita Basile, sister of Adriana.   *f* Giovanni Battista Bisucci.
g Vincenzo II, seventh Duke of Mantua.   *h* [*la vocale*] *de la gola*.
i A member of the choir of the basilica of St Mark's.

102

Venice, 31 July 1627
to [Alessandro Striggio, at Mantua]

Mantua, Archivio Gonzaga, Cassetta 6, fo. 349. Folio: 1 p.

Davari, 163; Malipiero, 265; Paoli, 269; Lax, 168

While a copy of the libretto of *La finta pazza Licori* was being made in Venice under Monteverdi's watchful eye, Count Fabio Scotti (major-domo at the court of Parma) was engaged in the complex arrangements for an entertainment of a quite different kind—a combination of tourney, play, and intermezzi to be produced with a degree of lavish display unknown to the rival court of the Gonzaga since the time of Vincenzo I. On the same day that Monteverdi wrote this letter to Striggio, Scotti wrote to the Marquis Enzo Bentivoglio, assuring him that once he had examined a collection of stage machinery left over from an abandoned project of 1618, and decided whether or not it could be repaired and put to good use, the principal part in the planning of these arrangements would lie in his hands.[1] And by 10 August or so, Monteverdi received from the Marquis an exploratory letter, asking whether he would be willing to assist with the music.[2]

My Most Illustrious Lord and Most Respected Master,

I handed over the play *La finta pazza* by Signor Giulio Strozzi[a] to be recopied, but in spite of my efforts (having received today, post-day, Your Lordship's request that I send it for you to look at) I have not been able to get it back again. By the next post, I hope without more ado to send Your Lordship either the original or the copy, on which the said copyist has been busily engaged for about six days.

I shall consider it a great favour if Your Lordship finds it compatible with his taste, which I desire to serve conscientiously with all my strength and energy. With the same affection I pray God that He may continually

---

[1] Reiner, 294.   [2] Cf. Letter 106.

[a] Venetian poet and librettist.

[347]

bless and preserve Your Lordship's most honourable self, and I humbly bow to you, and kiss your hands.

from Venice, 31 July 1627

Your Most Illustrious Lordship's

most humble and most grateful servant,

Claudio Monteverdi

103

Venice, 17 August 1627
to [Alessandro Striggio, at Mantua]

Mantua, Archivio Gonzaga, Cassetta 6, fo. 351. Folio: 1 p.

Davari, 163; Malipiero, 266; Paoli, 270; Lax, 169

Bisucci, the Bolognese bass, decided to take a calculated risk and place himself at the disposal of the Gonzaga. He took with him this letter, adding to it his own explanation of the continuing delay over the copy of *La finta pazza Licori*. Yet Bisucci cannot have stayed long in Mantua: he must have sensed the decay and distress from the moment he arrived, for the new Duke had only four months to live.

But if Mantua had begun its final decline, there was much activity in Parma, despite the equally unstable nature of their financial situation. Money or no money, the Farnese were determined to put on the most ambitious entertainment possible, and to this end there came about a growing involvement of court officials, poets, musicians, scenic artists, designers, and stage technicians. On 11 August the major-domo, Fabio Scotti, sent carriages to Reggio Emilia to meet the Marquis Bentivoglio,[1] and once in Parma he began the task of artistic organization that reached its climax sixteen months later.

Among the many letters that awaited his attention were two of particular interest as far as the music was concerned. One was from Monteverdi, expressing interest in collaboration and requesting an early opportunity to see the librettos to be set to music. This letter is unfortunately no longer extant. The other is preserved in the Archivio di Stato, Ferrara, as part of the Bentivoglio archive,[2] and it was written on 13 August by the Ferrarese composer, Antonio Goretti.

He expresses his regrets to the Marquis for having arrived in Ferrara just too late to see him and answer his questions about music and musicians. Regarding one in particular—Sigismondo d'India—he admits a certain degree of capability in the man, but qualifies this by a devastatingly frank character-sketch. D'India likes flattery and puffs himself up with it; but when it comes to the final stages of composition and the preliminary rehearsals, he is so indecisive as to drive the performers crazy. Goretti then offers his own services, reminding Bentivoglio that he set to music a libretto written for a previous festival, by which he seems to mean Alfonso Pozzo's intermezzi for *La difesa della bellezza* intended for performance in 1618, but subsequently abandoned.[3]

[1] Reiner, 295.   [2] Busta 208, fos. 241–2 (translation in Reiner, 286–7).   [3] Reiner, 288.

In the end, Goretti was engaged as Monteverdi's assistant, lending him valuable aid not only in preparing the scores but also by keeping his mind on the task in hand. A member of a noble family of Ferrara, Goretti possessed the means to indulge his propensity for music by arranging performances in his own house, which contained a useful library of printed and manuscript music as well as a fine collection of instruments.[4] Although few of his compositions have survived, numerous dedications to him indicate that he was highly regarded both for his musicianship and for his kindly nature.

Luigi Mazzi, organist of the Benedictine monastery in Ferrara, thanked him in the dedication of his *Ricercari . . . et canzoni* (1596) for encouragement to publish as well as for many other courtesies. Other complimentary allusions appear in publications by Orfeo Vecchi (*Motetti*, 1599), Vincenti's reissue of Victoria's hymns (1600), and Marsolo's *Madrigali boscarecci* of 1607. About the year 1598, Goretti was beginning to take an interest in Monteverdi's madrigals, many of which he included in Accademia concerts given at his house. Among the audience were musical connoisseurs of various camps, some conservative and others forward-looking and broadminded, but the most reactionary by far was Giovanni Maria Artusi, a canon of San Salvatore in Bologna, who became a stern critic of Monteverdi before being finally won over to the modern viewpoint.[5]

In 1603 Goretti published a speech he had given before the Accademia degli Intrepidi—'Dell'eccellenze et prerogative della musica'—and in the following year the Ferrarese composer Filippo Nicoletti dedicated to him a villanella, *Se ben parto mia vita*.[6] This work may have been a kind of *risposta* to Goretti's *Io parto, anima mia*, of which only a manuscript copy exists in Naples (Conservatorio San Pietro a Majella). Pozzo, writing to Bentivoglio about the projected entertainments for 1618, mentions Goretti briefly but implies that he was already much involved in the plans.[7]

But it is not until the preparations for the marriage festivities of Odoardo Farnese and Margherita de' Medici that Goretti emerges as an important and influential figure. By great good fortune many of his letters have survived, and fifteen of them have been partly or wholly published, either in Italian or in an English translation.[8] They give the impression of a sensitive, witty, and patient man, utterly devoted to the art of music and to helping its practitioners, however tiresome they must occasionally have proved. But he was reliable and conscientious; and for these reasons alone his role in the musical aspect of the entertainments was indeed a genuinely indispensable

---

[4] The music and instruments are mentioned in the dedication of G. B. Buonamente's *Sonate, et canzoni* of 1636 (Sartori, *Bibliografia*, 350).

[5] *L'Artusi, ovvero, delle imperfezioni della moderna musica* (Venice, 1600). The second discourse is translated in Strunk, 393–404. For a comprehensive account of these interchanges, see Palisca, 'Artusi', 133–66.

[6] Vogel, *Bibliothek*, ii. 21.   [7] Reiner, 288.

[8] 1627—12 Mar. (present whereabouts unknown; listed in the Succi Sale Catalogue as no. 481); 18 Apr. (summary in Kinsky, no. 457); 13 Aug. (Reiner, 286–7); 29 Oct. (Lavin, 146); 2 Nov. (Lavin, 146); 16 Nov. (Lavin, 146); 26 Nov. (Lavin, 147); 27 Nov. (Barblan, 'La vita' 140; translated in Reiner, 301); 7 Dec. (Lavin, 147). Six further letters belong to the following year, 1628—13 Feb. (Kinsky, no. 457); 18 Feb. (Lavin, 147); 25 Feb. (Lavin, 148); 9 Nov. (Lavin, 148); 28 Nov. (Lavin, 148); 15 Dec. (Lavin, 148).

one. Later he came into his own with the music of a tourney, *Discordia superata*, produced at Ferrara in 1635. He was still in touch with Bentivoglio in 1640,[9] but died before 1653, in which year his instruments were sold to the Archduke of Tyrol, eventually finding their way to Vienna.[10]

Bentivoglio spent only a few days in Ferrara, but was able to make a thorough inspection of the stage machinery originally built for Pozzo's *La difesa della bellezza* in 1618, and ordered it to be repaired in readiness for the vastly more ambitious project that would eventually be realized in 1628. On 16 August, less than a week after arriving, he wrote to his wife announcing his intention to return on the following day.[11]

My Most Illustrious Lord and Most Respected Master,

By the good offices of the present bearer[a] (the gentleman bass-singer who is coming at His Highness's[b] command) I wanted to let Your Lordship know that a great many tasks have engaged the attention of the copyist of the fable *La finta pazza Licori*, and because of this, I have still not been able to send it to Your Lordship, but I hope to do so very soon.

This gentleman bass-singer will be able to give you ample information regarding this busy state of affairs, and has insisted that I signify to Your Lordship by these same good offices how much he wishes to be considered as a faithful servant to Your Lordship, to whom with all affection I bow; and I reverently kiss your hands, praying God for your every perfect happiness.

from Venice, 17 August 1627
Your Most Illustrious Lordship's
most devoted and most grateful servant
Claudio Monteverdi

[9] Reiner, 288.   [10] Senn, 334, 340.   [11] Reiner, 295.

[a] Giovanni Battista Bisucci.   [b] Vincenzo II, seventh Duke of Mantua.

104

Venice, 28 August 1627
to [Alessandro Striggio, at Mantua]

Mantua, Archivio Gonzaga, Cassetta 6, fo. 353. Folio: 1 p. Enclosure: libretto of Acts II and III of *La finta pazza Licori*

Davari, 164; Malipiero, 267; Paoli, 271; Lax, 169

The libretto of Act I of *La finta pazza Licori* had already been sent with Letter 100; now Monteverdi sends Acts II and III, promising the remainder as soon as the copyist recovers from his illness sufficiently to complete the task. The last two acts follow on 10 September with Letter 106, which contains a lengthy discourse on Mantuan problems affecting his future. This was a crucial time in his career, for as the possibility of further commissions from Mantua grew slowly more remote, the composition of the music for Parma assumed persistently greater urgency.

Parma, the old enemy of Mantua, was now wooing the composer whose services Francesco Gonzaga had summarily dispensed with in 1613; and Monteverdi was in no mood to refuse their offer. He must have guessed that other names had occurred to the Dowager Duchess Margherita, and to her son Odoardo, the reigning Duke. Vincenzo Bonizzi, organist of the Steccata in Parma, had dedicated some vocal arrangements for viola bastarda to the Duchess in 1626,[1] while in the same year her son had been the dedicatee of a set of *Madrigali concertati* by G. B. Crivelli, organist of Santo Spirito in Ferrara, and of an opera—*La catena d'Adone*—by the Roman composer Mazzocchi.[2]

From Modena, where he was occupied in presenting one of his latest works to the Duke, Sigismondo d'India wrote to Bentivoglio on 26 August offering his services 'anywhere at all that you may think good', meaning of course that he had heard rumours of the music required for Parma and hoped to be invited.[3] Unknown to him at the time, this assignment had already gone to Monteverdi, with Antonio Goretti as his assistant.

My Most Illustrious Lord and Most Respected Master,

The copyist has been rather ill: because of this difficulty he has been able to give me the said play[a] written out only as far as the third act. By the next

---

[1] Sartori, *Bibliografia*, 307.   [2] Vogel, *Bibliothek*, i. 193, 440.   [3] Reiner, 286.

[a] *La finta pazza Licori*, by Giulio Strozzi.

post I shall send the remainder to Your Lordship, for this indeed he has promised me, and you will forgive me for the delay, which is not my fault. Awaiting after this Your Lordship's instructions regarding the said play, and here making a humble bow to Your Lordship, I pray God for the fulfilment of every happiness.

from Venice, 28 August 1627
Your Most Illustrious Lordship's
most devoted and most grateful servant,
Claudio Monteverdi

105

Venice, 10 September 1627
to [the Marquis Enzo Bentivoglio, at Ferrara]

Naples, Biblioteca del Conservatorio di San Pietro a Majella, no. 6829. Bifolio: 4 pp.

Caffi, ii. 135; Prunières, 275; Malipiero, 270; Paoli, 277; Fabbri 1985, 269; Lax, 170

This is the first of five letters addressed, as internal evidence shows, to the Marquis Enzo Bentivoglio.[1] Since the importance of his role in the development of Monteverdi's artistic career has not so far been given its due, a reassessment of the facts may not be out of place. The son of Cornelio Bentivoglio and Isabella Bendidio, Enzo seemed to inherit the administrative talents of his father, who held high office at the court of Alfonso II. He was born at Ferrara in 1575, and died in Rome on 25 November 1639, his life span being well within that of Monteverdi. Although he loved music, he never became a particular patron of the art or of its practitioners; and the total lack of printed dedications to him shows that he probably neither commissioned nor sponsored individual works.

His interest in the theatre (in the broadest sense of the word) was, however, considerable, and he also liked to write poetry, plan agricultural improvements, and supervise the construction of buildings such as the Capuchin monastery and the church of San Maurilio in his native city. His circle of influential friends included several princes of the Church—the cardinals Borghese, Caetani, Pio, d'Este, Serra, and Bevilacqua. His own brother Guido, after serving as apostolic nuncio in Flanders and in France, became a Cardinal in 1621, and their correspondence affords occasional glimpses of their joint concern for grandiose types of entertainment.[2]

In Letter 106 (apparently written on the same day as this one), Monteverdi refers to Enzo Bentivoglio as 'very much my lord for many years past', a phrase which has often been cited and as often misunderstood.[3] Indeed, the word 'many' suggests a much longer period of time than 'a few' or 'several' years; and as is frequently the case, Monteverdi's choice of words turns out to be sensible and significant, for he met Bentivoglio on several occasions during the latter part of his Mantuan period and almost certainly collaborated with him in some way.

[1] The other four are nos. 109, 111, 113, and 122. [2] Panigada (*passim*).
[3] Cf. Reiner, 285; 'it may denote nothing more than a long-standing esteem'.

Shortly before his marriage to Caterina Martinengo in 1602, Bentivoglio took a leading part in the founding of the Accademia degli Intrepidi, along with Francesco Saraceni and Guidobaldo Bonarelli.[4] He helped them by offering advice, perhaps even funds, towards the building of a theatre, and served the Accademia at certain times as its president or *principe*.[5] The link between Monteverdi and Bentivoglio is hinted at in the dedication of the Fourth Book of Madrigals (1603) in which the composer explains that since his wish to present some of his madrigals to Duke Alfonso was frustrated by the circumstance of that ruler's death in 1597, he intended to dedicate them to the members of the Accademia now that there had arisen in Ferrara a *principe* and head of a most noble band of chivalrous friends.

The identity of this *principe* has long remained obscure because it has always been assumed that the person referred to was either Alfonso's designated successor, Cesare I d'Este, or Vincenzo Gonzaga, first Duke of Mantua.[6] But when Clement VIII annexed Ferrara as a papal fief in 1598, Cesare moved his court to Modena, and from that time onwards Ferrara had no ruling prince or duke. Although Monteverdi established contact with Cesare at a later date, he could hardly have been referring to him in 1603. Nor could he have wished to bring into the picture his own 'padron collendissimo', Duke Vincenzo, for he had already dedicated the Third Book to him in 1592, and the whole point about the Fourth was its close association with Ferrara. The numerous madrigals with texts by poets associated with the city or living there— Guarini, Arlotti, Tasso—make this perfectly clear.[7]

Only one figure can convincingly fit the description: Enzo Bentivoglio, a vigorous, active, and wealthy young man of some 26 years who was indeed the chief and head of a distinguished group of noblemen and gentlemen intent upon cultivating the arts and letters through the formation of the Accademia degli Intrepidi. In their presence, Monteverdi had directed performances of his madrigals, and from them he had received approbation and hospitality; now he would present them with the fruits of his labour in the form of a set of part-books printed in unusually beautiful type by Amadino.

Apart from the further possibility of a meeting between composer and Marquis in 1610 when Monteverdi visited Rome (where Bentivoglio resided as Ambassador Extraordinary of Ferrara), there was another occasion in 1612 mentioned in a letter from Guido Bentivoglio, at that time a resident of Brussels. Enzo had been invited by Vincenzo Gonzaga to devise a tourney for Mantua, and since these displays of equestrian skill were invariably accompanied by suitable outdoor music, it is very likely that Monteverdi was called in as collaborator.[8] But even if they did not meet in 1610 or 1612, they must have done so in 1601 or 1602 at one or more of the meetings of the Ferrarese Academy.

Now, a quarter of a century later, Bentivoglio still displayed keen enthusiasm for tourneys, theatrical extravaganzas, and court entertainments. He gladly accepted the

[4] Vogel, 339 n. 3.　　[5] Paoli, 341.　　[6] Bettinelli, 79.

[7] Guarini's *Il pastor fido* may have been performed there in 1595. See Fenlon, 'Mantua', 161.

[8] Panigada, 430 (letter dated 12 Feb. 1612).

suggestion that he should supervise all the artistic arrangements for a performance of Tasso's *Aminta*, with a prologue (*Teti e Flora*) by Claudio Achillini of Bologna, and five intermezzi—*La Liberazione di Ruggero, Didone ed Enea, Diana e Venere, Gli Argonauti, I cinque continenti*—by Ascanio Pio di Savoia, Bentivoglio's son-in-law. For good measure, there was to be a tourney based on the subject of *Mercurio e Marte*, also by Achillini. The play was to be recited in the customary manner, but everything else called for music on the most elaborate scale, with soloists, choruses and instrumental ensembles dispersed throughout the area of action, whether above, below or behind the stage, or wherever the dramatic need might arise.[9] One man, with one assistant, had the task of composing all this music, orchestrating it, and seeing it through to the final performance.

The great occasion was to be the wedding, in Parma, of the young Duke Odoardo, who had at first been betrothed to Maria Cristina, eldest daughter of Cosimo II de' Medici, Grand Duke of Tuscany. Such matters were traditionally arranged when the unfortunate parties concerned were too young to know what was happening, and it may have been some years before Odoardo heard that Maria was a hunchback whose indifferent health was scarcely offset by a huge dowry. Loopholes in the marriage contract, rivalry from a French suitor—Gaston d'Orléans—and Maria's retirement to a convent and to an early death threw an unlucky shadow over negotiations that were already protracted, but in the end matters were satisfactorily resolved in Odoardo's favour, for whom the second of Cosimo's daughters, Margherita, was chosen.

One result of this matrimonial *imbroglio* was that the wedding had to be postponed from the spring of 1628 until October; and in consequence the play, intermezzi, and tourney did not take place until shortly before Christmas. *Aminta* and the intermezzi were given on 13 December in a specially constructed theatre within the first great courtyard of the Palazzo della Pilotta, principal residence of the Farnese, and it extended from the entire breadth of the façade of the Chiesa di San Pietro Martire (stage and proscenium) back to the row of pillars on the opposite side.[10] The tourney, *Mercurio e Marte*, took place on 21 December in what was then called the Teatro nel Salone, a wooden structure erected in 1618 to the designs of Giovanni Battista Aleotti and later modified by Bentivoglio. Although this auditorium situated on the upper main floor of the palace suffered extensive damage in World War II, it has now been satisfactorily restored.[11]

If Bentivoglio masterminded the entertainments as a whole, it was the Duchess of Parma who sought out and sifted the many ideas that must have been discussed at court as soon as the planning of a suitable spectacle received general approval. It is unlikely that Odoardo took much part in the deliberations, for in 1627 he was only 15 years old and probably more than content to leave such matters to his mother. Born Margherita Aldobrandini, she had married Ranuccio Farnese (1569–1622), fourth

[9] By a remarkable coincidence, three detailed and complementary studies of the events at Parma appeared in 1964: those of Lavin, Nagler, and Reiner.

[10] Buttigli, cited by Lavin, 153 ff. See also fig. 5, pl. III.

[11] Illustration from Ferrara, Biblioteca Comunale, in Lavin, fig. 7, pl. IV.

duke of Parma, in 1600, one of the humbler among her wedding gifts being a collection of musical epithalamia—*Sesto Himeneo ingemmato*—by Giulio Quintiani, organist and Director of Music at Piacenza cathedral.[12] Her fondness for music is shown by this and other dedications, and she was doubtless flattered by the final versions of the libretti by Ascanio Pio and Claudio Achillini, who between them brought in numerous direct or symbolic references to the name Margherita—her own name, that of her late husband's sister, and of her daughter-in-law, the future Duchess.

Monteverdi, in this reply to Bentivoglio's letter, makes a special point of mentioning the paragraph quoted from one of the Dowager Duchess's letters, which was clearly the source of the commission. Although she must have known something of Monteverdi's reputation, it seems that she allowed herself to be influenced by the strong recommendation of Settimia Caccini, who made it clear to those concerned that Monteverdi should be placed in charge at all costs. And in the end the singer had her way. The intermezzo enclosed with Bentivoglio's letter was the third of five by Ascanio Pio: *La favola pastorale di Diana e Venere.*[13] No time was lost in deciding on the kind of music for each of the four main sections of the intermezzo,[14] yet Monteverdi was quick to point out that certain passages would require the advice of Bentivoglio. The two references to 'next Wednesday' almost suggest a personal meeting, but they may mean no more than an unusual degree of urgency combined with reliance on the *corriere* (or rapid mail) rather than the slower *ordinario*.

The present letter, like the other four surviving ones from the composer to the Marquis, was evidently removed from the Bentivoglio archive in Ferrara at some time during the nineteenth century. Each letter now forms part of a different collection, in Naples, Oxford, Paris, Bologna, and Forlì; several more might also have been removed and have since disappeared completely. The curious fact about this letter is its date, written quite clearly as '1617' and so interpreted by some of Monteverdi's biographers. Frank Walker put matters right in a communication that confirmed the date as written but emphasized the fact that it was a slip of the pen (or the mind), for the subject-matter of the document clearly refers to the events of 1627 and 1628.[15]

Although Monteverdi rarely made mistakes of this kind, he did omit the day of the month in Letter 3, and the year is left out at the close of Letter 62. Many people find it difficult to advance the year when dating correspondence in the first week or so of January. But '1617' for '1627' is a little more difficult to explain when the month is September. Friday, 10 September, was in fact an unusual day because Monteverdi wrote three letters one after the other, and there is no similar instance of this in his entire life as a correspondent. All three letters were of considerable importance, and

---

[12] Vogel, *Bibliothek*, ii. 113.   [13] Solerti, *Musica*, 450.

[14] When these descriptions are compared with the libretto, it becomes clear that the first section begins with the opening words of the First Siren ('Fermate, O venti'); the second from Diana's words ('Fermate voi, fermate'); the third from Pluto's solo ('Cessin fra voi gli acerbi oltraggi'); and the fourth from Diana's solo ('Ma quale a gli occhi miei').

[15] Walker, 433.

a study of the handwriting reveals that he wrote them in an order corresponding to the rank of the addressee: first the Marquis, then the Count, finally the councillor (Marigliani having been promoted from secretary a short time previously). The most likely explanation is that he began with the letter to Bentivoglio early in the morning, and was still not quite awake when he came to the date. But as he warmed to his task, he put '1627' at the end of the letters to Striggio and Marigliani.

My Most Illustrious and Most Excellent Lord and Most Respected Master,

Yesterday, which was the 9th of this month, I received from the courier Your Excellency's package in which there was an intermezzo*a* and a letter from Your Excellency, doing me infinite kindness and honour, together with a copy of a paragraph from a letter of the Duchess of Parma,*b* written to Your Excellency, in which she deigns to honour me by commanding me (through Your Excellency) to set to music what will be ordered by Your Excellency. I have hardly been able to read the said intermezzo twice before having to write—this being the day when the courier leaves—yet I have seen so much beauty in it that, truth to tell, I was deeply moved and captivated by so fine a work.

Although time has been short, I have not been entirely useless in this respect, for I have already begun work, the modest results of which Your Excellency will see by next Wednesday. I have already taken into account the four kinds of music that will be used to adorn the said intermezzo: the first, which starts at the beginning and goes so far as the onset of the quarrel between Venus and Diana, and between their arguments; the second, from the beginning of the quarrel until the arguments are over; the third, when Pluto comes in to establish order and calm, lasting until Diana starts to fall in love with Endymion;*c* and the fourth and last, from the beginning of the said falling in love until the end.

But believe me, Your Excellency, there are passages which—without your sensitive aid—could, as you will see, cause me no little trouble, and I shall give Your Excellency more detailed information about this on Wednesday. For the moment I intend to do nothing more than to give thanks to God first of all, for having made me worthy of being able to

a *Diana e Venere*, the third of five written by Ascanio Pio for a performance of Tasso's *Aminta*.
b The Dowager Duchess Margherita, widow of Ranuccio Farnese.
c The name Endymion was replaced in the final version of the intermezzo by the designation *pastore*.

receive such distinguished commissions from such eminent gentlemen and patrons, praying him at the same time to make me worthy as much by the results as by my devotion, which will surely seek to serve patrons with the greatest power of which it is capable.

I render infinite thanks to Your Excellency for such a favour, at the same time praying God that he may always prosper Your Excellency's good grace, and I beg you to offer on my behalf the greatest thanks you can to the good graces of those Most Serene Highnesses to whom I make a most humble bow and deep reverence, binding myself to them as their most humble servant; and to Your Excellency I bow and kiss your hand.

from Venice, 10 September 1627[d]

Your Most Illustrious Excellency's

most devoted and most grateful servant

Claudio Monteverdi

[d] Monteverdi wrote '1617' in error.

106

Venice, 10 September 1627
to [Alessandro Striggio, at Mantua]

Mantua, Archivio Gonzaga, Cassetta 6, fos. 355–7. Bifolio + folio: 6 pp.
Enclosure: Libretto of Acts IV and V of *La finta pazza Licori*

Davari, 164; Vogel, 434; Malipiero, 267; Paoli, 273; Fabbri 1985, 267, 268;
Lax, 172

The comic opera libretto[1] is at last complete, and the dispute over singers appears to
have been resolved—at least for the moment, for Monteverdi's reference to the
strange behaviour of some of his choirmen almost ranks as a prophecy. Ten years later
he was to be insulted and attacked by one of them in St Mark's Square, once again
making his 'ability to control himself' desirable. He shows self-control in this letter,
although the invitation that prompted it must have upset him considerably. The
Gonzaga must have needed him desperately, for despite their earlier attempts and his
inevitable refusals, they were willing to try and persuade him even though the outlook
in Mantua had never been so discouraging, financially and politically.

Monteverdi therefore begins by playing up the situation at Parma for all it is
worth—his contacts with Bentivoglio, Duke Odoardo, and his mother; the fact that he
was chosen for the task by several other composers; his rapid progress on the first
intermezzo to be sent him. This leads to his customary eulogy of the Gonzaga, and in
particular the reigning Duke, to whom he may have taught music many years previously. Then follows a deliberate contrast between the security and stability of life in
Venice, and life at Mantua where speed of composition outweighs quality. With
regard to problems over his pension from Mantua, only one solution would be
acceptable: or rather two bound together as one single guarantee of good faith—his
fondo in the shape of land, and a canonry worth 300 scudi from Cremona. With these
he could work for a while and then retire to enjoy his well-earned leisure.

The political string-pulling necessary for such a move is then sketched in with
shrewdness and honesty, tempered, however, by a sanguine approach resulting from
unsuccessful earlier appeals for assistance linked to vacant ecclesiastical benefices at
Novara and Mantua.[2] This time the route is more complex and dangerous. He has in
mind an audience with Duke Vincenzo II, who would be asked for a letter of recommendation to his sister Eleonora, wife of the emperor Ferdinand II; she would
command the Duke of Feria (Governor of Milan) or His Eminence Cardinal Campori

[1] For this non-existent opera, see Tomlinson.   [2] Letter 11 and 49.

of Cremona, and the outcome might be a benefice for Monteverdi. But there were weak links in the chain, for the Emperor was not entirely in favour of the matter and had also to deal with his brother-in-law, King Sigismund III of Poland. For some reason Monteverdi, who had provided music for Sigismund in Venice, did not now wish to bring him into the orbit of discussion.

All this was to have been supported by the statutory gift of new compositions to the Empress, but the nature of these—sacred or secular, many or few—never becomes clear. Since no printed anthology qualifies at this time, they could have been works still in manuscript. Indeed, it was not until the *Selva morale* of 1641 that the Empress received a dedication from Monteverdi, and by then the need for a benefice no longer existed. There was no real hope of such a windfall in 1627, but the Gonzaga made their customary offer and the composer countered with his expected refusal. This was the last occasion on which the game would be played.

Parma too had its problems, but they were mainly matrimonial. Bentivoglio, on hearing that Monteverdi had definitely been chosen to write the music for the inter-mezzi and the tourney, wrote to the Duchess on 4 September: 'I cannot tell you how pleased I am about the decision taken to make use of Monteverdi, as much for the man's rare quality as also for being able to get down to work.'[3] In Monteverdi's daily round, Strozzi's libretto was now replaced by the verses of Ascanio Pio di Savoia, and another chapter of his life began.

My Most Illustrious Lord and Most Respected Master,

I am sending off to Your Lordship the remainder of *La finta pazza Licori*. I did not send it by the previous post, as the copyist was unable to let me have it in time for the departure of the courier. I have also paid heed to what Your Lordship was kind enough to tell me, yet even if you had not ordered me to be silent—since it was a matter such that talking about it could even have caused harm to my present occupation, for strange things go on amongst our crowd of singers—this ability to control myself would have been desirable for that very reason; but all the more so now that you ask it of me through your innate kindness.

The Marquis Bentivoglio,[a] very much my master for many years past, wrote to me as long as a month ago asking if I would set to music some words of his, made by His Excellency for use in a certain very important play that would be written for performance at a princely wedding. These would be intermezzi, not a play sung throughout. As he was very much

---

[3] Solerti, *Musica*, 193. Vogel, 385, quotes the same passage with slight variants, assuming the date to be 7 Sept. and the addressee the Dowager Duchess.

[a] Enzo Bentivoglio, Marquis of Gualteri from 1619.

my special master I replied that I would do everything possible to carry out His Excellency's orders. He answered with particular appreciation and told me it was going to be used at the wedding of the Duke of Parma.[b] I replied that I would do whatever he would be so kind as to ask of me.

He at once informed their Highnesses[c] of this, and I received a reply telling me to start work on the assignment, so he at once sent me the first intermezzo.[d] I have already half finished it, and shall compose it easily because they are almost all soliloquies. Their Highnesses do me great honour with such a commission, for I have heard that about six or seven applied for the appointment, but of their own accord these gentlemen were so kind as to elect myself, and that was how it happened.

I now reply to the paragraph that mentions the kind and special affection of the Most Serene Lord Duke Vincenzo,[e] my special master, for so he surely will be in every time and condition, and in no matter what circumstances, because of the particular reverence in which I shall always hold that Most Serene House, and which I hold now; and because of the special obligation I have to that Most Serene Highness, as I have received particular favours from his infinite kindness. And I shall affirm that His Highness will always be my master and patron without any expectation on my part other than His Highness's good grace, since I know for sure that he would not consent to my ruin or unhappiness.

Considering what I have, I have most securely whilst I live, whether or not I am able to work, because this security operates in such a way, that (as with the Director of Music, so with the singers themselves) they would never try to make anyone do what he cannot, never! I shall also affirm that I am very unlucky (and believe me truly, Your Lordship) in that my ill fortune—to play a joke on me—should interfere with the allowance which His Highness[f] deigned to grant me: nine times out of ten there would be no money for me in the Treasury. And so, thanks to this major misfortune I could in a short time be ripe for some internal illness, not to mention the misfortunes[g] attendant upon death, which would in fact leave me without any allowance whatever.

[b] Odoardo Farnese.   [c] Duke Odoardo and the Dowager Duchess Margherita.

[d] Actually the third of five, but the first to be sent.

[e] Vincenzo II, seventh Duke of Mantua.   [f] Vincenzo I, fourth Duke of Mantua.

[g] Dismissal from service and denial of pension, on the death of duke (cf. Letter 8).

Nothing could give my soul peace with satisfaction except to have a canonry at Cremona, in addition to my lands without anything of benefit from the Treasury; and I could have that canonry at once by means of an order from Her Majesty the Empress[h] to the Governor of Milan,[i] or to the Cardinal of Cremona[j] himself. The canonry would provide me with about 300 scudi in that currency. Thus feeling secure on this firm basis, and with the addition of my estate, I could be sure—after serving as long as I were able—of then having somewhere to retire, honourably and in godly manner, for the last days of my life.

Otherwise, as I told Your Lordship, I would always be in fear of some colossal trick that my ill fortune might play on me, and I could certainly expect it because I am no longer young. With this end in mind—of the said canonry—before its patronage[k] was allowed to die by His Majesty,[l] I was on the point of passing through Mantua to ask for letters of recommendation from His Highness to Her Majesty the Empress (since I was about to present her with some of my compositions, expressly in order to be favoured with that canonry), since the Lord Prince of Poland[m] became very involved in the matter; but ill luck called on me, because I did not wish to present his letters for a certain reason.

I am certainly not rich, but neither am I poor; moreover, I lead a life with a certain security of income until my death, and furthermore I am absolutely sure of always having it on the appointed pay-days, which come every two months without fail. Indeed, if it is the least bit late, they send it to my house. Then as regards chapel I do as I wish, since there is the sub-director, called Assistant Director of Music;[n] and there is no obligation to teach. Also, the city is most beautiful, and if I want to put myself to minimal trouble I come up with a further 200 good ducats.

Such is my condition: nevertheless the Lord Duke will always be my master, and I shall be his most faithful and most humble servant in every place and condition. And here making a most humble reverence to Your Lordship I pray God for the fulfilment of every happiness, while I render

[h] Eleonora Gonzaga, wife of Ferdinand II.
[i] Don Gomez Suarez di Figueroa e Cordova, fourth Duke of Feria.
[j] Pietro Campori, elected Bishop of Cremona, 1621.
[k] presulio [praesulium] in the sense of patronage.
[l] Ferdinand II, Holy Roman Emperor.
[m] Sigismund III, King of Poland.
[n] Giovanni Rovetta, appointed in 1627.

infinite thanks to you with infinite obligation, begging you at the same time to forgive me for being so lengthy, writing not being my profession.

from Venice, 10 September 1627

Your Most Illustrious Lordship's

most grateful servant

Claudio Monteverdi

107

Venice, 10 September 1627
to [Ercole Marigliani, at Mantua]

Mantua, Archivio Gonzaga, Cassetta 6, fos. 359–60. Bifolio: 3 pp.

Prunières, 275; Malipiero, 272; Paoli, 279; Lax, 175

The third letter written on 10 September 1627 is obviously intended for Ercole Marigliani, who is mentioned in affectionate terms just before the closing salutation. A more exalted level of address ('Illustrissimo') indicates that he had been promoted from the rank of secretary to that of councillor, and it is as such that he is referred to in Letters 115 and 119. This present communication is the last surviving one from Monteverdi to Marigliani, yet they almost certainly wrote to each other towards the end of September or the beginning of October regarding the sudden imprisonment of Massimiliano on the charge of having read a book that was on the Index.

The topic now is Parma,[1] where much remained to be done in what everybody thought would be a very short time, although in fact the chain of events dragged on so slowly that fourteen months were to elapse before the play and the tourney took place. Mention is made of Alessandro Ghivizzani, a singer and composer from Lucca, who had married Settimia Caccini with a dowry of 500 scudi from her father Giulio, and a promised 600 scudi from the Grand Duchess of Tuscany, wife of Cosimo I. Alas, she forgot to authorize payment of this sum. Her absent-mindedness might have been excused but for the fact that she arranged the marriage in 1609 with the express intention of keeping these two musicians together.[2]

On leaving Florence they settled in Lucca, then moved to Mantua in 1612, remaining there for the next seven years as part of Duke Ferdinando's musical establishment. Ghivizzani seems to have composed very little, apart from his contribution to *La Maddalena* in 1617 and three motets in Malgarini's Mantuan anthology of 1618.[3] After two years back in Lucca, the couple applied for leave to go to Parma, where Ghivizzani entered the service of Cardinal Farnese while his wife sang at court. In due course the leave was extended and eventually turned into a permanent situation, enabling Settimia to appear in various important roles during the festivities of

---

[1] Paoli, 279–80 considers these remarks to refer to a new work by Monteverdi. But the only new work for Mantua had been *La finta pazza Licori*. Ghivizzani's reference to a work that was not even begun must point unequivocally to the music for Parma.

[2] Boyer, 306.   [3] *Motetti a una, due, tre, e quattro voci* (Venice, Vincenti, 1618).

December 1628. Alessandro, who died in 1632, was survived by his wife, and she was active in musical circles until shortly after 1640.

Events in Parma, especially regarding music and musicians, gave rise to the expected tensions and rivalries between one artist and another, or between groups of them. Sigismondo d'India, who had offered his services to Bentivoglio, was evidently offended at having been passed over in favour of Monteverdi, so he appealed to Ghivizzani and his wife because they would certainly be involved as performers. Ghivizzani apparently replied to d'India, making it clear that he approved of Monteverdi's appointment, and adding that as far as his wife was concerned she preferred to work under the direction of Monteverdi rather than under any other musician.

The reason why his letter was enclosed with one from Marigliani may well be connected with a visit of Ghivizzani's to Mantua, where many of his former colleagues were still living. Discussing the matter with Marigliani, who was about to write to Venice, he could have requested that the two letters go together, and it seems that they did so, probably arriving about 7 September. As for the confusion over Ghivizzani's proper title, Monteverdi may have mistaken the word 'Eminenza' for 'Altezza' and assumed that Ghivizzani was on the court payroll, rather than that of the Cardinal. But whatever the error, Monteverdi looks forward to visiting Striggio and Marigliani in Mantua where preparations ought to be under way for the forthcoming première of *La finta pazza Licori*. For different and unrelated reasons, however, neither the visit nor the performance took place.

My Most Illustrious Lord and Most Respected Master,[a]

I have received Your Lordship's most esteemed and courteous letter, enclosing one from Signor Alessandro,[b] husband of Signora Settimia,[c] in which he speaks of little else but his certainty about the shortness of time for what those Most Serene Princes[d] intend to do, and as yet nothing in the way of poetry or any kind of beginning is to be seen.

Once again he kindly assures me that he will not allow his wife to obey anyone else but myself in singing, and that I should not be surprised about his having replied to Signor Sigismondo,[e] since he could not suffer the friend he loves to be hurt by anyone, either rightly or wrongly, beseeching me that if I knew anything I might try and pass the word on to him; and at the end of that letter he tells me that he is not one of His

---

[a] The use of *Illustrissimo* instead of the usual *Molto Illustre* shows that Marigliani has been promoted to *consigliere*.

[b] Alessandro Ghivizzani, composer.   [c] Settimia Caccini, singer.

[d] Duke Odoardo Farnese and the Dowager Duchess Margherita of Parma and Piacenza.

[e] Sigismondo d'India, composer.

Highness's*f* musicians, and would I please no longer give him the title of musician to His Highness. Little wonder that I had erred, not knowing about this; but when writing to him again (as I shall do by the next post) I shall try not to fall into my former error. But what made me err was seeing those precise words in his letter: 'If anybody—other than you yourself—has a right to look after that music, I should do so more than anyone else, because I am not inferior to the aforesaid (whom you mention) in any aspect of the art, so much the more because of the particular merits of my wife and my many years of service to that Most Serene House.' And, I repeat, since looking after music suits the musician and not the doctor, I have asked him this for these basic reasons; but when writing to him I shall be able to correct my error, and may he forgive me for it, since his letter was full of the greatest love and kindness.

I am invited to go to Mantua by the Most Illustrious Lord Count Alessandro Striggio,*g* very much my master, because of his desire to speak with me. The Feast of the Rosary*h* being over, and His Highness back from Maderno,*i* it will be easy for me to get to Mantua, and it will be most welcome to me, as much to enjoy that country which I so love, as to cheer myself up with Signor Marigliani, very much my master, ever rejoicing (as I shall ever go on doing) in his every complete happiness, which Our Lord grant him always, while with all reverence I kiss Your Lordship's hands.

from Venice, 10 September 1627
Your Most Illustrious Lordship's
most grateful servant
Claudio Monteverdi

f Odoardo Farnese, Duke of Parma. At this time Ghivizzani was in the service of Cardinal Farnese.
g Senior councillor of the Duke of Mantua.   *h* 7 Oct. See also Letters 108 and 111.
i Village on the west shore of Lago di Garda.

108

Venice, 18 September 1627
to [Alessandro Striggio, at Mantua]

Mantua, Archivio Gonzaga, Cassetta 6, fo. 362. Folio: 1 p.

Davari, 166; Malipiero, 273; Paoli, 284; Lax, 177

Marigliani having been promoted from secretary to councillor, his form of salutation now agrees with that hitherto accorded only to Striggio, and in consequence the problem of addressee becomes more acute. Nevertheless, there remains the evidence obtainable from the topic of each letter; and since Monteverdi tends to reserve specific matters either for Striggio or for Marigliani, a decision can usually be made as to which of the two is the more likely recipient.

The present letter, being the last to mention the comic opera, was obviously sent to Striggio, who for some reason or other had been obliged to cancel at short notice. This kind of occurrence was by no means unusual in Monteverdi's dealings with the Gonzaga, for between 1618 and 1620 he had spent countless hours working on *Andromeda* and *Apollo* without seeing any result whatever. That there may have been trouble at Mantua with some of the singers is a distinct possibility in view of the remark about variation in the vocal line being a prime consideration. Was the leading role too much for Margherita Basile? Or was Striggio's decision dictated by political confusion stemming from the Duke's chronic ill health? At this point Vincenzo II had only a few weeks to live.

In his letter condemning *La finta pazza Licori* to an undeserved oblivion, Striggio attempted to soften the blow by promising to do what he could about the canonry, but this (like the operatic project) quickly vanished from view. Replying in philosophical vein, the composer points to his continuing involvement with the music for Parma, mentioning Tasso's play *Aminta*, which he knew to be the framework for the prologue and intermezzi.[1] He lost no opportunity to inform the Mantuans of his prestigious commissions from other courts, and of his duties to the Serenissima.

My Most Illustrious Lord and Most Respected Master,

In truth, what Your Lordship thinks about *La finta pazza*, I had likewise thought, although everything could have been kept going with some vari-

[1] It has been suggested that *Aminta* is a slip of the pen, and that *Armida* was intended, but the latter was finished before May 1627, as is clear from Letter 92 (see Paoli, 285; Pirrotta, 23 n. 35).

ation of the vocal line. I have not completely finished *Aminta*[a]—it would take at least two months because I no longer enjoy those youthful powers of composition—but I have done a good part of it. I leave the entire matter of a canonry in Your Lordship's care, reserving a fuller discussion for the time when I can come to Mantua. This cannot be in October since I have to attend to certain feasts[b] ordered by our Most Serene Doge.[c] I shall nevertheless do everything possible to come. And here making a most humble reverence to Your Lordship, I pray Our Lord God for every happiness you desire and at the same time I kiss your hands devotedly.

from Venice, 18 September 1627

Your Most Illustrious Lordship's

most grateful servant

Claudio Monteverdi

[a] Monteverdi definitely refers to Tasso's play, although he was to set to music not the play itself but the prologue and intermezzi commissioned from Claudio Achillini and Ascanio Pio di Savoia.

[b] By far the most important was the anniversary of the Victory at Lepanto (1571) celebrated on 7 Oct. by the entire city. This coincided with the liturgical feasts of S. Giustina and the Most Holy Rosary.

[c] Giovanni Cornaro, installed Jan. 1625, died 23 Dec. 1629.

109

Venice, 18 September 1627
to [the Marquis Enzo Bentivoglio, at Ferrara]

Oxford, Private Collection of Albi Rosenthal. Bifolio: 4 pp.

Rosenthal, 103; Paoli, 282; Fabbri 1985, 269; Lax, 178

The existence of this letter was first mentioned by Vogel,[1] but although he knew that it formed part of a collection of autograph letters owned by D. G. Rossi of Rome, he was unable to study or copy it. At a later stage it came into the possession of Alexander Meyer-Cohn, and when his collection was dispersed in 1905 it was purchased by Karl Geigy-Hagenbach. The letter remained virtually unknown until 1961 when it was acquired by Albi Rosenthal, who first published the Italian text,[2] an English translation, and a facsimile of all four pages.[3]

This rediscovery, bringing the total number of Monteverdi–Bentivoglio letters then known to four, lends further support to the theory that the Ferrarese archives, with the gracious collaboration of one of its former custodians, yielded up valuable materials for autograph collectors during the latter part of the nineteenth century.[4] The intrinsic importance of the letter lies in its contribution to the story of the music for Parma, and in a possible first hint at the problem brewing in Mantua with regard to Monteverdi's son, Massimiliano.

Since Letter 115, dated 18 December 1627, states that Massimiliano's imprisonment on a trumped-up charge of reading a prohibited scientific book took place 'three months ago', the approximate date of this unfortunate episode would be 18 September. In 1973, new information was made available by Domenico De' Paoli, who found in the Mantuan archives a letter from the Imperial Resident

---

[1] Vogel, 388.

[2] The unusual word *barriera* seems to be employed here as the equivalent of 'tournament', by synecdoche, the part referring to the whole. The use of a barrier at jousts dates from 1430, when Philip the Good, Duke of Burgundy, presided over a tournament at the inauguration of the Order of the Golden Fleece. The mounted contestants ran their courses separated by a cloth-covered barrier intended to prevent collision. When the Medici staged *Eros and Anteros* in the Uffizi Theatre on 17 Feb. 1613 in honour of the baptism of the infant Giovan Carlo, the event was called a *barriera* in the anonymous description (possibly by Giovanni Villifranchi) printed that year in Florence. See *Descrizzione della barriera, e della mascherata, fatte in Firenze à XVII et à XIX di Febbraio MDCXII*, cited by Nagel.

[3] Rosenthal, 103–7. See also Cavicchi, 155–6 (in Monterosso, 'Monteverdi').

[4] Reiner, 273. Letter 105 is now in Naples, 109 in Oxford, 111 in Paris, 113 in Bologna, and a fifth letter, 122, in Forlì.

Nicolò Rossi, dated 18 October, and addressed to Ercole Marigliani at Mantua.[5] It is clear that both were trying to assist Monteverdi by making known his offer of a guarantee (or bail) of 100 scudi, so that Massimiliano could be released until the trial took place.

The present letter mentions a misfortune that had recently come upon the composer. In light of previous letters, this could refer to an illness or to some physical indisposition to which a 60-year-old man might well be prone. On the other hand, since the date of the letter corresponds fairly closely to the time when matters were becoming serious, it may be that the *acidente* referred to was indeed the trouble at Mantua, news of which would certainly have come to Monteverdi as an unexpected shock. Up to this time, his son's medical practice had flourished vigorously and his friends and protectors at court must have done their best to further his interests. There were no black clouds on the horizon. But life, as Monteverdi knew only too well, was capable of playing unpleasant tricks, and this proved to be one of the most devastating that could have happened at this particular time.[6]

In the midst of his work on the intermezzo *Didone ed Enea*,[7] he received the first instalment of Achillini's verses for *Mercurio e Marte*—presumably the opening section depicting a breakwater, beyond which Aurora (sung by Settimia Caccini) would appear in a chariot driven by Pegasus. He was immediately struck by the musical problems posed by the need to contrast the Months (who would sing in suave but suitable manner) with the figure of Discord, whose very name would rule out—even for Monteverdi—a slavishly exact imitation of her character as far as accompanying harmony was concerned.

Dissonance as a descriptive ingredient in madrigals and dramatic works was no stranger to Monteverdi, nor could he have easily forgotten the criticism it brought forth from Canon Artusi. But there was a difference between the occasional use of a dissonant chord within a basically harmonious texture, and the need to express discord in long soliloquies assigned to the singer of an eponymous role. So he thought seriously about depriving the character Discord of all harmony and instrumental support; and though he states that she should speak just as if she were actually singing, he may even have felt that a kind of *Sprechstimme* might be suitable in this unusual situation.[8] The loss of this music unfortunately makes it impossible to be sure about his final decision.

[5] Paoli, 295.

[6] See Letter 106: 'I would always be in fear of some colossal trick that my ill fortune might play on me . . .'.

[7] Lavin, 145: letter from Ascanio Pio to Bentivoglio, dated 8 Feb. 1628. The order of the five intermezzi was still under discussion, and since two of them featured Dido they had to be separated one from the other. The continual modification of plans and order must have caused havoc among the scenic artists, and it is certain that Monteverdi too found flexibility both a virtue and a necessity.

[8] The Testo part in his *Combattimento* is frequently far from melodic, and its success could have contributed to Monteverdi's readiness to try something not entirely dissimilar for the role of Discordia.

My Most Illustrious and Most Excellent Lord and Most Respected Master,

I am hoping, without more ado, to send Your Excellency by the next post, Saturday, the intermezzo of *Dido*[a] in its entirety. I thought that I might even send it by the present post, but a misfortune came upon me and has prevented me from composing for two days. I do hope this intermezzo will not displease Your Excellency, for not much has to be done to complete the first one. I further acknowledge receipt from Your Excellency, by courier, of the verses[b] sent to me for the use of the tournament.[c] These I have not read thoroughly as yet because of insufficient time, and because of my concentration on writing the said intermezzo of *Dido*.

I have, however, taken a quick glance at the Months and how they speak, and I have also looked at Discord. I have also thought a little about the representation of the aforementioned Discord, and it seems to me that it will be a little difficult. The reason is this: since the Months have to sing together in mellow harmony—and I shall seek out the kind that will provide the most plausible representation of each—I am going to assign the opposite kind of music to Discord (I mean opposite to that which is suitable for the Months). I cannot for the moment think of anything else but to have her declaim in speech and not in music.

This however is a first thought, which I wanted to let Your Excellency know about, so that with your most refined judgement you can assist my ability the better to serve Your Excellency's pleasure, which I desire with all my heart. Yet I would not deny that those speeches of the aforementioned Discord might be intensified by music; that is, she would have to speak just as if she were actually singing, but this singing of hers would not, however, be based on any instrumental harmony, and this (it seems to me) would be the way to represent Discord.

I would look upon it as the greatest favour to hear from Your Excellency regarding the time I can have for writing these songs, in order to fulfil your wishes in time, for here in Venice there is talk that the wedding of those Most Serene Princes[d] will take place next carnival time, in 1628. And

---

[a] The second of the five by Ascanio Pio di Savoia.

[b] *Mercurio e Marte*, by Claudio Achillini.

[c] *barriera*, referring to the cloth-covered barrier (or tilt) which served to prevent the horses and their riders from colliding as they moved towards each other in combat.

[d] Odoardo Farnese and Margherita de' Medici.

here making a most humble reverence to Your Excellency I kiss your
hand.

                    from Venice, 18 September 1627
                        Your Most Illustrious Excellency's
                            most humble and most grateful servant
                                Claudio Monteverdi

110

Venice, 25 September 1627
to [Alessandro Striggio, at Mantua]

Mantua, Archivio Gonzaga, Cassetta 6, fo. 364. Folio: 1 p.

Davari, 167; Malipiero, 274; Paoli, 286; Lax, 179

Striggio, urgently requiring a replacement for the abandoned comic opera, wrote to Monteverdi in the hope of being offered some suitable work already completed but never performed in Mantua. The *Armida* first mentioned in Letter 92 seemed the obvious choice, for it had come into being at the instance of Girolamo Mocenigo, in whose elegant palazzo the earlier and similar *Combattimento* had received its première in 1624. In the end Striggio accepted it, and Letters 115 and 118 continue the story of its brief career.

My Most Illustrious Lord and Most Respected Master,

I understand how much Your Lordship would like me to spend all the time I can in serving your sensitive taste. Rest assured that I shall not fail to do everything possible. It is true that these songs for Parma keep me very busy, but if Your Lordship would like to have something ready-made, then just possibly *Armida*[a] would not displease you, since it was written expressly for a taste similar[b] to Your Lordship's. And here awaiting advice with all affection I make a most humble reverence, praying Our Lord for your every perfect happiness.

from Venice, 25 September 1627
Your Most Illustrious Lordship's
most grateful servant
Claudio Monteverdi

[a] A work *in genere rappresentativo* based on Tasso's *Gerusalemme liberata* (see Letter 92).
[b] Girolamo Mocenigo, of Venice.

III

Venice, 25 September 1627
to [the Marquis Enzo Bentivoglio, at Ferrara]

Paris, Bibliothèque Nationale, Département de la Musique, lettre autographe Monteverdi. Bifolio: 4 pp.

Caffi, ii. 225–6; Prunières, 276; Malipiero, 274; Paoli, 287; Lax, 180

According to Caffi, the text of this letter (which he was the first to publish) was sent to him by the Ferrarese librarian, Giuseppe Antonelli. It is not clear how the original later became separated from the archives, or how it found its way to Paris, but its peregrinations cannot be too disconnected from those of the other Bentivoglio letters.

On Wednesday, 22 September, Monteverdi left Venice by boat for Chioggia shortly before the courier arrived with Bentivoglio's request that he proceed to Ferrara. No man can serve two masters, and it is perfectly obvious that Monteverdi could only with great difficulty have done his duty by the mayor of Chioggia—the son of the procurator Giovanni Battista Foscarini—as well as travelling to Ferrara to deal with the latest crisis over Duke Odoardo's wedding music. Not knowing of the arrival or the contents of Bentivoglio's letter, the composer set forth for his day in the picturesque fishing town at the southern end of the lagoon and enjoyed himself so much that he stayed the night, presumably as the mayor's guest, and returned to Venice on the following day, 23 September. But by the time he had found and read the letter, it was too late to send a reply by courier, so he waited for the Saturday *ordinario*.

We do not know what Monteverdi performed at Chioggia. But since the invitation came from the mayor rather than from an ecclesiastical dignitary, it is likely that the occasion was bound up with some secular festivity that might have included a concert and a banquet. No extant score, no lone libretto deprived of its music, refers to Chioggia or to Foscarini the younger: perhaps the concert was a relatively simple affair featuring a few madrigals and instrumental pieces. In any event this is Monteverdi's only recorded visit to the birthplace of two of his near predecessors at St Mark's—Giovanni Croce, also known as 'Il Chiozzotto', and Gioseffo Zarlino, who at one stage of his career nearly became Bishop of Chioggia.

The arrival of another intermezzo, probably that of *La liberazione di Ruggero* which was completed by 30 October (Letter 113), seems to have prompted Monteverdi to think seriously about a visit to Parma with the object of getting to know the acoustical problems of the inside and outside theatres. Bentivoglio's plan was to invite him to Ferrara for discussions about the casting of roles and deployment of musicians, then to travel on together and reassess the situation in Parma. But this was not possible until after 7 October, a day sacred to all Venetians as the anniversary of the naval victory in the Bay of Lepanto, where in 1571 the allies roundly defeated their common enemy, the Turkish fleet.

It so happened that 7 October was also the feast of S. Giustina, a Paduan lady who, having suffered martyrdom at the hands of a local Roman tyrant, was held in great honour throughout the Veneto, as is shown by the many churches dedicated to her, especially in Padua and Venice. Sansovino's account of S. Giustina on the Fondamente Nuove shows that it must formerly have been a splendid and richly endowed church associated with nuns who had come from Santa Maria degli Angeli on the island of Murano.[1] One of its relics was a stone, set into a wall near the baptistry, bearing the imprint of the saint's knees as she uttered her last prayer. Modern books on Venice usually have little to say about this historic edifice, for it has now been absorbed by the Istituto Tecnico.

The very first anniversary of Lepanto was observed on 7 October 1572, in a peculiarly Venetian way. The Doge Luigi Mocenigo, with the Signoria and all the officials of church and state, went in solemn procession, or *andata*,[2] to S. Giustina, where Mass was celebrated with choral and instrumental support from the musicians of St Mark's, under the direction of Gioseffo Zarlino. Monteverdi would have inherited this annual duty as part of his occasional and extra-liturgical commitments, and could not leave the city until after it had taken place. In addition to S. Giustina and the other saints who shared this joyful day, a commemoration of Santa Maria di Vittoria was authorized by Pius V, this in time giving place to the Feast of the Rosary during the pontificate of Gregory XIII.[3] This explains Monteverdi's reference to the feast in Letter 107, and his concern that he should remain in Venice and take charge of the music.

My Most Illustrious and Most Excellent Lord and Most Respected Master,

I beg Your Excellency not to be surprised if I did not reply to Your Excellency's most courteous letter by last Wednesday's post. The reason was that the Most Excellent Lord Procurator Foscarini,[a] my particular master, has a son who is mayor of Chioggia, and since this gentleman wanted to avail himself of my services in some musical function, I stayed

---

[1] Sansovino, 42–5.   [2] Ibid. 514.

[3] A letter to Marigliani, from a correspondent in Rome (13 Oct. 1629), links the feasts of church and state in a single sentence: 'On the evening of the first Sunday in this month, the district around the Chiesa della Minerva [Santa Maria sopra Minerva] was all lit up, in memory of the naval battle and the Feast of the Most Holy Rosary.' (Quazza, *La guerra*, i. 443).

[a] Giovanni Battista Foscarini, elected Procurator in 1625.

on in Chioggia a day more than I intended, which was the same day the courier left.

But when I returned last Thursday, instead of Wednesday, and received Your Excellency's package containing a beautiful intermezzo,[b] together with your instructions to be in Ferrara yesterday, which was the 24th of this month; and when I realized my shortcomings, believe me, Your Excellency, I felt extremely upset and shall continue so to feel until Your Excellency has once again deigned to inform me of your approval, for this brief lapse of time occurred against my will.

I wanted to ask Your Excellency to be so kind as to give me leave to remain in Venice until the 7th of the next month, for on that day the Most Serene Doge[c] goes in procession to S. Giustina[d] to give thanks to God our Saviour for the joyous naval victory.[e] He is accompanied by the entire Senate, and solemn music is sung. As soon as this function is over, I shall get on the boat with the courier and come to obey Your Excellency's commands.

It will be a prudent move to come and see the theatre in Parma, in order to be able to adapt (as far as possible) the music that is right and fitting for the vast area. It will not be such an easy task, in my opinion, to perform the many and varied soliloquies that I see in these very beautiful intermezzi. In the mean time I shall go on composing and writing, to be able to show Your Excellency something more, and the best that I can do. And here making a most humble reverence to Your Excellency, I pray Our Lord God with all my heart for the fulfilment of every supreme joy.

from Venice, 25 September 1627
Your Most Illustrious Excellency's
most humble and most grateful servant
Claudio Monteverdi

---

[b] Probably the first intermezzo in order of final publication, that of Ruggero's liberation and the intervention of Melissa and Bradamante.

[c] Giovanni Cornaro.   [d] A church on the Fondamente Nuove.

[e] Battle of Lepanto, 7 Oct. 1571.

112

Venice, 2 October 1627
to [Alessandro Striggio, at Mantua]

Mantua, Archivio Gonzaga, Cassetta 6, fo. 366. Folio: 1 p.

Davari, 167; Malipiero, 276; Paoli, 289; Lax, 182

The topic being *Armida*, Striggio is presumably the addressee. Finding the score neither properly presentable nor easily legible, Monteverdi arranges for it to be recopied, as he did many years before with *Arianna*. But in spite of the extra precautions and the additional copies, both works have disappeared from view. If Monteverdi felt any sorrow at the cancellation of *La finta pazza Licori*, he does not show it, one of the reasons (in all likelihood) being his complete involvement with the music for Parma, of which the libretto for the *torneo* had just been completed.[1]

My Most Illustrious Lord and Most Respected Master,

I have taken heed of what Your Lordship has commanded me. By the coming post*a* I shall send part of it to Your Lordship, and I am having it recopied because the manuscript is completely full of creases.*b* I do hope that this little work*c* will not displease Your Lordship, and if there is any need to add to it whatever you like, the better to adorn it, at the slightest sign you deign to send me I shall attend to it at once as is my duty and obligation; since I desire nothing more than to show myself, out of true affection, to be ever Your Lordship's servant. And here making a most humble reverence to Your Lordship, I pray Our Lord God for your every greater happiness.

from Venice, 2 October 1627
Your Most Illustrious Lordship's
most grateful servant
Claudio Monteverdi

---

[1] Reiner, 290. Fabio Scotti's letter, dated 29 Sept., contains the word *intermedio* instead of *torneo*, but mention of Achillini's name leaves no doubt as to the identity of the author.

a Saturday, 9 Oct. (no letter survives).

b *spegàzzamenti* (from *spiegazzare*).   *c* *Armida*.

113

Parma, 30 October 1627
to [the Marquis Enzo Bentivoglio, at Ferrara]

Bologna, Civico Museo Bibliografico Musicale, MS UU, scatola A. 24.
Bifolio: 4 pp.

Caffi ii. 171; Malipiero, 276; Paoli, 290; Lax, 182

The Lepanto anniversary and the *andata* to S. Giustina over and done with,
Monteverdi probably left Venice in what was, for him, unusual haste; he had to travel
to Parma, a distance of about 170 miles, by way of Ferrara, where Goretti would meet
him and keep him company for the rest of the journey. So he took the boat to Padua,
then a coach to Monselice, Ferrara, Modena (where he stayed long enough to compose an *entrata* with Goretti's aid), Reggio, and finally the city of the Farnese where
there was no talk but of the marriage—with whom it might be, and when. One
wonders what the 15-year-old Duke thought of all the confusion, the politics, and the
vacillation. These all too human elements certainly penetrated as far as the team of
designers and musicians whose various and considerable talents were already being
put to good use, as the rich collection of documents ably demonstrates.[1]

In his letter to Marigliani dated 10 September, the composer had expressed his
pleasure at the prospect of a visit to Mantua, but this was not to be. Unpleasant news
concerning his son Massimiliano, held in prison by the Inquisitors on a charge of
reading a prohibited scientific treatise, put such a journey out of the question. Nor
could a bold rescue be planned. Monteverdi knew that the only possible approach was
to be cautious and discreet, availing himself of whatever power ploy could be brought
to bear on the situation. But it was worrying and wearing, causing an additional
burden at a time when his mind should have been completely free for the task ahead
at Parma.

If he left Venice about 9 October, he would have reached Parma (after brief stops
in Ferrara and Modena) by 12 or 13 October. In two weeks he had settled down in
pleasant and comfortable quarters, with all the attentions and services that befitted an
honoured guest, and he is quick to thank Bentivoglio for seeing to it that the welcome
was so warm. Towards the end of October he went to look at the new theatre under
construction in the courtyard of the church of S. Pietro Martire, and Goretti (who was
with him) wrote to Bentivoglio on 29 October: 'I marvelled at the new theatre and the
new stage—we went there with Signor Claudio, and all will be well.'[2] But almost at

---

[1] See especially Lavin, 119–58.   [2] Ibid. 146, no. 27.

once he added a comment about the possible threat to the acoustics when the roof was put on, fearing that neither voices nor instruments would fare well in such dampened circumstances.

Otherwise the music was making steady progress, with some of the intermezzi already completed and part of the tourney planned. Rehearsals cut into all this, however, and on the near horizon there loomed a return to Venice with its concomitant load of heavy Christmas duties. No time had been lost on the journey, as is clear from the postscript inserted between the final salutation and the signature—Goretti and Monteverdi had arrived in Parma with a new *entrata* ready to rehearse.

The original letter, now in Bologna, was first published by Caffi after a copy sent to him by Giuseppe Antonelli, librarian of the Bentivoglio archive at Ferrara.

My Most Illustrious and Most Excellent Lord and Most Respected Master,

I come to do reverence to Your Lordship, and at the same time to give you the greatest thanks I know and am capable of, for the particular and extraordinary honours received from the Most Serene Duchess and Duke,[a] who have not only issued instructions to the Lords Ministers that every comfort be given me, but have assured me personally of this singular favour.

The Most Illustrious Signor Major-domo[b] thereafter left no stone unturned in carrying out the good wishes of his masters, but the kindness of Your Excellency has seen to my needs to an even greater extent, so that there is nothing lacking from the hand of God, except for results in my own work that correspond partially (I shall not say totally, for that would not be possible) to so many and such outstanding favours.

Devoted reverence is certainly by no means lacking in me, for in truth I burn with desire to do something that may be pleasing both to Their Most Serene Highnesses, and to the delicate taste of Your Excellency; and this, if you were here in person, I would hope to pursue to an even greater extent. As for what the Duchess had in mind, I believe she was anxious that Your Excellency should come to Parma, because on presenting to her Your Excellency's letter, she said: 'And when will the Lord Marquis be in Parma?'

I find that I have finished the first intermezzo,[c] which is about Melissa and Bradamante, but not that of *Dido*; this will be the second. I am busy

---

[a] The Dowager Duchess Margherita and Duke Odoardo.
[b] Count Fabio Scotti.   [c] *La liberazione di Ruggero.*

with the third, and when that is done, I shall start rehearsing something. During the period of these first rehearsals I shall also (please God) finish the fourth. As yet I have not had the fifth, but I think it will be given to me as soon as possible. Nor have I so far neglected to do some work on the tourney,^d and since at any rate the greater part—if not all of it—is planned, I would like to have leave to be able to go to Venice to attend to my duties on Christmas Eve at St Mark's (since this solemn feast is the greatest that the Director of Music has in the entire year) and then at once return to the service of those Most Serene Highnesses, and of Your Excellency.

Concerning all that I have done and am doing, I have told Their Highnesses and the Most Illustrious Major-domo; and they have expressed their satisfaction, for which I have given thanks to God, and likewise I pray with every fervent emotion that He may always bless and preserve Your Excellency, whose hand I reverently kiss, bowing most humbly.

from Parma, 30 October 1627
Your Most Illustrious Excellency's

[PS] I must also tell Your Excellency about the beautiful *entrata* that we made, the most courteous Signor Goretti^e and I, in Modena. This having obtained the approval of all, the journey was undertaken joyfully. Now we are working on this cheerfully and with determination to obtain the result that this gentleman and I warmly desire, in order to serve the commands of those Most Serene Highnesses and of Your Excellency, for in truth the Lord God had sent me help according to my needs.

most humble and grateful servant
Claudio Monteverdi

---

^d *Mercurio e Marte*, by Claudio Achillini.
^e Antonio Goretti, the Ferrarese composer appointed to assist Monteverdi.

114

Parma, 8 November 1627
to [a Procurator of St Mark's, at Venice]

Venice, Archivio di Stato, Procuratori di S. Marco de Supra (Chiesa), Filza 91, Processo 208, fos. 88–9. Bifolio: 4 pp.

Caffi, i. 243; Sommi-Picenardi, 157; Malipiero, 278; Paoli, 293; Lax, 184

Having spent some time at the new theatre under construction in the courtyard, Goretti and Monteverdi, led by the Duke's major-domo Count Fabio Scotti, made a tour of inspection in the upstairs part of the Palazzo della Pilotta where the *salone*, or Teatro Farnese, was situated. On 2 November Goretti wrote to Bentivoglio; 'Today we were in the *salone* with Count Fabio Scotti, and it is indeed admirable! Signor Claudio was completely bowled over. They tried out the Three Furies, which is something really tremendous.'[1]

It was during the course of that busy week that Monteverdi realized how much still remained to be done, what with composing, orchestration and rehearsals. He therefore decided to apply as soon as possible for extra leave beyond the twenty days already granted, and which—by the time this letter had been written—had already expired. To make assurance doubly sure, he addressed his request not to the procurators *de supra* as a group, but to one particular procurator whom he knew well enough to ask for a special favour.[2] He then backed this up with a letter from the Duke of Parma to the Doge. This is not the letter published by Canal,[3] but another written a month earlier, and referred to in the opening lines of the request dated 9 December ('Some days ago I requested Your Serenity . . .'). The Duke's earlier letter seems not to have survived.

A simple extension of leave is not the only matter to be touched here: more time will be needed after the Christmas celebrations, for not only are the intermezzi to be completed, but the tourney as well. Fortunately for Monteverdi, the officials in Venice found it possible and politic to grant him the request, although by the time they had made up their minds it was a *fait accompli*. Presumably he was allowed a further twenty days, which should have seen him back in Venice by 19 or 20 November at the latest. But once again he overstayed his leave, and after a week the procurators sent him a sharp reminder of his duties and obligations.[4]

---

[1] Lavin, 146, no. 28.

[2] Not perhaps Foscarini or Contarini, whom he knew well, for they dealt with matters outside the chapel as procurators *de citra*.

[3] Canal, 121 n. 2.   [4] See commentary to Letter 115.

My Most Illustrious and Most Excellent Lord and Most Respected Master,

I came to Your Excellency to get leave for some twenty days so that I could visit Parma, having been invited by those Most Serene Highnesses*a* who had done me the honour of commissioning me to set to music a quite considerable number of verses for use in a most beautiful play that they are staging. Having seen the theatre and given an account to Their Highnesses of the method I wanted to follow in setting these words to music, I thought that I could return at once; but when I had arrived, the Most Illustrious Major-domo*b* did his best to persuade me to stay until I had completed those five intermezzi for the said play, as there were still more words to set to music.

I told him by way of reply that I had leave from Your Excellencies for only twenty days, but the gentleman answered that Their Most Serene Highnesses would request leave for at least all of this month, in which time I promised to get it done, and that they would write to Your Most Illustrious Excellencies and to His Serenity the Doge.*c* I replied that it would be necessary for me to be able to leave at the end of this month, so as to arrive in time for the Christmas Eve Mass in Venice. He answered that this would certainly be possible.

I wanted to let Your Excellency know all about it, as likewise I have told His Serenity, so that you may be accurately informed about me. Signor Major-domo has assured me that those Highnesses are writing to Venice by this post, and that their letter will include a special request that, once the first week of Christmas is over, you may let me return to Parma to perform the works composed. And here making a most humble reverence to Your Excellency, I pray for your every perfect happiness from God Our Lord.

from Parma, 8 November 1627
Your Most Illustrious Excellency's
most humble servant
Claudio Monteverdi

a The Dowager Duchess Margherita and Duke Odoardo.
b Count Fabio Scotti.   *c* Giovanni Cornaro.

[383]

115

Venice, 18 December 1627
to [Alessandro Striggio, at Mantua]

Mantua, Archivio Gonzaga, Cassetta 6, fos. 368–9. Bifolio: 4 pp.

Davari, 168; Vogel, 435; Prunières, 277; Malipiero, 279; Paoli, 295; Fabbri 1985, 259; Lax, 186

A competent and conscientious musician who works for the theatre knows that he must always be prepared to adjust his contribution, whether creative or performing, to the challenging demands of his colleagues on or behind the stage. Questions of acoustics, including the carrying power of voices and instruments, not to mention the problem of synchronization and ensemble, are now dealt with almost effortlessly thanks to electronic aids; but in Monteverdi's day such matters called forth a spirit of sharp practicality honed by near-desperation. Not that he was unused to the theatrical world and its peculiar demands. Since his involvement with *Il pastor fido* in Ferrara and in Mantua, some thirty years before the assignment for Parma came his way, he had enjoyed (if that is the word) more than ample opportunity to reconcile the claims of pure music with the customs of pure theatre. Parma, however, was a testing ground whose intractability could hardly be compared with anything he had previously known.

The middle of November found him still ensconced in the comfortable lodgings prepared for him by the Farnese staff, and from this musical headquarters he sallied forth from time to time in order to find out exactly where his musicians would have to secrete themselves—below, behind, or within the scenery. The assistant architect, Francesco Mazzi, wrote to Bentivoglio on 16 November: 'Monteverdi has been to see the place for the musicians, but there is considerable difficulty in giving him satisfaction as regards his ideas, and at first he began to say that the players cannot be fitted in there; however, we shall not fail to try and satisfy him whatever happens.'[1]

This little problem of accommodation in the Teatro Farnese arose because the structure in the courtyard (*da basso*) was still incomplete. On the same day, 16 November, Goretti sent his impressions to Bentivoglio, enlarging somewhat upon the explanation given by the assistant architect: 'We have been several times to the *salone*, in order to begin to arrange the places for the musicians, as much to accompany the people as to provide ornament where there is need of it, and we have always found great difficulty because of the narrowness of the place for this blessed music, which is

---

[1] Lavin, 131, no. 12.

partly essential yet has this ill fortune—that no thought is ever given to its location, as if it did not have to make any contribution. Yet it is so necessary!'[2]

Nicola Sabbatini, who published his highly original treatise on stage sets and machines at Ravenna in 1638 (*Pratica di fabricar scene e machine ne' teatri*), mentions organs and other musical instruments in a section dealing with the best placing for musicians:

> We must consider a position for the Musicians, since we do not want them on the stage, where they will get in the way of the Machinery, both in themselves and with their Organs or other instruments. We can place them off-stage on either side, and for that purpose we can make two balconies out of solid timber, with filled-in partitions, large enough for them and their instruments. These can be associated with corbels, balustrades and shutters . . . so that the music and singing can be heard better, and so that they can adorn the Set. If however we need them on-stage, we will have to design the Set to accommodate the Organs from the outset . . . Make two boxes, namely on either side of the set, as large as is necessary, and scale all the other houses accordingly . . . make sure that the [supporting] Beams pass through holes in the stage, so that they do not end up touching it; since if they were fixed to it they would disrupt the Organs and other instruments when Morescas were danced. Moreover make them high enough above the stage . . . so that [the musicians] will not be seen inside, as experience convinces us that this is the best policy.[3]

Adjustments and modifications were under way a week later, when Mazzi sent news to Bentivoglio about the work still to be done. A laconic note on a supplementary sheet (written in another hand) says: 'Adjust the balconies for the musicians. Signor Monteverdi and I will arrange them; indeed, we have already begun.'[4] But the narrowness of the balconies was only one of the composer's problems: he had also to contend with the narrow and egotistic minds of some of the imported singers, among whom was the famous castrato Gregorio Lazzarini. A member of the papal chapel since 1619, Lazzarini soon afterwards entered the service of Cardinal Francesco Borghese, by whose permission he was allowed to sing at Parma. His career, long and active, saw him in the title-role of Filippo Vitali's *Aretusa* in 1620 (when his angelic voice so perfectly echoed the concept of chastity) and much later in 1640 when he sang the part of Esther in Pietro della Valle's *Dialogo d'Ester* performed on the Monday of Holy Week in the Oratorio del Santissimo Crocifisso, in Rome.[5]

True to type, he arrived in Parma with no illusions about his reputation and no particular feelings of restraint with regard to the power that a virtuoso can wield. He was assigned the role of Mars in the third of Ascanio Pio's intermezzi (*Diana e Venere*) one of the high points of which was a love scene with Diana, but for reasons that are not explained by the documents, this section was cut and Lazzarini appealed to Bentivoglio to have it restored. This small detail of the complex musical mosaic is known only through brief extracts from a letter of his dated 26 November, originally part of the Bentivoglio archives. Presumably owned thereafter by Antonelli,[6] it later passed into the Succi collection (no. 551 in the catalogue published in 1888) and then

---

[2] Ibid. 146, no. 29.   [3] Quoted and translated in Maguire, 60–1.
[4] Lavin, 134, no. 13 (23 Nov.).   [5] Ziino, 109.   [6] Lavin, 109.

to the Wilhelm Heyer collection in Cologne. When this was dispersed in 1927, the sale catalogue gave a brief description of Lazzarini's letter as no. 510.[7]

If Monteverdi had problems in dealing with Lazzarini, more were soon to follow, for on 27 November the Procurators sent him a letter asking for his immediate return to Venice: 'We have taken note of what you tell us in one of your letters, but since your absence from this chapel can, for various reasons, no longer be extended, we are obliged to inform you that you free yourself as soon as possible, and come to attend to your duties, knowing full well the terms of your contract, and how necessary is your presence here.'[8]

In spite of pressures, Monteverdi contrived to lead a fairly quiet life, as is evident from Goretti's letter to Bentivoglio, also dated 27 November:

> I shall do what I can about hurrying the workmen along, as Your Most Illustrious Lordship bids me, but understand that I have so much to do that I do not have time to breathe. We never go out of doors, and I alone go, with effort, to Mass. Signor Claudio composes only in the morning and the evening: during the afternoon he does not wish to do anything at all. I urge him, and I relieve him of such labour—which means taking the work from under his hands, after having discussed and arranged it together; and I find it so intricate and tangled that I give Your Most Illustrious Lordship my word that I labour more than if I were to compose it all by myself; and that if it had to be left to him to write it, it would take time and plenty of it (and if I were not at his heels so much, he would not have done half of what he has done). It is true that the labour is great, and tedious; but still, he is a man who likes to talk things over in company at great length (and about this, I make it a rule to take the opportunity away from him during working hours)—so that I wish to say that my job is no small one.[9]

Goretti's deft sketch of the 60-year-old composer reveals endearing as well as stubborn traits in his character, and there is no reason to disbelieve this testimony, coming as it does from a fellow musician competent enough to be an impartial judge of a situation, and yet independent enough not to feel the pangs of envy or jealousy. On the bureaucratic front, however, matters were rapidly coming to a head, for the procurators' letter had to be answered quickly and by a responsible personage. Monteverdi spoke to Scotti, and he in turn to the Duke himself, who wrote a letter to the Doge, Giovanni Cornaro, on 9 December:

> Some days ago I requested Your Serenity to consent that Monteverdi might remain here until Christmas. Now he is coming away to fulfil the duties of his post. And I humbly ask you to kindly permit the same Monteverdi to return here, once the festive season is over, as it is necessary for him to be here for the performance of what he, with such loving devotion and talents, has begun for the festival to be held at my wedding.[10]

---

[7] Kinsky, 94. 'Monteverdi habe ihm soeben gesagt (*mi vien detto dal Monte Verde . . .*), in der ihm zugedachten Rolle sei die Liebesszene mit Diana—*è che quella fosse il più bello di quella parte . . .*— gestrichen worden, weshalb er (Lazzarini) bitte, sich seiner anzunehmen, d.h. die Streichung dieser Szene rückgängig zu machen.'

[8] Arnold, 203.   [9] Reiner, 301. The original Italian is quoted by Barblan, 'La vita', 140 n. 45.

[10] Canal, 121.

Having left Parma on or about 10 December, Monteverdi made his way back to Venice via Ferrara, where he spent some time giving Bentivoglio a *viva voce* report on what had been accomplished over the past eight weeks. When he arrived at his apartment in the canonry of St Mark's, preparations for the Christmas music were already in progress thanks to the aid of his assistant Rovetta, for it was already the middle of the month and there was much to be done. Within three days he was back at his writing-desk, reopening the final chapter in his long correspondence with Striggio. He had received two letters in Parma, but delayed answering them until his return to Venice.

Armida is still being discussed, strangely enough, although Duke Vincenzo was gravely ill and would die in a few days, leaving the world to its daily round and Mantua to its grim and unavoidable fate. Dutifully, Monteverdi sends the manuscript to be recopied and informs his friend about the state of the musical market, especially as regards castrati. He names Lazzarini, as might be expected; but holds out little hope for borrowing Antonio Grimano, whose principal patron in Rome was Monsignor Ciampoli, who adored music and wrote poetry for his favourite composers.[11] Monteverdi's acutely critical assessment of singers comes to the fore in his dismissal of the two youngsters, Pietro di San Pietro and Marc'Antonio Malagigi, who were looked after in Parma by their respective teachers. The official notices show somewhat greater enthusiasm, as well as gifts to the teachers of 100 ducats or more.[12]

The success of Monteverdi's music at Parma had reached Florence by early December, for Luigi Inghirami, one of Gian Carlo Medici's secretaries, wrote to the Archduchess Magdalene (the mother of Princess Margherita) that 'the music was remarkable and the voices exquisite, the work of Monteverdi, today the greatest musician in Italy'.[13]

Finally the veil that has covered Massimiliano's shame for three long months is now drawn aside. Marigliani had tried to intervene, but without success, and nothing is left but to appeal to Striggio and then promise to pay 100 ducats by way of ransom. The arrangement seems at first to be a simple one, but complications were to ensue and the files were not closed until July of the following year.

My Most Illustrious Lord and Most Respected Master,

I received at Parma two of Your Lordship's letters: in the one you instructed me to let you have *Armida*,[a] which was so much to the liking of

---

[11] Vogel, *Bibliothek*, i. 338 (Kapsberger); 436–9 (Mazzocchi 1, 2, 4); ii. 196 (Savioni, 2).

[12] Vogel, 437–8. Malagigi, later in the service of Cardinal Barberini, grew to be jealous of Leonora Baroni, the daughter of Adriana; so too were the Lolli sisters, under the protection of Cardinal Borghese. The hirelings of Malagigi and Lolli wrote obscenities on the walls of Leonora's house. (Ademollo, 326.)

[13] Vogel, 387.

[a] A work, probably similar in style to the *Combattimento*, and based like it on verses from Tasso's *Gerusalemme liberata*.

the Most Serene Lord Duke[b] my master, and likewise that I should come to Mantua; and in the other Your Lordship instructed me to busy myself getting hold of a male soprano of the best quality. I answered neither the one nor the other because I was doing my best, day after day, to return to Venice and serve you from there.

On my return to Venice three days ago, I at once handed over *Armida* for recopying: I shall be sending this to Your Lordship by the next post, and informing you about the castrato, for in Parma the best is said to be Signor Gregorio,[c] who is in the service of His Eminence Cardinal Borghese,[d] but could (with considerable effort) get away, I should think. There is also Signor Antonio Grimano,[e] but you could hardly hope to engage him. There are two others who have also come from Rome: some castrato[f] who sings in St Peter's, but he seems not very good to me because he has a voice that suffers from catarrh—not too clear, stiff ornaments, and very little *trillo*; then there is a boy of about 11,[g] but he seems not to have a pleasing voice either—he can do little ornaments and something of a *trillo* but everything is pronounced with a somewhat muffled voice.

Regarding these two, I shall put out a feeler if Your Lordship wishes, but concerning the others I think I would not do anything. Nevertheless I have let them know about it, and since I am returning (if it please God) on the 2nd or 3rd of next month, I shall be better able to inform Your Lordship, as I have been late in receiving Your Lordship's very kind letters.

About my coming to Mantua, I shall also have to be excused at present, for because of my reputation I am not allowed to go there since my son Massimiliano[h] is in the prisons of the Holy Office. He has been there for three months, the reason being that he read a book which he did not know was prohibited. He was accused by the owner of the book, who got himself imprisoned, and was deceived by the owner who said that the book dealt only with medicine and astrology. As soon as Massimiliano was in prison, the Father Inquisitor wrote to me saying that if I gave him a pledge of 100

[b] Vincenzo II Gonzaga, seventh Duke of Mantua.
[c] Gregorio Lazzarini (b. Ancona, ?; d. Rome, 1686).
[d] Cardinal Francesco Borghese, to whom Monteverdi had been given a personal introduction in 1610.
[e] A castrato in the service of Cardinal Ciampoli, and formerly at St Mark's.
[f] Pietro, a young singer accompanied by his teacher.   [g] Marc'Antonio Malagigi.
[h] Monteverdi's younger son, now 23 years old.

ducats for being legally represented until the case was dispatched, he would release him at once.

In one of his letters, Signor Ercole Marigliani,[i] the councillor, offered of his own accord to protect my son, and because of this known partiality of his, I begged him to pass on the task of arranging for my security payment to the Father Inquisitor to come out of the annual income paid to me by that Most Serene Prince my master, but since two months have gone by without my receiving an answer either from the Father Inquisitor or from Signor Marigliani, I am turning (with the greatest possible reverence) to Your Lordship's protection in delegating this particular matter to Signor Marigliani, in Massimiliano's favour and in accordance with his interests.

If he does not wish to undertake this security settlement, I shall always be ready to deposit 100 ducats so that my son can be released. I would indeed have done this already had I received a reply from Signor Marigliani. While Your Lordship will be helping my son (and of this I am most certain), I shall pray Our Lord for your well-being on this most holy feast of Christmas, and for a happy new year, making a most humble reverence to you and kissing your hand.

from Venice, 18 December 1627
Your Most Illustrious Lordship's
most grateful servant
Claudio Monteverdi

[i] Formerly court secretary, recently promoted councillor.

116

Venice, 1 January 1628
to [Alessandro Striggio, at Mantua]

Mantua, Archivio Gonzaga, Cassetta 6, fos. 372–4. Bifolio + folio: 5 pp.

Prunières, 278; Malipiero, 281; Paoli, 298; Fabbri 1985, 260; Lax, 188

Notwithstanding differences of opinion regarding the addressee, this letter must have been intended for Striggio since Marigliani had earlier proved to be an insufficiently weighty personage to deal with the Inquisitor. Monteverdi's offer of a necklace worth 100 ducats, and his reference to the continuing problems of the pension (worth 100 scudi), almost make it seem as if he were intent on setting off one against the other, for the scudo was worth only slightly less than the ducat. As for the necklace, could this have been the one given to him by the Duchess Caterina in 1620?[1] If so, a gracious reward for a welcome book would help to buy off the shame brought about by a book that was more than suspect.

It says much for Striggio's magnanimity that he was able to find time to help Monteverdi when the affairs of state and the general morale in Mantua had never been worse. Vincenzo's attempt to have Isabella of Novellara assassinated had failed, and in the eyes of the papacy he was a doomed man. The Gonzaga succession too was doomed, and the armies of the candidates for this impoverished dukedom were being drawn up for possible action. Carlo Gonzaga of Nevers, later eighth Duke of Mantua, a descendant of Ludovico (brother and rival of Duke Guglielmo), naturally received the support of his own countrymen in France, together with the approval of Venice. On the other side, Spain and the Emperor Ferdinand supported Cesare Gonzaga, Prince of Molfetta.

Vincenzo, on his deathbed, witnessed the marriage of Carlo of Nevers and Maria Gonzaga, daughter of Duke Francesco and Margherita of Savoy. And when he died, on Christmas Day 1627, he escaped both the wrath of the church and the shame and terror that was to descend on his dukedom. Monteverdi expresses his sorrow at Vincenzo's death, but he immediately launches into the inevitable corollary: without the Duke there will be no chance to appeal for the *fondo*. Striggio, for his part, knew the composer better, and probably smiled to think how soon Carlo of Nevers would hear about this ancient bone of contention.

---

[1] See Letters 53 and 54; also Stevens, 'Necklace'.

My Most Illustrious Lord and Most Respected Master,

You will be doing me a favour, Your Lordship, to forgive me for not sending by the previous post an immediate reply to Your Lordship's most kind and courteous letter, the reason for this being that the postman did not give me mine until the outgoing post had left.

I am, however, writing now—not having been able to do so before—to give your Lordship boundless thanks for such a favour as you have shown yourself so willing to do me by helping that poor unfortunate son of mine, Massimiliano,[a] so that he may come out of prison: a favour so great that I do not know how I shall ever be able to repay even the smallest part, for it will hold me so indebted that I shall always be bound at least to pray God for the continual preservation and exaltation of yourself and of all your most Illustrious House.

The favour which I now beg of Your Lordship's great authority, with all due affection, is this: only that you may be so kind as to influence the Father Inquisitor so that he lets Massimiliano go back home, by virtue of the pledge which he himself requested of me. I desire nothing else of Your Lordship's grace, since I have handed over a necklace worth 100 ducats to Signor Barbieri[b] (a rich dealer in precious stones who is here in Venice, both a countryman of mine, and a close friend for many years) so that he may write by this post asking Signor Zavarella,[c] who looks after the customs duties of His Most Serene Highness[d] of Mantua and is a very close friend of the aforesaid Signor Barbieri, to come to Your Lordship and offer to look after the said pledge personally.

I do not intend to inconvenience you, or beg for anything, otherwise than to induce the Father Inquisitor to let Massimiliano go back home. If I am too bold with Your Lordship's grace, blame the great need that I have of your favour, and blame that great kindness and gentleness of yours which gave me a mind to be so bold.

To change the subject, I heard with extreme sorrow of the death of the Most Serene Don Vincenzo[e] (may God receive him in heaven!) not only because of the special affection I bore to all those noble masters, in particular to this Most Serene Lord—because of that spontaneous goodwill with

---

[a] Monteverdi's younger son, born in 1604.   [b] See also Letter 118.
[c] Giulio Cesare Zavarella.   [d] Carlo Gonzaga of Nevers, eighth Duke of Mantua.
[e] The seventh Duke had died on 25 Dec. 1627. The prefix 'D' for Don may indicate that Monteverdi always thought of him as the young prince: Duke Vincenzo, his particular master, was the fourth Duke.

which he was moved to remember my feeble self, by showing that he took pleasure both in seeing me and in my poor compositions—but also because I hoped that through his kindness I might get the capital sum for that pension or remittance of mine, of 100 scudi.

So, to obtain that favour with greater ease, I endeavoured to put on one side a few small sums of money, and it was for this reason—to add a little more—that I went as I did to toil away for those princes of Parma.*f* But my fate, which has always been rather more unfavourable than otherwise, insisted on giving me this great mortification when least expected. Thank God I have not lost both my master and that little security which, through grievous toil, has been granted me by God, whom I pray and beseech with all my heart that the present Most Serene Lord may live in blessed tranquillity.

For as I am very sure that he is very just, being of that Most Serene House, I do not believe nor ever will believe that he would take away what is mine, so reliant am I upon the favours of Your Lordship, who (I confidently hope) will be most gracious in helping me if the need arise. Dear Sir, comfort me with a word about this matter, because it will give me life; and here making a humble reverence I pray God with all my heart for your every continued happiness.

from Venice, 1 January 1628

Your Most Illustrious Lordship's

most humble and most grateful servant

Claudio Monteverdi

[PS] I said above that Signor Zavarella will come to Your Lordship to take care of the pledge, but I now have to say that it will not be him, but rather Signor Giovanni Ambrogio Spiga,*g* His Highness's jeweller. It will be this man who will come to take care of the pledge. For the love of God, forgive me for such inconvenience: again I turn to make you a most humble reverence.

f The Dowager Duchess Margherita and Duke Odoardo.

g A Milanese goldsmith who settled in Mantua.

117

Venice, 9 January 1628
to [Alessandro Striggio, at Mantua]

Mantua, Archivio Gonzaga, Cassetta 6, fos. 376–7. Bifolio: 3 pp.

Prunières, 280; Malipiero, 283; Paoli, 301; Fabbri 1985, 275; Lax, 190

Striggio, bowed down as he was by the Mantuan problems that beset him from all sides, gave security for Massimiliano's release and talked the Treasury into sending Monteverdi his pension. This letter affects an indebtedness far beyond the usual expressions of humble thanks, and the composer assures him that the court jeweller, Giovanni Ambrogio Spiga,[1] will come and repay the security money, received from the Venetian jeweller Barbieri. At last Massimiliano is out of prison, and able to return to his medical practice.

At Parma, the two theatres were still being worked on, though as Monteverdi hints to Striggio, plans for the wedding had entered into an indecisive period and the pessimists went so far as to say that it would never take place at all. But one Medici daughter was about to be replaced by another on the political and matrimonial chessboard that provided every gossip with a ready topic of idle conversation. The lines of communication reached far and wide; and even Monteverdi's letters prove that a procurator of St Mark's, Venice, and a count in Mantua were willing to devote a little time to speculation and the exchange of useful ideas. If the marriage were to fall through, so would Monteverdi's music. But this kind of situation was by no means unknown to him, coming as it did as the dubious reward for devotion to a private patron rather than to a public theatre. For this new approach, Monteverdi was fortunately in the right city at the right time.

My Most Illustrious Lord and Most Respected Master,

I have received a favour from Your Lordship at a time when it was almost impossible for you to keep your own affairs in mind—a sure proof that with benign affection Your Lordship deigned to do me one of the most remarkable and confidential favours that I could ever hope for from my

---

[1] Spiga was probably the son of Michelangiolo Spiga of Milan (see Bertolotti, 'Arti minori', 88). He was working for Duke Ferdinando by 1619, and seven years later received from Duke Vincenzo II a licence to carry arms (ibid. 78, 83).

greatest good fortune. I did not deserve it because I am the most feeble subject in the world, but God has granted me recognition of the fact that I owe a very great debt; and this will not be denied me by His Divine Majesty, whom I pray and beseech that I may at least confess it, if I cannot pay it. Nevertheless I offer to Your Lordship's great goodness not only my few worldly possessions but also my life-blood, while to God I offer my prayers, feeble though they are.

Signor Spiga[a] will come to relieve Your Lordship of the security, since he will receive by this post special instructions to act in this way. Otherwise I would feel grieved, desiring (as I do) nothing from your innate kindness beyond your protection, and even this is too much. I have heard that Massimiliano[b] is out of prison, and I am awaiting his letter to give you an explanation, together with mine, considerably different from what you imagine. Moreover, I am twice comforted, having heard that I shall also see my remittance in the same letter, and am that much more aided by Your Lordship's good grace, in which I pray that God may deign to keep me, since I ever desire to try with all diligence to maintain and preserve it for myself.

I hope that, within two days, I shall return to Parma to prepare for Their Most Serene Highnesses[c] the music for the tourney[d] and the intermezzi[e] of the play that is going to be produced. From there, if it please you, I shall send news of the outcome of these events. From Venice, through the Most Excellent Lord Procurator Contarino,[f] my master (as he is procurator of St Mark's), I heard yesterday by word of mouth that His Excellency[g] not only believes, but fears, that the wedding will not take place this carnival time, nor this May—letters from Ferrara say it will take place then—and perhaps not even at all. Anyway I shall go and prepare the music that I have been given, for more than this I cannot, nor must I do. May God bless Your Lordship, while with all my heart I kiss your hands and pray for your every greatest happiness.

from Venice, 9 January 1628
Your Most Illustrious Lordship's
most grateful servant
Claudio Monteverdi

[a] A Milanese goldsmith who settled in Mantua.   [b] Monteverdi's younger son, born in 1604.
[c] The Dowager Duchess Margherita and Duke Odoardo.   [d] *Mercurio e Marte.*
[e] For Tasso's *Aminta*.   [f] Simone Contarino, elected procurator in 1620.
[g] The Marquis Enzo Bentivoglio.

118

Parma, 4 February 1628
to [the Marquis Alessandro Striggio, at Mantua]

Mantua, Archivio Gonzaga, Cassetta 6, fos. 379–80. Bifolio: 4 pp.

Davari, 169; Vogel, 436; Prunières, 280; Malipiero, 285; Paoli, 303; Fabbri 1985, 266, 275; Lax, 192

Arriving in Parma about the middle of January, Monteverdi resumed his task with renewed vigour, but with no more certain news about a performance date than he could discover from gossips, whose guesses ranged between May and September. Information concerning the musicians invited to take part shows that the net had indeed been cast wide—as far as Rome, Modena, and Piacenza, to which cities Venice and Ferrara should be added with respect to the composer and his assistant. But since the marriage negotiations were taking place in Florence as well as in Parma, it is perhaps strange to find no mention of Florentine musicians: the casting of Settimia Caccini for several important roles shows that they were undoubtedly considered to be part of the general scheme of things. Having resided in Parma for many years with her husband Ghivizzani (from Lucca), Settimia was probably regarded as an adopted daughter of the city of the Farnese, despite her Florentine origins.

In this letter, *Armida* is mentioned for the last time. Monteverdi excuses himself for not sending the score earlier because the death of Duke Vincenzo II on 25 December inevitably cast a shadow over the plans for performance at carnival time. The score was now at Mocenigo's house in Venice, where it had probably received its première shortly before 1627, but Rapallino—Mocenigo's chaplain—would have a copy made and sent to Striggio. Rapallino, alerted by Monteverdi on 12 February, wrote to the Marquis promising to see to the matter immediately.[1]

Striggio's elevation to the marquisate, which he was to enjoy only for two years, came as the reward of a lifelong devotion to the political affairs of the Gonzaga. The good news prompts Monteverdi to pen a lengthy and sincere eulogy, but oddly enough there is no change in formal address—no 'Eccellentissimo' in the salutation, and no 'Vostra Eccellenza Illustrissima' in the letter.

My Most Illustrious Lord and Most Respected Master,

The news given me by the Most Illustrious Marquis Enzo,[a] who has just

[1] Davari, 128.

[a] Enzo Bentivoglio of Ferrara.

passed through Mantua and arrived at Parma, about Your Lordship's having been made a marquis by the new duke, cheers and comforts my heart. The infinite obligation that I owe, and shall owe as long as I live, and the long and unbroken friendship of which you have always deigned to make me worthy, by offering me continual proofs of particular and extraordinary favours; and the long service which I have ever professed to maintain by always desiring to be worthy of being known, through your grace, as your true and genuine servant; let them plead and speak for me, and assure Your Lordship of my consolation.

I beg you most urgently to be so kind as to keep me in that same state of grace, in the future also, assuring Your Lordship that if I cannot serve you in any other way (being a most feeble subject) I shall never fail in my feeble prayers to pray the Lord that he maintain and prosper you in this and greater happiness by His holy grace.

How distressing it was, then, for me to receive Your Lordship's renewed instructions that I send *Armida*,[b] because of my being (as I am) in Parma, and having *Armida* in Venice—may God be my witness! I refrained from sending it to Your Lordship this Christmas, because of the death of the Most Serene Lord Duke Vincenzo[c] (may he be in glory!) as I would never have thought that you might wish to enjoy it at carnival time. This failure on my part, if Your Lordship could see into my heart, upsets me very much, believe me truly. *Armida* is, however, in the hands of the Most Illustrious Signor Mocenigo,[d] my very affectionate and special master.

Now by this post, which leaves today for Venice, I am writing very urgently to the said gentleman, that he honour me with a copy of it, and that he give it to Signor Giacomo Rapallino[e] the Mantuan, very much Your Lordship's servant, a singer at St Mark's and my very dear friend, to whom I am now writing persuasively to see if he can get it from the aforesaid Signor Mocenigo (very much his master and much befriended by him), and without loss of time—if possible—send it off in my name to Your Lordship. And knowing this nobleman to be most polite, and Signor Rapallino to be very keen on having himself known as Your Lordship's

---

[b] A stage work based on verses from Tasso's *Gerusalemme liberata*.
[c] Seventh Duke of Mantua, d. 25 Dec. 1627.
[d] Girolamo Mocenigo, a Venetian nobleman and patron of the arts.
[e] Baritone singer and chaplain to Mocenigo.

servant, I have not the slightest doubt, Your Lordship, that as soon as ever possible it will be sent to you.

Here in Parma the music is being rehearsed, having been written by me in haste—Their Most Serene Highnesses[f] believing that the noble wedding might have to take place some time before the appointed date—and these rehearsals are being held because in Parma there are Roman and Modenese singers, instrumentalists from Piacenza, and others. Since Their Highnesses have seen how these musicians fulfil their needs, and the success they are having, and their confident outlook upon the event that they are preparing in a very few days, it is considered that we—all of us—could go home, until firm news of the outcome, which they say could be this May, though others favour this September.

There will be two most beautiful entertainments—one a complete spoken play, with the intermezzi set to music (there is no intermezzo that is not at least 300 lines in length, and each has a different character, the words having been written by the Most Illustrious Don Ascanio Pio,[g] son-in-law of the Marquis Enzo Bentivoglio, and a most worthy and gifted nobleman); the other will be a tourney, in which four squadrons of knights will take part, and the master of ceremonies will be the Duke himself. Signor Achillini[h] has written the words for the tourney, and there are more than a thousand lines, which is very nice for the tourney but very long drawn out as regards the music. They have given me a great deal to do.

Just now they are rehearsing the music for this tourney.[i] Whenever I could not find enough emotional variety, I tried to change the instrumentation, and I hope this will give pleasure. I entrusted Signor Barbieri,[j] a rich merchant of Venice, to do his best to relieve Your Lordship of the pledge made for Massimiliano, and to this end he is keeping on hand for you a necklace worth 100 ducats. I am waiting for a reply about this: may Your Lordship forgive me for the delay. And here making a most humble reverence I kiss your hand and pray for your every happiness.

from Parma, 4 February 1628

Your Most Illustrious Lordship's

most grateful servant for ever

Claudio Monteverdi

[f] The Dowager Duchess Margherita and Duke Odoardo.

[g] Related to the Guastalla branch of the Gonzaga as well as to the Bentivoglio family of Ferrara.

[h] Claudio Achillini (Aquilini in Monteverdi's autograph), a Bolognese lawyer and poet.

[i] *Mercurio e Marte.*   [j] See also Letter 116.

119

Venice, 1 July 1628
to [the Marquis Alessandro Striggio, at Mantua]

Mantua, Archivio Gonzaga, Cassetta 6, fos. 382–3. Bifolio: 3 pp.

Prunières, 282; Malipiero, 287; Paoli, 307; Fabbri 1985, 260; Lax, 194

If the general feeling among the musicians lodged at Parma was that it might soon be possible for all of them to go home, more concrete evidence can be found in one of Goretti's letters to the Marchioness Bentivoglio. This letter, dated 13 February 1628, was put up for auction in 1927 and has since been lost sight of,[1] but the single phrase quoted in the catalogue sufficiently reveals Goretti's mood: 'I hope to be back [in Ferrara] towards the end of carnival, for I am dying to go to the theatre.' He and Monteverdi may indeed have made their escape by the first week in March, for Goretti's last winter letter from Parma is dated 25 February, and Monteverdi would have had to return to Venice to prepare for the Easter music at St Mark's. On the other hand, there are letters from Francesco Guitti discussing the musical problems and mentioning Monteverdi's name as late as the middle of March.

On 18 February both Guitti (chief architect to the Farnese) and Goretti sent off reports to Bentivoglio, still ensconced in his domain near Ferrara and probably quite content to witness the confusion at a safe distance. One can almost hear Guitti's sigh of relief as he writes: 'At last Monteverdi has found the right sound-effect, because I made a place ready for his use and he very much likes it.'[2] His diagram and explanation make it clear that the stage would be surrounded by a balustrade whose main purpose was to shield the instrumentalists from the audience's view. In addition, it would enable the singers and players to see and hear each other and so contribute towards a perfect ensemble.

Goretti's letter, besides providing fascinating details of the acoustic and practical problems of the Teatro Farnese, tells how he and Monteverdi adapted not only the music but even the instruments to the existing situation. 'We have once again adjusted the musical effect to suit the theatre by having some pipes made to help the harpsichords, and we also set them up in front of the stage balcony, in the space between the stairways.'[3] He also mentions that a sturdy wall will be needed to protect the instruments and the claviorganum from the water—for the final scene of the tourney calls for a flood, in which fantastic sea creatures disport themselves to the accompaniment of appropriate music and outlandish aquatic adventures.

---

[1] Kinsky, no. 457.   [2] Lavin, 126, no. 7 (see also fig. 3).   [3] Ibid. 147, no. 32.

Another letter from Goretti to Bentivoglio, dated 25 February, confirms that special instruments are still being built and fixed into place, the object of the exercise being to achieve the best possible sound-effect (*armonia*) in spite of unfavourable acoustics. His main concern is with the two pipe-organs placed in small balconies in front of the stage area.[4] But as time went on, the building and rehearsing lost some of its impetus, yielding to other interests in view of the approaching carnival season. Duke Odoardo's future brother-in-law was invited to take part in a splendid masquerade, featuring a float laden with musicians and a ship large enough to contain twenty men. Achillini was pressed into service along with Monteverdi, and between them they produced a madrigal that was performed by two castrati, Grimano and Lazzarini, a bass from Rome (probably Bartolomeo Nicolini), and a group of instrumentalists from Piacenza. Guitti's description of this reference to the special arrangements for Carnival Sunday (5 March) stresses the fact that all available talent should be pressed into service, for the musicians were, after all, on the temporary payroll of the Farnese and could therefore be asked to provide occasional entertainment.[5]

In the end, however, it was a case of *post carnelevarium triste*, as the temporary euphoria gave way to another round of trials, discussions, alterations, and rehearsals. By 15 March Guitti was telling Bentivoglio that 'since the roles of the singers have been changed, and they are inexperienced as well as frightened, and Monteverdi's musical effects do not in fact work out, I have noticed that the Duke has less than mediocre regard for the music, which has come down to words rather than deeds'.[6] Perhaps Monteverdi had already left for Venice; and without his guidance and supervision, the musicians were unable to give of their best. Guitti complains about their failure to co-ordinate tempos with the moving of the machines, so that much effort has to be wasted and the machines suffer as a result.

Meanwhile in Mantua the new Duke Carlo was having his own troubles with musicians. Intending to make a gracious, indeed harmonious gesture of homage to the Empress, he sent to Prague some of the violinists she would remember from Mantua—a group headed by the brothers G. B. and Orazio Rubini (the *casaleschi*) mentioned indirectly in one of Monteverdi's letters of 1611.[7] But not long after the arrival of the musicians, a dispute broke out among them over the currency in which they were to be paid, the promised thalers having been exchanged for florins, and as a result they left Prague (and a bad impression) contributing little if anything to the cause of Imperial and Mantuan relations.[8] Further to the south, another musical memory of Mantua was fading into oblivion as Ferdinando's widow, the Dowager Duchess Caterina, wrote from Siena to Adriana Basile in Naples—a polite exchange of greetings with never a hint of music.[9]

---

[4] Ibid. 148, no. 33.   [5] Ibid. 126, no. 8.

[6] Ibid. 127, no. 9.   [7] Letter 11 (22 Jan. 1611).

[8] Quazza, *La guerra*, ii. 95. On their return to Mantua, the musicians petitioned the Duke for 200 scudi, probably for travelling expenses (Bertolotti, 103).

[9] Ademollo, 315.

For all his loyalty to Venice, Monteverdi apparently set great store by his Mantuan citizenship, originally granted him by Duke Vincenzo in 1602. Since this honour extended to his sons, nephews, and heirs whether male or female, it must have come as a shock to the composer when he discovered that the original deed had been lost, so he promptly applied to Duke Carlo for a new one, which was granted on 8 June.[10] This proved to be of considerable importance in view of a fresh attempt by the Inquisition to question Massimiliano, who was admitted to the Medical College of Mantua on 17 June.[11] Marigliani has already lent his support, but once again Monteverdi turns to Striggio for extra leverage.

My Most Illustrious Lord and Most Respected Master,

Urged on by the misfortune that weighs upon my soul, and trusting in Your Lordship's infinite kindness, I am writing to beg you to honour me by reading these few words, and by helping me with your favour: this I beg with all my heart. The misfortune is that I thought my son Massimiliano[a] was in fact freed from his wretched plight, and in consequence from the pledge and all other problems.

But as long as two weeks ago he wrote to me that, because the case of the rogue who brought the prohibited book for him to read has not yet come up, he fears he may have to return to prison again. I do not know why, since he already let it be seen that he was not to blame. Now because of this fear I begged Signor Marigliani[b] the councillor, my master, to try and arrange for my son to come and stay with me. Having obtained this favour, he kindly informed me of the fact, and discussed it with the Fathers Inquisitors at Padua, who have assured me that my son is not guilty and did not deserve to be in prison at all.

Now, anxious that he should not return to prison (although confirmed by Signor Councillor Marigliani), I am writing again to beg Your Lordship to deign to arrange this business with Signor Councillor Marigliani, and ask him for the love of God to try and help me in this, further considering that my son has not only not erred, but that he is a Mantuan who entered the College of Physicians, and is very much a servant of Your Lordship's. I beg this much-needed favour of you, while with true heart

---

[10] Davari, 84.   [11] Ibid. 129.

[a] Monteverdi's younger son, aged 24.
[b] Ercole Marigliani, court official and librettist.

I make a most humble reverence and pray God for your every true happiness.

from Venice, 1 July 1628
Your Most Illustrious Lordship's
most grateful servant
Claudio Monteverdi

120

Venice, 8 July 1628
to [the Marquis Alessandro Striggio, at Mantua]

Mantua, Archivio Gonzaga, Cassetta 6, fos. 385–6. Bifolio: 4 pp.

Prunières, 283; Malipiero, 288; Paoli, 309; Lax, 196

This letter, the last extant letter from Monteverdi to Striggio (and the last in the long series preserved at Mantua) ranks as the most heartfelt and pathetic of all his pleas for help—far more intense even than the lengthy and elaborately reasoned documents setting forth his preference for Venice as a place to live and work, or his exasperation at the delays in payment of his pension. Massimiliano, whom he believed at one time to have escaped the taint of imprisonment and suspicion, has now been called back for further questioning by the Inquisition, and although the authorities maintain that a mere two days will suffice to clear up the entire matter, Monteverdi is at the point of losing heart and courage because he fears that torture might be used to extract a confession—a by no means unusual procedure.

   Apparently the intervention of the Marquis saved the situation. Massimiliano, however, had to leave Mantua and live with his father in Venice, and it was from there that he wrote, probably to Marigliani, for assistance in arranging for his medical books to be sent, presumably in order to open a new practice.[1] In the early part of October he was in Parma, to see about the books and about his father, but it is not clear whether this was a special journey, or whether he travelled there en route to some other city. Yet he did eventually return to Mantua, presumably after the year of plague and destruction, and led a relatively peaceful life until 1661, when the parish records of SS. Siro e Sepolcro note his demise at the age of 57.[2]

My Most Illustrious Lord and Most Respected Master,

So tremendous are the favours I receive, that the need I have for Your Lordship's good grace makes uneasy feelings weigh me down—for thus it has pleased God to afflict me to my great mortification—and this misfortune makes me fear greatly. I cannot do so, however, while I know that

---

[1] For an untraced letter from Monteverdi, dated 22 July 1628 (and another from Massimiliano, at that time in Venice), see Paoli, 312.

[2] Pontiroli, *Monteverdi*, 55.

Your Lordship so greatly rewards and honours me. By heaven, no sooner did I beg you for a favour than at once, without losing time, you granted it both with efficacious results and with extreme kindness of heart. I am conscious of my great debt, and shall always be as long as I live; and having no other way to repay you, I shall pray God to help me with his good grace by blessing Your Lordship and making you rise to the highest position you could possibly desire, and all of your Most Illustrious House as well.

I understand from your most considerate letter that you happened to speak personally to the Most Reverend Father Inquisitor (a favour so great that it makes me blush) who replied to Your Lordship that a mere two days of Massimiliano's[a] being in prison will in fact be enough to free him. I doubt, Your Lordship—and forgive me if I speak so plainly within Your Lordship's great confidence—I doubt, and he also (that is, my son) doubts that it will come to torture, or any kind of unusual fine, or any imprisonment of much more than two days—so as to question him about something he had never thought of, let alone done—so that this doubt might still have had a quite different outcome. Nevertheless the fear concentrated in his mind scares him terribly, and believe me Your Lordship, hardly a day goes by without my weeping and grieving because of that mental anguish.

The Most Reverend Father Inquisitor wrote to me by this post these actual words: that he is happy to release my son for as long as I wish. As long as I wish! For ever, I tell Your Lordship! If then he has this good intention, and has put this boy's spirit to the test by boarding him[b] for six months, why does he not release him, and relieve him of this tribulation, and me as well, and let him practice medicine to his and my satisfaction? And if it were necessary for me to pay 20 or 25 ducats as a reminder of the punishment, so that he would never in future go and find such vain and unseemly things to read (although I know for sure that he would certainly never go back to them again), I would pay him willingly.

Dear Sir, if such an outstanding favour could come my way, I beg you with all my heart and soul to do me the kindness of letting me receive it, for I assure you that it will give life both to the boy and to me, since I truly feel my mind tormented because of this thought. Comfort me, I beg of

---

[a] Monteverdi's youngest son.

[b] boarding him: *in donzina*, which usually means 'board and lodging', but is used here as a euphemism for imprisonment.

you, if it is at all possible, for greater grace than this there cannot be. The benefits of this world are most precious to me, but more precious still is peace of mind and my own honour. Forgive me, I beseech you, for so much inconvenience, while with all my heart I make a most humble reverence and kiss your hand.

from Venice, 8 July 1628

Your Most Illustrious Lordship's

most humble and most grateful servant

Claudio Monteverdi

121

Venice, 23 February 1630
to [?Don Ascanio Pio di Savoia, at Ferrara]

Present location unknown. Folio: 1 p.

Malipiero, 290; Paoli, 313; Lax, 198

Formerly among the Arrigoni collection of autographs, this letter was listed in the sale catalogue of 1881 and later became part of the library of Carlo Lozzi.[1] It subsequently passed to the Heyer collection in Cologne. When this was dispersed in 1927, the letter was purchased by Henri Hinrichsen, who passed it on to his son Walter in New York. Although the letter cannot now be traced, a facsimile was fortunately printed as pl. XVII of the Heyer sale catalogue.[2] Neither Malipiero nor De' Paoli divulges the source of his version.

Certain problems are posed by the identification of the addressee. The brief description in the Heyer catalogue and the caption below pl. XVII suggest that Bentivoglio might be the most likely recipient, for the word 'Eccellentissimo' appears in the opening and closing salutations. But the other five extant letters to Bentivoglio embody characteristics that, if they are only slightly different from those of the present letter, nevertheless set them well apart from it. In Letters 105, 109, 111, 113, and 122, the references to Bentivoglio within the document are invariably abbreviated as 'V.E.Illma', whereas in this case the corresponding references are 'V.S.Illma'— pointing to a slightly lower rank than that of a marquis. In addition, the five letters known to have been directed to Bentivoglio end with two qualifying superlatives, placed before or after the word 'servitore', whereas this letter—in common with many to Striggio and Marigliani—has only one adjective: 'servitore obbligatissimo'.

De' Paoli postulates Striggio as the most likely recipient,[3] but the salutation (as we have seen) is not quite consistent with that reserved for a marquis; and in any event the letters written to Striggio after his elevation to the marquisate continue with the same salutations as before. Another reason for ruling out Striggio is that Mantua was at war in February of 1630, and a high official of a virtually besieged city could hardly expect to be bothered with the musical setting of a canzonetta.

[1] Olschki, 234.

[2] Kinsky, item 509, referring also to the Arrigoni collection. I am indebted to Albi Rosenthal for the information about the Hinrichsen purchase, which is recorded in a copy of the Heyer catalogue forming part of the Otto Haas library. Mrs Walter Hinrichsen of New York kindly looked for the letter but was unable to discover to whom it had been sold.

[3] Paoli, 313.

There are, however, among Monteverdi's extant letters three that combine the 'Eccellentissimo' element with the use of 'V.S.Illma' in the body of the text. These are Letters 29, 30, and 33, all of which are addressed to Don Vincenzo Gonzaga. The recipient of the present letter being therefore in all probability the younger son of a nobleman, it is for this reason that I suggest Don Ascanio Pio, who was the son-in-law of the Marquis Enzo Bentivoglio, and a poet whose verses had been set not only by Monteverdi but by other composers of the time. A further reason is that the few letters not preserved in Rome or Mantua can be traced back to the Bentivoglio archives at Ferrara, a city that in 1630 was not desperately affected by the imperial troops. Ascanio Pio, as a friend and relative of Bentivoglio, could certainly have contacted Monteverdi in the hope of persuading him to set a canzonetta to music.

Previous requests for canzonette had come to Monteverdi from Cesare I d'Este, Duke of Modena, in 1624 (see Letter 81), but if this particular request originated in Modena the opening salutation of the reply would have had to begin with 'Serenissimo Signore'. Whether Monteverdi eventually complied with the demand is not known, for the only examples of his canzonette published after the date of this letter were the three-part compositions in Book IX. If the poems upon which these were based could be shown to be the work of Ascanio Pio, the letter would take on additional significance. The only trio for female voices, *Come dolce oggi l'auretta spira*, is based on verses from Giulio Strozzi's *Proserpina rapita* (1630). Those scored for male voices still lack a poetical attribution.

If there is doubt about the existence or identity of Monteverdi's canzonetta, his ecclesiastical music for the nuns of S. Lorenzo shrouds itself in total mystery. The church and nunnery of S. Lorenzo, situated between the Rio S. Lorenzo and the Rio della Pietà, enjoyed a fair musical reputation in Monteverdi's day, for Zarlino had been buried there, though no stone survives to mark his grave or memorial.[4] Nor is there any trace of Monteverdi's music in the church itself or in his published works. For a choir of nuns, however, he would probably have written music that could easily be sung by a unison choir of soprano voices, such as the hymn *Sanctorum meritis* (first setting) or the motet *Jubilet tota civitas* published in the *Selva morale* of 1641. An even stronger candidate might be the solo motet in honour of an unnamed martyr (St Lawrence?) published with the title *Venite, videte martyrem* in 1645.[5]

The nineteen months that separate Letters 120 and 121 were highly eventful for Monteverdi, a fact which makes the sparse survival of documents regrettable, to say the least. On 16 August 1628 he was again involved in the providing and performing of music for the Feast of S. Rocco, but his total fee amounted to only 146 lire, whereas in 1623 it had been much higher—620 lire.[6] Late in September, he may have returned to Parma for further rehearsals, in view of the revival of interest in the Farnese–Medici wedding and the need to offer counsel to the uneasy marriage of music and

---

[4] A far more famous tomb in S. Lorenzo was that of Marco Polo. See Sansovino, 79.

[5] It appeared posthumously in a miscellaneous collection: *Motetti a voce sola* (1645), and was first edited in modern times by Wolfgang Osthoff in *12 composizioni vocali profane e sacre* (Milan, 1958), 24.

[6] Arnold, 202.

stage machinery. Towards the end of October, Heinrich Schütz arrived in Venice on his second visit to the city that had taught him to respect and emulate the vitality of northern Italian polychoral music.[7] His first master had been Giovanni Gabrieli; his second was now to be Monteverdi.

Although the Venetian archives are silent (as might be expected) with regard to Schütz's period of study with Monteverdi, evidence in German sources provides both direct and indirect proof of this association between two great musicians, one of them 61 and the other 43 years of age. Schütz would have known many of his teacher's madrigals, either in their original form, or in Coppini's versions with Latin texts. *Una donna fra l'altre*, which appeared in borrowed ecclesiastical robes even before it saw the light of day as a madrigal, so captivated the Germans that it acquired a third text, this time from Eccles. 32:6—*Wie ein Rubin*. This was the very text chosen by Schütz for a soprano and alto duet in the second set of his *Symphoniae Sacrae* (1647).[8]

In addition to his acquaintance with Monteverdi's music, Schütz could easily conjure up a picture of the man himself, for among fourteen portraits of musicians in the instrument chamber on the third floor of the Dresden palace one was of the Director of Music at St Mark's, having been placed there at some time between 1614 and 1629.[9] Apparently Schütz worked in various musical genres, sacred and secular, under Monteverdi's guidance. Early in 1633, writing to Friedrich Lebzelter in Hamburg about his desire to compose music for the wedding of the Danish Crown Prince, the future Christian V, with Princess Magdalene Sybille of Saxony, he explained how on his latest visit to Italy he 'undertook a special form of composition, namely, how a comedy of all kinds of voices could be presented in recitative style, brought upon the stage and enacted with singing'.[10]

This special form of composition was of course the very same that Monteverdi was hoping to perfect in his projected opera *La finta pazza Licori* of 1627, and in the intermezzi and tourney of 1628—these also being intended for a princely wedding. One can imagine the enthusiasm with which Monteverdi communicated his ideas and theories to the mature but none the less eager student, for some of the most vital teaching is born of the discovery of some new method or technique. Schütz almost certainly heard a performance of the *Combattimento*, for he not only copied out the music (at that time still in manuscript) but with great skill and sensitivity translated it and underlaid the German text.[11]

From two works which first appeared in print in the *Scherzi musicali* of 1632— *Armato il cor* and *Zefiro torna*—Schütz created a brilliant vocal concerto, *Es steh Gott auf*, acknowledging his indebtedness to Monteverdi in the preface to *Symphoniae Sacrae II*. He understood the possibilities of this music only too well, even if he missed the finer points of his teacher's remarks in the famous preface to the *Madrigali guerrieri et amorosi* of 1638. He read there a statement which he interpreted as meaning

---

[7] He wrote home soon after arrival to ask the Elector for money with which to purchase 'new and beautiful music'. See the letter dated 3 Nov. 1628 in Müller von Asow.

[8] Moser, 564.   [9] Ibid. 138.   [10] Ibid. 137.   [11] Osthoff, 195.

that music had now reached its final perfection ('die Music nunmehr zu ihrer etlichen Vollkommenheit gelanget seyn soll'), though Monteverdi's words merely affirm that he was waiting for greater perfection in the [warlike] style ('la mia bona volontà . . . starà attendendo . . . maggior perfettione in natura del detto genere'). Nevertheless the relationship of teacher and pupil is confirmed by David Schirmer's poem published with other funeral odes and the oration of Martin Geyer in 1672: 'the noble Monteverdi gladly instructed him, and showed him with genuine delight the course he so often sought after'.[12]

When Schütz arrived in Venice, Monteverdi was still very much occupied with musical affairs in Parma. Goretti's three letters of 9 and 28 November and 15 December 1628 communicate something of the growing excitement, especially with regard to the equestrian exploits of Cornelio Bentivoglio and the urgent need to correlate the timing of the machines and the music. On the whole, however, he feels that the music is very successful and that outstanding problems will be settled well before the deadline.[13] Monteverdi, for his part, had to contend with two productions at Parma and the forthcoming rehearsals for Christmas music in St Mark's.

On 13 December, the day of the performance of *Aminta* and its new prologue and intermezzi in the specially constructed theatre near S. Pietro Martire, the procurators wrote to Monteverdi requesting his immediate return to Venice. Following up a letter from his assistant Rovetta, they pointed out that a major feast such as Christmas required the attendance of the Director of Music in person if St Mark's was to retain its good name.[14] It is likely, therefore, that he stayed in Parma long enough to direct the music for *Aminta*, leaving soon afterwards for Venice and entrusting *Mercurio e Marte* to Goretti. The tourney finally took place on 21 December, in the *salone*, apparently with great success in spite of fears that either the machines might not do what was expected of them, or the weight of water released into the theatre for the *naumachia* would bring the entire building down in ruins.[15]

So ended the year 1628 for Monteverdi—a year in which he had knowingly cut down his duties and responsibilities at St Mark's to the bare minimum, in exchange for triumphs elsewhere both within and without the city. Aside from his labours in connection with the feast of S. Rocco, he had provided choral music, since lost, for a banquet given at the Arsenal by the Doge Giovanni Cornaro. *I cinque fratelli* celebrates all five sons of the Grand Duke Cosimo II—Ferdinando, Gian Carlo, Mattia, Francesco, and Leopoldo. Only two of the brothers were able to be present, but the event was well attended and successful. In the same year Calvo's *Quarto raccolta de canti sacri* included two motets by Monteverdi: *Exulta filia Sion* and *Exultent caeli et gaudeant angeli*.

In 1629 Mantua, now bereft of her greatest paintings, headed for final disaster and the loss of even more of her art treasures by pillage and destruction. Venice too was in an increasingly dangerous situation, and even Parma had left its mark in a negative

---

[12] 'Der edle Mont de verd wies ihn mit Freuden an | Und zeigt ihm voller Lust die oft gesuchte Bahn'.
[13] Lavin, 148, nos. 34–6.   [14] Arnold, 203 (doc. no. 5).
[15] For a description of the festivities see Nagler, 153 ff.

sense, for the tremendous effort involved in the festival left the composer exhausted both physically and mentally, and ready only for repose.

My Most Illustrious and Most Excellent Lord and Most Respected Master,

I received Your Lordship's instructions with such special and personal pleasure that I am writing to thank Your Lordship with all my heart, since you have deigned to give me sure proof of that good grace with which Your Lordship is so kind as to befriend me. I have not been able immediately to write music for the very beautiful words sent to me, because I was a little taken up with certain ecclesiastical compositions for some of the nuns of S. Lorenzo[a] who insisted no little on my doing it.

I shall certainly hope to send Your Lordship, by the next post, the canzonetta[b] which you requested of me. May it please God that the results correspond to the intention, the infinite obligation and the special reverence with which I desire (and shall always desire) to show myself worthy of Your Lordship's grace, and here bowing with all humble reverence to Your Lordship I kiss your hand, praying God for your every greatest happiness.

from Venice, 23 February 1630
Your Most Illustrious Excellency's
most grateful servant
Claudio Monteverdi

[a] A church in the Sestiero di Castello, rebuilt in 1590.

[b] Presumably for three voices, as were the early ones of 1584 and the ten published in the *Madrigali e canzonette* of 1651.

122

Venice, 9 March 1630
to [the Marquis Enzo Bentivoglio, at Ferrara]

Forlì, Biblioteca Comunale Aurelio Saffi, Fondo Piancastelli, Autografi sec. XII–XVIII, *ad vocem* Monteverdi. Folio: 1 p.

Vitali, 404; Lax, 199

The rediscovery of this letter, apparently yet another that may have formed part of Giuseppe Antonelli's collection deriving from the archives at Ferrara, was first announced by Carlo Vitali in 'Una lettera di Vivaldi perduta e ritrovata; un inedito monteverdiano del 1630 e altri carteggi di musicisti celebri, ovvero splendori e nefandezze del collezionismo di autografi', *Nuova rivista musicale italiana*, 14 (1980), 404–12. The opinion there expressed with regard to the most likely recipient of the letter—Enzo Bentivoglio—is borne out not only by the references to Parma and to Goretti, who had given so much in the way of moral and practical assistance to Monteverdi while the Farnese music was being composed, copied, and rehearsed, but also by the initial, medial, and final salutation formulae. Indeed they correspond exactly with those employed in Letters 105, 109, 111, and 113; and by the same token they reconfirm the supposition that Letter 121 was written to a person of slightly less exalted rank than the marquis. A comparison of the final phrases of 121 and 122 suffices to show that Monteverdi found it expedient, in the latter case, to adopt a more elaborate and flowery cadential formula.

Despite the coincidence that Letters 121 and 122 both mention delays in the composition of a canzonetta, it is clear that Monteverdi is working on two different canzonette for two different patrons; and in case they might happen to know one another (as they would if the recipient of Letter 121 were Ascanio Pio—Bentivoglio's son-in-law), he gives two separate excuses: music for the nuns of S. Lorenzo, and a bad leg. This is the first time we hear of a leg hurt at Parma, but it comes as no great surprise because the letters written by Francesco Guitti, Francesco Mazzi, and Antonio Goretti make it clear that Monteverdi often went on tours of inspection to ensure that the two amphitheatres at Parma could really and truly accommodate his musicians.[1] It would not have been difficult for a 61-year-old man to fall while attempting to reach some of the more inaccessible and dangerously placed balconies, and apparently the accident was serious enough to cause pain more than a year after it had happened.

[1] Lavin 126, 131, 134, 146.

My Most Illustrious and Most Excellent Lord and Most Respected Master,

You will forgive me if I have been a little tardy in sending Your Excellency the canzonetta[a] which you kindly requested of me, for (much to my displeasure) it was advisable for me—because of my leg—to stay in bed for a few days; and again it is the leg which I slightly damaged at Parma, as indeed Signor Goretti[b] can confirm to Your Excellency.

Please God that I may have found favour with your most refined taste, but if not, may there be some recompense in that I did not know what it was really intended for; otherwise I would have written it more suitably. And my mind—with which I long to serve you with the greatest integrity in everything—will be what would intervene to assist me; with which also I pray fervently for Your Excellency's greater happiness and pleasure, while with all my heart I make a most humble reverence and kiss your hand.

from Venice, 9 March 1630
Your Most Illustrious Excellency's
Most humble and most grateful servant
Claudio Monteverdi

[a] A different canzonetta from the one mentioned in Letter 121, but possibly printed later in Book IX.
[b] Antonio Goretti, composer and collector of instruments at Ferrara.

123

Venice, ?1 May 1632
to [the Doge Francesco Erizzo and Councillors, at Venice]

Venice, Archivio di Stato, Collegio, Lettere comuni, filza 170. Folio: 1 p.

Tiepolo, 141; Paoli, 317; Lax, 200

Between November 1629 and March 1630, the Venetian republic spent some 638,000 ducats in attempting to resist and exhaust the enemy that thronged its borders and beset its neighbour and ally, Mantua. But the strength of Venice lay in her excellence as a sea power. Dedicated for centuries to the maintenance of law and order throughout the *terra firma*, she now found the imperial hordes of the Holy Roman Emperor a serious threat, and even though the city was never in immediate danger, there was a widespread feeling of unease. This was shared by the Marquis de Cœuvres, Ambassador Extraordinary sent by Richelieu to ensure that diplomatic lines of communication were kept busy and open at all times; and since he was also concerned with the morale of his considerable entourage he petitioned the senate for a short theatrical season during Lent.

Such a request from the representative of a powerful ally could not be refused, and so it was that on 3 March 1630 the famous actor Scapino, at the head of a newly formed troupe, launched a series of plays at the Teatro Vendramin near San Salvatore.[1] Monteverdi may have attended one or more of these performances, for he gives the impression of being acquainted with Scapino's virtuosity in Letter 125, addressed to G. B. Doni. He devoted most of his time, however, to the successful staging of a new opera commissioned by his special patron, Girolamo Mocenigo, whose daughter Giustiniana (the only child of his first marriage with Elisa de Alvise Pisani) was to celebrate her wedding in April. The bridegroom, another friend and patron of the composer, was Lorenzo Giustiniani, whom he had tried so hard to assist in the matter of hiring Mantuan actors in 1622.

Monteverdi was singularly fortunate in most of his Venetian contacts. His work was much admired and constantly sought after, and he frequently had the pleasure of providing music for brilliant social events attended by eminent citizens and members of the old patrician houses. In addition, he was usually able to work with writers and

---

[1] Letter from G. P. Codebò, the Modenese Resident in Venice, to the Duke of Modena (2 Mar. 1630). See Gaetano Cozzi, 'Scapino', 190. For further details of Scapino, see commentary to Letter 125.

artists with whom he found himself in sympathy, and in this case it was his old friend Giulio Strozzi who provided the libretto for *Proserpina rapita*. Girolamo Scolari was in charge of the dancers, while the scenery and stage-machines came to life in the hands of Giuseppe Schioppi, one of the outstanding designers of the day. Monteverdi's music is lost, with the exception of a posthumously published trio,[2] but the libretto (with a dedication dated 16 April 1630) not only survived in its first printing but was reissued in 1644 when Francesco Sacrati wrote a new opera around it for the Teatro San Moisè.

Within two months of this festive occasion, Monteverdi had to face a personal tragedy that was also a major disaster. A man who had been his staunch friend and faithful ally for nearly forty years, who had come from Mantua to Venice via the disease-ridden route of Aldringen's rabble in the hope of persuading the Doge and Senate to grant more money and troops for the besieged city of the Gonzaga— Alessandro Striggio, librettist of *Orfeo*, succumbed to the plague and died during the night of 15–16 June in Venice. Whether the two men met, even briefly, on this final and fateful occasion is not known; but by the time Striggio's wasted corpse had been carried by boat to the little island of S. Clemente, not far from the southern shores of Venice, Lelio Arrivabene in Verona had already sent a dispatch announcing to Duke Carlo the death of his senior statesman.[3]

Just over a month later, on 18 July, Mantua gave way to the siege which it had so valiantly withstood for many months. The city, proud and beautiful for centuries, suffered every possible indignity at the hands of the imperial troops, losing in that final agony the little that remained of its artistic life-blood and its precious treasures. Those who could escape did so: among them were several court musicians, including the Rubini family, Margherita Basile, and Francesco Dognazzi, all of whom sought refuge in Vienna.[4] Less fortunate was G. F. Busenello, at that time the Venetian Resident in Mantua. He was captured and held for some time before being allowed to return to Venice, where he soon decided to give up diplomacy for literature, later working with Monteverdi on *L'incoronazione di Poppea* in 1642.

The death of Striggio and the destruction of Mantua, so ironically interrelated, led to a third event that was also dependent upon the other two. By 28 July the plague had fastened its deathly grip on Venice, taking the lives of 46,000 citizens over the next sixteen months. Monteverdi and his two sons managed to survive, but how they did so is a matter for conjecture. Possibly they left the city for a time, in view of the closing down of many public services and the strict enforcement of health and sanitation laws. Certainly there is no hint of artistic or musical activity on Monteverdi's part between the *Proserpina rapita* of April 1630 and the Gloria and Credo performed at the Thanksgiving Mass in St Mark's on 28 November 1631. The choir was joined on this solemn occasion, which celebrated the longed-for disappearance of the plague, by an unusually brilliant group of instrumentalists, among whom were players of trom-

---

[2] *Come dolce oggi l'auretta spira* (Book IX). For a contemporary description of this event see Zoppelli, *passim.*

[3] Quazza, *La guerra*, ii. 112.   [4] Bertolotti, 103.

bones, called 'trombe squarciate' by one who was present.[5] The complete Gloria and fragments of the Credo were printed later in the *Selva morale e spirituale* (1641), whose dedicatee was the Empress Eleonora, wife of the man who had unleashed so much death and destruction.

The dissension over Mantua was resolved in October, Carlo Gonzaga being granted the Duchy of Mantua and Monferrato in return for Luzzara, Dosolo, Reggiolo, and Solara, which became part of the territories owned by the Gonzaga of Guastalla, while Trino, Alba, and a few minor holdings near Monferrato went to the House of Savoy. On 21 September 1631 the Duke and his retinue made their way into a sacked and ruined city, which in spite of the devoted labours of all who worked for reconstruction, could never be the same as it was when Monteverdi first set eyes upon it during the early and glorious years of the reign of Vincenzo I.

Towards the end of April, or perhaps even early in May 1632, the composer felt that he ought to revisit Mantua, where life was gradually returning to some semblance of normality. He sought permission to travel there, with letters of recommendation to the Duke, giving as his reason a 'business matter', which was undoubtedly the recovery of his pension and capital.[6] On 7 May the Doge Francesco Erizzo sent a letter to Carlo of Nevers, eighth Duke of Mantua and Monferrato, requesting that Monteverdi be given all possible assistance.[7] He probably left Venice shortly afterwards, spending the latter part of May, all of June and July, and most of August in Mantua, where the settling of his financial problems proceeded at a much slower pace now that his greatest supporter, Striggio, was no longer there. During his absence, Bartolomeo Magni dedicated Monteverdi's second collection of *Scherzi* (on 20 June) to Pietro Castello, mayor of Capo d'Istria, lauding the absent composer as 'so worthy a subject that our century can rejoice at having been so singularly favoured by Heaven as to enjoy the talents of so famous a man; so much the more because his excellence is praised and admired by you'.

It was the title-page of this collection, containing five songs and two duets, that announced for the very first time Monteverdi's ecclesiastical title—*Molto Reverendo*—indicating that he had recently taken holy orders. In fact permission to proceed had been received from Mantua as early as 8 May 1629, and on 9 March 1631 the tonsure was bestowed by the Patriarch, Giovanni Tiepolo. Two witnesses attested to Monteverdi's good character (4 April), and arrangements were well in hand when Tiepolo, who had known the composer for nearly twenty years, died of the plague. Federico Corner succeeded in office but took some time to assume full responsibilities since the city was almost in chaos. But by 10 April 1632 something like normal life had

---

[5] The account of Antonio de' Vescovi (Vogel, 393) has given rise to varying interpretations of the term, but it is certain that brass instruments were used. This theory is elaborated in Morre, 'Venezia', 342 ff., and in Kurtzmann, 63 ff. Cf. Guarini's description of the intermezzi for a production of *Il pastor fido* at Mantua in 1592, where the following phrase occurs: 'abbia in mano trombone di quelli che chiamano "squarciati"' (*Opere di Battista Guarini* (Turin, 1950), 266).

[6] The letter was discovered by Maria Francesca Tiepolo. See Tiepolo, 135–43.

[7] Bertolotti, 78.

been resumed, and Monteverdi was made deacon and finally priest, on 16 April, in the church of S. Maria del Giglio.[8] Almost certainly he had been moved to make this decision by the course of events in 1630: the death of Striggio, the sack of Mantua, and the plague in Venice, from which he had been miraculously spared. But he was far from being totally well, and the rigours of travel combined with the stress of being once more in Mantua caused some illness in July of 1632. He wrote of his plight to the procurators, and they answered him in mid-August, offering sympathies with regard to his past illness, and his problems with the treasury, but expressing hope that he would soon return to Venice and to St Mark's.[9]

Most Serene Prince, Most Illustrious and Most Excellent Lords,

I, Claudio Monteverdi, a very devoted servant of Your Serenity, having great need to travel to Mantua, and having the kind favour and permission of yourself and of the Most Excellent Procurators my masters, for a business matter which greatly concerns me,[a] most reverently beg Your Serenity and Your Most Illustrious Excellencies to be so kind as to favour me with a letter[b] of recommendation for a speedy and successful journey, so that I may return as soon as possible to my very devoted service, which must be uninterrupted throughout my lifespan.

With thanks, etc.

Claudio Monteverdi

[8] Vio, 392 ff.   [9] Arnold, 203 (doc. 6).

[a] His pension.

[b] Dated 7 May 1632, and send to Carlo of Nevers, Duke of Mantua, by Andrea Rosso, secretary to the Doge.

124

Venice, 22 October 1633
to [Giovanni Battista Doni, at Rome]

Florence, Conservatorio di Musica 'Luigi Cherubini', fondo Basevi 2438, vol. xv, fos. 7–9. Bifolio: 4 pp.

Vogel, 438; Prunières, 284; Malipiero, 291; Paoli, 320; Fabbri 1985, 61, 291; Lax, 200

On the same day that Monteverdi wrote this letter, he entered into a contract with a friend in Cremona about a property that required management, and revived an earlier interest in a canonry there. His native city continuing to interest him, he contacted the Emperor Ferdinand II by writing to his Gonzaga Empress. Results appeared with a minimum of delay in a letter from Ferdinand (19 December 1633) warmly recommending Monteverdi's suit to another Ferdinand, the Cardinal Infanta, who belonged to the Spanish Habsburgs and was then governor of Milan. Mild pressure could thus be applied to the Bishop of Mantua, who in turn controlled the canonry at Cremona. In this way wires continued to pull wires, the Monteverdian bait being an advance instalment of his Eighth Book, to be published five years later. The Empress Eleonora received the manuscript madrigals, had them performed, and at once the Italian-Austrian contingent began to copy their salient stylistic features. The effect of works such as *Hor che'l ciel* on certain of the court composers is too obvious to be dismissed as fortuitous. Monteverdi was clearly a closely-watched composer.[1]

Vogel, who first published this letter (and its sister no.125), refrained from guessing the identity of the addressee. But he rightly stressed the importance of the two letters, which are linked together naturally by nearness in date, provenance, and topic. Prunières thought that they could have been written to G. B. Doni (see Pl. 8), an authority on musical theory and inventor of the Lyra Barberina.

The way in which Monteverdi begins and ends a letter frequently provides valuable clues as to the identity of the intended recipient. Letters 5 and 11, addressed to Cardinal Ferdinando Gonzaga, open with the words 'Illustrissimo et Reverendissimo'; in the present case 'Molto Illustre et Reverendissimo' would seem to indicate someone not far removed from the status of a cardinal. Doni, although he was no ecclesiastic, certainly mixed with members of the Sacred College and worked under the patronage of one of its greatest luminaries, Cardinal Francesco Barberini, so that the form of address used by Monteverdi was in every way appropriate.

[1] This information was kindly communicated to me by Dr Steven Saunders, who hopes to publish it in *Music and Letters*.

IO.BAPT.
PATR.FL.

DONIVS
A.AET.L.

8. Giovanni Battista Doni. Anonymous engraving. Milan, Civica Raccolta delle Stampe A. Bertarelli

It was so considered by others who corresponded with Doni, as is evident from a letter of Count Pietro de' Bardi who wrote to him on 16 December 1634, on the subject of the origins of musical drama.[2] Bardi begins with a salutation that corresponds exactly with the one employed by Monteverdi in Letters 124 and 125, excepting only the last word, which is 'Osservandissimo' rather than 'Collendissimo'.

<hr />

[2] Solerti, *Origine*, 143. First printed in Bandini, who adds a letter from the Biship of Padua to Doni, dated 8 July 1633, on the subject of the Accademia di Ricoverati (col. 109, Letter no. LXVI). Doni is addressed here as 'Molto Illustre e Molto Reverendo Signore'.

Further evidence in support of the candidacy of Doni is as follows: both letters are now in Florence, where Doni was born and died, and they were given to the Conservatorio by the critic and composer Abramo Basevi, who died in Florence in 1885, after spending most of his life there as an editor of musical periodicals and a tireless advocate of musical performance. He probably acquired the letters from a local collector who had purchased them from a series of intermediaries reaching back to the seventeenth century.

In addition, the dates of Monteverdi's two letters coincide broadly with the period during which Doni was writing to well-known experts on ancient music and drama, such as Marc'Antonio Cornaro (Bishop of Padua), Count Bardi of Florence, and Nicolas Peiresc, at Aix-en-Provence.[3] Not content with conversations and study alone, Doni laid great store by his correspondence with scholars both in Italy and in other countries, constantly gleaning and sifting materials that later appeared in his lectures and treatises.[4] It has not been generally noticed that Doni, in the Appendix to *Lyra Barberina*, discusses 'the Lament of Arianna' with regard to the rival claims of its two versions, solo and polyphonic, reaching the conclusion that Monteverdi can scarcely be blamed for the madrigal arrangement because he made it to please others rather than himself, 'as he himself confesses in one of his letters'.[5]

The Lament is of course mentioned in the present letter, but the absence of any confession resembling the one referred to by Doni suggests that Monteverdi sent him further correspondence in which this topic was broached. Doni can hardly be discussing letters that the composer sent to other musicians, since they were at that time unpublished and perhaps unknown. It is therefore reasonable to suppose that the meeting of these two great minds was not restricted to the two letters from Monteverdi and the three that Doni wrote to him, these three having since been lost.

From September 1632 until September 1633 Monteverdi's biography presents little more than a blank page to the reader. There are no important events, no publications, no letters. But the one sent to Doni, marking the beginning of their relationship by correspondence, affords a glimpse of how that time might have been spent: in reading treatises by earlier writers on music (notably Vincenzo Galilei, and probably Zarlino as well), in planning the scope and size of the book, and in talking over its proposed contents with other musicians residing in Venice. Monteverdi apparently mentioned his self-imposed task to Benedetto Erizzo, Vicar-General of St Mark's, on learning from him that Doni was about to embark on a similar treatise. Erizzo—who was in touch with the Bishop of Padua whom he had known well as Dean of St Mark's from 1619 until 1632—passed this information along because he knew that news about music (and Monteverdi) would be welcome.

It is strange that the Bishop's name has been so frequently mistranscribed in Italian and English versions of this letter, for the composer's handwriting is no less clear than usual at the point where 'Cornaro' is spelled out. The reading 'Cervaro' is impossible

[3] For a transcription of the letter to Peiresc, see Schaal, 89.
[4] Complete bibliography in the article by A. A. Abert, *MGG* 3, cols. 675–6.
[5] Doni, ii, App. 26.

in view of the way in which Monteverdi shaped the 'o' and 'n', and the succession of Paduan bishops is in any event well documented in ecclesiastical records.[6] Marc'Antonio Cornaro's enthusiasm for music was a matter of common knowledge in Venice, where Monteverdi had provided music for his private oratory,[7] and in Padua, where his staff included an excellent violinist and cornetto-player who had given lessons to Pietro della Valle.[8] It was also known as far afield as Rome, and this explains how a chance remark made by Monteverdi to Erizzo eventually found its way via Padua to the Sacred College of Cardinals. Doni lost no time in replying to Cornaro, and enclosed in his letter one for Monteverdi, whose reaction was predictably enthusiastic.

Doni's eminence in scholarship notwithstanding, Monteverdi could not have known his work since the bulk of it remained unpublished for many years. The *Compendio del trattato de' generi e de' modi della musica* did not appear until 1635, and the *Annotazioni sopra il compendio* only in 1640. Works of this nature did not circulate in manuscript, except to Doni's closest friends, and Rome was far from Venice in more senses than that of mere distance. Doni, on the other hand, was well acquainted with certain key works in the Monteverdian canon, as is clear from his many references to *Arianna*, *Orfeo*, the *Lettera amorosa*, and *Partenza amorosa* throughout the posthumously published volumes of the *Lyra Barberina* of 1763.[9]

Monteverdi's treatise on the *seconda prattica* suffered the same fate as so much of his theatre music, as far as can be gathered. The difference is that whereas proof exists of the composition and performance of the music, there is nothing to show that Monteverdi ever finished his projected treatise. He seems to have drawn on a vital part of it, however, in the famous preface to his *Madrigali guerrieri et amorosi* of 1638, where a careful discussion of declamation and rhythm culminates in a recommendation that performance should concern itself with three principal matters: text, harmony, and rhythm; a theory deriving from Plato's *Republic*, book iii, which is also the source of Monteverdi's comments on imitation in the present letter, and of the 'cithara–tibia' quotation in Letter 19. These three main headings are reflected in his plan for the book, each section of which would correspond to one aspect of the art of music: word-setting, harmonization, and rhythmic patterns.

Doni's approach was largely academic, for after early training in classical philology and literature, he studied modern and oriental languages as well as jurisprudence. He was not a musician, though his knowledge of musical theory and his devotion to the art stood him in good stead when he came to examine the principles of Greek melodrama and their relationship with the new genre of opera, with which he had literally grown up. Steadily occupied from about 1632 until 1638 with the research for (and writing of) his *Lyra Barberina*, Doni attempted to rationalize in theory what he had to some degree already put into practice by his invention of the instrument of that name. Its alleged ability to combine ancient modes (Dorian, Phrygian, Lydian) with modern practice undoubtedly aroused Monteverdi's interest, as did the promise of a

---

[6] Gams, 798.   [7] See Letter 50.   [8] Solerti, *Origine*, 158.
[9] Doni, i. 124; ii. 25, 65, 80, 104, 128; App. 26, 63, 98.

copy of Doni's treatise, which was probably the *Compendio del trattato de' generi e de' modi della musica*, published at Rome in 1635.

My Very Illustrious and Most Worshipful[a] Lord and Most Respected Master,

Enclosed with a most kind letter from the Most Illustrious Lord Bishop Cornaro,[b] my particular lord and most revered master, sent to me from Padua, there was one from Your Worship addressed to me, so abundantly fruitful in honour and praise of my feeble self that I was almost lost in wonder at it; but considering that from a most virtuous and kindly tree such as Your Worship's person there could grow no other fruit but that of like nature, I kept quiet, accepting the harvest not so much because I was worthy of it, but rather to preserve it for the singular merit of Your Worship, knowing myself to be something of a green shrub,[c] and of such kind that I produce nothing other than leaves and flowers without scent.

Please be so good, therefore, as to accept from me by way of reply the praises which your most noble letter deserves, for I deem it a great favour that you do me the honour of accepting me as your most humble servant. Monsignor the Vicar of St Mark's,[d] who was so kind as to tell me about Your Worship's noble qualities and particular virtues, mentioned that you were writing a book on music; at which point I added that I too was writing one, though with fear that through my weakness I would fail to reach the desired conclusion. This gentleman being very devoted to the Most Illustrious Lord Bishop of Padua, I imagine that this is how His Grace may have heard of my writings, for I know of no other way, and I make no effort to let people know. But since His Grace has been kind enough to honour me so in Your Worship's favour, I beg you to consider the rest of what I have to say.

You should know, therefore, that I am indeed at work—but under compulsion, however, inasmuch as the event which years ago spurred me to begin was of such a kind that it caused me unawares to promise the world something that (once I had become aware of it) my feeble forces

---

[a] Monteverdi uses the word *Reverendissimo*, but since Doni was not a priest (though secretary to the College of Cardinals) a secular appellation is perhaps preferable.

[b] Marc'Antonio Cornaro, Bishop of Padua from 1632 until his death in 1636, and formerly Primicerius at St Mark's (see also Letters 48 and 50).

[c] A pun on the composer's name.   [d] Benedetto Erizzo, abbot of San Crisogono of Zara.

could not manage. I promised, as I said before, in a printed work of mine to let a certain theoretician[e] of the First Practice know that there was another way (unknown to him) of considering music, and this I called the Second Practice. The reason for this was that he had been pleased to criticize (in print!) one of my madrigals,[f] as regards certain of its harmonic progressions, on the basis of tenets of the First Practice (that is to say, the ordinary rules, as if they were exercises[g] written by a youth beginning to learn the first species of counterpoint) and not according to a knowledge of melody.

But on hearing of a certain exegesis published in my defence by my brother,[h] he calmed down in such a way that from thenceforward not only did he stop overruling me, but—turning his pen in my praise—he began to like and admire me. Since the promise was public, I could not neglect it, and for this reason I am compelled to pay the debt. I beg you therefore to consider me excused for my boldness.

The title of the book will be as follows: *Melody, or the Second Musical Practice*. I mean the second as regards numerical order, in modern style; first in order, in the old style. I am dividing the book into three parts corresponding to the three aspects of Melody. In the first I discuss word-setting, in the second, harmony, and in the third, the rhythmic part. I keep telling myself that it will not be unacceptable to the world, for I found out in practice that when I was about to compose 'the Lament of Arianna'—finding no book that could show me the natural way of imitation, not even one that would explain how I ought to have been an imitator, other than Plato, in one of his shafts of wisdom, but so hidden that I could hardly discern from afar with my feeble sight what little he showed me)—I found out (let me tell you) what hard work I had to do in order to achieve the little I did do in the way of imitation, and I therefore hope it is not going to be displeasing, but—let it come out as it will in the end—I shall be happier to be moderately praised in the new style, than greatly praised in the ordinary; and for this further presumption I ask fresh pardon.

Well, what pleasure I felt on learning that in our own times a new instrument[i] had been invented! May God be my witness—whom I pray

[e] Canon Giovanni Maria Artusi, of Bologna.

[f] *Cruda Amarilli* (Book V).   [g] *solfe* (plural of *solfa*).

[h] Giulio Cesare Monteverdi, in the *Dichiaratione* printed at the end of the *Scherzi musicali* of 1607.

[i] The Lyra Barberina, whose three sets of strings could be tuned to the Dorian, Phrygian, and Lydian modes.

[421]

with all my heart to maintain and bless the most virtuous person of the inventor, who was none other than Your Worship—I have indeed often thought about the reason for its discovery, on which (I mean to say, where) the ancients based their ideas in order to find so many differences*j* in it (as they did), because not only are there many that we use, but many that have been lost. Nor has there been even one theorist of our times (yet they have professed to know all about the art) who has shown even one to the world. I hope, however, in my book, to say something about this point that perhaps will not be displeasing.

From the pleasure I have told you about, Your Worship can decide for sure whether it will be precious to me—the favour promised me in due course through your kindness—that is, in being favoured with a copy of such a worthy treatise, containing new and recondite things. Wherefore I beg you for the promised favour, even as I beg you to consider me as your most humble and most grateful servant, and here making a most humble reverence, with all my heart I kiss your most honourable hands.

from Venice, 22 October 1633

Your Most Illustrious Worship's

most devoted and most grateful servant

Claudio Monteverdi

---

j In tuning to different modes.

125

Venice, 2 February 1634
to [Giovanni Battista Doni, at Rome]

Florence, Conservatorio di Musica 'Luigi Cherubini', fondo Basevi 2438, vol. xv, fos. 13–15. Bifolio: 4 pp. Enclosure: single page containing descriptions of instruments

Vogel, 439; Prunières, 285; Malipiero, 294; Paoli, 325; Fabbri 1985, 291; Lax, 203

To Monteverdi's letter of 22 October, Doni appears to have replied about the middle of December, following up with another letter a month later. But the composer is slow to reply because of an unexpected illness—a recurrence of the catarrh he suffered in 1627.[1] Nevertheless, he outlines carefully the scope of his studies and in particular his reactions to the *Dialogo della musica antica e della moderna* (1581) by Vincenzo Galilei, an author who would have appealed to Doni through the discussions of Greek music and theory, and to Monteverdi because monody (that is to say, melody, which coincides with the name of his treatise) is extolled over classical polyphony.

The 'best philosophers' to whom Monteverdi turned were Plato (whose *Republic* he knew well) and Boethius, who begins the first book of his *De institutione musica* with a discourse on the natural relationship between music and mankind.[2] The composer's interpretation of their theories is of course entirely his own, for his main intent—as he explains to Doni—is to base new ideas on old principles and create effects that cleave closely to nature and the natural order. His aim is therefore practical, and he has tried to avoid the pitfalls of obscure signs and ideas of remote antiquity, just as he turned away from the rigid contrapuntal rules that he was obliged to learn in his youth.

It is not known whether, in the eleven years that remained to him, Monteverdi fulfilled his vow to visit Loreto, going on to Rome for a meeting with Doni. By 1640 Doni had returned to Florence and to the academic life he had so long desired, but by then Monteverdi had practically ceased to travel, and the only proven journey he made in those latter years was the one to Mantua in 1643. It is therefore unlikely that the two men ever met.

Doni's remarkable experiments with ancient and modern instruments, which he sometimes attempted to combine, led not only to the Lyra Barberina but also to new kinds of violins and harpsichords, but the brilliance of his inventions was largely offset

---

[1] Letter 99.   [2] Both authors are cited in the Preface to Book VIII.

by the sheer impracticality of his methods. The instruments could certainly be seen and admired; to play them was quite another thing. Yet he continually sought after new information and ideas. He wanted Monteverdi to obtain drawings of the many instruments played by the actor Francesco Gabrielli, known as Scapino, whose father Giovanni Gabrielli ('Il Sivello') had been in the service of Cardinal Bonifacio Caetani in Rome many years previously. Scapino, warmly recommended by the Cardinal in a letter to Duke Vincenzo Gonzaga I,[3] left Rome in the late spring of 1611 and travelled via Florence—where he gave several performances[4]—to Mantua, undoubtedly meeting Monteverdi, who became an admiring friend.

In 1633, when Monteverdi began to correspond with Doni, a Milanese engraver named Carlo Biffi portrayed Scapino holding a mask in one hand and a stringed instrument in the other (see Pl. 9), this vignette being surrounded by pictures of some of the strange musical inventions that apparently endeared the actor to his thronging audiences. It so happened that in February 1634 Scapino was appearing in Modena; and Monteverdi, unable to travel there, had to rely on descriptions of the instruments as recalled by various friends, and these he enclosed on a separate sheet of paper. It may be asked why the composer himself was unable to supply these details, for they were after all musical matters, and he would have known enough about them to write a simple description, especially if he had seen Scapino's performances in 1630.

Perhaps the most likely explanation is that Monteverdi knew Scapino best in the earlier part of the actor's career, before he had developed his fantastic instrumentarium to the full. Yet he shows himself ready and willing to go to some trouble in obtaining suitable drawings direct from Modena, probably through his friend Bellerofonte Castaldi, who united within himself the talents of musician and artist-engraver. To this he adds the unexpected but welcome description of a cittern-like instrument from the Middle East, which he had seen and heard played at Mantua about the year 1604. It was perhaps a variant of the Islamic short lute, whose soundboard 'divided by a cross line into two halves, probably of wood and of skin',[5] corresponds fairly closely to Monteverdi's description.

My Very Illustrious and Most Worshipful[a] Lord and Most Respected Master,

I have received two letters from Your Worship: one before Christmas—at a time when I was entirely taken up with writing the mass for Christmas Eve (a new mass being expected of the Director of Music according to a custom of this city)—and the other one two weeks ago from the courier, who found me not properly recovered from a catarrhal descent which started to appear over my left eye just after Christmas, and this kept me far

---

[3] Bertolotti, 93.   [4] Ademollo, 62.   [5] Sachs, 252.

[a] *Reverendissimo* (but Doni was not a priest).

9. Francesco Gabrielli detto Scapino. Engraving by Carlo Biffi, 1633. Milan, Civica Raccolta delle Stampe A. Bertarelli

not only from writing but also from reading, for many a long day. Nor am I yet free from it, in fact, for it still keeps troubling me to some extent, and because of these two real impediments I am writing to beg Your Worship to forgive this fault of mine in replying so tardily.

[425]

Only two weeks ago I read Your Worship's first letter, most courteous and most helpful, from which I gathered the most kindly advice, all of it worthy of my careful consideration; and for this I am sending you my infinite thanks. I have, however, seen the Galilei[b]—not just now, but rather twenty years ago—the part where he mentions that scant practice of ancient times. I valued seeing it then, perceiving in that same part how the ancients used their practical signs in a different way from ours, but I did not try to go any further in understanding them, being sure that they would have come out as very obscure ciphers, or worse, since that ancient practical manner is completely lost.

Whereupon I turned my studies in another direction, basing them on the principles of the best philosophers to have investigated nature. And because, in accordance with my reading, I notice that the results agree with those reasonings (and with the requirements of nature) when I write down practical things with the aid of those observations, and really feel that our present rules have nothing to do with those requirements, I have for this basic reason given my book the title of Second Practice; and I hope to make this so clear that it will not be censured by the world, but rather taken seriously.

I keep well away, in my writings, from that method upheld by the Greeks with their words and signs, employing instead the voices and characters that we use in our practice, because my intention is to show by means of our practice what I have been able to extract from the mind of those philosophers for the benefit of good art, and not for the principles of the First Practice, which was only harmonic.

Would to God that I might find myself near to Your Worship's singular affection and singular prudence and advice, for I would tell you all, by word of mouth—begging you to hear me out, I mean in everything—as much about the plan, as about the principles and the divisions of the parts of my book; but my being far away prevents it. Because of a special favour received of the Most Holy Virgin's consummate goodness in the year of the plague[c] at Venice, I am bound by a vow to visit the Most Holy House of Loreto.[d] I hope soon, with the Lord's help, to fulfil it; on which

---

[b] Vincenzo Galilei, Florentine composer and theorist (d. 1591), author of several treatises, the one referred to here being in all likelihood *Dialogo della musica antica e della moderna* (1581; 1602).

[c] July 1630 until Nov. 1631.

[d] Episcopal see and pilgrimage city a few miles south of Ancona.

occasion I would come on to Rome (if it please the Lord to grant me the favour) in order to be able to present my service personally to Your Worship, and enjoy both the sight and the most beautiful sound of your most noble instrument,[e] and be honoured by your most brilliant conversation.

I have seen a drawing of the instrument on the piece of paper you sent me, which—far from diminishing my eagerness—has on the contrary made it grow. And since in the aforesaid second letter you ask me to engage the services of Scapino[f] in order that I may send Your Worship drawings of the many extraordinary instruments that he plays, because of my great desire to find an opportunity of serving you, and being unable to do this as he is performing in Modena, not in Venice, I therefore feel very disappointed.

Nevertheless I have used a little diligence with certain friends so that they can at least describe to me the ones they are able to remember, and so they gave me the enclosed sheet of paper which here and now I am sending off to Your Worship. Nor did I neglect to write to a friend[g] about trying to obtain drawings of those most different from the ones in use. I have never seen them myself, but from the little information I am sending, it seems to me that they are new as regards shape but not in sound, since all fit in with the sounds of the instruments that we use.

What I did seen in Mantua thirty years ago, played and put together by a certain Arab who had just come from Turkey (and this man was lodged at the court of the Duke of Mantua,[h] my master) was a cittern, the size of ours, strung with the same strings and similarly played, but it had this difference—its belly was half of wood around the part near the neck, and half of sheepskin around the underneath part, well stretched and glued about the rim of the cittern, the strings of which were attached rather to its lower rim, and rested upon a bridge which was placed in the centre of that sheepskin; and the small finger of the quill hand[i] making the said sheepskin dance while he stopped the chord, those chords came out with a tremolo motion which gave a very pleasing effect. I have heard nothing more novel that was to my liking.

[e] The Lyra Barberina, invented by Doni and described by him in a book of that name.

[f] Stage name of the actor-musician Francesco Gabrielli.

[g] Probably Bellerofonte Castaldi of Modena, who was a gifted artist and engraver besides being a virtuoso on the theorbo.

[h] At that time (about 1604) Vincenzo I, fourth Duke.   [i] *mano de la penna.*

I shall remain alert, and if I am notified of anything that might bring you pleasure I shall not fail to send you a little drawing at once. I beg you to maintain me as a servant in your good graces, while with all my heart and very reverently I kiss your hand and pray from Our Lord your every perfect happiness.

from Venice, 2 February 1634
Your Most Illustrious Worship's
most devoted servant
Claudio Monteverdi

126

Venice, 9 June 1637
to [the Procurators of St Mark's, at Venice]

Venice, Archivio di Stato, Procuratori di San Marco de Supra (Chiesa), Busta 91, Processo 208, fasc. 1, fo. 96^{r-v}

Sommi-Picenardi, 159; Weiss, 44; Paoli, 337; Fabbri 1985, 296; Lax, 206

Towards the end of 1636 Monteverdi was putting the final touches to a group of vocal and instrumental works presumably commissioned by the Habsburgs for the coronation of Ferdinand III, first as King of Hungary and later as Emperor. He had previously had very little to do with the Habsburgs, apart from a single motet contributed to Giovanni Battista Bonometti's anthology of 1616,[1] and the music for the intermezzi in *Le tre costanti*, devised to celebrate the imperial wedding in 1622.[2] Now, for use at various festive occasions in Regensburg and Vienna, he prepared three new works: *Altri canti d'Amor* (based on a sonnet of anonymous authorship, but clearly written in imitation of Marini's *Altri canti di Marte*), the cantata *Ogni amante è guerrier*, and the ballet *Movete al mio bel suon*. Nino Pirrotta has shown that the cantata and the ballet are based on poems written by Rinuccini in honour of Henry IV of France,[3] and much altered by Monteverdi to conform with a totally different political situation. He had achieved something similar in 1628, when the Mantuan opera-ballet *Il ballo delle Ingrate* underwent topographical text changes in order to render it suitable for a Viennese performance.

Of Monteverdi's artistic involvements in the early part of 1637, nothing is known for certain, but he cannot have failed to take a more than passing interest in an operatic venture by Francesco Manelli, a bass singer and composer from Rome who would later be invited to become a member of the choir of St Mark's. Having set to music Benedetto Ferrari's libretto *Andromeda*, the enterprising Manelli had the idea of providing operatic entertainment that would draw upon the best designers and singers (one of these was his wife Maddalena, another was the Bolognese bass, G. B. Bisucci), and appeal to the general public as well as to the aristocracy. Not far from the church of San Cassiano, or Cassano, which had originally been dedicated to Saint Cecilia and contained a splendid organ built by Father Urbano, stood the Teatro San Cassiano, a short distance only from the Rialto Bridge and a perfect meeting-place for the arts and music in Venice. On 6 March *Andromeda* filled the theatre to capacity and

---

[1] *Parnassus Musicus Ferdinandaeus.* See Federhofer, 167.   [2] See Letters 65, 66, 68–70.
[3] Pirrotta, 55–7. See also Stevens, 'Madrigali', 174–8.

made operatic history. Form then onwards, opera came to be considered an entertainment of unrestricted appeal and interest.[4]

It would be more than two years before Monteverdi re-entered the theatrical world as a priest in his early seventies but still in full possession of his musical faculties. In the mean time, the innumerable churches of Venice constantly sought his aid. On 17 May 1637, the body of St John the Martyr, Duke of Alexandria, was translated with due solemnity from its original sepulchre in S. Daniele, a nunnery far to the eastern part of the city in the district of Castello, further even than the Arsenal whose massive walls were visible from its cloister. The relic had been brought to Venice by Rodoaldo, Prior of S. Daniele in 1112, before the buildings were handed over to the Benedictine nuns. Now it was placed in a magnificent sepulchre over an altar in the centre of the church. The altar frontal, by Alessandro Varotari, depicted the saint in prison, being baptized by Christ. Although Martinioni's additional matter in *Venetia città nobilissima*[5] briefly notes the occasion, no mention is made of the presence at Vespers of the choir of St Mark's, who were presumably under Monteverdi's direction. But his letter, or memorandum to the procurators, makes it quite clear that the singers were present, and that their fees were collected by Boniventi for distribution on 8 June.

Some eight years before this event, Dr John Earle, Bishop of Salisbury, called singers 'a bad society, and yet a company of good Fellows, that roare deepe in the Quire, deeper in the Taverne'.[6] If there were a few rough characters among the choirmen of St Mark's, one in particular had been a source of trouble since the year when Monteverdi was appointed. In 1613 Domenico Aldegati had denounced another singer named Savolchi because he was not a regular member of the choir, and denied him the privilege of going with his tenured colleagues to sing in other churches.[7] Still jealous and quarrelsome nearly a quarter of a century later, he allowed his dissatisfaction over the fee to unleash his temper, which was directed at Monteverdi, who claimed to have nothing to do with the financial arrangements for outside engagements.

Aldegati's attack, fortunately only a verbal one, took place in front of a crowd near the great door of St Mark's. Monteverdi suffered an affront to his honour and an accusation of dishonesty: his report to the procurators was justified, and they took the necessary action on 19 June, reprimanding Aldegati for his unseemly behaviour. Like so many of Monteverdi's letters, this document contains matters of musical, social, and historical interest; yet it is much more rhetorical in style than the majority of them, and so planned that the subject of the exordium is separated from the main verb by nearly half the length of the letter. Some of the words are hard to decipher due to

---

[4] Further on Manelli and his *Andromeda*: Worsthorne, 24–9, 168–9. Monteverdi's growing involvement with opera at this time is recorded in the anonymous *Satire, et altre raccolte per l'Academia de gl'Unisoni in casa di Giulio Strozzi* (possibly written by Busenello) found in manuscript copies at the Biblioteca Marciana and the Museo Correr, Venice. For bibliographical details and the excerpts concerning Monteverdi, see Rosand, 250–1.

[5] Sansovino, 22–3.   [6] Earle, 'The Common Singing Men'.   [7] Prunières, 106, 213 n. 104.

the ravages of damp, and even certain legible ones pose problems of interpretation because of unusual vocabulary. Pietro Canal drew attention to the document as early as 1881,[8] and it was published fourteen years later by Guido Sommi-Picenardi.[9] More recently it has appeared in many collections of Monteverdi's letters in Italian, English, and German. Its value lies in the fact that it affords definite evidence concerning Monteverdi's occasional problems with the choir, and incontrovertible proof of the vulnerability of a great musician face to face with an uncontrolled display of temper, invective, and jealousy.

Most Illustrious and Most Excellent Lords and Most Respected Masters,

I, Claudio Monteverdi, Director of Music at St Mark's, most humble servant of Your Excellencies and of the Most Serene Republic, come humbly unto your presence to set forth to you how Domenico Aldegati,[a] a singer at St Mark's, a bass[b]—yesterday morning which was the 8th of the present month of June 1637, before the great door of that church, at the time of the greatest concourse of people, among whom there was a large number of singers and players (and there was also a certain Bonivento Boniventi,[c] a musician who was handing out to the singers and players certain moneys given to him by the Most Illustrious Nuns of S. Daniele[d] for the Vespers service they held before the processional raising of the body of St John, Duke of Alexandria), whether the reason for this was perhaps because he did not get the said moneys, or because his share was less in comparison with the other shares, I do not know, because I never interfere with the money affairs of singers—beyond all reason and justification, and having respect neither for the office that I hold from the Most Serene Republic nor for my age and my priesthood, nor for the honour of my family and of my virtue, but spurred on by a wild fury and with a loud raucous voice, after a few minutes of first insulting my person (and having brought together in a semicircle more than fifty people, part of whom were strangers, among whom those present were:

---

[8] Canal, 96.   [9] Sommi-Picenardi, 159.

[a] This singer had already proved troublesome in 1613, the year of Monteverdi's arrival in Venice. He may also have penned the denunciation of Monteverdi in 1623 (see commentary to Letter 81).

[b] The main verb does not appear until note *i* below.

[c] He contributed a song to Vincenti's *Arie di diversi* (1634), which also contained two songs by Monteverdi and others by Venetian composers.

[d] A Benedictine nunnery, where the body of St John the Martyr, Duke of Alexandria, was brought in 1112.

Sig. Giovanni Battista,^e called the Bolognese singer of the chapel
Sig. Gasparo Zorina,^f a Brescian, who plays the double bass
Sig. Alovisi Lipomani^g
Sig. Don Anibale, a Roman, singer of the chapel
Sig. Giovanni Battista the Paduan,^h who plays trombones

and the said Sig. Bonivento Boniventi who was handing out the said moneys) spokeⁱ these exact words, as indeed some of the said witnesses reported to me: 'The Director of Music comes from a brood of cut-throat bastards,^j a thieving, fucking he-goat',^k with many other wicked insults, and then he added: 'And I shit on him and whoever protects him, and so that everyone can understand me, I say that Claudio Monteverdi is a thieving fucking he-goat, and I am telling you, Bonivento, so that you can go and report it as coming from me.'

I come therefore to Your Excellencies' feet not as Claudio Monteverdi the priest, for as such I shall forgive him all and pray that God may do the same; but as Director of Music, whose authority deriving from the royal hand of the Most Serene Republic I would not allow to be ill used and insulted in such a way, nor my virtue nor the honour of my family, which is protected by the most serene hand of this Most Serene Republic; and with a mind to this man, that the other singers may take care to limit themselves to honourable terms regarding anyone, especially him who holds the name of Director of Music. Otherwise, for the sake of my honour, I would be forced to avoid a second occasion of hearing him or the likes of him, and ask for an honourable discharge, to go away under the protection of my freeholds, left to me by my ancestors, which are few but nevertheless sufficient to support me far from such evils and licentious occasions. Hoping this to be a just cause I here bow to the ground before you.

I, Claudio Monteverdi, have written this and beg that this man's life may not be harmed.

---

^e Giovanni Battista Bisucci.

^f Probably Gasparo Serena, a member of St Mark's orchestra until after 1652.

^g Double bass player in the orchestra until 1642.

^h A member of the orchestra until after 1652.   ⁱ Main verb of sentence.

^j Although not clear, the word seems to be *bojenona* (from *boia* meaning executioner or clumsy surgeon, and therefore a possible reference to the fact that Monteverdi's father was a doctor).

^k *ladro becco fotuto*. Strange that these words, once unfairly applied to the composer, might now be used with some justification to describe the more unruly among his interpreters.

127

Venice, ?20 August 1643
to [the Doge Francesco Erizzo, at Venice]

Venice, Archivio di Stato, Collegio, Lettere comuni, filza 180. Folio: 1 p.
Enclosure: copy of Duke Vincenzo's decree of 1609

Tiepolo, 142; Paoli, 332; Lax, 209

This memorandum to the Doge, together with the one dating from 1632, was discovered by Maria Francesca Tiepolo in the Venetian State Archives. It is the last surviving document written by (or for) Monteverdi, preceding his death by only a few months. His final years in the city he loved so much are not closely documented, but this is of little moment when one recalls the masterpieces he composed or compiled. In 1637, his colleague G. B. Buonamente was thoughtful enough to write two short works named for Monteverdi: the first Sonata and the first Sinfonia in his *Sonate, sinfonie* . . . (Book 7), whose dedication is dated 3 December.[1] The Sonata 'La Monteverde', for two violins in strict canon and basso continuo, was first performed in modern times at the inaugural concert of the Accademia Monteverdiana at the City of Bath Festival, 4 June 1961, by Yehudi Menuhin, Robert Masters, and Kinloch Anderson. In the following year an edition was published by Hinrichsen, London.

Monteverdi, accepting Buonamente's tribute with gratitude, nevertheless continued to pour his finest inspiration into vocal rather than instrumental music. Had he wished to do so, he could have taken an important part in the further development of the solo sonata and the trio sonata, perhaps of the sinfonia too as it grew in stature and significance.

But he was too busy compiling the last two works that he would see through the press himself: the Eighth Book of Madrigals (1638), and the *Selva morale e spirituale* (1641). Both rank as colossal achievements, offering a wide variety of styles within the bounds of secular and sacred music respectively, and reaching back to his days at Mantua.[2] Both were dedicated to members of the Habsburg dynasty, the madrigals to the Emperor Ferdinand III, and the church music to the widow of Ferdinand II— Eleonora Gonzaga. Aside from these published anthologies, there were the operas *Le nozze d'Enea in Lavinia*[3] in 1641 and *L'incoronazione di Poppea* (Busenello) in 1642— both at the Teatro SS. Giovanni e Paolo far off to the northern shore of Venice, on the

---

[1] Sartori, *Bibliografia* i. 355; ii. 101.

[2] On the *salmi spezzati* in this collection see Moore, 'Vespers', 272.

[3] Text anonymous, music lost.

Fondamente Nuove. At the Teatro San Moisè, happily only a short walk from the Piazza San Marco, Monteverdi saw a new production of *Arianna* in 1639 and 1640. Then, at the Teatro San Cassiano—the scene of Manelli's triumph in 1637—Monteverdi too enjoyed an enthusiastic reception in 1640 when *Il ritorno d'Ulisse in patria* (Badoaro) received its first performance. There was a successful revival in 1641.

This is mentioned in an informative and discursive *Lettera dell'autore ad alcuni suoi amici* ('The author's letter to some of his friends') which introduces the printed scenario of *Le nozze d'Enea in Lavinia* (Venice, 1640). The document praises Monteverdi for his immense contribution to opera: theatrical music is much indebted to him for its rebirth in even greater perfection than with the ancient Greeks—he will be sighed for in future ages, for his compositions will surely outlive the ravages of time.

The last three years of the composer's life saw his waxing renown and his waning health. It was a time of ripe success coloured by the dark hue that betrays the beginning of the end. Just as the ghosts of Mantua returned for a brief obeisance, so too did the spirit of the Farnese—that same Duke Odoardo, now a grown man, for whom Monteverdi had written the festive music of 1628. This time it was a commission for a ballet on a libretto by Bernardo Morandi, to be performed in Piacenza as part of a celebration for the birth of a prince. *La vittoria d'Amore* was given in carnival time, 1641, just after the birth of the child, Ottavio Angelo Maria Felice Farnese, who did not live beyond August of the same year.[4]

In Mantua, Carlo, the eighth Duke, had died on 21 September 1637, leaving as heir his grandchild born in 1629 to Carlo, Prince of Nevers and Rethel, and Maria Gonzaga, daughter of Francesco, fifth Duke of Mantua. This prince might have become duke had he enjoyed greater longevity, but his death in 1631 left Maria a widow, and since her son—the future Carlo II, ninth Duke of Mantua—was too young to assume the cares of state she became Regent of Mantua. It was to her that Monteverdi decided to appeal in 1643, as a last-ditch attempt to obtain his *fondo*. He supplicated for leave in order to visit Mantua in person, and this was granted along with a letter of commendation penned by the doge's secretary Paulucci. Hoping to strengthen his case, the composer enclosed with his memorandum a copy of Vincenzo's decree.[5]

If Maria acted on the pleas of Monteverdi and his protectors, she did so too late, for he fell ill and returned to Venice, where he died on 29 November 1643. A Requiem Mass, composed by his pupil Rovetta, was held in St Mark's; and two weeks later, on 15 December, G. B. Marinoni organized and directed solemn obsequies in the church of S. Maria Gloriosa dei Frari, where Monteverdi, a Mantuan citizen born in Cremona, was laid to rest in the tomb reserved for men of Lombardy, and dedicated to St Ambrose.

Other commissions under consideration were thrust aside by the hand of death.[6] Yet many of his friends remembered him in literary tributes, brought together in a

---

[4] Solerti, 'Balletto', 24.   [5] Tiepolo, 136.

[6] One was a further commission from Piacenza to a text by Morandi, cited by Bianconi and Walker, 420. Another seems to have been a parergon to *Il ritorno d'Ulisse*, again with a libretto by Badoaro.

little volume entitled *Fiori poetici* and printed in Venice by Francesco Miloco in 1644. Marinoni (known as 'Giove' after playing that part in an opera) acted as editor and included sonnets, free verse, an epigram in dialogue, and a musical sonnet using the names of notes ('Longa e la pena, breve il godimento') by the Reverend Maestro Paolo Piazza. Antonio de Vescovo, priest of S. Maria Zobenigo (S. Maria del Giglio, where Monteverdi himself became a priest in 1632), contributed two examples of a quaint literary-numerical form called 'Vaticinium Arithmeticum', in which the year of Monteverdi's death is 'prophesied' by a short Latin poem, the letters of each word being keyed to a simple number system (A = 1, B = 2, and so on), so that both poems add up to 1643.

This unusual but obviously sincere collection is prefaced by a funeral oration extolling Monteverdi's high qualities by the parish priest of S. Tomà, Mattteo Caberloti, with a dedication to the three procurators of St Mark's, Francesco Molini, Giovanni Nani, and Giovanni Pesaro. The engraved frontispiece, with the title surmounted by a medallion portrait based on a reversed image of the Strozzi painting, shows all the composer's favourite instruments—violin, viola bastarda, harp, lute, spinet, trumpet, cornetto, trombone, lute, and his beloved theorbo (facing away from us as if in sorrow). Also notable are the three organs, the 'organi di legno' mentioned in Letter 11 as providing the perfect accompaniment, with theorboes, for voices—a combination which seems permanently to elude Monteverdi's modern interpreters.

Some admirers who missed contributing to the 'Fiori poetici' made their offerings at a later date. One of these was Giuliano Bezzi, whose 'Mille e mille nel sen Claudio chiudea' appears in his *Il torneo et altre rime* printed in 1645 at Bologna by Giacomo Monti.[7] Another is by the Venetian poet Leonardo Quirino: 'O tu che in nere spoglie':[8]

> O you, clothed in black, who call to mind the funeral rites of the great father of rhythms and harmonies, and my mourning, perform the sad and sorrowful offices, but quietly, so that you wake him not; for he has not left us as you seem to think, but tired of singing gives his senses over to sleep.

Most Serene Prince:

In the year 1632 Your Serenity consented, through exceeding kindness, to favour me—Claudio Monteverdi, Your Serenity's most humble and most devoted servant—with letters of recommendation for the late Most Serene Duke Carlo of Mantua,[a] so that I might obtain a donation granted me by Duke Vincenzo I,[b] and of this His Highness ordered immediate im-

---

[7] For a summary see Fabbri 1994, 267. A sermon mentioning Monteverdi in 1653 appears in Monterosso, 3.

[8] 'In morte di Claudio Monteverdi, padre della musica', from his *Vezzo d'Erato: poesie liriche* (Venice, 1653).

[a] Carlo of Nevers, eighth Duke of Mantua (d. 1637).   [b] Fourth Duke of Mantua (d. 1612).

plementation. But having been postponed by his ministers and impeded by his death, it could not provide the desired satisfaction that was due to me.

Wherefore I am ready to turn once more to the highest protection and unparalleled kindness of Your Serenity, most humbly beseeching your kind consent to favour me with new letters of recommendation for the Most Serene Princess[c] now reigning, so that I might obtain that which was granted me by the kindness of that Prince. This I trust I shall be able to obtain the more rapidly by means of Your Serenity's benign grace from which alone I acknowledge so much good. And so I humbly bow to Your Serenity.

With thanks, etc.
Claudio Monteverdi

[c] Maria Gonzaga (1609–60) daughter of Duke Francesco, and Regent of Mantua after the death of Carlo of Nevers.

Bibliography

Ademollo Alessandro Ademollo, *La bell'Adriana ed altre virtuose del suo tempo alla corte di Mantova* (Città di Castello, 1888).

Adler Guido Adler (ed.), *Musikalische Werke der Kaiser Ferdinand III, Leopold I und Joseph I* (Vienna, 1892–3).

Anthon Carl Anthon, 'Some Aspects of the Social Status of Italian Musicians during the Sixteenth Century', *Musica Disciplina* [*Journal of Renaissance and Baroque Music*], 1 (1946), 111–23, 222–34.

Antonicek Theophil Antonicek, 'Claudio Monteverdi und Oesterreich', *Oesterreichische Musikzeitschrift*, 26 (1971), 266–71.

Arnold Denis Arnold, *Claudio Monteverdi* (London, 1963).

Arnold, 'San Rocco' —— 'Music at the Scuola di San Rocco', *Music and Letters*, 40 (1959), 229–41.

Arnold, 'Singers' —— 'Monteverdi's Singers', *The Musical Times*, 111 (1970), 982–5.

Arnold, 'Succession' —— 'The Monteverdian Succession at St Mark's', *Music and Letters*, 42 (1961), 205–11.

Askew Pamela Askew, 'Fetti's "Portrait of an Actor" Reconsidered', *The Burlington Magazine*, 120 (1978), 59–65.

Banchieri Adriano Banchieri, *Lettere armoniche* (Bologna, 1628).

Bandini Angelo Maria Bandini, *Commentariorum de vita et scriptis Joannis Bapt. Doni* (Florence, 1755).

Barblan, 'La vita' Guglielmo Barblan, 'La vita di Monteverdi', in *Claudio Monteverdi* (Turin, 1967).

Barblan, 'Lamento' —— 'Un ignoto "Lamento d'Arianna" mantovano', *Rivista italiana di musicologia*, 2 (1957), 217–28.

Baschet Armand Baschet, *Les Comédiens italiens à la Cour de France* (Paris, 1882).

Bellonci Maria Bellonci, *A Prince of Mantua*, trans. Stuart Hood (New York, 1956).

Bertolotti Antonio Bertolotti, *Musici alla corte dei Gonzaga in Mantova dal secolo XV al XVIII* (Milan, 1890).

[437]

Bertolotti, 'Arti minori' —— *Le arti minori alla corte di Mantova nei secoli XV, XVI, e XVII* (Milan, 1889).

Bettinelli   Saverio Bettinelli, *Delle lettere e delle arti mantovane* (Mantua, 1774).

Bianconi and Walker   Lorenzo Bianconi and Thomas Walker, 'Dalla "Finta pazza" alla "Veremonda": Storie di Febi-armonici', *Rivista italiana di musicologia*, 10 (1975), 379–454.

Bombarda   Domizio Bombarda, *Teatro delle glorie della Sig. Adriana Basile* (Venice, 1623).

Boyer   Ferdinand Boyer, 'Les Orsini et les musiciens d'Italie au début du XVIIᵉ siècle', in *Mélanges de philologie, d'histoire, et de littérature offerts à Henri Hauvette* (Paris, 1934), 301–10.

Briccio   Giovanni Briccio, *Il pianto e la mestitia dell'alma città di Roma per la morte dell'Ill. e Rev. Sig. Alessandro Perretti card. Montalto* (Rome, 1623).

Brunelli   Bruno Brunelli, *I teatri di Padova* (Padua, 1921).

Buttigli   Marcello Buttigli, *Descrittione dell'apparato fatto per honorare la prima e solenne entrata in Parma della Serenissima Principessa Margherita di Toscana* (Parma, 1629).

Caffi   Francesco Caffi, *Storia della musica sacra nella già Cappella Ducale di S. Marco in Venezia dal 1318 al 1797* (Venice, 1854–5).

Calvo   Lorenzo Calvo, *Symbolae Diversorum Musicorum* (Venice, 1620).

Cametti   Alberto Cametti, 'Chi era l'"Hippolita", cantatrice del cardinal di Montalto', *Sammelbände der Internationalen Musikgesellschaft*, 15 (1913–14), 111–23.

Canal   Pietro Canal, *Della musica in Mantova: Notizie tratte principalmente dall'Archivio Gonzaga* (Venice, 1881). [Page references are to this book, not to the work as published earlier in the form of an article.]

Carter   Tim Carter, '*Possente spirto*: On Taming the Power of Music', *Early Music*, 21 (1993), 517–23.

Cavalcabò   Agostino Cavalcabò, 'I "pifferari" cremonesi e i probabili e possibili loro rapporti con i cornamusari scozzesi', *Bollettino storico cremonese*, 32 (1961–4), 278–92.

Cavicchi	Adriano Cavicchi, 'Teatro monteverdiano e tradizione teatrale ferrarese', in *Claudio Monteverdi e il suo tempo* (Verona, 1969), 139–56.
Champigneulle	Bernard Champigneulle, *Les Plus Beaux Écrits des grands musiciens* (Paris, 1946).
Coniglio	Giuseppe Coniglio, *I Gonzaga* (Mantua, 1967).
Cosenza	Mario Emilio Cosenza, *Biographical and Bibliographical Dictionary of the Italian Printers* (Boston, 1968).
Coussemaker	Edmond de Coussemaker (ed.), *Scriptorum de musica medii aevi nova series* (Paris, 1864–76).
Cozzi, 'Scapino'	Gaetano Cozzi, 'Scapino a Venezia', *Bollettino dell'Istituto di Storia della Società e dello Stato Veneziano*, 1 (1959), 190–2.
Damerini	Gino Damerini, 'Venezia al tempo di Monteverdi', *Musica*, 2 (1943), 105–20.
Davari	Stefano Davari, 'Notizie biografiche del distinto maestro di musica Claudio Monteverdi, desunte dai documenti dell' Archivio Storico Gonzaga', in *Atti della R. Accademia Virgiliana di Mantova* (Mantua, 1885), 79–183.
Doni	Giovanni Battista Doni, *Lyra Barberina* (Florence, 1763).
Earle	John Earle, *Micro-cosmographie* (London, 1629).
Einstein	Alfred Einstein, *The Italian Madrigal* (Princeton, 1949).
Einstein, 'Emissär'	—— 'Ein Emissär der Monodie in Deutschland: Francesco Rasi', in *Festschrift für Johannes Wolf zu seinem sechzigsten Geburtstage* (Berlin, 1929), 31–4.
Einstein, 'Grillo'	—— 'Abbot Angelo Grillo's Letters as Source Material for Music History', in *Essays on Music* (London, 1958), 159–78.
Errante, 'Forse che sì'	Vincenzo Errante, 'Forse che sì, forse che no', *Archivio storico lombardo*, 42 (1915), 15–114.
Errante, 'Il processo'	Guido Errante, 'Il processo per l'annullamento del matrimonio tra Vincenzo II duca di Mantova e donna Isabella Gonzaga di Novellara', *Archivio storico lombardo*, 43 (1916), 645–764.
Eubel	Conrad Eubel, *Hierarchia Catholica medii aevi, sive summorum Pontificum, S.R.E. Cardinalium, ecclesiarum antistitum series* (Münster, 1898–1913).

Fabbri 1985 Paolo Fabbri, *Monteverdi* (Turin, 1985).

Fabbri 1994 —— *Monteverdi*, trans. Tim Carter (Cambridge, 1994).

Fabbri, 'Inediti' —— 'Inediti Monteverdiani', *Rivista italiana di musicologia*, 15 (1980), 71–86.

Federhofer Hellmut Federhofer, 'Graz Court Musicians and their Contributions to the *Parnassus Musicus Ferdinandaeus* (1615)', *Musica Disciplina*, 9 (1955), 167–244.

Fenlon, 'Mantua' Iain Fenlon, *Music and Patronage in Sixteenth-Century Mantua* (Cambridge, 1980). [References are to vol. i.]

Fenlon, 'Vespers' —— 'The Monteverdi Vespers: Suggested Answers to some Fundamental Questions', *Early Music*, 5 (1977), 380–7.

Frey Hermann-Walther Frey, 'Das Diarium der Sixtinischen Sängerkapelle in Rom für das Jahr 1594', *Analecta Musicologica*, 14 (1974), 445–505.

Gallico, 'Assalito' Claudio Gallico, 'Assalito da briganti Monteverdi sulla via di Venezia', *Civiltà mantovana*, 1 (1966), 24–6.

Gallico, 'Contra C. M.' —— 'Contra Claudium Montiviridum', *Rivista italiana di musicologia*, 10 (1975), 346–59.

Gallico, 'Dazi' —— 'Monteverdi e i dazi di Viadana', *Rivista italiana di musicologia*, 1 (1966), 242–5.

Gallico, 'Documents' —— 'Newly Discovered Documents concerning Monteverdi', *Musical Quarterly*, 48 (1962), 68–72.

Gallico, 'Lettera' —— 'La Lettera amorosa di Monteverdi', *Nuova rivista musicale italiana*, 1 (1967), 287–302.

Gams P. Pius Bonifacius Gams, *Series Episcoporum Ecclesiae Catholicae* (Regensburg, 1873).

Giustiniani Vincenzo Giustiniani, *Discorso sopra la musica*, trans. Carol MacClintock (Rome, 1962).

Glixon Jonathan Glixon, 'Was Monteverdi a Traitor?', *Music and Letters*, 72 (1991), 404–6.

Grillo Elio Durante and Anna Martellotti, *Don Angelo Grillo O.S.B. alias Livio Celiano: Poeta per musica del secolo decimosesto* (Florence, 1989).

Guarini Giambattista Guarini, *Opere* (Turin, 1950).

Hansen Henny Harald Hansen, *Costumes and Styles* (New York, 1956).

Hazlitt   W. Carew Hazlitt, *The Venetian Republic* (London, 1915).

Hitchcock   H. Wiley Hitchcock, 'Caccini's "Other" *Nuove musiche*', *Journal of the American Musicological Society*, 27 (1974), 438–60.

Honour   Hugh Honour, *Venice* (New York, 1966).

Jeppesen   Knud Jeppesen, 'Monteverdi, Kapellmeister an S.ta Barbara?', in *Claudio Monteverdi e il suo tempo* (Verona, 1969), 313–22.

King   Archdale A. King, *Liturgies of the Religious Orders* (London, 1955).

Kinsky   Georg Kinsky, *Versteigerung von Musikbüchern praktischer Musik und Musiker-Autographen des 16. bis 18. Jahrhunderts aus dem Nachlaß des Herrn Kommerzienrates Wilhelm Heyer in Köln* (Berlin, 1927).

Kirkendale   Warren Kirkendale, *L'aria di Fiorenza, id est Il ballo del Gran Duca* (Florence, 1972).

Kirkendale, 'Rasi'   —— 'Zur Biographie des ersten Orfeo, Francesco Rasi', in *Festschrift Reinhold Hammerstein zum 70. Geburtstag* (Laaber, 1986), 297–335.

Kurtzmann   Jeffrey G. Kurtzmann, 'Monteverdi's "Mass of Thanksgiving" Revisited', *Early Music*, 22 (1994), 63–84.

Lavin   Irving Lavin, 'Lettres de Parme (1618, 1627–8) et débuts du théâtre baroque', in *Le Lieu théâtral à la Renaissance* (Paris, 1969), 105–58.

Lax   Éva Lax, *Claudio Monteverdi: Lettere. Edizione critica* (Florence, 1994).

Lea   Kathleen M. Lea, *Italian Popular Comedy* (Oxford, 1934).

Levi Pisetzky   Rosita Levi Pisetzky, *Storia del costume in Italia* (Milan, 1964–9).

Litta   Pompeo Litta, *Famiglie celebri italiane* (Mocenigo di Venetia: Dispensa 157) (Milan, 1868).

Luisi   Leila Galleni Luisi, 'Il Lamento d'Arianna di Severo Bonini (1613)', in *Claudio Monteverdi e il suo tempo* (Verona, 1969), 573–82.

Luzio   Alessandro Luzio, *La galleria dei Gonzaga venduta all'Inghilterra nel 1627–8* (Milan, 1913).

MacClintock, Communication   Carol MacClintock, Communication, *Journal of the American Musicological Society*, 23 (1970), 360–1.

MacClintock, 'Songbook'   —— 'A Court Musician's Songbook: Modena MS C 311', *Journal of the American Musicological Society*, 9 (1956), 177–92.

MacClintock, *Wert*   —— *Giaches de Wert (1535–1596): Life and Works* (Rome, 1966).

Maguire   Simon Maguire, 'The Bumper D.I.Y. Book of Stage Sets', *Opera Now* (July 1991), 60–1.

Malipiero   Gian Francesco Malipiero, *Claudio Monteverdi* (Milan, 1929).

Mantova: Le lettere   *Mantova: Le lettere*, ed. Emilio Faccioli (Mantua, 1962).

Marinoni   Giovanni Battista Marinoni (ed.), *Fiori poetici* (Venice, 1644).

MGG   *Die Musik in Geschichte und Gegenwart*, 16 vols. (Kassel, 1949–79).

Monterosso   Raffaello Monterosso, *Mostra bibliografica dei musicisti cremonesi* (Cremona, 1951).

Monterosso, 'Monteverdi'   —— (ed.), *Claudio Monteverdi e il suo Tempo* (Venice, Mantua, Cremona, 1968).

Monteverdi Companion   *Monteverdi Companion, The*, ed. Denis Arnold and Nigel Fortune (London, 1968).

Monteverdi Companion, New   *New Monteverdi Companion, The*, ed. Denis Arnold and Nigel Fortune (London, 1985).

Moore, 'Venezia'   James H. Moore, '*Venezia favorita da Maria*: Music for the Madonna Nicopeia and Santa Maria della Salute', *Journal of the American Musicological Society*, 37 (1984), 299–356.

Moore, 'Vespero'   —— 'The *Vespero delli Cinque Laudate* and the Role of *Salmi Spezzati* at St Mark's', *Journal of the American Musicological Society*, 34 (1981), 249–78.

Moser   Hans Joachim Moser, *Heinrich Schütz: His Life and Work*, trans, C. F. Pfatteicher from 2nd rev. edn. (St. Louis, 1959).

Müller von Asow   Erich Hermann Müller von Asow, *Heinrich Schütz: Gesammelte Briefe und Schriften* (Regensburg, 1931).

Musica II   *Musica II* (Florence, 1943).

Nagler   Alois Maria Nagler, *Theatre Festivals of the Medici, 1539–1637* (New Haven, Conn., 1964).

Nani	Battista Nani, *Storia della Repubblica di Venezia* (Venice, 1662–79).
New Grove	*The New Grove Dictionary of Music and Musicians*, ed. Stanley Sadie (London, 1980).
Newcomb	Anthony Newcomb, *The Madrigal at Ferrara, 1579–1597* (Princeton, NJ, 1980).
Nuovo Vogel	Emil Vogel, Alfred Einstein, François Lesure, and Claudio Sartori (eds.), *Bibliografia della musica italiana vocale profana dal 1500 al 1700* (Pomezia, 1977).
Olschki	Leo S. Olschki, 'Una visita alla collezione del Comm. C. Lozzi . . .', *La Bibliofilia*, 3 (1901–2), 231–59.
Osthoff	Wolfgang Osthoff, 'Monteverdis *Combattimento* in deutscher Sprache und Heinrich Schütz', in *Festschrift Helmuth Osthoff zum 65. Geburtstage* (Tutzing, 1961), 195–227.
Padoan	Maurizio Padoan, 'Tarquinio Merula nelle fonti documentarie', in *Contributi e studi di liturgia e musica nella regione padana* (Bologna, 1972), 229–330.
Palisca	Claude Palisca, 'The Artusi–Monteverdi Controversy', in *The Monteverdi Companion* (London, 1968), 133–66; repr. in *Studies in the History of Italian Music and Music Theory* (Oxford, 1994).
Panigada	C. Panigada (ed.), *Guido Bentivoglio: Memorie e lettere* (Scrittori d'Italia, no. 150; Bari, 1934).
Paoli	Domenico de' Paoli, *Claudio Monteverdi: Lettere, dediche, e prefazioni* (Rome, 1973).
Paoli, *Monteverdi*	—— *Monteverdi* (Milan, 1979).
Pirrotta	Nino Pirrotta, *Scelte poetiche di Monteverdi* (Rome, 1968). [Page references are to this book, not to the articles in *Nuova rivista musicale italiana*, 2 (1968), 10–42, 226–54.]
Pontiroli, *Monteverdi*	Giuseppe Pontiroli, *Notizie sui Monteverdi, su personaggi ed artisti del loro ambiente: La casa natale di Claudio Monteverdi* (Cremona, 1968).
Pontiroli, 'Musicisti'	—— 'Notizie di musicisti cremonesi dei secoli XVI e XVII', *Bollettino storico cremonese*, 22 (1961–4), 149–92.
Portioli	Attilio Portioli, *Viaggio e nozze del Duca di Mantova Ferdinando* (Mantua, 1882).
Possenti	Pelegrino Possenti, *Canora Sampogna* (Venice, 1623).

Prod'homme — Jacques-Gabriel Prod'homme, *Écrits de musiciens* (*XVᵉ–XVIIIᵉ siècles*) (Paris, 1912).

Prunières — Henry Prunières, *Monteverdi: His Life and Works*, trans. Mary D. Mackie (London and New York, 1926).

Prunières, *La Vie* —— *La Vie et l'œuvre de Claudio Monteverdi* (Paris, 1926).

Prunières, *Monteverdi* —— *Claudio Monteverdi* (Paris, 1924; rev. edn., 1931).

Quazza, *Diplomazia* — Romolo Quazza, *La diplomazia gonzaghesca* (Milan, 1941).

Quazza, *La guerra* —— *La guerra per la successione di Mantova e del Monferrato (1628–1631)* (Mantua, 1926).

Quazza, *Mantova* —— *Mantova e Monferrato nella politica europea alla vigilia della guerra per la successione (1624–7)* (Mantua, 1922).

Rasi — Luigi Rasi, *I comici italiani* (Florence, 1897).

Read — John Read, *Prelude to Chemistry* (London, 1937).

Redlich — Hans Redlich, *Claudio Monteverdi*, trans. Kathleen Dale (London, 1952).

Reed — Henry Reed, '*Vincenzo*', in '*The Streets of Pompeii*' *and Other Plays for Radio* (London, 1970).

Reiner — Stuart Reiner, 'Preparations in Parma—1618, 1627–8', *Music Review*, 25 (1964), 273–301.

Reiner, 'Angioletta' —— 'La vaga Angioletta', *Analecta Musicologica*, 14 (1974), 26–88.

RISM — Répertoire International des Sources Musicales, *Receuils imprimées, XVI–XVIIᵉ siècles: I. Liste chronologique* (Munich, 1960).

Rosand — Ellen Rosand, 'Barbara Strozzi, *virtuosissima cantatrice*: The Composer's Voice', *Journal of the American Musicological Society*, 31 (1978), 241–81.

Rosenthal — Albi Rosenthal, 'A Hitherto Unpublished Letter of Claudio Monteverdi', in *Essays Presented to Egon Wellesz* (Oxford, 1966), 103–7.

Rovetta — Giovanni Rovetta, *Salmi concertati* (Venice, 1626).

Sachs — Curt Sachs, *The History of Musical Instruments* (New York, 1940).

Sansovino — Francesco Sansovino, *Venetia città nobilissima* (with

	additional material by Giustinian Martinioni) (Venice, 1663).
Santoro, *Iconografia*	Elia Santoro, *Iconografia Monteverdiana* (Cremona, 1968).
Santoro, *Monteverdi*	—— *Claudio Monteverdi: Note biografiche con documenti inediti* (Cremona, 1967).
Sartori, *Bibliografia*	Claudio Sartori, *Bibliografia della musica strumentale italiana stampata in Italia fino al 1700* (2 vols., Florence, 1952, 1968).
Sartori, *Dizionario*	—— *Dizionario degli editori musicali italiani* (Florence, 1958).
Sartori, 'Monteverdiana'	—— 'Monteverdiana', *Musical Quarterly*, 38 (1952), 399–413.
Sartori, 'Salò'	—— 'Giulio Cesare Monteverdi a Salò: Nuovi documenti inediti', *Nuova rivista musicale italiana*, 1 (1967), 3–14.
Schaal	Richard Schaal, 'Ein unbekannter Brief von G. B. Doni', *Acta Musicologica*, 25 (1953), 88–91.
Schneider	Louis Schneider, *Claudio Monteverdi* (Paris, 1921).
Selfridge-Field	Eleanor Selfridge-Field, *Venetian Instrumental Music from Gabrieli to Vivaldi* (Oxford, 1975).
Senn	Walter Senn, *Musik und Theater am Hof zu Innsbruck* (Innsbruck, 1954).
Solerti, *Albori*	Angelo Solerti, *Gli albori del melodramma* (Palermo and Milan, 1904–5).
Solerti, 'Balletto'	—— 'Un balletto musicato da C. Monteverde', *Rivista musicale italiana*, 11 (1904), 24–34.
Solerti, *Musica*	—— *Musica, ballo e drammatica alla corte Medicea del 1600–1637* (Florence, 1905).
Solerti, *Origine*	—— *L'Origine del melodramma* (Turin, 1903).
Sommi, *Monteverdi*	Giorgio Sommi-Picenardi, *Claudio Monteverdi a Cremona* (Milan, 1895).
Sommi-Picenardi	Guido Sommi-Picenardi, 'D'alcuni documenti concernenti Claudio Monteverde', *Archivio storico lombardo*, 22 (1895), 154–62.
Stattkus	Manfred H. Stattkus, *Claudio Monteverdi: Verzeichnis der erhaltenen Werke* (Bergkamen, 1985).
Stevens, '1993'	Denis Stevens, 'Monteverdiana 1993', *Early Music*, 21 (1993), 565–75.

Stevens, 'Ballet' —— 'Monteverdi's Earliest Extant Ballet', *Early Music*, 14 (1986), 358–66.

Stevens, 'Bracciano' —— 'Monteverdi, Petratti, and the Duke of Bracciano', *Musical Quarterly*, 64 (1978), 275–94.

Stevens, 'Church Music' —— 'Monteverdi's Venetian Church Music', *Musical Times*, 108 (1967), 414–17.

Stevens, Communication —— Communication, *Journal of the American Musicological Society*, 26 (1973), 501–3.

Stevens, 'Madrigali' —— 'Madrigali Guerrieri, et Amorosi', *Musical Quarterly*, 53 (1967), 161–87.

Stevens, *Monteverdi* —— *Claudio Monteverdi: Sacred, Secular and Occasional Music* (London, 1978).

Stevens, 'Necklace' —— 'Monteverdi's Necklace', *Musical Quarterly*, 59 (1973), 370–81.

Stevens, 'Ornamentation' —— 'Ornamentation in Monteverdi's Shorter Dramatic Works', in *Bericht über den siebenten internationalen musikwissenschaftlichen Kongress Köln 1958* (Kassel, 1959), 284–7.

Strozzi, *Fratelli* Giulio Strozzi, *I cinque fratelli* (Venice, 1628).

Strunk Oliver Strunk, *Source Readings in Music History* (New York, 1950).

Tagmann Pierre Tagmann, 'La cappella dei maestri cantori della basilica palatina di Santa Barbara a Mantua (1565–1630)', *Civiltà mantovana*, 4 (1971), 376–400.

Talbot Michael Talbot, 'Ore Italiane: The Reckoning of the Time of Day in Pre-Napoleonic Italy', *Italian Studies*, 40 (1985), 51–62.

Tiepolo Maria Francesca Tiepolo, 'Minima Monteverdiana', *Rassegna degli Archivi di Stato*, 29 (1969), 135–43.

Tomlinson Gary Tomlinson, 'Twice Bitten, Thrice Shy: Monteverdi's "finta" *Finta pazza*', *Journal of the American Musicological Society*, 36 (1983), 303–11.

Vecchi Giuseppe Vecchi, *Le accademie musicali del primo seicento, e Monteverdi a Bologna* (Bologna, 1969).

Vio Gastone Vio, 'Ultimi ragguagli Monteverdiani', *Rassegna veneta di studi musicali*, 2–3 (1986–7), 347–64.

Vitali Carlo Vitali, 'Una lettera di Vivaldi ... un inedito Monteverdiano del 1630', *Nuova rivista musicale italiana*, 14 (1980), 404–12.

Vogel Emil Vogel, 'Claudio Monteverdi', *Vierteljahrsschrift für Musikwissenschaft*, 3 (1887), 315–450.

Vogel, *Bibliothek* —— *Bibliothek der gedruckten weltlichen Vocalmusik Italiens aus den Jahren 1500–1700* (Berlin, 1892).

Walker Frank Walker, Letter to the Editor, *Music and Letters*, 29 (1948), 433–4.

Weiss Piero Weiss, *Letters of Composers through Six Centuries* (Philadelphia, 1967).

Whenham John Whenham (ed.), *Claudio Monteverdi: Orfeo* (Cambridge, 1986).

Whenham, 'Gonzagas' —— 'The Gonzagas Visit Venice', *Early Music*, 21 (1993), 525–42.

Wistreich Richard Wistreich, '"La voce è grata assai, ma . . .": Monteverdi on Singing', *Early Music*, 22 (1994), 7–19.

Worp J. A. Worp, 'Constantijn Huygens' Journal van zijne Reis naar Venetie in 1620', *Bijdragen en Mededeelingen van het Historisch Genootschap*, 15 (1894), 128–9.

Worsthorne Simon Towneley Worsthorne, *Venetian Opera in the Seventeenth Century* (Oxford, 1954).

Wotton Sir Henry Wotton, *Elements of Architecture* (London, 1624).

Ziino Agostino Ziino, 'Pietro della Valle e la "musica erudita": Nuovi documenti', *Studien zur italienisch-deutschen Musikgeschichte*, 4 (1967), 97–111.

Zoppelli Luca Zoppelli, 'Il Rapto Perfettissimo: un'inedita testimonianza sulla "Proserpina" di Monteverdi', *Rassegna veneta di studi musicali*, 2–3 (1986–7), 343–5.

List of Works by Monteverdi mentioned in the Letters and Commentaries

*denotes music lost, or never composed

General Index

compiled by Lillian Elizabeth Stevens